# 成为安迪·沃霍尔
# BECOMING ANDY WARHOL

# 成为安迪·沃霍尔
## BECOMING ANDY WARHOL

UCCA 北京：2021年7月3日—2021年10月10日
UCCA EDGE：2021年11月6日—2022年3月6日

UCCA 尤伦斯当代艺术中心 Center for Contemporary Art 编

浙江摄影出版社

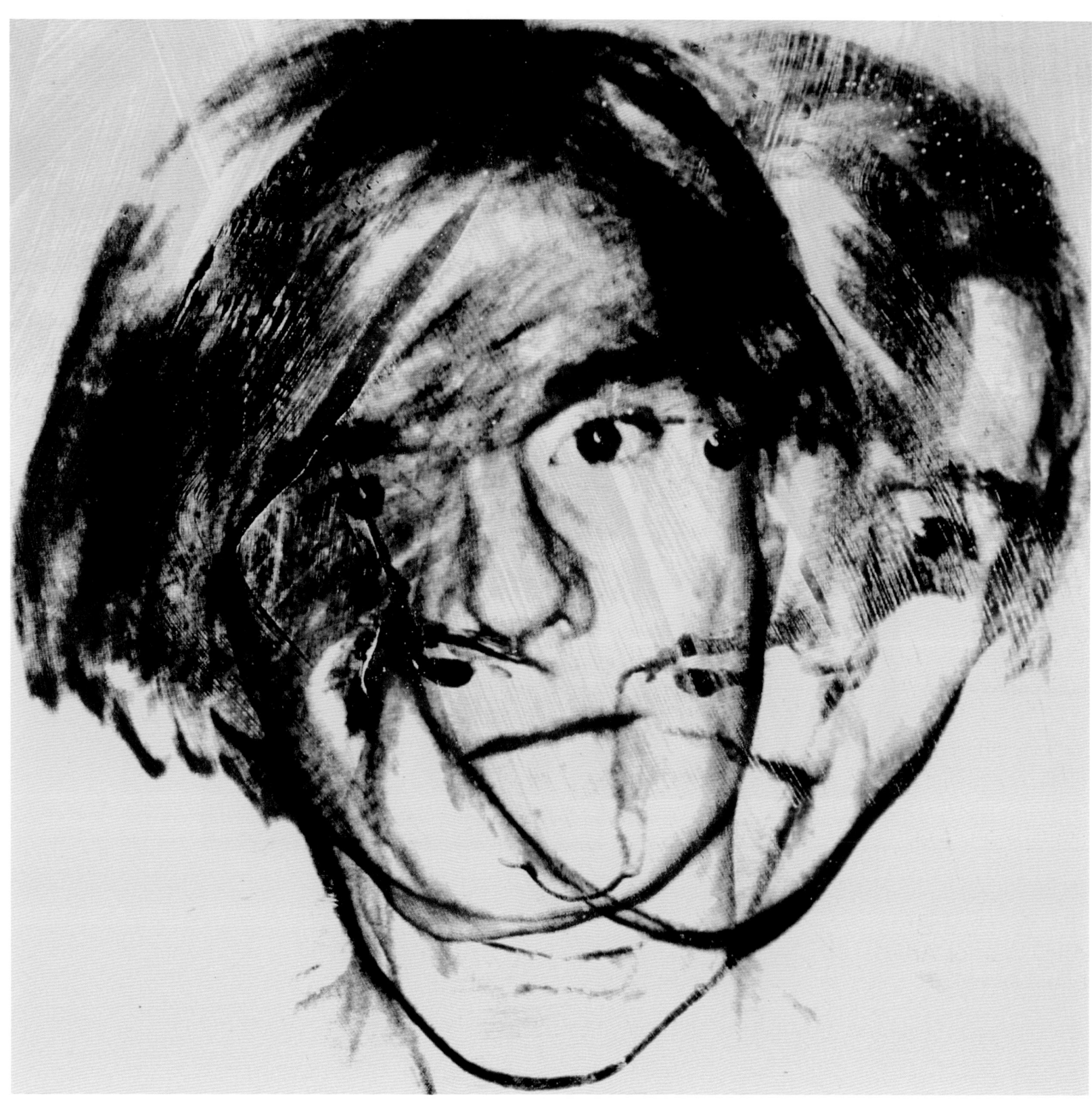

《自画像》
*Self-Portrait*
1978

布上丙烯和丝印油墨
Acrylic and silkscreen ink on linen
101.6 × 101.6 cm

# 目录
# CONTENTS

## 前言
## FOREWORDS

田霏宇
Philip Tinari — 7

帕特里克·摩尔
Patrick Moore — 9

## 文章
## ESSAYS

今天是他的生日
何塞·卡洛斯·迪亚兹
Birthday Boy
José Carlos Diaz — 11

安迪·沃霍尔,一位艺术家
布莱克·戈普尼克
Andy Warhol, Artist
Blake Gopnik — 17

我们与安迪·沃霍尔的距离
周婉京
The Distance Between Warhol and Us
Stefanie Chow — 27

## 参展作品
## EXHIBITION

缘起
Origins — 35

摄影师沃霍尔
Warhol the Photographer — 107

电影作为客体
Cinema as Object — 211

沃霍尔重塑
Warhol Remixed — 247

非物质
The Immaterial — 301

## 文献
## DOCUMENTATION

展览现场
Installation Views — 333

参考文献
Bibliography — 360

作品索引
Index of Works — 364

除非另有说明,本书中所有作品由安迪·沃霍尔创作。
Unless otherwise noted, all artworks are by Andy Warhol.

# 前言

田霏宇

# FOREWORD

Philip Tinari

在因疫情而被限制国际旅行之前，我经常有机会去往世界各地，欣赏在不同地方举办的重要展览。最让我记忆犹新的一次展览是参观纽约惠特尼美术馆的"安迪·沃霍尔：从A到B，反之亦然"。那是2018年11月的一个周六下午，我在人潮涌动的展厅里重新认识了这位我自以为已经很了解的艺术家。

与这场展览相遇的时刻其实是一个至关重要的时间节点：UCCA尤伦斯当代艺术中心（以下简称"UCCA"）在新赞助人的支持下重获新生，以徐冰回顾展宣告了我们的回归；我们的第一个分馆——UCCA沙丘——在几周前开馆；我为古根海姆美术馆策划的"1989年后的艺术与中国：世界剧场"刚刚在旧金山现代艺术博物馆拉开巡回展的最后一站；不久之前举办的美国中期选举中，民主党在众议院的胜利，体现出大部分美国人民对国家前进的方向所感受到的不安。我在惠特尼美术馆里还碰到了艺术家彼得·韦恩·刘易斯，2016年UCCA曾举办过他的展览。我们在一个展出了1980年代初氧化画的展厅里站了半个小时，一边聊天一边看美术馆会员预览场次的展览——这是一个多么典型的疫情前时代的场景，人们在美术馆里试图理解艺术作品和周遭残破的世界。

惠特尼美术馆举办的这场具有历史意义的展览，也是自1989年以来美国博物馆举办的第一个沃霍尔回顾展，有人如此评论道："这是沃霍尔的世界，我们只是生活在其中。"他把深邃与肤浅合而为一，对名利既批判又崇敬，拥有令人不安的直觉——所有的现实都可以被媒介化，自我可以通过不断地表演而被无限地表达：这一切已经从艺术家的直觉变成了普遍的社会现状。虽然其中的很多"症状"原本是非常具有美国特性的，但由于在他去世后三十年间蓬勃的全球化进程而逐渐扩散到了全世界。

参观完那场展览后，我坚定了UCCA需要举办一场沃霍尔展览的决心。虽然之前在中国也曾举办过几次沃霍尔的展览，包括2012年的巡回展"15分钟的永恒"，但还没有一场展览能抓住沃霍尔创作中所涵盖的全部艺术形式，也没有得到唐娜·德·萨尔沃和她在惠特尼美术馆的同事们于2018年带来的当代批判性学术研究的启发。此前UCCA已经举办过"杜尚与/或/在中国"（2013）、"劳森伯格在中国"（2016）与"毕加索——一位天才的诞生"（2019）等展现20世纪关键艺术人物的展览，现在是时候将对沃霍尔的全新理解带给中国的观众们了。当时开始

In the era before the world closed up, I often had the chance to travel inter-nationally, seeing important exhibitions around the world. One moment that sticks out vividly is a visit to "Andy Warhol: From A to B and Back Again" at the Whitney Museum of American Art in New York. That Saturday afternoon in November 2018, I walked through the packed galleries, turning corners into new discoveries about an artist I thought I knew well.

This exhibition came at a pivotal moment. UCCA, freshly revitalized by new patrons, had just finished its Xu Bing retrospective, the show that announced our rebirth. Our first satellite location, UCCA Dune, had opened weeks earlier. Another exhibition I had co-curated for the Guggenheim, "Art and China after 1989: Theater of the World," had just opened for its last stop, at SFMOMA. The midterm elections had happened earlier in the week, a Democratic victory in the House of Representatives signaling much of the nation's discomfort with the direction of the country. Walking the floors of the Whitney, I ran into the artist Peter Wayne Lewis, whose exhibition we had mounted at UCCA in 2016. We stood for half an hour in a gallery of early 1980s oxidation paintings, chatting and watching the members-preview, pre-pandemic crowd make sense of the work and their damaged world.

One refrain in the commentary on that historic exhibition – the first Warhol retrospective organized by a U.S. museum since 1989 – was that "it's Warhol's world; we're just living in it." His conflation of depth and shallowness, his critical reverence for fame, his uncanny intuition that all reality could be mediated and the self infinitely articulated through constant performance: these had gone from artistic intuitions to endemic social conditions. And while some of these pathologies were distinctly American, others, owing to the globalization that had flourished in the three decades since his death, were approaching universal.

Seeing that exhibition convinced me that a Warhol show needed to happen at UCCA. While several had been mounted in China before, notably including the 2012 traveling exhibition "15 Minutes Eternal," none had captured the artist's full range nor been informed by the contemporary, critical scholarship that Donna De Salvo and her Whitney colleagues brought to bear in 2018. Having previously engaged with key positions from twentieth-century art through exhibitions such as "DUCHAMP and/or/in CHINA" (2013), "Rauschenberg in China" (2016), and "Picasso – Birth of a Genius" (2019), we felt the moment was right to bring a new understanding of Warhol to our audience. What we did not yet know is that in 2021, UCCA would grow to include another location in Shanghai, and that this would become the first exhibition in our history to travel between UCCA venues.

Thanks to a kind introduction by Meg Maggio, we connected with Patrick Moore and his team at The Andy Warhol Museum, and the task before us became immediately clear. I went to Pittsburgh to visit Patrick and his colleagues in August 2019. Spending time there with chief curator José Carlos Diaz and

筹备这场展览时未曾料到的惊喜是，2021年UCCA在上海开启了另一家全新分馆，而"成为安迪·沃霍尔"也将成为我们历史上第一个在UCCA不同场馆巡回的展览。

感谢梅格·马吉奥的介绍使我们得以与帕特里克·摩尔和他在安迪·沃霍尔美术馆的团队建立合作关系，让我们共同办展的目标变得清晰。2019年8月，我曾前往匹兹堡拜访帕特里克和他的同事们，与首席策展人何塞·卡洛斯·迪亚兹及其同事一起工作与讨论的过程让我备受启发，这不仅因为他们对沃霍尔的生活与创作提供了新的见解，也因为我有机会近距离看到这个具有开创性精神的机构是如何持续地向不同的观众群体讲述一个充满开创性的美国艺术家的故事。作为一个不断寻求成长与突破的机构，UCCA从与安迪·沃霍尔博物馆的长期合作中获益匪浅。遗憾的是，由于2020年和2021年的全球大环境，我们之间的交流与合作几乎完全以线上形式进行，这也需要我们彼此之间有着在疫情前无法想象的相互信任与创造力。

在此，我要感谢每一位为实现此次展览而付出努力与承担风险的合作者与同事。感谢帕特里克和何塞策划了这样一个充满活力而且细致入微的展览；感谢安迪·沃霍尔美术馆团队的瑞秋·巴伦-霍恩、安柏·摩根和肯尼·马歇尔的团队和合作精神。也感谢UCCA的团队，特别是郭希、赖柏圣、关健、游骁、孔令祎、黄洁华、徐丹羽、杨懏然和刘楷韵，感谢他们卓越的奉献和专业精神。

由衷感谢每一位赞助商的支持，感谢美国的传奇汽车品牌凯迪拉克支持北京站与上海站的展览。感谢首席赞助商香奈儿，作为一个与沃霍尔同样热爱艺术也与之有着深厚联系的品牌，此次赞助也是庆祝香奈儿五号香水百年纪念的各项活动的一个部分。感谢联合赞助商摩根士丹利和苏富比继2019年支持毕加索的展览之后，再次回归我们的赞助队伍。我们还要感谢各位赞助人、基金会理事会成员、国际委员会和青年赞助人的持续支持。我们愿把此次展览视作对于跨文化的以及在困难环境下积极合作的信念，并以此追求更持续的交流与更深刻的理解。

田霏宇
UCCA尤伦斯当代艺术中心馆长
UCCA集团CEO

other colleagues was revelatory, not just for the new insights it offered into Warhol's life and work, but for the chance to see up close how this inspired institution was mobilizing itself to tell the story of a groundbreaking American artist to diverse new audiences. As an institution that is constantly seeking to grow and improve, UCCA has benefitted greatly from the extended collaboration with The Andy Warhol Museum that produced this exhibition. Unfortunately, owing to the global circumstances of 2020 and 2021, this engagement has been all but entirely virtual. This has required levels of trust and creativity not previously imaginable.

I am grateful to everyone who has worked hard and taken risks to make this exhibition a reality: to Patrick and José for curating such a dynamic and nuanced exhibition; to the team at The Andy Warhol Museum including Rachel Baron-Horn, Amber Morgan, and Keny Marshall for their collaborative collegiality; to Xiaoxi Chen for a beautiful exhibition design; and to the UCCA team, especially Guo Xi, Patrick Rhine, Edward Guan, Christina You, Kong Lingyi, Huang Jiehua, Xu Danyu, Anna Yang, and Karen Kaiyun Liu for their unparalleled dedication and professionalism.

We are grateful for the support of our sponsors. We are pleased to collaborate with the iconic American automobile Cadillac to present the exhibition in both Beijing and Shanghai. Chanel, which shares a love of art and a deep connection with Warhol, has generously joined us as Executive Sponsor, in keeping with a wide program of celebrations surrounding the centennial of CHANEL No°5. We welcome back our Presenting Sponsors, Morgan Stanley and Sotheby's, with whom we successfully worked on our Picasso exhibition in 2019. As always, we are indebted to our patrons, members of the Foundation Council, International Circle, and Young Associates for their continued camaraderie. We offer the exhibition as a testament to the power of spirited collaboration, across cultures and against difficult circumstances, in pursuit of sustained dialogue and deeper understanding.

Philip Tinari
Director, UCCA Center for Contemporary Art
CEO, UCCA Group

# 前言

## 帕特里克·摩尔

# FOREWORD

## Patrick Moore

安迪·沃霍尔美术馆是匹兹堡四个卡内基博物馆之一，在卡内基研究院、安迪·沃霍尔视觉艺术基金会和迪亚艺术基金会的合作下于1994年开馆。安迪·沃霍尔美术馆的藏品囊括了安迪·沃霍尔的全面创作成果和档案资料，最早的作品可以追溯到艺术家家族移民到美国之时，可以说是世界上最大和最全面展示沃霍尔艺术遗产的机构。

自成立以来，沃霍尔美术馆一直为能在全球各地展出其藏品而感到自豪，其中一些地区是我们尤为重视的。随着亚洲特别是中国成为当代艺术世界的重地，我们越来越关注向更多的中国观众展示安迪·沃霍尔的创作和遗产的机会。沃霍尔本人也曾访问过中国，亚洲文化对他的整个艺术生涯产生了重要影响。

"成为安迪·沃霍尔"是沃霍尔作品在中国最大和最具雄心的展览。在田霏宇的支持下，何塞·卡洛斯·迪亚兹和我希望能够关注沃霍尔创作生涯中不那么为人熟知的方面，包括电影、摄影和艺术生涯后期的作品。我们在策展方面的构想也以沃霍尔的出生地以及沃霍尔美术馆的所在地——匹兹堡为重点。我们希望此次展览能够提供一次对于沃霍尔创作的全面观察，并为深受艺术熏陶的中国观众们带来新的视角。

我谨感谢沃霍尔美术馆的工作人员为此次展览所付出的努力，特别是我的联合策展人何塞·卡洛斯·迪亚兹。与此同时，我也要感谢馆长田霏宇带领下的UCCA尤伦斯当代艺术中心的工作人员，你们是出色的合作者，充满热情与专业精神，在整个展览的筹备过程中不懈追求卓越与完美。

最后，我由衷地希望沃霍尔，这位最具美国特色的艺术家，能够成为中美两国之间持续友好关系的象征和助力。

帕特里克·摩尔
安迪·沃霍尔博物馆馆长

The Andy Warhol Museum, one of the four Carnegie Museums of Pittsburgh, opened its doors in 1994 as a collaboration between the Carnegie Institute, The Andy Warhol Foundation for the Visual Arts, and Dia Art Foundation. The Warhol's collection represents Andy Warhol's entire creative output and archival materials reaching back to the Warhola family's immigration to the United States. In total, The Warhol's collection is the largest and most complex representation of Warhol's legacy in the world.

Since its inception, The Warhol has been proud to share its collection globally, but certain parts of the world are of particular importance. As Asia generally and China in particular have become powerhouses in the world of contemporary art, The Warhol has become increasingly interested in opportunities to showcase Andy Warhol's work and legacy to the growing audience there. Warhol himself visited China, and Asian culture was a significant influence for him throughout his career.

"Becoming Andy Warhol" is the largest and most ambitious showing of Warhol's work in China. With the support of Philip Tinari, José Carlos Diaz and I were encouraged to look at lesser-known aspects of Warhol's creative enterprise including film, photography, and later work. Our curatorial vision for the exhibition also had a heavy focus on Pittsburgh, where Warhol was born and The Andy Warhol Museum is located. It is our hope that "Becoming Andy Warhol" will present a complex view of Warhol and bring new perspectives to the already sophisticated audiences in China.

I wish to thank the staff of The Warhol for helping to realize this exhibition, especially my co-curator José Carlos Diaz. Similarly, the staff of UCCA Center for Contemporary Art, led by Director Philip Tinari, have been exemplary collaborators, remaining steadfast in their commitment to excellence and proving themselves to be gracious and professional partners.

It is my hope that Warhol, the most American of artists, will serve as a symbol of and an inspiration to continued fellowship between China and the United States.

Patrick Moore
Director
The Andy Warhol Museum

《挤压过的金宝汤罐头（牛肉面味）》
*Crushed Campbell's Soup Can
(Beef Noodle)*
1962

棉布上酪蛋白颜料和石墨
Casein and graphite on cotton canvas
182.6 × 132.1 cm

## 今天是他的生日

何塞·卡洛斯·迪亚兹

## BIRTHDAY BOY

José Carlos Diaz

他是怎样成为安迪·沃霍尔的？也许一切都是与生俱来的，可以追溯到 1928 年 8 月 6 日他出生的日子。又或许要归功于 58 年间人生阅历的积累，从初生到直面死亡，先是 1968 年一次近乎致命的枪杀未遂，最终于 1987 年 2 月 22 日离世。他的传记人尽皆知：安德鲁·沃霍拉祖籍在今属斯洛伐克的一个小村庄，出身于一个有着宗教背景的卢森尼亚家庭，在宾夕法尼亚州的匹兹堡出生长大，后来蜕变为美国式的波普偶像——安迪·沃霍尔。然而，尽管许多细节都很清楚，他成长的过程仍旧难以捉摸。要成为安迪·沃霍尔，意味着这个匹兹堡出身的脆弱同性恋者需要打磨关于自己的一切，事实与虚构，从出生到死亡，同时也需要他人参与到他的人生建构中。从出身平凡到在艺术界声名赫赫，沃霍尔成了最多才多艺的博学家。他在 20 世纪美国进行了跨领域的艺术实践，包括电影制作、摄影、雕塑、绘画、版画、出版，等等。而这一切也都有赖于在这众多领域里奉献、消费和曾为他点燃灵感的人们。

"成为安迪·沃霍尔"是一个特别的展览，分为五个部分，通过位于他家乡的安迪·沃霍尔博物馆提供的艺术品、物品和影像资料来探索沃霍尔的生活与事业。此次展览包括他年轻时期的稀有档案物品，后期发展成丝网印刷风格的那些试水之作，鲜少放映的 16 毫米胶片，关注度较低的作品如实验性的线缝相片，以及意外去世前最后十年的行动绘画。重新审视这位因涂画金宝汤罐头、拍摄 1960 年代美国风月场以及流连于权贵之间而为人熟知的艺术家，本次展览拼凑出他的长篇传记中那些缺失的缝隙。

如果说沃霍尔的许多生活方式和作品仍然被错误解读，部分原因是他默许了舆论对自己的捏造和模糊化，促成了围绕他的神秘感。例如，这位艺术家曾说，汤给了他身体需要的营养，也激发了他早期的波普创作。而几十年后再次被问及这个问题时，沃霍尔维持了这个谎言，"哦，是的，我每天中午都喝金宝汤罐头，大约有二十年了。"[1] 即使在他死后，他的身世对他同时代的人来说仍然模糊得不可思议。一份讣告写道："他早年的细节仍不清晰。根据三个已知的版本，他于 1928 年、1929 年或 1930 年在宾夕法尼亚州的某个地方出生。"[2] 尽管他的曝光率很高，但仍有大量的空白留给我们填补。

在一个经典的欧洲童话故事中，一位旅行者在一个村

How did Andy Warhol become? Perhaps it all began on his date of birth, August 6, 1928. Or perhaps, he became thoroughly himself as a result of a lived experience sometime between his childhood and the sudden surfacing of death, first in a near-fatal assassination attempt in 1968 and for eternity on February 22, 1987. The biography is well known: Born into a religious, Carpatho-Rusyn family from a village in modern-day Slovakia, Andrew Warhola was born and raised in Pittsburgh, Pennsylvania, and later metamorphosed into the All-American Pop icon – Andy Warhol. Yet while many of the details are clear, the process of becoming remains elusive. To become Andy Warhol required the vulnerable, gay man from Pittsburgh to nurture every detail about himself, both fact and fiction, from birth until the end, and let others contribute in the construction of his development. From humble beginnings to artistic fame, Warhol became the ultimate Renaissance Man, who established a multidisciplinary practice in twentieth-century America that included filmmaking, photography, sculpting, painting, printmaking, publishing, and more. None of this could have been possible without the countless people who contributed, consumed, and ignited his surroundings.

"Becoming Andy Warhol" is a special exhibition divided into five sections that explore the life and career of Warhol using artworks, objects, and films exclusively from The Andy Warhol Museum, located in the artist's hometown. It includes important archival items from his youth; provisional paintings that developed into his silkscreen style; rarely screened 16mm films; underappreciated work, such as experimental stitched photography; and gestural paintings from the final decade before an unexpected passing. This exhibition fills in the gaps when reconsidering a lengthy and dense biography of an artist recognized primarily for painting Campbell's Soup cans; filming the demimonde of 1960s America; and companioning the rich and famous.

If much of his life and work remains misunderstood, it is in part because Warhol encouraged fabrication and ambiguity about himself, which has contributed to the mystery and mythology. For example, the artist embellished that soup nourished him in his childhood as well as inspired his early Pop art. When asked decades later, Warhol maintained the deception, responding, "Oh yeah, I had Campbell's Soup every day for lunch for about twenty years."[1] Even upon his death, his origins remained surprisingly vague to his contemporaries. One obituary wrote: "The earliest facts of his life remain unclear. He was born somewhere in Pennsylvania in either 1928, 1929, or 1930, according to three known versions of his life."[2] Despite his cultivated outsized exposure, there are massive lacunae left for us to address.

In a classic European folk tale a traveler stops to rest in a village and begins to simmer a metal cauldron filled with water and a large stone from the ground. The mysterious stranger offers to share the "stone soup" with the villagers.

子里停下来休息,煮起一锅水,往水里丢了一块地上捡的大石头。这个神秘的陌生人提出要与村民分享"石头汤"。他建议,如果再多加一些配料,就能让汤的味道更丰富。村子里每个人都带来了一点点配料,最后大家都心满意足地分享了这锅美味的汤。与这个故事类似,沃霍尔的第二个工作室——著名的"银色工厂",成了一个避难所,为那些路过的、生活艰苦的、自由奔放的、特立独行的、被歧视的、怪异的和极为优秀的人服务,他们都为沃霍尔这锅"石头汤"带来了一点自己的配料。事实上,他的艺术创作正依赖于他身边的人们,沃霍尔也因此成为波普教皇。[3] 一位沃霍尔的"超级明星"曾说:"安迪实现了他的愿望。他成了掌控品味、魅力、性、时尚、摇滚、电影、艺术八卦和夜生活的大祭司,也是那些迷失在毒品、性、金钱、家庭等问题中的孩子们的告解神父。在忏悔室里,安迪神父在他的白金主教冠冕下低着头,他让人倾诉,但从不用心听,只是记录着。'告诉我你的罪过,'他说,'我将赦免这些罪过。'"[4]

与其说是汤为沃霍尔提供了养分,不如说是获得的所有关注让他成长。艺术家、评论家、藏家,以及随后涌现的媒体见证了这位年轻艺术家带着他的波普画作登场,成为安迪·沃霍尔。诗人约翰·焦尔诺在最近的一本回忆录中写道:"1962 年,所有的波普艺术家都已经举办了他们的首场个展,到 1963 年,他们迎来了第二次展览,同时也变得更加成熟。"[5] 作为沃霍尔早年的男友,焦尔诺证实波普艺术于 1963 年已经确立下来。也是在这一年,沃霍尔拍摄了他的第一部电影《沉睡》,在沃霍尔新买的 16 毫米宝莱克斯电影摄像机的注视下,焦尔诺昏睡了五个多小时。1964 年初,沃霍尔还准备搬迁工作室,并建立他的"银色工厂"。这个银色喷漆与铝箔包裹的空间成为沃霍尔派对和创作的中心舞台,同时也是数以百计的试镜影片的拍摄场地。这些影片记录了每个参观者在这个金属圣地——可能是当时最具享乐主义和最有创造力的空间——展现出的个人本质。虽然当代观众可能不会认出黑白胶卷记录下来的拍摄对象,但一定可以体会到他们不同的情绪,并注意到沃霍尔选角的多样性。例如实验性舞台演员鲁夫斯·科林斯、享誉国际的黑人时尚模特多尼尔·卢纳,以及他的同性恋朋友们,如舞蹈家弗雷迪·赫科和摄影师彼得·于亚尔。在沃霍尔人生轨迹中出现的人们也提升了他的影响力。这些人同样充满天赋,以各种方式做出了贡献,时常为他的跨领域实践带来主题灵感,并强化了波普的氛围感(和潮流感)。许多人出现在沃霍尔的电影、摄影、画布上,或成为他有影响力的杂志《访谈》的封面。沃霍尔的明星好友,也是他的缪斯女神丽莎·明尼里回忆说:"他对周围的事物很着迷,我为此很欣赏他。他很有趣,对一切都很好奇……"[6]

成年后,数不清的人在不同的时间点成为沃霍尔选中的家庭成员。不过,沃霍尔的母亲也在儿子的生活中扮演了重要的角色,直到她 1972 年去世。沃霍尔小时候,朱莉娅·沃霍拉就鼓励他画画和填色,甚至给他买了相机和投影机。沃霍尔 1952 年搬到纽约后,她也随之搬了过去,与他同住了近 20 年。也许鲜有人知,沃霍尔终生信奉天主教,与他的父母一起埋葬在匹兹堡的圣约翰浸礼会天主教公墓。人们仍然会去那里朝圣,并留下自己的纸条和汤罐以纪念这位艺术家。[7]

"大萧条"和"二战"期间,沃霍尔在匹兹堡这座钢铁城中长大。在这个经济和家庭状况都十分困难的年代,家庭与宗教仍是维系沃霍拉一家的核心。就在沃霍尔上高中之前,他的父亲因身体欠佳猝然离世。尽管家境艰难,沃霍尔依旧坚持学习,最终从卡内基理工学院毕业(他的父亲曾专门存钱确保沃霍尔能顺利上大学,沃霍尔也是家中第一个大学生)。无

He suggests that it would benefit from just a few more ingredients to help develop the flavors. Contributions from the entire community (a pinch of this, a dash of that) result in a satisfying stew shared by all. In a similar way, Warhol's second studio, the celebrated Silver Factory, served as a sanctuary to the transient, needy, free-spirited, exceptional, discriminated, freaky, and fabulous, all giving a little bit of themselves to Warhol's metaphorical melting pot. In fact, his artistry depended mostly on his surroundings as he developed into the Pope of Pop.[3] "Andy got his wish. He became the high priest officiant of taste, glamour, sex, fad, fashion, rock-and-roll, movies, art gossip, and nightlife. He was father confessor of the lost kids with all their problems – drugs, sex, money, family. In the confessional, Father Andy, head bowed under his platinum miter, always lent an ear, never interrupted, just recorded. 'Tell me your sins,' he was saying. 'I will absolve them,'" noted former Superstar Ultra Violet.[4]

Rather than soup, much of Warhol's nourishment came from all the attention he received. Through others (artists, critics, collaborators, and collectors), as well as through the outpouring of media that followed, the young artist was observed *becoming* Andy Warhol as his Pop paintings made their debut. "In 1962, all the Pop artists had had their first one-person shows, and in 1963, they were having their second shows and becoming more established," poet John Giorno penned in a recent memoir.[5] An early boyfriend of Warhol, Giorno affirmed that by 1963, Pop had officially arrived. This was also the year that Warhol made his first film, *Sleep*, featuring over five hours of Giorno slumbering under the gaze of Warhol's newly purchased 16mm Bolex movie camera. Warhol was also preparing to move studios and establish his Silver Factory in early 1964. The silver-foiled space became Warhol's center stage for parties and production, but also for the hundreds of filmed Screen Tests. These films documented the individual essence of each visitor in this metallic sanctuary, arguably the most hedonistic and creative space of the time. While contemporary audiences will not likely recognize the young sitters in the black-and-white film reels, they can relate to their varied emotions and note the vast diversity in Warhol's periphery, including Rufus Collins, an experimental stage actor; Donyale Luna, international Black fashion model; as well as queer friends, like the dancer Freddy Herko and photographer Peter Hujar. Those in Warhol's orbit elevated his artistry because they too were gifted and contributed in one way or another, often inspiring themes in his multidisciplinary practice and reaffirming the ambiance (and trendiness) of Pop. Many appeared as subjects in film, photography, canvas, or the cover of *Interview*, his influential magazine. Liza Minnelli, a celebrity friend and muse, reminisced, "He was fascinated by things around him, and I admired him for that. He was fun, you know. Curious about everything…".[6]

By adulthood, and depending on the decade, countless people made up Warhol's chosen family. However, his mother too played an active role in her son's life until her death in 1972. As a child, Julia Warhola encouraged him to draw and color, and even bought Warhol a camera and a film projector. In 1952, after Warhol had relocated to New York, she moved in with him and stayed for almost twenty years. It is not widely known that Warhol, a life-long practicing Catholic, is now buried alongside his parents at St. John the Baptist Byzantine Catholic Cemetery in Pittsburgh. Pilgrimages to the site are still made, and offerings of personalized notes and soup cans are left in commemoration of the artist.[7]

Young Warhol grew up in the Steel City during the Great Depression and World War II. Family and religion were central to the Warhola's during these years of financial and familial hardship. Just before attending high school, his father unexpectedly died from poor health. The family struggled financially, but Warhol continued his studies and eventually graduated from Carnegie Institute of Technology (his father had established a savings bond to fund college, a first in the family). Holidays, both religious and secular, including Christmas and birthdays, were celebrated at home and would have been modest. Warhol's birthday is worth exploring because he seemed to constantly prefer distractions around his date of birth. On his fortieth birthday in 1968, while recovering in bed from gunshot wounds inflicted by Valerie Solanas, he spent the day calling friends and ignoring sympathy and tears, preferring "light gossipy" chatter.[8] Much earlier, Marilyn Monroe's death made frontpage headlines on Warhol's birthday in 1962.[9] Familiar with her persona and career, Warhol would go on to immortalize the Hollywood blonde's image, at times on gold surfaces, akin to Byzantine icons.[10] Around the same period, he also depicted the unforgettable mushroom cloud on a single silkscreened red canvas, recalling August 6, 1945,

论是宗教还是世俗的各种节日，包括圣诞节和生日，沃霍拉一家都是在家中简单庆祝的。沃霍尔的生日很值得我们研究，因为他似乎一直喜欢让大家误会他的出生日期。1968 年的 40 岁生日，沃霍尔是在病床上度过的，彼时他还在恢复瓦莱丽·索拉纳斯带来的枪伤，他花了一天时间给朋友打电话，并未理会同情和眼泪，而更喜欢聊一些"轻松的八卦"。[8] 更早的时候，玛丽莲·梦露的死亡在 1962 年沃霍尔生日当天成为报纸的头版头条。[9] 沃霍尔熟悉梦露的个性和事业，将通过画作使这位好莱坞金发女郎的形象永垂不朽，有时是在纯金色的表面上，仿佛拜占庭圣像。[10] 大约在同一时期，他还在一块丝网印刷的红色画布上描绘了令人难忘的蘑菇云，以此来回顾 1945 年 8 月 6 日他 17 岁生日当天投放在日本广岛的原子弹，这场伤亡惨重的灾难最终导致了日本的投降。

在他去世后出版的《安迪·沃霍尔日记》中记录了他在 1976 年至 1987 年间过生日时那些充满厌世感的自白。"我的生日，这是一个令人沮丧的日子，"[11] 他写道。两年后又记下，"我甚至不想提起今天。我已经告诉所有人我不想听到'生日'这个词。"[12] 另一年，"今天是我的生日。我告诉了办公室的每个人，如果他们提到生日，我就会解雇他们。"[13] 还有，"今天是我的生日，但我没有想起来，还是文森特打电话提醒了我。"[14] 尽管沃霍尔很喜欢社交，是聚会的主角，但唯独抗拒 8 月 6 日举办的庆祝活动："我的生日又来了。我一到办公室就马上切蛋糕，这样我就不用在大家面前切了。蛋糕很难吃。"[15] 然而就在一天后，他的好友，时装设计师霍尔斯顿就在声名狼藉的迪斯科舞厅 54 俱乐部为沃霍尔举办了一场无比浮华且热闹十倍的生日派对。[16]

一年之后的 1980 年，当迪斯科的热潮逐渐退去，这位年迈的艺术家说："今天是我的生日……这次我真的觉得自己是个老前辈了。"[17] 看起来，渐长的年龄与收益颇丰的事业虽然并行不悖，但要在当代艺术领域保持前卫对沃霍尔来说却越来越难，他当时主要制作客户指定内容的委托作品。作为一个社交变色龙，沃霍尔经常默许那些虚构他生活方式的内容，甚至给它们添油加醋。但也不总是如此。有一次，一位国际记者与他对谈后报道了他的出身和背景，而非他近期的那些耀眼成就与影响力。"我向她倾诉了我的心声，她却写了那些陈词滥调，就'父亲在煤矿病死 / 沃霍拉 / 卡内基理工学院'这些——我可是向她倾诉了我的心声！"雪上加霜的是，沃霍尔坚持认为这场采访中完全剔除了所有他讨论的那些"现代的"和"年轻的"东西。[18]

死亡是贯穿沃霍尔波普艺术的显要主题。也许他并不像害怕衰老、孤独、默默无闻那样惧怕死亡，特别是周遭不再有什么需要他去编排、去培育、甚至在某种程度上，去控制。如果每个人都不再关注或崇拜沃霍尔，他是否会仅仅成为一个记忆中的话题？尽管沃霍尔经常在画中描绘自己，但它们并不是沃霍尔精心呈现的自我形象，而是更直观地记录了这个男人的日渐衰老，甚至有可能失去一切。在遭到枪击并死里逃生的十年后，沃霍尔创作了 60 多幅自画像。画中的沃霍尔显得焦躁不安、心烦意乱、脆弱且略带玩世不恭，身边放一个假头骨，或假装被助手掐住脖子。在另一个版本中，沃霍尔将自己的三张宝丽来照片叠加在一起，戴着拖把头的假发，穿着《访谈》杂志的 T 恤。他生命中最后时期的肖像画中那些分层图像给人以无声运动的感觉，让人回想起他 1960 年代的早期试镜影片，只是少了青春和美丽。在 1986 年，沃霍尔最后一次描绘了他自己。画中是一个巨大的头像，严厉地凝视着观者。

1986 年 8 月 6 日，也就是他最后一个生日那天，沃霍尔写道："一整天，人们只是悄悄说着'生

his seventeenth birthday, when the atomic bomb was dropped on Hiroshima, Japan, killing vast numbers of people and leading to Japan's surrender.

*The Andy Warhol Diaries*, published posthumously, records a cluster of his birthdays between 1976-87 with cynical confessions. "It was a depressing day, my birthday," he wrote.[11] Two years later, "The unmentionable day. I'd told everyone I didn't want to hear the word 'birthday.'"[12] Another, "It was my birthday and I'd told everyone at the office that if they even mentioned it they'd be fired,"[13] and, "It was my birthday but I didn't think of it until Vincent called and reminded me."[14] He seemed to enjoy socializing, being the life of the party, but oddly deterred celebration when it centered exclusively on August 6: "My birthday. When I got to the office I cut the cake right away, so that I wouldn't have to do it in front of everybody. It tasted awful."[15] A day later, however, friend and fashion designer Halston organized a birthday party for Warhol, tenfold more effort, at the notorious discotheque Studio 54 that included glitz and gifts.[16]

The following year in 1980, as disco was fading, the aging artist reflected, "It was my birthday... I really feel like an old-timer this time."[17] It appears that growing older each year ran parallel to a lucrative career, yet Warhol struggled to remain edgy in the contemporary art scene and relied mostly on paid commissions with the content dictated by his clients. As a social chameleon, Warhol often allowed and assisted with the fiction surrounding his lifestyle. However, one instance, an interview with an international journalist, reported his origins and not the recent accomplishments and relevance. "I mean, I poured out my heart to her and she wrote the kind of rehashed article, you know – 'Father dies in coal mines/Warhola/Carnegie Tech' – and I poured out my heart to her." Adding salt to the wound, Warhol insisted that the interview excluded all the "modern" and "*young*" things that he had discussed.[18]

Artworks throughout his Pop career blatantly emphasized death. Perhaps he did not fear death as much as aging, loneliness, and fading from popularity, especially if there was no longer any entourage to curate, cultivate, and, in some ways, control. If everyone ceased their attention and admiration for Warhol, would he simply be a topic of the past? Although Warhol frequently depicted himself in paintings, they not only reflected self-representation but literally the man growing older each year and at risk of losing it all. A decade after surviving gunshot wounds from an attack, Warhol created over sixty self-portraits. Warhol appears restless, distracted, vulnerable, and slightly playful, with a fake skull at his side or pretending to be choked by an assistant. In another version, Warhol superimposed three Polaroid photos of himself, wearing a mop top wig and *Interview* magazine t-shirt. The layered images in the final portraits give the sensation of silent movement, reminiscent of his early Screen Tests from the 1960s, yet lacking youthfulness and beauty. Warhol would live long enough to depict himself once more in 1986, as a monolithic head with a stern gaze at the viewer.

On August 6, 1986, what would be his final birthday, Warhol wrote, "All day people just whispered 'Happy birthday,' they didn't say it out loud." He continues that "the day got strange" after the artist Keith Haring informed him that a mutual friend, Martin Burgoyne, was "sick" with "it," referring to HIV. Pop sensation Madonna, a best friend of Burgoyne, was seen buying books for "a sick friend," Warhol includes in the diary.[19] Perhaps loneliness struck Warhol that day, as he was aware of the effects of AIDS epidemic devastating the gay community. By then, his last romantic relationship had fizzled with Jon Gould, a Paramount Studios executive. Gould had been diagnosed with AIDS in 1984 and eventually returned to Los Angeles.

One month after Warhol's birthday, the Pyramid Club hosted an event to celebrate and raise funds for the wildly popular but deteriorating Burgoyne. "The news that yet another friend was seriously ill seemed all too familiar in the neighborhood. Nearly everyone at the party early yesterday morning, where about $6,000 was raised for Mr. Burgoyne's medical and living expenses, could list the names of several friends who have died of AIDS," the *New York Times* published. Warhol, in attendance, was credited for drawing Burgoyne's portrait on the invitation of the event. Haring, Kenny Scharf, and Madonna also attended.[20] A little over a week later Warhol heard that his ex-boyfriend Gould had died on September 18. Warhol left this out of his diary for that particular date, but later noted, "...the Diary can write itself on the other news from L.A., which I don't want to talk about."[21] Burgoyne would also pass away from AIDS-related complications by November 1986.

日快乐'，他们并没有大声说出来。"他继续说，在艺术家凯斯·哈林告诉他一个他们共同的朋友马丁·伯戈因得了"那种病"（指艾滋病）之后，"这一天就变得很奇怪。"流行天后麦当娜是伯戈因的好朋友，沃霍尔也在日记中提到，她被看到为"一个生病的朋友"买书。[19] 也许那天沃霍尔深感孤独，他意识到了艾滋病对同性恋群体的蚕食。那时，他与派拉蒙影业的执行制片人乔恩·古尔德的最后一段浪漫关系已经破灭了。古尔德在 1984 年被诊断出患有艾滋病，最终回到了洛杉矶。

在沃霍尔生日的一个月后，金字塔俱乐部举办了一次庆祝活动，为受人欢迎但健康状况急剧恶化的伯戈因筹集资金。《纽约时报》这样报道："又一个朋友身患重病的消息对这个群体来说似乎太熟悉了。在昨天清晨的聚会上，几乎每个人都能列出几个死于艾滋病的朋友的名字。这次聚会为伯戈因先生的医疗和生活费用筹集了约 6000 美元。"沃霍尔参加了这场筹款，为邀请函画了伯戈因的肖像。哈林、肯尼·沙尔夫和麦当娜也都出席了这次活动。[20] 一个多星期后，沃霍尔听说他的前男友古尔德于 9 月 18 日去世。当天的日记里沃霍尔并没有提及，后来才写到，"……那些洛杉矶的新闻报道不言自明，我不想谈论它们。"[21] 伯戈因也在 1986 年 11 月因艾滋病并发症去世。

沃霍尔本人于 1987 年 2 月离世。不是因为艾滋病，而是因为一场失败的胆囊手术，全世界都为之震惊。沃霍尔的葬礼在匹兹堡的圣灵拜占庭天主教堂举行，与在纽约圣帕特里克大教堂举行的声势浩大的追悼会相比，这场葬礼仍然是一个主要由家人和亲友参加的私人场合。数以千计自认为是亲密朋友的人参加了纽约的追悼会，并对它记忆犹新。一位不知所措的客人形容那场追悼会："……就像一颗星星，这个城市的一部分，就这样消失、爆炸了。"在散场后的聚会上，她生动地回忆道："沿环形楼梯走向地下，仿佛置身于电影场景中，有一种来自早年间曼哈顿的衰败魅力的光环。里面是这个世界上最有名的人：流行歌星、皇室成员、富豪、电影明星、政治家。你无法相信自己在同一时间与所有这些人共处一室，简直不可思议。但他们都是这个谦逊的人的朋友，一个因为秃头感到窘迫而戴着白色假发的人。"[22]

"成为安迪·沃霍尔"意味着什么，这个问题的核心仍旧是个复杂的拉扯：舞会落单的人与幕后策划；前卫艺术家和派对动物。沃霍尔的一位前同事曾讲述了他们如何在沃霍尔位于纽约蒙托克的海滨度假别墅为沃霍尔举办了一个亲密的生日派对。这场派对将沃霍尔身上的矛盾展现得淋漓尽致：简单的晚宴后是蛋糕和香槟。经典摇滚乐唱片响起，人群开始跳舞。然而寿星不愿意加入，他观察了一下，咕哝着说："天啊……你们这些孩子相处得真好。"然后他从自己的派对上溜走去睡觉了。[23] 沃霍尔大概很清楚，即使没有他，派对也会继续下去。

何塞·卡洛斯·迪亚兹是安迪·沃霍尔美术馆的首席策展人，曾策划展览"法哈德·莫希里：向西行""安迪·沃霍尔：启示""梦幻美利坚"及"波拉·彼薇：渴望一切"。他还担任美国艺术博物馆策展人协会理事，并于 2018 年担任策展领导力研究中心的研究员。迪亚兹拥有旧金山州立大学艺术史学士学位及利物浦大学文化史硕士学位。

Warhol himself would pass away in February 1987, not from AIDS, but from a failed gallbladder procedure at a New York hospital. The world was shocked. Warhol's funeral, at the Holy Ghost Byzantine Catholic Church in Pittsburgh, remained mostly a private occasion with family and close associates, in comparison to the over-the-top memorial service that followed at St. Patrick's Cathedral in New York. Thousands who considered themselves close friends attended and remember that occasion. One bewildered guest described the memorial service "...like a star, a part of the city, just vanishing or exploding." At the after-party, she vividly recalls, "You went down a sweeping circular staircase leading underground, and you could have been on a movie set with an aura of decayed glamour from an earlier era of Manhattan. The people inside were the most recognizable on the planet: pop stars, royalty, the fabulously wealthy, movie stars, politicians. You couldn't believe you were in a room with all these people all at the same time – it made no sense. But all of them were friends with this modest man who wore a white wig because he was embarrassed about being bald."[22]

At its core, the question of what it meant to become Andy Warhol hinges upon this still perplexing dialectic of wallflower and impresario, avant-garde artist and party animal. One particular celebration captures the contradiction well. A former colleague of Warhol described how they threw him an intimate party for his forty-ninth birthday at his beach retreat in Montauk, New York. A casual dinner was followed by cake and champagne. Classic rock-and-roll records blasted, and dancing was inevitable. The birthday boy, reluctant to dance, observed and allegedly cooed, "Gee... you kids get along so well." He then slipped away from his own party and went to bed.[23] Perhaps Warhol knew the party would go on, even without him.

José Carlos Diaz is the Chief Curator at The Andy Warhol Museum. There he has curated "Farhad Moshiri: Go West"; "Andy Warhol: Revelation"; "Fantasy America"; and "Paola Pivi: I Want It All." He serves on the Board of Trustees for the Association of Art Museum Curators and was a 2018 fellow at the Center for Curatorial Leadership (CCL). Diaz received a MA in Cultural History from the University of Liverpool, and a BA in Art History from San Francisco State University.

## 注释

1. 格伦·奥布莱恩,《访谈:安迪·沃霍尔》,《高峰月刊》,1977年8月,收录于肯尼思·戈德史密斯编辑,《我将是你的镜子:安迪·沃霍尔访谈选集》,纽约:卡罗尔与格拉夫出版社,2004年,第242页。
2. 道格拉斯·C. 麦吉尔,《波普艺术家安迪·沃霍尔去世》,《纽约时报》,1987年2月23日。
3. 安迪·沃霍尔,《安迪·沃霍尔的哲学(从A到B,再到A)》,纽约:哈科特出版社,1975年,第193页。
4. 伊莎贝尔·C. 迪弗雷纳,《15分钟的名望:我与安迪·沃霍尔的那些年》,纽约:哈科特出版社,1988年,第17页。
5. 约翰·焦尔诺,《伟大的魔鬼王:关于诗歌、性、艺术、死亡和启蒙的回忆录》,纽约:法拉,施特劳斯和吉鲁,2020年,第86页。
6. 埃莉莎·里皮斯基-卡拉斯,《莉莎·明尼利的纽约》,《时尚芭莎》,2011年2月17日。
7. 艺术家马德琳·勒里希管理着墓地以及其他献祭的详细目录,更多信息参见 http://www.andyfigments.com/。
8. 安迪·沃霍尔与帕特·哈克特,《波普主义:沃霍尔的六十年代》,纽约:哈科特出版社,1980年,第355—356页。
9. 霍华德·赫特尔与唐·内夫,《讣告:玛丽莲·梦露去世》,《洛杉矶时报》,1962年8月6日。
10. 布莱克·戈普尼克,《沃霍尔》,纽约:哈珀柯林斯出版社,2020年,第282页。
11. 安迪·沃霍尔与帕特·哈克特,《安迪·沃霍尔日记》,1982年8月6日。
12. 同上,1984年8月6日。
13. 同上,1981年8月6日。
14. 同上,1978年8月6日。
15. 同上,1979年8月6日。
16. 同上,1979年8月7日。
17. 同上,1980年8月6日。
18. 同上,1981年6月16日。
19. 同上,1986年8月6日。
20. 威廉·E. 盖斯特,《关于纽约:在瘟疫面前》,《纽约时报》,1986年9月6日。
21. 安迪·沃霍尔与帕特·哈克特,《安迪·沃霍尔日记》,1986年9月21日,第760页。
22. 《还记得快乐吗?:在我们焦急地等待快乐回归之时,一篇关于最近记忆中最棒派对的口述史,也可能是未来派对一瞥?》,《城镇与乡村杂志》,2021年4月。
23. 鲍勃·科拉切洛,《神圣的恐惧:安迪·沃霍尔小传》,纽约:库珀广场出版,1990年,第344—345页。

## Notes

1. Glenn O'Brien, "Interview: Andy Warhol," *High Times* (Aug. 1977), in *I'll Be Your Mirror: The Selected Andy Warhol Interviews*, ed. Kenneth Goldsmith (New York: Carroll & Graf Publishers, 2004), 242.
2. Douglas C. McGill, "Andy Warhol, Pop Artist, Dies," *New York Times*, February 23, 1987.
3. Andy Warhol, *The Philosophy of Andy Warhol (From A to B and Back Again)* (New York: Harcourt, 1975), 193.
4. Ultra Violet, *Famous for 15 Minutes: My Years with Andy Warhol* (New York: Harcourt, 1988), 17.
5. John Giorno, *Great Demon Kings: A Memoir of Poetry, Sex, Art, Death, and Enlightenment* (New York: Farrar, Straus, and Giroux, 2020), 86.
6. Elisa Lipsky-Karasz, "Liza Minnelli's New York," *Harper's Bazaar*, Feb. 17, 2011.
7. Artist Madelyn Roehrig manages the gravesite and inventories the offerings. More info at: http://www.andyfigments.com/.
8. Andy Warhol and Pat Hackett, *POPism: The Warhol Sixties* (New York: Harcourt, 1980), 355–356.
9. Howard Hertel and Don Neff, "Marilyn Monroe Dies; Pills Blamed, *Los Angeles Times*, Aug. 6, 1962.
10. Blake Gopnik, *Warhol* (New York: Harper Collins, 2020), 282.
11. Andy Warhol and Pat Hackett *The Andy Warhol Diaries* (New York: Warner Books, 1989), entry for Aug. 6, 1982.
12. Ibid, entry for Aug. 6, 1984.
13. Ibid, entry for Aug. 6, 1981.
14. Ibid, entry for Aug. 6, 1978.
15. Ibid, entry for Aug. 6, 1979.
16. Ibid, entry for Aug. 7, 1979.
17. Ibid, entry for Aug. 6, 1980.
18. Ibid, entry for June 16, 1981.
19. Ibid, entry for Aug. 6, 1986.
20. William E. Geist, "About New York: In the Face of a Plague, A Party," New York Times, Sept. 6, 1986.
21. Andy Warhol and Pat Hackett, *The Andy Warhol Diaries* (New York: Warner Books, 1989), entry for Sept. 21, 1986, 760.
22. "Remember Fun?: As we anxiously await its return, an oral history of the best parties in recent-ish memory – and maybe a glimpse of its future?", *Town & Country Magazine*, T&C House Rules column, April 2021.
23. Bob Colacello, *Holy Terror: Andy Warhol Up Close* (New York: Cooper Square Press, 1990), 344–345.

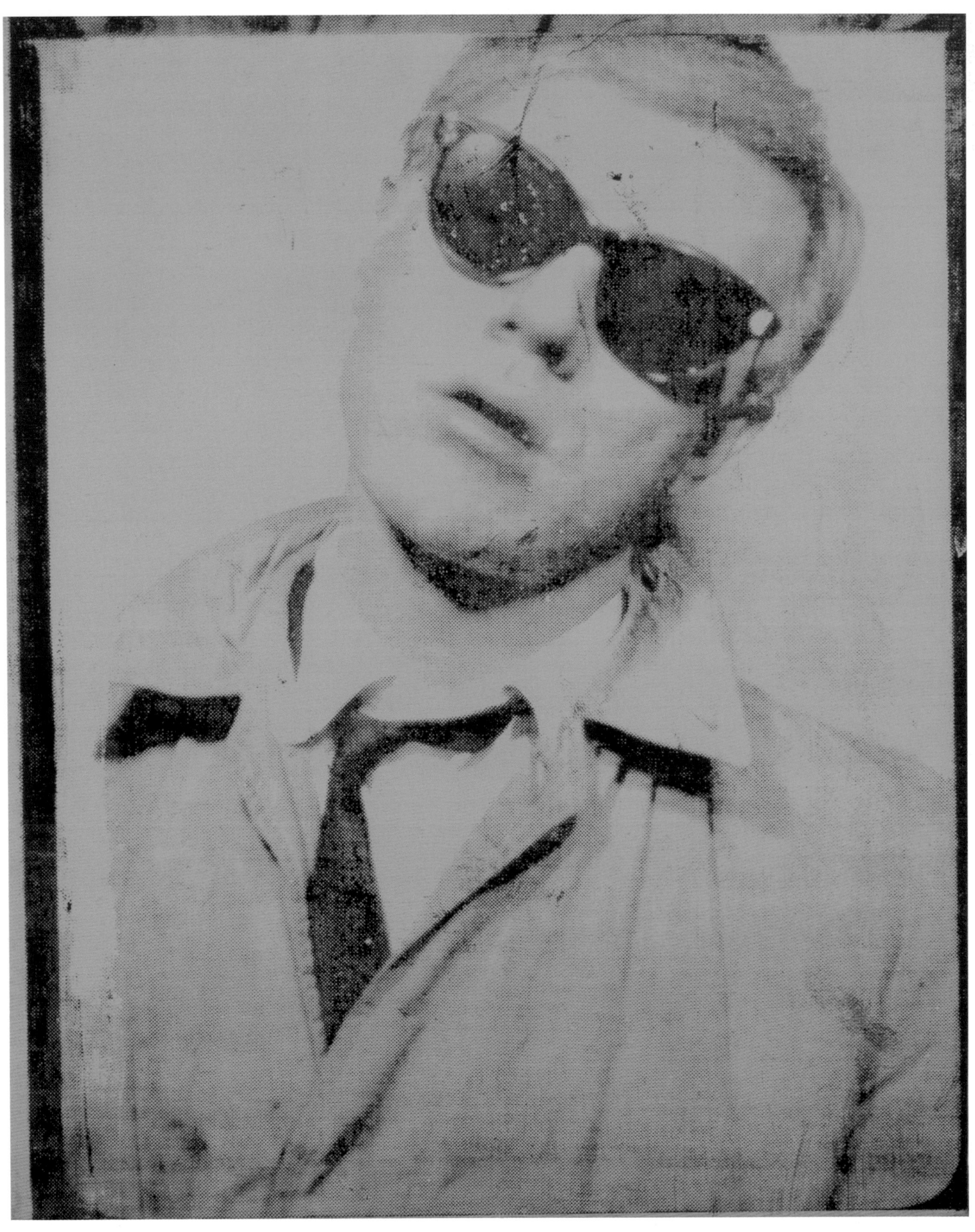

《自画像》
*Self-Portrait*
1963—1964

布上丙烯和丝印油墨
Acrylic and silkscreen ink on linen
50.8 × 40.6 cm

# 安迪·沃霍尔，一位艺术家

布莱克·戈普尼克

# ANDY WARHOL, ARTIST

Blake Gopnik

安迪·沃霍尔，一位艺术家。

这样的概述看似不言而喻，但其实点明了有关沃霍尔的一个最为重要，却经常为人所忽略的事实。从他开始波普艺术实验的那一年到2021年春天，已经过去了近六十个年头，然而无论是他的拥护者还是批评家似乎都未能完全认清的一点，那就是沃霍尔终其一生信奉的都是艺术以及艺术的不断革新，这个信念影响到了他所做的一切。

一些沃霍尔的拥趸往往将他作为真正艺术家所付出的努力视为其职业生涯的附录，或是一篇波普的序言，而他们显然更关心之后的章节：他是流行文化中无法撼动的存在，是众多名流怪咖中最特立独行的一位。他们看重那个1960年代的派对狂人，带着银色假发，和瘦得笔杆儿一样的模特跳扭摆舞；又或者那个地下的原型朋克（proto-punk）嬉皮士，打破社会道德范式，将地下丝绒呈现在我们面前；又或者那个上流社会的附庸，被54俱乐部（Studio 54）里的那些漂亮的人儿吸引，随后让我们在他的《访谈》（Interview）杂志里对着美人垂涎三尺。在看重这些"沃霍尔"的同时，拥趸们觉得大可以把艺术抛在脑后；有些人可能还为能够避而不谈艺术感到庆幸。

对于这些拥趸的解读，沃霍尔的批评家或多或少地表示了赞同，尽管他们因为这些表征谴责沃霍尔背离了高雅艺术（High Art）的阳春白雪，投身于流行文化的流俗与浅薄之中。即便是艺术世界的怀疑者已经承认了沃霍尔早年在波普艺术上取得的成就（至今仍有人并不认可），也会认为他之后的种种作为是为了追名逐利渐渐偏离、背叛了艺术。1964年，当沃霍尔的"布里洛盒子"系列面世之时，已经有一位《纽约时报》的批评家抱怨他"把大写的艺术摧毁了。"[1] 从那时起，这样的观点已经被重复了无数次，重复者或是因此振奋，或是为之感伤。

然而，更近地观察沃霍尔和他的一生，我们就会看到，从一开始，他就着迷于艺术（the Art），并且在他的想象里，艺术一直都是当得起以大写字母的伟丽来书写的。沃霍尔创造的不论种类的几乎每一件物品，暴露在公众视野的每一步举措，都可以透过他的艺术家之眼来观察审视。他绝非是要"摧毁"艺术——现今已是2021年了，回望过去，不用说"摧毁"，我们连他阻碍了艺术发展的迹象都找不到，不是吗？——终其一生，他的雄心壮志都是要尽可能地拓宽艺术的边界、丰富艺术的内涵，使艺术宽广到甚

Andy Warhol was an artist.

If that seems obvious, it is actually one of the most significant and sometimes most neglected facts about him. Since his first experiments in Pop Art, which celebrated their sixtieth year this spring, both fans and critics have had a tendency to lose track of how much his lifelong commitment to art, and to its constant renewal, touched almost everything he did.

Certain Warhol fans have tended to see his labors as a fine artist as almost a sideline in his career, or maybe as a kind of Pop Art preface to another aspect they care more about: his presence deep inside popular culture, as maybe the kookiest in its vast pool of celebrity kooks. They value the 1960s party animal in the silver wig, frugging with stick-thin models. Or the underground, proto-punk hipster, master of anomie, who brought us the Velvet Underground. Or the high-society hanger-on who gaped at the Beautiful People of Studio 54, then let the rest of us ogle them in *Interview* magazine. In valuing those "Warhols," fans feel they can leave art to one side. Some may even count themselves lucky to have escaped it.

Warhol's critics have more or less agreed with the reading of those fans, although they look at those same aspects of Warhol's career and condemn them as signs of how deeply he sold out, surrendering the high values of High Art to the superficialities of popular culture. Even when art-world doubters have recognized the virtues of Warhol's first years in Pop Art (some still don't), they have seen almost everything that occupied him later as a slide away from art, and a betrayal of it for the sake of fame and wealth. Already by 1964, when Warhol's great Brillo boxes first went on view, one *New York Times* critic was complaining that Warhol had "destroyed Art with a capital A."[1] That view has been repeated countless times since, either with glee or dismay.

A closer look at Warhol and his life shows, however, that from the very beginning he was obsessed with Art and always imagined that it deserved the most magnificent of capital letters. Almost every object Warhol created, of any kind, and almost every public move he made can be seen through his artist's eyes. Rather than "destroying" art – in 2021, are there signs he even slowed it down? – Warhol's passionate, lifelong ambition was to broaden its reach and meaning as widely as possible, even wide enough to include a life's worth of living. This was not for the sake of the wig or the leather or the disco balls, or even for the dollars and amusement those brought him, but for the sake of the art – the Art – he could turn them all into. The modern artist in Warhol saw room to move in his later exploits in weak portraiture, worse television, and execrable commercialism, just by virtue of their distance from the traditional ideals of Western art. By reaching and breaching this far frontier, he could help modern art prove its power. That was his true obsession.

"Anything bad is right,"[2] said Warhol in 1971, and, in 1977, "New things are always much better than old things."[3] That same year, Studio 54 certainly

至足以涵盖一个人一生的存在价值。他活着可不是为了戴假发、穿皮衣，或是在闪耀的迪斯科球下起舞，甚至不是为了金钱以及随之而来的娱乐消遣，而是为了艺术——大写的艺术，沃霍尔可以将身边的一切化作艺术。沃霍尔体内的那个现代艺术家，在拙劣的肖像画、糟糕的电视节目和令人不齿的消费主义中看到了可供他挥洒的空间，因为这些与传统的西方艺术理想之间相去甚远。沃霍尔可以抵达并打破传统艺术理想的边界，证明现代艺术的威力。这才是真正让他着迷的地方。

"任何坏的事物都是对的。"² 沃霍尔在 1971 年如是说道。1977 年时他又说："新事物总是比旧事物要好得多。"³ 那时，比起纽约索霍区的任何一个敞间，54 俱乐部都绝对算得上是一处更新的、"更坏的"（也因此是更好的）艺术创作场所。沃霍尔通过在那儿闲晃创造出来的"艺术"拥有特别的力量，因为它正处在整个文化的中心；在流行文化的极深处生长也使这样的艺术和它的创造者在先锋艺术的最前线上获得了一席之地。

沃霍尔的目标并非那种常见的不切实际的理想：希望用艺术的种种美妙设想来给生活施加养分，使其变得更好；也不是文化激进分子怀抱的神圣志向：想要从艺术的桎梏中完全脱身，专心致志于生活本身，把它过得丰富多彩。沃霍尔志在推进艺术，扩大其边界以容纳生活的全部，实现它全部的先锋潜能——结果越"坏"、越荒诞，就越好。如果说在 1917 年，马塞尔·杜尚（Marcel Duchamp）迈出了荒诞主义的一步，向我们展示了甚至小便器都能被归于艺术范畴之内，那么自 1960 年代开始，沃霍尔则着手让艺术拓展到厕所、厕所所在的建筑、建筑所处的城市，以及任何他所能够踏足的地方和一切他所能够置身其间的领域。如果我们认同杜尚真正的兴趣是在艺术而非厕所管道，那么我们也应该认同沃霍尔更看重的是艺术，而不是扭摆舞和美丽的人儿，甚至可能也不是钱。

深植于沃霍尔心中的对于现代艺术以及打破现代艺术边界的信仰——换句话说，对于一个经典意义上的"先锋"的信仰——是在他创作出伟大的波普艺术之前的几十年里形成的。本文接下来将展现他是怎样集齐诸般要素，成长为成熟的"沃霍尔"，能够将生活的全部都当作艺术的源泉：年轻的安德鲁·沃霍拉（Andrew Warhola）⁴，一个匹兹堡工人阶级家庭的孩子，需要获得一种对于艺术超凡价值的坚定信仰、一个不断拓展其边界的艺术定义、一份先锋派无止境革新的执着以及一种坏与荒诞可以击败美与好的观念。沃霍尔的家乡刚好提供了这四项要素。

一切全都从他的母亲开始。

关于朱莉娅·沃霍拉（Julia Warhola，她本姓扎瓦奇 [Zavacky]）我们了解得不多，不过以我们所知道的来看，沃霍尔的母亲似乎有着天生并有意自我强化的作为波西米亚人的身份认同。⁵ 她"一战"前的年轻岁月是在喀尔巴阡山的穷乡僻壤度过的，现有的故事在谈到这一时期时，都说她十分热衷并擅长绘画，甚至将教堂装饰这种典型的男人工作承担了过来。她又是如此渴望自己的声音能够被听到，加入了通常只对男人开放的唱诗班。已为人妻的朱莉娅 1921 年在匹兹堡安顿下来，她走街串巷地售卖从铁皮罐里剪下来的鲜花，以此捱过大萧条带来的贫困。你很难想象一个平凡的移民家庭的主妇，会将艺术表达视为维持生计的理所当然的手段。（说起来，平凡主妇的想法很可能是对的：朱莉娅的鲜花生意似乎并没有赚到多少钱。）

沃霍尔从他母亲那里学不到太多"正经的"艺术——她只受过极为有限的教育，但她向沃霍尔展

counted as a newer, "worse" (and therefore better) site for artmaking than any SoHo loft could. The "art" Warhol made by hanging out there gained special power because of its existence right at the heart of the culture at large; by living so deep inside popular culture, this art and its maker also gained a presence at the far edge of the vanguard.

Warhol's goal wasn't the standard utopian one of improving life by fertilizing it with art's best ideas. And it wasn't the hallowed ambition of cultural radicals, who aimed to altogether escape the narrow confines of art in favor of life itself, richly lived. Warhol's aim was to improve art, and to realize its full avant-garde potential, by letting it expand to include all of life – the "worse" and more absurd the result, the better. If, in 1917, Marcel Duchamp took the absurdist step of demonstrating that art could expand enough to include even a urinal, in the 1960s and beyond, Warhol set out to have it include the entire bathroom, the building it was in, the city around it, and anything and everything he could get up to in them. And if we imagine that Duchamp's true interest was in art, not sanitary plumbing, we should credit Warhol with caring more about art than about frugging, Beautiful People, or even, just possibly, money.

Warhol came to his deep belief in modern art and its boundary-busting – in other words, a belief in a quite classic avant-gardism – over the decades that preceded his great works in Pop Art. The rest of this essay will show how he first came upon the components that were necessary for his mature self to count all of life as an art supply. Young Andrew Warhola, son of Pittsburgh's working class, needed to acquire an unyielding and unlikely faith in the supreme worth of art; a definition of art that expanded its boundaries; an avant-garde commitment to its endless updating; and a notion that the bad and the absurd could trump the Beautiful and the Good. Warhol's hometown supplied all four.

It all began with Mom.

We don't know a lot about Julia Warhola, née Zavacky, but it looks as though Warhol's mother had a strong identity as some kind of natural-born, self-made bohemian.⁴ Stories about her youth before World War I, in the backwoods of the Carpathian mountains, show her so eager to paint, and so talented at it, that she took on the typically male job of church decoration. She was so keen on making her voice heard that she sang in choirs normally reserved for men. After marrying and then settling in Pittsburgh in 1921, she confronted the deprivations of the Great Depression by going door-to-door selling flowers that she'd cut from tin cans. It's hard to imagine your average immigrant housewife seeing artistic expression as an obvious way to make ends meet. (That housewife would have been right: The flowers don't seem to have yielded much profit.)

Warhol couldn't have learned much about "serious" art from his mother – she'd had the most meager of educations – but she exposed him, maybe almost by accident, to a generic cultural frontiersmanship. The eccentricities of Julia Warhola's self-made culture (her siblings seem to have shared it) happened to map unusually well onto the perfected and professionalized eccentricities of the modern avant-garde, born in the same era that she was. Warhol may have got more from Julia's inchoate urge for eccentric expression than he would have gotten from a mom who frequented MoMA. His later excellence didn't come from his work's clean insertion into the modern canon but rather from the breadth of his vision of what art could be. His success lay in an ethos of invention rather than in a particular practice as inventor, and it looks as though he first learned that ethos at home.

It got outside reinforcement. From about the age of nine, Warhol's Saturdays all began with a walk up the road to the great beaux-arts bulk of the Carnegie Institute and its art museum, where he joined other junior culturati as one of the "Tam O'Shanters" who were granted art lessons there. (The name seems to have been a weird "translation" of the bohemian berets of Montmartre into the headgear of Andrew Carnegie's youth in Scotland; it's another sign of the confused but potent commitment to the avant-garde that young Andy found all around him in Pittsburgh.)

"I looked for the boys and girls to express themselves in their own ways. In other words, I didn't say that a drawing had to be this way, or that way ... but I did say it had to be excellent,"⁵ recalled Joseph Fitzpatrick, one of the young men who taught the classes, expressing a distinctly modern, even modernist, view that his Victorian predecessors would have found incoherent or even dangerous. On the other hand, colleagues in the most rigorously up-to-date art

现了一个在文化的边缘地带摸索的人可能展现的风范，虽然这也许只是无心之举。朱莉娅·沃霍拉那种自创自立的文化带有的种种怪癖（她的兄弟姐妹似乎也有着同样的怪癖），刚好可以近乎完美地和现代先锋派的那种精雕细琢的、专业化的古怪相映照——先锋派和她是同一时代的产儿。朱莉娅对于异乎寻常的表达具有原始而强烈的欲望，沃霍尔从这里面得到的滋养，恐怕比从一位经常去纽约现代艺术博物馆（MoMA）的母亲那里所可能得到的还要多。他之后所取得的卓越成就并不因为他的作品可以干净利落地楔入现代经典之中，而是因为他对艺术可以怎样延伸这个问题具有宽广的视野。他的成功在于他拥有一种创造的精神气质，而不在于他可以做出一个两个具体的发明，而这种精神气质他最初也是在家里学到的。

此外，这种精神气质还在外界得到了强化。从大约9岁开始，沃霍尔在每个星期六都会动身前往卡内基学院（Carnegie Institute）和学院的艺术博物馆。那里有宏富的艺术收藏，还有和他一样在那儿接受艺术教育的小小文化人，他们被称作"绒球软帽"（Tam O'Shanters）。（"绒球软帽"这一名号似乎是对蒙马特[Montmartre]的波西米亚贝雷帽的一个古怪的"转译"，将其变为了安德鲁·卡内基[Andrew Carnegie]年轻时在苏格兰戴的帽子；这是年轻的沃霍尔在匹兹堡虽然迷茫但坚持"先锋"的又一例证。⁶）

"我希望这些男孩女孩以他们自己的方式表达自我。换句话说，我没跟他们说过一幅画一定要画成这样或者那样……不过我确实说过必须要画得出色才行。"⁷约瑟夫·菲茨帕特里克（Joseph Fitzpatrick）回忆道。他曾是在那里教课的诸多年轻人中的一位，而他表达的这一观点显然是现代的，甚至可以说是现代主义的。这样的观点要是让他维多利亚时代的前辈听到了，肯定会觉得颠倒错乱，乃至于十分危险；而要是让他的同代人，让那些在最新式的艺术学校里教书的同行听到的话，他们会觉得他这是在迎合一种没有明确形态的异端——但你可能会说做一个"没有明确形态的异端"成了他最出色的学生在处理艺术和事业时所遵循的根本原则。一名"绒球软帽"在回忆菲茨帕特里克时说，他让所有小孩"都对作为一种观念的艺术……燃起了一团火"⁸，而沃霍尔在之后取得的卓越成就得益于他避免了将自己与任何一种单一的艺术实践绑定，转而依靠一种关于艺术的笼统"观念"，将其运用到文化的全部领域。

相比于菲茨帕特里克，他的一位同事的关注点就要具体得多。他专注于新近的艺术潮流（至少以匹兹堡标准而言），在钢琴上演奏德彪西，让他的"绒球软帽"就音乐做出"反应"，画下"听到那引人遐想的音符时跃入脑海的"⁹抽象画面。尽管成年沃霍尔定会抨击其"俗套"（"俗套"在沃霍尔的骂人语汇里是最为发自内心的一个），这位教师的教学法却可以帮我们理解沃霍尔从一般意义上的艺术教育中得到的领悟：区隔不同美学领域的边界正在崩解。这种崩解在沃霍尔的家乡似乎已然上演，而在日后也成为沃霍尔的一个标志：他几乎触及了每一个文化领域，其中不仅有显然是后德彪西的、激进的音乐，还有绘画和雕塑、电影和出版、戏剧和电视，甚至还有餐厅设计。

让沃霍尔度过无数个星期六的卡内基学院，在致力于向匹兹堡市民普及关于文化和智慧的笼统观念这件事上具有相当的自觉。正如安德鲁·卡内基在学院献词中所言，学院的用意在于提供"阶梯"，"有抱负的人沿此梯攀爬，可以体验到美的享受与和谐的愉悦，由此变得富有感受力，变得彬彬有礼；他会来到知识之海，智慧由此喷涌而出；他将广阔而宏伟的人类生活尽收眼底，生而为人由此得到了升华。"¹⁰

schools of his era might have thought he was courting a shapeless heterodoxy – but you might say that "shapeless heterodoxy" became the governing principle behind the art and career of his greatest pupil. One Tam O'Shanter recalled that Fitzpatrick had the kids "all on fire ... about art, as an idea,"[6] and Warhol's later excellence depended on avoiding any single artistic practice, instead relying on a generalized "idea" of art that he could then apply to all of culture.

A colleague of Fitzpatrick's might have counted as more narrowly committed to recent artistic trends – or recent, at least, by Pittsburgh standards – when he played Debussy on the piano while his Tam O'Shanters "responded" to the music with abstract forms "that sprang into life from hearing the inspiring notes."[7] While the adult Warhol would have blasted this as "corny" (one of the most heartfelt insults in his arsenal), it represented something that did sink in from his more general artistic education: a collapse of boundaries between aesthetic disciplines. That seems to have been very much in play in Warhol's hometown and became the trademark of a man who went on to touch on almost every cultural discipline that came his way, including radical and distinctly post-Debussian music but also painting and sculpture, film and publishing, theater and television, and even restaurant design.

The Carnegie Institute, where Warhol spent all those Saturdays, was quite self-consciously committed to promoting a generalized concept of Culture and Wisdom to Pittsburghers. It was meant to provide "ladders," as the steel baron Andrew Carnegie put it at his Institute's dedication, "upon which the aspiring may climb to the enjoyment of the beautiful and the delights of harmony, whence come sensibility and refinement; to the sources of knowledge, from which spring wisdom; and to wider and grander views of human life, from whence comes the elevation of man."[8] The Institute's single building included galleries for the display of art and others for natural history. It also housed a Hall of Architecture with life-size reproductions of some of the great façades of Europe, a free library (a favorite haunt of Warhol's), and the great music and lecture hall where the Tam O'Shanters took their lessons. Walking up to the grand building on all those Saturdays, the young Warhol was greeted by a façade that bore, as it still does, the names of a buffet of creators ranging from Rembrandt and Velazquez to Bach and Beethoven to Shakespeare and Goethe. In a metropolis like New York, such cultural patron saints would have been divided up between specialized institutions, thereby teaching New Yorkers that culture itself ought to stay siloed. Pittsburgh's syncretic approach, which Warhol continued to bathe in right through university, has echoes in his later embrace of almost every medium, discipline and approach in art and culture.

If those art lessons at the Carnegie let Warhol discover the pleasures of artmaking, "as an idea," they also plunged him into the specifics of what professional artists got up to, across a vast range of practices. As the older Tam O'Shanters gained skills, they were rechristened "Palettes" and sent to draw and paint in the Carnegie's art galleries, copying what was on display there. (One fuzzy old photo seems to show an 11-year-old Warhol doing just that.) The Carnegie's own art collection was barely worth notice, so curators brought in ambitious loan exhibitions that would have trumpeted the greatness of great art, of all stripes, as well as the vast cultural prestige that came with it. These loan shows gave Warhol exposure to European Old Masters such as Rembrandt, Rubens, and Poussin and, more importantly, to such icons of the Western avant-garde as Honoré Daumier, Henri Rousseau, and, most importantly, Pablo Picasso. The world-famous Spaniard was an obsession of the adult Warhol; *Guernica* itself, ultimate symbol of the avant-garde's success, had made a pit-stop at the Carnegie when Warhol was in eighth grade.

Warhol got exposed to a full range of up-to-date work once a year in the vast Carnegie International, an invitational survey of contemporary art that had been running since 1896 – just one year after the founding of its only global rival, the Venice Biennale. By the standards of Paris or New York, the art that the Carnegie's curators brought in might have appeared fairly tame – there was relatively little of the latest abstraction, for instance – but Pittsburgh treated the yearly selection as almost intolerably novel. In the 1930 edition, the prize awarded to a quite restrained Picasso portrait had caused a furor with the local audience, known to "spit at 50 yards at a modern painting,"[9] according to the International's longtime director. In following decades, that same audience came to decry his annuals' artists as having "pink" or even "red" politics.[10] Warhol himself adopted distinctly pink positions in his college years and never quite gave them up.

置身于一栋单体建筑中的卡内基学院有多个陈列艺术及自然历史的展厅;此外还容纳一个建筑大厅,厅内摆放着伟大的欧洲建筑的微缩模型;一个免费的图书馆(这是沃霍尔很喜欢去的地方);一个音乐和演讲大厅,"绒球软帽"就在这个大厅里上课。每逢星期六,沃霍尔都会沿着这座宏伟建筑拾级而上。迎接年轻的沃霍尔的,是一个镌刻有无数创造者姓名的立墙,这些名字今天也还在其上熠熠生辉:从伦勃朗(Rembrandt)和委拉斯开兹(Velazquez),到巴赫(Bach)和贝多芬(Beethoven),再到莎士比亚(Shakespeare)和歌德(Goethe)。若是在纽约那样的大都会,这些文化巨擘肯定会分别由不同的专门机构和场馆纪念,纽约人由此得到的教导是:文化是要分门别类、各自安放的。沃霍尔直到上大学都一直沐浴在匹兹堡这种融会贯通的理念之下,而这种融会贯通也在他之后的人生中激起了回响——他几乎拥抱了文化和艺术中的每一种媒介、每一个领域和每一种方法。

如果说那些卡内基的艺术课让沃霍尔发现了"作为一种观念"的艺术创作的乐趣的话,它们还通过一系列的艺术实践让他获得了职业艺术家必须经受的训练。随着年纪渐长,"绒球软帽"获得的技能也不断增多,并有了"调色板"(Palettes)这一新的代称,被送到卡内基的艺术展厅里画画,临摹在那里展出的作品。(我们在一张模糊的老照片上似乎还能看到正在接受这一训练的 11 岁的沃霍尔)。卡内基自己的艺术收藏不怎么值得一提,所以策展人会从各处借来出色的展品展览,这些展览彰显了各种类型的伟大艺术的精妙之处,以及伴随而来的文化声威。这些展览让沃霍尔接触到包括伦勃朗、鲁本斯(Rubens)、普桑(Poussin)等人在内的欧洲古典大师;更为重要的是,这些展览还使他得以观摩西方先锋派中的标志性人物,例如奥诺雷·杜米埃(Honoré Daumier)、亨利·卢梭(Henri Rousseau),以及最为重要的——巴勃罗·毕加索(Pablo Picasso)。这位举世闻名的西班牙人是成年沃霍尔的迷恋对象,他的《格尔尼卡》(Guernica),先锋派成就的终极象征之作,在沃霍尔八年级时曾在卡内基短暂展出。

在一年一度的盛大的卡内基国际展(Carnegie International)上,沃霍尔可以一览各类艺术的最新力作。卡内基国际展创办于 1896 年——仅比它唯一的国际对手威尼斯双年展晚一年——实行邀请制,旨在审视当代艺术。以巴黎或者纽约的标准来看,卡内基的策展人挑选的艺术也许有些过于驯顺和乏味了。比如,相对而言,展会上不太看得到最新的抽象作品。但是对于匹兹堡来说,这些每年挑选出来的艺术品几乎新奇到了不可容忍的地步。以 1930 年那届展会为例,奖项颁给了毕加索的一幅肖像画,尽管这幅画相当收敛,却使当地观众一片哗然,据国际展常任总监说,他们"从 45 米外朝一幅现代绘画啐口水"[11]。在其后的几十年里,这些观众还会因国际展的年度艺术家具有"粉红"[12] 或"红色"政治立场而对其加以谴责。[13](沃霍尔自己在大学期间明确了"粉红"立场,并终身坚守。)

卡内基的年度展览让沃霍尔感受到了新艺术的力量,同时并没有将新艺术呈现为只有单一的方向或目标。卡内基国际展总是相当折中且兼收并蓄的。它倾向于将各种现代画法混在一起一并推出:从保罗·克利(Paul Klee)的梦幻之境,到本·沙恩(Ben Shahn)的激进象形,再到像摩西奶奶(Grandma Moses)这样的素人画家的作品,还有像卡罗尔·布兰查德(Carol Blanchard)这种假充素人艺术家的戏作——这些都对 1950 年代创作仍相对保守的沃霍尔产生了肉眼可见的影响。而在六十年代及之后的岁月里,随着沃霍尔波普艺术的诞生以及其后种类

If the Carnegie's annuals taught Warhol the power of the new, they didn't portray it as having a singular direction or goal. The show was always quite eclectic: It tended toward a mix of options in modern figuration, from the dreamscapes of Paul Klee to the activist imagery of Ben Shahn to work by outsider artists such as Grandma Moses and of faux-outsiders such as Carol Blanchard – all the above having had a visible influence on Warhol in the 1950s, when his art would have still counted as fairly conservative. In the 1960s and beyond, with the advent of Warhol's Pop Art and the vast range of creations that followed, Warhol turned the Carnegie International's open-armed embrace of the new into something closer to a conceptual gambit and polemic. He rejected single directions and approaches in favor of treating modern artmaking as capacious enough to include just about everything he got up to. In Warhol's hands, the almost Victorian eclecticism of the early Carnegie surveys became a proto-postmodern polymorphism.

Beyond the almost accidental breadth that Warhol witnessed at the Carnegie, a remarkable Pittsburgh gallery called Outlines offered him a more self-conscious yoking of cultural range with avant-garde sophistication. Described by one Pittsburgh art student as "the gallery of tomorrow,"[11] Outlines operated from 1941 to 1947, just when Warhol would have been forming his first impressions of "serious" contemporary art and culture.

At Outlines, Warhol got the chance to see the abstract sculpture of Alexander Calder; the Surrealism of Max Ernst, André Mason, and Joseph Cornell; and the proto-Pop paintings of Stuart Davis, built around household products and ads. (A college professor of Warhol's gave a talk at Outlines on "Modern Advertising in Art" almost two decades before Warhol became famous for that same combination.)

Most importantly, Outlines displayed work by Marcel Duchamp, whose Dada appropriations – his famous urinal, bicycle wheel, and snow shovel – were by far the single most important influence on Warhol's entire career. (In 1944, the founder of Outlines bought a deluxe, signed, and inscribed copy of Duchamp's *Boîte-en-valise*, the complete survey-in-a-box of the Frenchman's career, with each of his works reproduced in miniature. Warhol later bought his own.)[12] If the Carnegie Institute's annual show suggested that modern art included a vast range of options, Duchamp let Warhol know that there was simply nothing that modern art could not pull into its orbit.

In its programming, Outlines offered almost as capacious a view.

Modernist authors came within its scope: The gallery hosted such events as a reading from James Joyce's newly published *Finnegans Wake* and a concert performance of Gertrude Stein's *Four Saints in Three Acts*.

Outlines sponsored performances and a residency by composer John Cage and choreographer Merce Cunningham, a team, and a couple, who were central figures in the New York avant-garde when Warhol joined it in the 1960s. The gallery also had a deep commitment to the artistic potential of photography when most of the art world would still have seen that as a quite radical position. Outlines went far out on that limb by collapsing the distinction between "art" photographs by Edward Weston and Man Ray and more "commercial" works by Eugene Atget and Henri Cartier-Bresson. The gallery's final event, as it shut down, was a presentation titled "The Illiterate of The Future Will Be The Man Who Cannot Use The Camera," given by Beaumont Newhall, curator of photography at the Museum of Modern Art, and by László Moholy-Nagy, one of photography's great promoters at Germany's Bauhaus. Much of Warhol's mature art was built around camera work and the modern viewer's supreme skill at reading it.

Outlines had an equally profound and unlikely commitment to the full range of contemporary film, screening both Hollywood movies and more experimental works by Sergei Eisenstein, Jean Cocteau, and Maya Deren. Later, Warhol's own work as a filmmaker came to embrace both ends of the spectrum, bringing them together into a single practice. Warhol's love of Hollywood's Golden Age was not, or not only, the starry-eyed worship of a fan-boy, although that's almost always how it has been seen. Instead, it was also, or mostly, the steely-eyed appreciation of a committed avant-gardist: Screenings at Outlines had taught Warhol that a Greta Garbo movie could have just as vital a place in vanguard culture as any film by Eisenstein or Cocteau – and that this collapse of high and low was a central avant-garde gesture.

Outlines' deepest commitment, however, was to the art and design – and especially the *principles* – of the Bauhaus, which the Nazis had recently forced into

繁多的创造,沃霍尔将卡内基国际展对于新艺术的热情拥抱化为观念先导,就此展开论争:他拒绝单一的方向和方法,认为现代艺术创作辽阔宏大到几乎可以容纳他所接触的每一样东西。在沃霍尔手中,早期卡内基国际展所遵行的几近维多利亚式的折中主义(eclecticism),变为了原初形态的后现代多态(proto-postmodern polymorphism)。

沃霍尔在卡内基认识到了几乎是偶然呈现的艺术广度,而匹兹堡的一家名为"廓线"(Outlines)的不同寻常的画廊则更为自觉地将文化的广度与先锋派的繁复精深结合了起来。被一位匹兹堡的艺术生形容为"画廊明日"[14]的廓线在1941到1947年间营业,这一时期的沃霍尔正在形成对"严肃的"当代艺术和文化的最初印象。

在廓线画廊,沃霍尔得以看到亚历山大·考尔德(Alexander Calder)的抽象雕塑,马克斯·恩斯特(Max Ernst)、安德烈·马松(André Masson)和约瑟夫·康奈尔(Joseph Cornell)的超现实主义作品,以及斯图尔特·戴维斯(Stuart Davis)的那些体现了波普的原初形态(proto-Pop)的、围绕着家居用品和广告创作的画作。(在沃霍尔将艺术和广告相结合而举世闻名的近20年前,沃霍尔的一位大学教授做过一场题为《艺术中的现代广告》的演讲。)

最为重要的是,廓线展出过马塞尔·杜尚的作品。杜尚的达达式的挪用——他知名的小便器、自行车轮、雪铲——在当时对沃霍尔的整个职业生涯产生了最为重要的影响。(1944年,画廊的创始人买了一件杜尚的豪华限量签名版《手提箱中的盒子》[Boîte-en-valise],盒子里是这位法国艺术家的艺术生涯重现,容纳了他每件作品的微缩模型。后来沃霍尔自己也收藏了一件。)[15] 如果说卡内基学院一年一度的国际展表明了现代艺术有着纷繁多样的路数,那么杜尚则让沃霍尔了解到没有什么是不能被现代艺术纳入自己轨道的。

在廓线画廊的规划里,它提供了一个几乎同样广阔的视野。

现代主义作家在它的关注范围之内:比如朗读詹姆斯·乔伊斯(James Joyce)最新出版的《芬尼根的守灵夜》(Finnegans Wake),演奏格特鲁德·斯坦(Gertrude Stein)的《三幕四圣》(Four Saints in Three Acts)等活动,廓线全都举办过。

廓线还赞助过作曲家约翰·凯奇(John Cage)和编舞家莫斯·坎宁安(Merce Cunningham)的演出和驻留。他们既是一个团队,也是彼此的伴侣,在沃霍尔于1960年代粉墨登场时已是纽约先锋运动的中心人物。

这家画廊还对摄影的艺术潜力深信不疑,这被当时艺术界的大部分人视为相当激进的立场。廓线画廊冒着很大的风险,抹除了爱德华·韦斯顿(Edward Weston)和曼·雷(Man Ray)的"艺术"摄影与尤金·阿杰(Eugène Atget)和亨利·卡蒂埃-布列松(Henri Cartier-Bresson)的"商业"作品之间的分野。这家画廊关张前举办的最后一次活动,是一个名为"未来的文盲将是那些不会使用相机的人"的分享会,纽约现代艺术博物馆摄影策展人博蒙特·纽霍尔(Beaumont Newhall)和在德国包豪斯极力推动摄影艺术的拉兹洛·莫霍利-纳吉(László Moholy-Nagy)都参与其中。沃霍尔成熟期的艺术创作有许多都围绕摄影展开,而且有赖于现代观众拥有的读解摄影的高超能力。

廓线对于当代电影的各类形态也有着同等深度的关注,这着实令人难以置信。它既放好莱坞大片,也放更具实验色彩的电影,如谢尔盖·爱森斯坦(Sergei Eisenstein)、让·科克托(Jean Cocteau)和玛雅·黛伦(Maya Deren)的作品。后来,沃霍

an American afterlife at the School of Design in Chicago and Black Mountain College in North Carolina. The gallery's embrace of film and photography, of modernist music, dance, writing, and design, was of a piece with the Bauhaus "educational method" cited in the review of an Outlines show dedicated to the school's American heirs. Outlines shared the Bauhaus ideal of dissolving the distinctions between fine art and design, between the elevated and the functional, so that an enlarged field of art could benefit modern society.

It's obvious that Warhol's mature antics and gambits had almost nothing in common with the utopian sobriety of Bauhaus productions. Sophisticated Bauhausers would have cringed at his explicitly foolish and garish cow wallpaper; ditto at his deliberately ham-fisted efforts in film. (Warhol barely tried to keep his camera in focus, let alone figure out new ways to use it.) But the very fact that Warhol, the dedicated and successful fine artist, felt an urge to expand his art practice to embrace design and film, photography and publishing, depends on a Bauhaus model that he learned early and then got busy enlarging—and deliberately corrupting—once he truly came of age in art.

The modernist expansiveness on view at Outlines was reinforced for Warhol when he entered the art department of the Carnegie Institute of Technology in the fall of 1945. Many of Warhol's instructors showed and spoke at Outlines, while all their best students hung out there. The department's pedagogy was explicitly based on Bauhaus principles—on "the ideal that there was no line between the fine and the applied arts and that there [are] certain fundamental principles of design and certain aspects of creative expression that all work together," according to a classmate of Warhol's.[13]

In 1947, Moholy-Nagy, a frequent guest at Outlines who had been tasked with bringing the exiled Bauhaus to Chicago, published a book of his principles called *Vision in Motion*, and we know Warhol read and admired it.[14] The book's account of the modern avant-garde was capacious in the extreme, even by the standards of Outlines and Carnegie Tech: It included Voltaire, Lenin, Einstein, Beethoven, Joyce, Picasso, Mondrian, and many other similar giants. All these pioneers of an "advanced" human culture were to be gathered under a single umbrella, said Moholy-Nagy, with the goal of "restoring the basic unity of all human experiences" by deploying "scientists, sociologists, artists, writers, musicians, technicians, and craftsmen" toward "a new unity of purpose" for and in culture.

"The new specialist will have to integrate his special subject with the social whole," Warhol read, and he took that to heart by getting it backward: He went on to integrate the "social whole"—every last bit of life—into his "special subject" of art, thereby guaranteeing his place in the vanguard Moholy-Nagy had taught him about.

When Warhol started college, all of Tech was being reconceived around a new "critical-thinking" pedagogy that, like the Bauhaus, favored a curriculum built around a general set of "problems" and how to approach them, rather than around the practical skills and approaches enshrined in any one discipline.

In Warhol's program in "Pictorial Design"—note the deliberately generic name; it had recently been changed from "Painting and Illustration"—studio classes were designed to encourage "the development of habits of observation and analysis and the acquisition of skills necessary to the most effective expression of ideas."[15] The curriculum deliberately blurred the lines between commercial and fine art and between the various subfields in each. (While making clear that fine art was still the elite and most desirable practice, as Warhol always believed, even when he was making a killing in illustration.) Rather than train dedicated painters or sculptors or illustrators, the school would mold the young artist into a "social participator and collaborator."[16] That essentially conceptual approach, agnostic as to medium and discipline, governed all the best art that Warhol went on to make. It became the officially "advanced" position in the art of the 1960s and beyond, and Warhol came primed to embrace it and take it further than anyone.

The academic offerings that Warhol encountered at Tech were equally ambitious and all-encompassing. Every day for a year, Warhol attended a course with the grand name of "Arts and Civilization," and he later recalled it with affection. The course textbook and surviving lesson plans show that it introduced the full range of "advanced" modern culture, from Stravinsky to Brecht to Picasso. Rather than taking a traditionally connoisseurial approach, the textbook described art history as "cultural and social geography," ready to deal with just about anything humans make. The book made such advanced,

尔自己作为电影制作人的作品也是同时拥抱两极,将它们融合成一种实践。沃霍尔对于好莱坞黄金时代的爱并不是——或者并不只是——一个闪着星星眼的男孩的粉丝式的崇拜,尽管大家几乎总是这样认为。实际上,他的爱也是——甚至可以说主要是——对笃定的先锋派目光坚定的欣赏:在廓线举办的那些放映活动教会了沃霍尔,一部葛丽泰·嘉宝(Greta Garbo)的电影在先锋文化中可以和一部爱森斯坦或科克托的电影具有同等重要的地位;而这种折叠高雅与凡俗的做法,正是一种重要的先锋姿态。

然而,廓线最为深沉的关怀还是专注于包豪斯的艺术和设计,特别是融贯其间的包豪斯理念。在纳粹的催逼之下,有关包豪斯的种种此时正在美国的芝加哥设计学校(School of Design in Chicago)和位于北卡罗来纳州的黑山学院(Black Mountain College)获得重生。正如廓线画廊为包豪斯的美国继承者所办展览的一篇展评所言,画廊拥抱电影和摄影,拥抱现代主义的音乐、舞蹈、写作和设计,这一做法和包豪斯的教学方法是相通的。廓线和包豪斯有着同样的理想,他们都希望可以消融艺术和设计之间的分别,消融艺术性和功能性的分别,这样,扩展了涵盖范围的艺术将更有益于现代社会。

显而易见的是,沃霍尔那些老练的戏谑与编排几乎和包豪斯作品所显示出的那种理想化的冷静和克制没有丁点相同之处。考究的包豪斯人在沃霍尔那浮夸又过分艳丽的大牛壁纸前肯定会感到局促不安,而面对他那些故意拍得笨手笨脚的电影应该也平静不到哪里去。(沃霍尔甚至都没打算把摄影机的焦距对准,更不要指望他会研究使用摄影机的新方式了。)但是这位专注的、成功的艺术家感到的强烈冲动,想要扩大他的艺术实践,将设计和电影、摄影和出版统统容纳进来,却是因为他在之前学到的包豪斯范式。虽然沃霍尔在艺术上真正成熟后就开始忙于扩充,并且有意识地破坏这一范式。

沃霍尔在廓线画廊领略到的现代主义的宽阔视野在 1945 年秋天入读卡内基理工学院(Carnegie Institute of Technology)艺术系后更加凸显。给沃霍尔上课的很多老师在廓线办过展览和讲座,而他们最出色的那些学生也在此流连。艺术系的教学法很明显是基于包豪斯的理念设计的,用一位沃霍尔的同学的话来说,追寻"这样的一个理想:在纯艺术和应用艺术之间没有分界线,而设计中的一些最为基本的原则和创造性表达的一些特定方面是共同作用的"。[16]

1947 年,廓线画廊的常客——将流离失所的包豪斯带到芝加哥来的莫霍利-纳吉出版了一本名为《运动中的视觉》(Vision in Motion)[17] 的书。他在书中阐述了他的一些原则和理念,沃霍尔读过这本书并且十分喜欢。[18] 此书对于现代先锋运动的论述,视野极为宏大——即使以廓线和卡内基理工学院的标准来看也是这样:它将伏尔泰(Voltaire)、列宁(Lenin)、爱因斯坦(Einstein)、贝多芬、乔伊斯、毕加索、蒙德里安(Mondrian)和众多巨擘统统囊括了进来。按照莫霍利-纳吉的说法,所有这些探索人类文化"更高阶段"的人物都应该被归拢到同一运动之下,通过对"科学家、社会学家、艺术家、作家、音乐家、技术人员和工匠"的有效部署,朝向文化的"一个全新的共同目标"进发,以期"将人类的全部经验重新统一起来"。

"新时代的专家必须将他的专业和社会的整体相结合。"沃霍尔这样理解,将其记在心间并反向操作起来:他将"社会的整体"——生活中的每一个点滴——和艺术这一"他的专业"结合起来,确保了他在莫霍利-纳吉教授带给他的先锋运动中取得一席之地。

syncretic claims as that the traditional "plastic" arts of painting and sculpture were bound to give way to "the more dynamic dance, music, and drama in a development which has come ... to find its most satisfying synthesis in the colored talking motion picture."[17]

In fact, the students at Tech outpaced even their most advanced instructors in their love of film, arranging to screen "experimental motion pictures" and getting together to make one of their own that sounds, in surviving accounts, like a full-blown nod to Dada – a movement the students learned about in their yearlong Arts and Civ. course. Its textbook described Dada artists, including Marcel Duchamp, as creating a "specifically unintelligible form" that deployed "the debris of modern life ... to convince mankind of its lunacy"[18] – not, as it happens, a bad précis of much of Warhol's later art and activities.

Two of Warhol's classmates went on to do graduate work on Dada; in the early 1950s, that would still have been seen as the most unlikely and esoteric of choices and can only have come from tastes they had acquired at Tech. Warhol, graduating as a star student, had also acquired a taste for artistic disruption: One of his final college paintings is a nude of himself, full-frontal and wearing only a girl's Mary Janes, with a finger jammed up his nose.

To give an absurdist, Dada spin to the Bauhausers' utopian vision of an all-encompassing avant-garde – that was the project of Warhol's mature career, as the most ambitious and committed of artists. His years in Pittsburgh made him uniquely prepared to go there.

After Andy Warhol's move to New York in the summer of 1949, it took more than a decade for him to realize his education's full potential.

His commitment to art remained as great as ever. Despite a frenetic and very profitable career in commercial illustration that began right after his move, Warhol always made work he could count as fine art and hunted for galleries that would show it. The common notion that Warhol's career as an exhibiting artist only began in the 1960s, with his Pop Art, is simply wrong: He'd had at least eight shows in the previous decade, many of them solos. But despite the keen artistic ambition that survived from Warhol's Pittsburgh training, an expanded definition of art did not. Everything he showed in the 1950s stood safely in the traditional fine-art categories of painting, drawing, printmaking, and sculpture. (Although the content of the work was often unsafe in the extreme, by '50s standards – it was close to explicitly gay.) If Warhol occasionally blurred the distinctions *between* the categories he worked in – his paintings were partly printed and his sculptures were folded drawings – he didn't step outside of those categories into the culture at large, as his exposure to Outlines and Tech might have encouraged. In the 1950s, Warhol made art that was far more concerned with charming style than with redrawn boundaries. And there was certainly no hint of the "unintelligible form" or "debris of modern life" favored by Dada, or of any Duchampian interest in "lunacy" or the absurd.

All that seemed to arrive almost at once, in the spring of 1961. Throughout the 1950s, Warhol had got occasional work as a department-store window dresser. When yet another window contract came along early in '61, he decided to fill the rear of his display with big paintings that riffed on images from comic strips and tabloid ads. The canvases he made for his window channeled recent developments in vanguard art by "proto-Pop" figures such as Jasper Johns and Robert Rauschenberg – Warhol's interest in the avant-garde had never lapsed – while also serving the store's marketing, which was pitched at the kind of young girls who read comics and tabloids. Brightly colored paintings matched the lively dresses set in front of them.

In that high-end store window, Warhol's with-it paintings were functioning as highly effective props, of a piece with other modern paintings that window dressers had placed behind merchandise over the previous decade. And then Warhol took things much further. Somehow he came to realize that those prop paintings, reeking of their origins in commercial display – in fact *because* of the odor of commerce that clung to them – could, in a gallery setting, do great work as vanguard fine art.

An avant-garde ethos Warhol had imbibed in Pittsburgh (almost with his mother's milk, you might say) led him to embrace the radical novelty of his act. Pittsburgh's expansive vision of what art could include left him open to the notion that his window props might find a place in his fine-art practice, much more narrowly conceived until then. And his Pittsburgh encounters with Dada

与包豪斯的主张类似,当沃霍尔开始他的高校生活时,整个理工学院都在重构一种新的"批判性思维"的教学理念。依据这一理念,课程体系的搭建应该围绕着一组笼统的"问题"展开,学习如何解决它们,而不是专注于让学生掌握在某一特定领域中被奉为圭臬的实用技术和方法。

沃霍尔就读于"图画设计"(Pictorial Design)系——这一有意为之的通用名称是最近才更改的,过去叫作"绘画和插图"(Painting and Illustration)。该系的工作室实践意在"培养学生观察和分析的习惯,帮助他们获得可以最有效地表达观念的技能"。[19] 整个课程体系有意模糊商业艺术和纯艺术之间,以及这两个领域之下不同子领域之间的界限。(与此同时,也明确地表示了纯艺术仍然是精英的且最受人追捧的,而这也是沃霍尔所认同的,甚至在他凭借画插画赚大钱的时候也未曾动摇。)学院并不着意于培养一心想要成为画家、雕塑家或插画师的人,而是希望将这些年轻艺术家塑造为一个"社会的参与者和合作者"。[20] 这种教育说到底采用的是一种概念性的方法,不限定所使用的媒介和所处的领域,这在沃霍尔之后创作的所有出色的艺术作品中都有体现。在 1960 年代及之后的艺术中,在"观念"之上发力正式成为艺术的"更高阶段",而沃霍尔早已为此做好了准备,并且在这条路上走得比任何人都远。

理工学院提供给沃霍尔的学术资源也同样彰显着它的勃勃雄心与广阔视野。曾有一个学年,沃霍尔每天都会上一门名称宏大的课程——"艺术与文明",他在其后的岁月里也曾充满感情地回忆起这门课。从课程所使用的教材以及遗留下来的大纲来看,它介绍了处于"更高阶段"的现代文明的方方面面,从斯特拉文斯基(Stravinsky)到布莱希特(Brecht)再到毕加索。与以往同类课程所惯常采取的鉴赏式的教学有所不同,这门课程的教材将艺术史以"文化和社会地理"的形式描述,随时准备对人类所创造的任何事物加以探讨。这本教材还从融合的视角出发做出了这样一个先进的论断:绘画和雕塑这类传统的"造型"艺术,必将让位给"更具动态的舞蹈、音乐和戏剧……而这一发展历程已然来到了最令人满意的综合阶段——彩色有声电影。"[21]

实际上,理工学院的学生对电影的喜爱程度甚至超过了最先进的教员。他们不仅安排放映,还共同拍摄自己的实验电影。依照现存的记述,这部电影像是一曲达达主义的赞歌;在那门为期一年的"艺术与文明"课上,达达运动也是教学内容的一部分。教材中是这样描述包括马塞尔·杜尚在内的达达艺术家的:他们运用"现代生活的碎片"创出出"特别令人费解的形式……以此来向人类证明自己的疯狂"[22]——这也精巧概括了沃霍尔后来大部分的艺术和活动。

沃霍尔的两位同学都选择围绕达达完成毕业作品。在 1950 年代早期,这可能是最少人会做的,也是最为艰深的选择,深受理工学院品味的影响。沃霍尔这位明星毕业生,也形成了自己的品味——他对艺术的干扰和破坏有着特别的偏好:他大学期间的最后画作中有一幅自己的裸体,正面全裸,只穿了一双女孩常穿的玛丽珍鞋(Mary Janes),一只手指正在挖鼻孔。

包豪斯那种理想化的、认为先锋可以包容一切的观点,需要被赋予一种荒诞主义的、达达式的诠释,这将是成熟期的沃霍尔致力完成的事业;而在所有的艺术家之中,他也是最具雄心、也最为笃定这一事业的那位。匹兹堡的岁月使他为此做好了准备。

安迪·沃霍尔在 1949 年夏天搬去纽约后,花了十多年的时间,才发挥出他所受教育的全部潜能。

and Duchamp gave him permission to elevate "mere" display props to count as art. His hometown training had left him able to recognize the absurdist energy of such elevation.

It was another six months or so before Warhol began to show his new Pop Art to gallerists, and a full year before it earned him a solo exhibition, in Los Angeles, of his new Campbell's Soup paintings. And once he did begin to show this new work, many observers were no happier to accept a painted Campbell's Soup can as art than they were to accept Duchamp's urinal. But for Warhol, the Tech-trained Duchampian avant-gardist, that rejection itself registered as a sign he was onto something. Easy acceptance was more problematic and always signaled a need to move on. Once Pop came to be accepted as just the latest art, according to a new definition that Pop itself had proposed, Warhol shifted to underground film. As that, too, began to fall within accepted ideas of an artist's practice – or at least *Warhol's* ideas of such a practice – he moved on to pop-music promotion, then to funding feature films, and eventually to such projects as opening a string of diners (which never quite happened), selling portraits to the rich and famous (which happened, often), and appearing in ads and on bad TV shows.

It's not quite right, or even coherent, to say that we should count everything that Warhol ever made or did as Art with a capital A. Sometimes he was just making money; sometimes he was just living life. But his singular achievement, as the most dedicated and highly trained of modern artists, was to always leave us wondering what was his art, and what wasn't.

Blake Gopnik is the author of *Warhol*, a comprehensive biography of the Pop artist published in 2020. He is a regular contributor to arts coverage at the New York Times.

他对于艺术的信奉与之前任何时期一样坚定。尽管在搬去纽约后,沃霍尔就立刻开始了他那狂乱而收入极丰的商业插画事业;他一直都在创作他自己认为是纯艺术的作品,并且一直都在寻找可以展出这样作品的画廊。人们普遍抱有一个错误的观念,认为沃霍尔直到1960年代才开始他作为展览艺术家的职业生涯,展出他的波普艺术。实际上,他在五十年代已经有过至少八个展览了,其中好几个都是个展。尽管沃霍尔保有着从匹兹堡带来的艺术上的勃发雄心,匹兹堡的教育赋予他的扩展定义的艺术观念却并未在这一时期得以展现。他在1950年代展出的每一件作品都十分安全地落在传统的艺术类别里:油画、素描、版画和雕塑。(尽管以五十年代的标准而言,他作品的内容常常是极为危险的——他近乎直白地展示着同性恋。)如果说沃霍尔确实偶尔会模糊类别之间的边界的话——他画作的一部分是印刷的,他的雕塑是折叠起来的素描——他并不会从这些类别之中跨越而出,像廊线画廊和理工学院鼓励的那样,进入到更为宽泛的文化领域之中。在1950年代,沃霍尔的艺术创作更着意于表现一种惹人喜爱的风格,而非重新绘制艺术的边界。这些创作中丝毫没有达达偏好的"令人费解的形式"或是"现代生活的碎片",也没有展现出一丁点儿杜尚式的对于疯狂或荒诞的兴趣。

印着"沃霍尔"标签的一切似乎是在1961年春天一下子开始出现的。在整个1950年代,沃霍尔偶尔会为百货公司做橱窗设计。当1961年春又一个橱窗设计的工作合约找上门来,他决定在橱窗展示品的后部以大尺幅的画作来作衬托,即兴复制漫画片段和小报上登载的广告。他为橱窗展示品创作的这些背景画,与贾斯珀·约翰斯(Jasper Johns)和罗伯特·劳森伯格(Robert Rauschenberg)等"波普原初形态"代表人物当时所倡导的先锋艺术不谋而合——沃霍尔对于先锋的兴趣从未止歇,同时对帮助店铺招揽生意也颇有成效,目标对准那些读小报和看漫画的年轻女孩。色彩明亮的背景画极好地衬托了摆放在它前面的那些活泼俏皮的连衣裙。

在那个高档商场的橱窗里,沃霍尔那些时髦的画作为道具极为有效,与此前十年橱窗设计师放置在商品背后的别样的现代绘画在功能上一脉相承。之后,沃霍尔往前迈了一大步,他开始意识到那些作为道具的,有着无法掩盖的商业展示本质的画作——实际上,正因为附着在画作之上的独特的商业气息——可以在画廊的情境中作为先锋艺术发挥重大作用。

沃霍尔在匹兹堡汲取的先锋气质(你也可以说这样的气质是与生俱来的)引导着他,做出新奇而激进的举动。直至当时,关于如何定义艺术的范畴,人们大多还抱有相当狭隘的理解。但匹兹堡拓展了沃霍尔的视野,这让他对于橱窗道具也可以在艺术实践中占据一席之地的想法保持了开放的心态。他从匹兹堡接触的达达和杜尚那里获得了灵感,将"仅仅"用于展示的道具抬升到艺术的高度。在家乡所经受的训练使他可以认识到这样的升华中蕴含的荒诞的力量。

还要再过约六个月,沃霍尔才开始向画廊主展示他那新颖的波普艺术;而还要再过整整一年,才有了这一新艺术的个展——在洛杉矶展出他最新创作的"金宝汤"系列。当他真正开始展出这组新作时,许多观众并不认为金宝汤罐头画作为艺术品比杜尚的小便器更令人愉悦。但是对于沃霍尔这位接受过理工学院训练的、杜尚式的先锋派来说,这种拒斥本身就表明他其实已经步入正轨了。轻轻松松就被接受了才更成问题,意味着需要继续突破。当波普被接受为最新的艺术——按照它自身所提出的有关艺术的新的定义——沃霍尔就转向了地下电影。而当地下电影也开始被接纳为艺术家的实践时——至少在沃霍尔的观念里是这样的——他便开始投身流行音乐的推广。之后他开始赞助剧情长片,最终涉足的项目包括了开连锁餐厅(实际搁浅)、卖肖像画给富人和名人(时常发生)、接广告、上不入流的电视节目等等。

如果有人说我们应该把沃霍尔做过的每一件事、创作的每一样东西都算作大写的艺术,那是不准确的,甚至是说不通的。有时他只是在挣钱,有时他只是在生活。但是,作为现代艺术家中训练有素而且最为投入的一个,他所取得的独一无二的成就,总是不禁让我们揣想:什么算是他的艺术,而什么不是。

布莱克·戈普尼克是《沃霍尔》(*Warhol*)一书的作者,此书出版于2020年,是一部关于这位波普艺术家的翔实传记。此外,戈普尼克还经常为《纽约时报》撰写艺术报道。

## 注释

1. 斯图尔特·普雷斯顿，《观看事物的新旧方式》，《纽约时报》，1964年4月26日。——原注。本文无特殊说明的均为原注。
2. 安迪·沃霍尔和大卫·鲍登，两人通电话时的笔记（1971年12月11日），大卫·鲍登卷宗 II.3，现代艺术博物馆档案，纽约。
3. 格伦·奥布赖恩，《访谈：安迪·沃霍尔》，《高峰月刊》，1977年8月，第36页。
4. 安迪·沃霍尔本名安德鲁·沃霍拉。——译者注
5. 有关朱莉娅·沃霍拉的更多细节，请看我的《沃霍尔》一书（纽约：Ecco，2020年）。本文有关沃霍尔、他身边的人以及他的事业的种种细节，均以这本书为依据，后文不会再一一注明。
6. 中文"贝雷帽"的"贝雷"是对 beret 这种形制的帽子的音译，因为这种形制的帽子常为画家所戴，所以在中文里又有以"画家帽"来作为译名的——或者至少是作为商品名。Tam O'Shanter 这种顶上带有绒球的软帽虽然在形制上和贝雷帽（画家帽）有相似之处，但它最常引起的联想是苏格兰军队，而非艺术家。所以作者这里说，在卡内基学院上艺术课的这帮小孩儿被称作"绒球软帽"似乎是对于贝雷帽（画家帽）的一种古怪的"转译"。——译者注。
7. 约瑟夫·菲茨帕特里克，《约瑟夫·菲茨帕特里克，去看，要看见、记住、享受》，《卡内基杂志》，1987年4月，第22页。
8. 菲利普·佩尔斯坦，本文作者所做采访，2014年8月18日。
9. 《卡内基杂志》，1945年1月，第229页。
10. 安德鲁·卡内基，出自罗伯特·甘奇韦尔所著《文化的殿堂》一书，匹兹堡：匹兹堡大学出版社，2011年，第22页。
11. 霍默·圣-高登斯，出自道格拉斯·内勒的《匹兹堡市民不再朝现代艺术"离着50码远啐口水"了》，《匹兹堡新闻》，1950年7月2日。
12. 这里的"粉红"，原文是 pink，用来形容左派政治观。——译者注
13. 苏珊·普拉特，《赌博、圈地和伪装：霍默·圣-高登斯和卡内基国际展，1922—1950》，收录在维基·A. 克拉克主编的《国际遭遇：卡内基国际展和当代艺术，1896—1996》，匹兹堡：卡内基艺术博物馆，1996年，第88页。
14. 标示了1946年的一份剪报，概要画廊，剪贴簿（未标日期），罗克韦尔家族藏品。除非另行说明，本文有关概要的种种记述均来自这本剪贴簿。
15. 罗克韦尔买的这个《手提箱中的盒子》于2015年5月15日经佳士得拍卖售出。参看"马塞尔·杜尚（1887—1968），马塞尔·杜尚或罗丝·塞拉维作品（《手提箱中的盒子》）[A 系列] 未命名"，https://www.christies.com/lotfinder/lot_details.aspx?intObjectID=5893256，2019年2月28日访问。
16. 贝蒂·阿舍·道格拉斯，口述史，由本文作者和马特·沃比肯采访，数字录音，2014年7月2日，安迪·沃霍尔博物馆档案。
17. 利用 vision 一词所具有的多重相关含义——视觉能力、视野、见解等，莫霍伊-纳吉在本书的书名中压缩进了他的许多主张，中文暂译为《运动中的视觉》。——译者注
18. 帕特里克·S. 史密斯引述杰克·威尔逊，参看史密斯的《沃霍尔：关于他的对话》，艺术研究系列第59号，安阿伯：UMI 研究出版社，1988年，第21页。
19. 《卡内基理工学院公告：艺术学院》，1945年2月1日，第14页。
20. 同上，第43页。
21. 雷蒙德·萨默斯·斯蒂茨，《艺术与人》，伦敦：麦格劳-希尔，1949年，第819页。
22. 同上，第738页。

## Notes

1. Stuart Preston, "Old and New Ways of Seeing Things," *New York Times*, April 26, 1964.
2. Andy Warhol and David Bourdon, typed notes from a telephone call (December 11, 1971), David Bourdon Papers, II.3, Museum of Modern Art Archives, New York.
3. Glenn O'Brien, "Interview: Andy Warhol," *High Times* (Aug. 1977): 36.
4. For details on Julia Warhola, see my *Warhol* (New York: Ecco, 2020). This essay's other biographical details on Warhol, his associates, and his career depend on that book, which will not be cited again.
5. Joseph Fitzpatrick, "Joe Fitzpatrick, Look, to See, to Remember, to Enjoy," *Carnegie Magazine* (April 1987): 22.
6. Philip Pearlstein, interview by author, Aug. 18, 2014.
7. *Carnegie Magazine* (Jan. 1945): 229.
8. Andrew Carnegie, quoted in Robert Gangewere, *Palace of Culture* (Pittsburgh: University of Pittsburgh Press, 2011), 22.
9. Homer Saint-Gaudens, in Douglas Naylor, "Pittsburghers Have Quit 'Spitting at 50 Yards' at Modern Art," *Pittsburgh Press*, July 2, 1950.
10. Susan Platt, "Gambling, Fencing and Camouflage: Homer Saint-Gaudens and the Carnegie International, 1922–1950," in *International Encounters: The Carnegie International and Contemporary Art, 1896–1996*, ed. Vicky A. Clark (Pittsburgh: Carnegie Museum of Art, 1996), 88.
11. Clipping dated 1946, Outlines Gallery, scrapbook (n.d.), Rockwell family collection. Unless otherwise indicated, references to the programming at Outlines derive from this scrapbook.
12. The Rockwell *Boîte* was sold at Christies on May 15, 2015 – see "Marcel Duchamp (1887–1968), de Ou Par Marcel Duchamp Ou Rrose Sélavy (La Boîte-En-Valise) [Series A] Untitled," accessed Feb. 28, 2019, https://www.christies.com/lotfinder/lot_details.aspx?intObjectID=5893256.
13. Betty Asche Douglas, oral history, interview by author and Matt Wrbican, digital audio, July 2, 2014, Andy Warhol Museum Archives.
14. Jack Wilson quoted in Patrick S. Smith, *Warhol: Conversations About the Artist*, Studies in the Fine Arts, no. 59 (Anne Arbor: UMI Research Press, 1988), 21.
15. *Bulletin of the Carnegie Institute of Technology: College of Fine Arts*, Feb. 1, 1945, 14.
16. Ibid, 43.
17. Raymond Somers Stites, *The Arts and Man* (London: McGraw-Hill, 1940), 819.
18. Ibid, 738.

《安迪·沃霍尔正在拍摄电影
<泰勒·米德之臀>》
弗雷德·麦克达拉
*Andy Warhol Filming Taylor Mead's Ass*
Fred McDarrah
1964

明胶银盐相纸
Gelatin silver print
40 × 30 cm

# THE DISTANCE BETWEEN WARHOL AND US

## Stefanie Chow

If he exalts himself, I humble him.
If he humbles himself, I exalt him.
And I go on contradicting him until he understands
that he is monster that passes all understanding.
–Blaise Pascale, *Pensées*

### The 1960s Pursuit of the New

In 1982, Andy Warhol visited China. He never could have anticipated, however, that four decades later, the distinctly Warholian technology of livestreaming would be used in a wide range of fields and industries across China. Public WeChat accounts, livestream marketing, Tik-Tok videos – all have become platforms for the expression of individual desire. On one level, we are interested in the oddball figure of Warhol because we are fascinated by his multifaceted identity: painter, filmmaker, author, aphorist, media mogul, trendsetter. But in truth, we are more curious about the secret of how, in one fell swoop, the young Andrew Warhola became the master of the Factory and the Pope of Pop. It is rare in art history to find artists like Warhol who lived under the sun for nearly their entire lives.[1] What's more, he didn't just share his work with his fans – he revealed to them the process by which these works were made and exposed his ambition to succeed and become a star.

Warhol was New York's first influencer in the modern sense, and this exhibition at UCCA captures traces of his rise to fame and his golden age. Photograph after photograph of party scenes recreate Warhol's 1960s life and tell the story of how his Factory on 231 East 47th Street quickly became the salon of the most fashionable celebrities. Taking the decrepit elevator to the top floor, when the doors opened, you were walking into Warhol's world. Every surface was covered in tin foil and outfitted with shattered mirrors. Countless celebrities, politicians, and businessmen passed through this space. The Velvet Underground rehearsed here, and Truman Capote sat on the only red couch reading. Hungover young men and women lazed on the floor drinking until the next day. And Warhol, he could be found in the corner, silently observing it all. It was when Pop artist Tom Wesselmann, Roy Lichtenstein, James Rosenquist, and Claes Oldenburg pulled him into a group photo in front of his work *Thirteen Most Wanted Men* that he emerged from the shadows to stand in the limelight.

We often don't know how to talk about Andy Warhol. Or rather, we do not know which Warhol should we should believe in. It's often hard to avoid discussing the relationship between the artist and his era, the artist and the people around him. He was a wallflower, famously remarking that he'd prefer to watch parties on a monitor alone. Yet because he was Warhol, you can never completely take him at his word.

部电影",但因为他是沃霍尔,他的话还是不能完全取信于人。

然而有些事,确确实实发生在他的"工厂"里。自从沃霍尔将开派对比作拍电影,他就愈发对电影着迷。他在"工厂"架设了一台摄影机,邀请朋友和客人坐在镜头前进行称作《试镜》的摄像。拍摄对象被要求坐在明亮灯光下尽可能保持3分钟不动,而且得一直看着摄影机。沃霍尔会离开现场让"试镜者"单独面对摄影机,其中有一些人就会忍不住动起来或者做其他手势。1964年至1966年期间,沃霍尔和他的工作室助理杰拉德·马兰加共拍摄了472位试镜人物,其中包括我们熟悉的鲍勃·迪伦和萨尔瓦多·达利,也包括这次展出的我们不那么熟悉的演员艾薇·尼科尔森和"垮掉的一代"诗人安·布坎南。大部分的受访者在镜头面前看起来非常紧张,这种紧张反而满足了沃霍尔作为一个窥私癖者、煽动者的兴奋。沃霍尔也许并没有意识到,他对人的兴趣与他所生活的1960年代——充斥着毒品、性解放、变装、电影、音乐和喧嚣狂乱生活的时代——开始重叠在一起。

他喜欢拍摄对象带给他的惊喜,尤其是像诗人安·布坎南这样极其听从他指令的对象。当布坎南因为不能眨眼的压力而落泪时,沃霍尔觉得拍电影简直棒极了。正如麦克卢汉对1960年代所下的定义:"在这个以信息和规划产业为特色的新电子时代,商品本身就能呈现出越来越多的信息特征。"沃霍尔理解这种变革,而且不介意把当时泾渭分明的高雅艺术与低俗文化放在他的"搅拌机"里。他将"工厂"发展成一个反主流文化的阵地,由一些合同演员、一个外景场地和一个不太稳定的技术人员团队组成。这个团队所拍摄的作品,就包括这次在UCCA展出的他于1963年拍摄完成的首部电影《沉睡》与1964年的《帝国大厦》。

沃霍尔对电影的热忱很大一部分原因在于它的新,它不仅代表了麦克卢汉预言的技术上的革命,还变成一个可以提供"一炮而红"机会(被沃霍尔称作"Big Time")的场域。他明明知道所有"新艺术一旦被做出来就不新了",[2] 但他依旧沉迷于新生事物,或者更确切一点说是关于"新"的悖论。沃霍尔想成为的是写下《1845年的沙龙》并在书中衷心呼唤"新之诞生"的波德莱尔,他也可能想要成为大声疾呼"创新!"(make it new!)的庞德,他那些表面上看来是把艺术商业化的做法,实际上却是为了将自己打造成一台永不过时的机器。亦因于此,玛丽莲·梦露、伊丽莎白·泰勒以及《花》等一系列形象在他的波普"工厂"里迅速制作出来。这种制作的新工艺是丝网印刷图像,简单、快速、效果不俗。沃霍尔也不避讳对新工艺的夸赞,他说,"选一张照片,把它放大,用胶水粘在丝绸上,然后用滚轴将墨水涂抹在上面,这样墨水就可以穿透丝绸层,但又不会渗透胶水层。这样你可以得到相同的图像,但每一次会略微不同。制作如此简单、快速且充满偶然性。"[3]

在沃霍尔成为美国波普文化的代表之前,曾有评论家试图用"新达达主义派""新现实主义"或"通用主义者"将其归类。其中"通用主义者"一词因为常被美国艺术界用来批评苏联艺术,于是首先被排除在外。但剩下的两个词似乎也不足以传达沃霍尔作品中的聪明、时髦感。直到评论家劳伦斯·阿洛韦和艺术家理查德·汉密尔顿从全新的"摇摆伦敦"(Swinging Sixties)引入"波普"(Pop)的概念,这个原本被用来描述伦敦新兴艺术氛围、俏皮且流行的消费主义文化的词,忽然跃然纸上。[4] 汉密尔顿在定义波普艺术时写道:"波普艺术,即流行的(面向大众的)、转瞬即逝的(短期方案)、可随意消耗的(易忘的)、廉价的、批量生产的、年轻人的(以青年为目标)、诙谐风趣的、性感的、恶搞的、魅惑人的。"[5]

We can be assured that certain events took place in his Factory. Since the moment Warhol compared parties to movies, he became increasingly enamored of filmic art. In his Factory, he installed a stationary camera, inviting friends and guests to sit for the lens and film what he called Screen Tests. The subject of each Screen Test was asked to sit under a bright light and stay as motionless as possible for around three minutes, staring at the camera. Warhol would walk away as the sitter faced the camera alone. Some subjects couldn't keep still, and others deliberately made gestures at the camera. Between 1964 and 1966, Warhol and his studio assistant Gerard Malanga shot 472 subjects for his Screen Tests, including luminaries such as Bob Dylan and Salvador Dalí as well as lesser-known figures like the actress Ivy Nicholson and Lost Generation poet Ann Buchanan, both of whom are featured in this exhibition. Many of the subjects appear tense, and this strain satisfied Warhol's voyeuristic and a provocateur proclivities. What Warhol himself perhaps did not realize is that his interest in those around him had begun to fold into the very character of the 1960s itself – a generation of frenzy, drugs, sexual liberation, gender bending, film, and music.

Warhol delighted in the unanticipated moments of his sitters. Ann Buchanan, for instance, followed his instructions to the letter. Struggling to keep her eyes open, she began crying in her Screen Test, which Warhol found spectacular. Just as Marshall McLuhan defined the 1960s, "In the new electric Age of Information and programmed production, commodities themselves assume more and more the character of information." Warhol understood this revolution, and he didn't hesitate to take the once distinct categories of fine art and low culture and toss them into the blender together. His Factory – a motley crew of contract players, a backlot, and a not-so-reliable team of technicians – began to adopt an anti-mainstream strategic position. This group went on to create his first film, *Sleep* (1963), and *Empire* (1964), both on view here at UCCA.

Warhol's passion for film was in large part due to its "newness." Film did not just represent McLuhan's prophesized technical revolution; it also became a site where one was given the opportunity to make it big instantly (what Warhol called the Big Time).[2] He clearly knew that "new art's never new when it's done," yet he still threw himself into new things, or, more accurately, into the paradox of the new. Warhol wanted to become what Charles Baudelaire passionately advocated for in his *Salon de 1845*: "the advent of the new." He wanted to follow Ezra Pound's call to "make it new!" His methods, which superficially seem to commercialize art, in truth served to reconstruct himself into a machine of timelessness. It is also for this reason that the Pop Factory quickly began to manufacture its iconic images: Marylin Monroe, Elizabeth Taylor, and *Flowers* among other series. The new technology that empowered this facture was the silkscreened image – simple, quick, and stunning. Warhol was quick to praise these new technologies, noting, "With silkscreening, you pick a photograph, blow it up, transfer it in glue onto silk, and then roll ink across it so the ink goes through the silk but not through the glue. That way you get the same image, slightly different each time. It all sounds so simple – quick and chancy."[3]

Before Warhol became a Pop icon, critics tried to label him as Neo-dada or Neo-realist, or even Universalist. Universalist was a term that American art circles used to denounce Soviet art. The former two also seem insufficient to convey the wit and sense of fashion in Warhol's work. Until the critic Lawrence Alloway and the artist Richard Hamilton introduced the concept of Pop to the Swinging Sixties, the term had been used to describe the new art atmosphere of London and a certain slick, hip consumerist culture.[4] Suddenly, it started to pop up everywhere in criticism. Attempting to define Pop Art, Hamilton in particular once wrote, "Pop Art is: Popular (designed for a mass audience), transient (short-term solution), expendable (easily forgotten), low cost, mass produced, young (aimed at youth), witty, sexy, gimmicky, glamorous."[5]

### The Involution of Andy Warhol

One reason that Warhol was virtually ignored by the most influential critic of his era, Clement Greenburg, lies in the artist's interest in the new. Greenberg could not imagine that when he delivered his famous treatise "Modernist Painting" in 1960, Warhol was already beginning to use Pop to make contemporary art. In his text, Greenberg looked to the state of painting in the 1950s and early 1960s as a way to reflect on the history of Modernist painting. He preferred to

## "内卷"的安迪·沃霍尔

沃霍尔被当时最有话语权的评论家格林伯格视而不见的一个原因,还在于他对"新"充满了兴趣。格林伯格料想不到,当他那篇著名的《现代主义绘画》在 1960 年发表时,沃霍尔就已经借由"波普"来建构"当代艺术"了。文章中,格林伯格从 1950 年代和 1960 年代初的美国绘画现状来回顾现代主义绘画发展,宁愿分析杰克逊·波洛克是如何像马奈那样在绘画的内在逻辑层面不断走向平面化,也没有提及新兴的波普艺术,甚至到他晚年也鲜少提及沃霍尔和他的波普同行的"平面化"创作。对格林伯格这样的现代主义理论家来说,迷恋新鲜事物的沃霍尔,无论是在英文的"现代传统"还是"古典传统"中都难以找到立足之地。沃霍尔的"新"很自然地将他区隔于经典艺术史的藩篱之外。随之而来的除了沃霍尔作为人、作为个体的孤独,还有"新"对他的背叛——这个"波普教皇"被"新"紧紧包围着,迫使他疲于更新,在这种情况下,新的真正价值还能剩下几许?这让人不得不想起向现代性发难并冠之以堕落之名的尼采口中所说的"永恒轮回",新旧交替,旧的东西自以为新,逐新也因此失去了意义。而"新"的悖论也让沃霍尔时常陷入难以自洽的境地,他不得不将自己的孤独暴露在外——尽管簇拥于曼哈顿名流之中,却被他的文学偶像杜鲁门·卡波特形容为"我这辈子见过的最孤独、最没有朋友的人"。

沃霍尔身上另一个常为人诟病的地方是,他打破了"艺术家"与"名人"之间的边界,让艺术与商业混为一谈。在他那里,似乎只有名人才能拥有姓名和故事,其他人不过是陪他消磨一段时光的无名者,那些被他称为"B"的人们。6 他在这些人身上也看到了自身的矛盾,他一方面沉迷于让人意识到他作为名人的独特气场,7 另一方面又对成为名人不屑一顾。他嘲讽一个身份普通的朋友——从新泽西来的英格丽,给她起名"英格丽·超级巨星"(Ingrid Superstar),然后让她用这个新名字回到自己的圈子中间,在一次又一次的派对中逐渐扬名立万,影响力之大甚至使"超级巨星"这个词成了当时媒体的新宠。就像今天许多人把"内卷"挂在嘴边一般,那时的纽约媒体圈开始频繁使用"超级巨星"一词。后来这个英格丽消失了,但她的新名字却一直沿用至今。沃霍尔的讽刺可谓是一种反思性的批评,他在指认他人的问题之时,也牵引出他自己的身世——他何尝不是一个改名换姓的小镇青年?那个来自匹兹堡的小镇青年何尝不是将"沃霍拉"偷偷改成"沃霍尔"?我们可以看出,沃霍尔对名利的纠结让他始终处于名利场的中央,而他自我否定的态度竟有点像阿多诺在否定辩证法中暴露的问题,即现代艺术虽然体现的是一种不断自我否定的精神,但它最终也会带来一种悖论,如果艺术只负责批评,那么没有一种艺术可以自称"艺术"。

沃霍尔在不断用"新"来替换"新"时,实际上也在"新"的内部否定着"新"。这有点像福柯在《知识考古学》中提及的句式——"它不是……也不是……也不是……"。8 布朗肖认为阿多诺和福柯这类拒绝"价值"的态度,最后会让他们变得"无话可说",并带来单一、循环的陈述:"陈述是稀少的、单一的;受其严格意义上的外在的可能性状况(外界,外在性)所限,陈述只会要求被描述,或者仅仅要求被重写。"9

"内卷"这个本来用来形容农业社会精耕细作、重复劳动、只有缓慢的渐进式增长而没有发展到工业化和资本主义,现在用来形容当代社会的"过度且内耗式的竞争"。按照这一标准,沃霍尔的"新"无疑是"内卷"的。沃霍尔创作时依赖的技术手段——丝

analyze Jackson Pollock and how he embodied a movement toward flatness that first emerged in the logic of the paintings of Manet. He did not, however, mention the newly emergent Pop Art movement, and even in later years he only rarely mentioned the flatness of Warhol and his Pop peers. To a modernist theorist like Greenberg, Warhol and his obsession with the new had no place in either the Modernist or classical tradition. Warhol's form of "new" would inevitably keep him out of the annals of art history. Relatedly, outside of his social and professional isolation, there was another way in which the "new" betrayed Warhol – the Pope of Pop was consumed by this obsession with newness, constantly toiling away at finding new ways to refresh his work. Yet under these circumstances, what value could the new be said to have? One is reminded of Nietzsche, how he rebelled against the coming of modernity and called it degenerate, and his theory of the eternal return. The new is always replacing the old, and old things propose themselves as new, gradually losing meaning in this dynamic. And the paradox of the new often trapped Warhol in inescapable loops, in which he was compelled to expose his own loneliness – even though he was surrounded by the glitterati of Manhattan, he was once described by his literary idol Truman Capote as "the loneliest, most friendless person I'd ever seen in my life."

Another oft-castigated aspect of Warhol's work is that he broke down the borders between artist and celebrity, conflating art and commerce. In his orbit, it seemed that only celebrities had names and stories, while everyone else was just an anonymous character who would associate with him for a time, whom he referred to as "B."[6] He also saw his own contradictions in these B's. He luxuriated in the distinctive aura that surrounded him, one that forced people to recognize his celebrity.[7] At the same time, however, he held a certain contempt for the idea of becoming a celebrity. In a tongue-in-cheek gesture, he called a certain friend of his who came from an ordinary New Jersey upbringing Ingrid Superstar, and asked her to use this new name as she moved through her social circles. With party after party, she gradually became famous herself. His influence grew so great that the media began using the buzzword "superstar" as well. 1960s New York media circles use of the word in some ways parallels China today and how "involution" is increasingly used to describe a certain professional burnout and ennui. Ingrid Superstar would later disappear, but people continue to use her new name to this day. Warhol's sarcastic humor could be seen as a self-reflective form of criticism – when he was pointing out other people's problems, he was also indicting his own origins. Was he not also a kid from a provincial city who had changed his name? Did this Pittsburgh boy not also quietly drop the "a" from his family name? It's clear that Warhol's vexed relationship with fame is exactly what ended up placing him at the center of it. And this attitude of negation has something in common with the central problem proposed by Theodore Adorno's critique of dialectics, that while modern art embodied a spirit of constant self-negation, it ultimately raises a paradox: if art only is responsible for critique, then nothing can make a claim to being "art" unto itself.

While Warhol was constantly using the new to replace the new, he was also negating the new from inside the new. This posture recalls Michel Foucault's *The Archaeology of Knowledge* and its oft-used sentence structure, "It's not..., nor is it..., nor is it for that matter...".[8] Maurice Blanchot believed that Adorno's and Foucault's rejection of "value" will ultimately deprive them of discursive ability, culminating in single-minded, circular statements: "The statement, which is rare, singular, asking only to be described or merely rewritten, in relation to its strictly *external* conditions of possibility (the outside, exteriority)."[9]

Involution was a term that originally described a dynamic in agrarian societies in which more intensive cultivation and repeated labor only leads to slow, gradual growth in the absence of industrialization and capitalism. Today, it is used to describe a condition of excessive, exhaustive professional competition. According to this standard, Warhol's newness was undoubtedly involuted. The technological strategies that Warhol relied upon for his work – the silkscreen and reproduced images – only exacerbated this involution. And Warhol's involution is something we still struggle to understand, how he expended all his energy trying to earn the recognition of commercial and popular culture. The logic that animates Warhol's involution is similar to its many manifestations in Chinese society today: the constant pressure on kids to excel, buying expensive homes just for the nearby schools, students who are only good at taking

网印刷与图像复制——更加剧了这种内卷。我们无法理解沃霍尔的一点就在于他的"内卷",他几乎在日常生活中拼尽全力去赢得商业文化与流行文化的认可。沃霍尔的"内卷"跟当下中国社会普遍存在的"鸡娃""学区房""小镇做题家"背后的逻辑有着相似性,那就是无论他用何种媒介进行创作,他的创作逻辑背后都有高度一体化的东西——"价值评价体系高度单一,竞争方式高度单一,奖惩方式高度单一"。这样的名利生产模式不允许失败和停滞不前 [10],如果沃霍尔活在当下的中国,如果他是直播间里的主播,那么他一定会 24 小时不厌其烦地直播他的生活。因为他对媒介敏感,时刻想要用媒介将自己作品的价值最大化。以媒介为基础,以逐新为目的,沃霍尔的"内卷"是完全自愿的。

而事实上,沃霍尔已经在 58 年前完成了这种类似直播的电影创作——1963 年,《沉睡》这部长达 5 小时 21 分钟的电影,画面中只有一个始终在睡觉的男人,他是沃霍尔当时的同居男友约翰·焦尔诺,其他什么也没有。类似的情况也发生在《帝国大厦》中,沃霍尔将镜头对准帝国大厦。尽管沃霍尔的"直播式影像"是相对静止的——他巧妙地将电影叙事压缩成一种感受,一种摩天大楼般静止的感受。他用慢镜头放映摄制的图像,改变了观看电影的传统,强调我们对时间的感知。这种片刻的静止又跟沃霍尔置身名流之中而观看名流的习惯出奇的相似,他的观看本身就有两个层次,一个是对于镜头下的人和物,另一个是对于观看自身。夹在这两种观看之中的空隙,时间静静流过。

正是这种对时间张力的考量,让沃霍尔的作品有别于当下流行的直播。沃霍尔仍然在挑战时间与影像、实体与表现的问题,而我们现在所面对的直播更多是电商和算法操纵的倾销。换句话说,沃霍尔通过丝网印绘汤罐头、纸钞、可乐瓶拓展了艺术的边界,却仍是在一个相对本体论的范畴里来探讨艺术;而发生在中国当代社会的直播却是将产品的物之属性全部剥落,再用最前沿的算法来提升交易速度,最后将直播平台上的物彻底转化为一串代码或一条点击就可以即时购买的链接。相比之下,沃霍尔的"直播"最终变成了战后新美国文化的一面镜子,他用日常生活的琐碎无聊、社会名人的困境、死亡与疾病等内容,迫使我们去面对消费主义文化及其带来的虚假意义。而国内由电商平台发起的直播在一路的加速中狂飙突进,没有停歇,却不能像沃霍尔那般以"直播"的方式来批评"直播"。

## 欲望复制的肖像画家

"内卷"的沃霍尔并非完全不关心他的创作对象。相反,他很关心他们。只不过,他的关心明显带着目的性。因其随时准备将这些人做成作品,这让他的关心时常停留在视觉再现的阶段。1962 年 8 月 5 日,玛丽莲·梦露去世,当沃霍尔收到这一消息时,他的第一反应不是悲伤,而是当即决定为这位悲剧明星画一幅"她的漂亮脸蛋丝网印刷画"。同年 11 月,当斯泰博画廊为沃霍尔举办个展时,玛丽莲·梦露已经化身《金色玛丽莲》,并被摆放在展厅的正门口。梦露的形象之后贯穿了沃霍尔毕生的创作,在不同年代、系列的丝网印刷品中,都能唤起我们最基本的情感:对名声的欲求,对肉体的渴望,以及对图像再现的期待。梦露眨着她彩色的眼睛,嘟着微翘的嘴唇,她的脸庞宛如沃霍尔童年在教堂瞻仰的圣像。经由沃霍尔之手,梦露又活了一回。机械复制技术的普及自然而然地与"内卷"联系起来——作为艺术界明星的沃霍尔复制了大众文化领域的性感女神梦露,这让复制不

tests. No matter what medium Warhol adopted, the logic behind his work was something highly unitary – unitary in its system of value judgment, mode of competition, and means of success and failure. This production of fame and wealth does not permit failure or stagnation.[10] If Warhol lived in China today, if he were the host of some livestreaming channel, he would tirelessly broadcast his life 24 hours a day. But it was his sensitivity to media that also empowered him to maximize the value of his art. Pursuing the new on the basis of innovations in medium, Warhol's involution was completely voluntary.

In truth, Warhol already created a form of livestream art 58 years ago with his film *Sleep*. This work from 1963 is five hours and twenty-one minutes long, yet from start to finish it depicts only the figure of a sleeping man, Warhol's live-in boyfriend John Giorno. Nothing else occurs in the film. A similar scene unfolds in *Empire*, in which Warhol trains his lens on the Empire State Building. Even as Warhol's livestream-like films are relatively still, he cleverly condenses filmic narrative into a feeling, a skyscraper-like stillness. He uses these images built of slow shots to alter habits of filmic viewing, emphasizing our perception of time. These moments of stillness are surprisingly similar to his habit of observing celebrities even as he was ostensibly part of their crowd. His concept of observation itself has two dimensions: the literal observation of the people and objects in front of his camera, and the observation of observation itself. Lingering in the interstice between these two modes of observation, time passes slowly.

It is this interest in temporal tension that differentiates Warhol's works from livestreaming today. Warhol is still challenging the relationship between time and film, object and surface, while livestreaming is merely the mass commerce of online retailers and algorithmic manipulations. In other words, Warhol uses silkscreen prints of soup cans, dollar bills, and cola bottles to expand the limits of art – he is exploring the concept of art as an ontological category. The livestreaming of contemporary China strips away the material properties of the product while using constantly renewed algorithmic means to quicken transactions, ultimately transforming all of the featured objects into a string of code or a quick-buy link. In comparison, Warhol's "livestreams" ultimately became a mirror onto the new culture of post-war America, pushing audiences to confront consumerism and its hollow meanings. In China, the livestreaming of online retail platforms only contributes to the consumerist frenzy. Advancing without pause, it cannot employ livestreaming to critique livestreaming as Warhol once did.

## A Portrait Painter of Reproduced Desire

The involuted Warhol was not uninterested in his creative subjects. On the contrary, he was very interested in them, but his interest was purposeful. Because he was turning them into artworks, his attention often ended at the level of visual representation. On August 5, 1962, Marilyn Monroe passed away. When Warhol received this news, his first reaction was not one of grief, but to transform this tragic star into "screens of her beautiful face." In November of the same year, for a solo show organized by the Stable Gallery, Monroe was transformed into *Gold Marilyn* and placed at the entrance of the gallery. Monroe's figure would reappear in Warhol's work throughout his life. Silkscreens from different decades and series all seem to conjure emotions foundational to the artist: desire for fame, yearning for corporeality, and hope for imagistic representation. Monroe blinks her colorful eyes, pouts her full lips, appearing like an icon Warhol would have gazed up at in reverence in the churches of his childhood. By Warhol's hand, she was resurrected. The universality of mechanical reproduction also has a natural connection to involution. As an art world celebrity, Warhol chose to repeatedly reproduce a sexual icon of mass culture. This was not just a reproduction of the image itself, but also a reproduction of the forces of fame and desire on the grandest scale possible.

Following this first phase of involution, Warhol hit a high point in his career in 1964 and 1965. In December of 1964, he made the cover of *Artforum*, appearing very unlike a conventional artist. For one thing, his striking good looks could rival his contemporary superstar Dennis Hopper. Around the same time, his newly signed gallery, Leo Castelli, sold all of his recent artworks, and even collectors who didn't manage to snag a piece flooded his opening at the gallery, just to catch a glimpse of the red-hot Pop artist.[11] Warhol's Big Time had quietly arrived. In 1964, he used his own photograph to produce a set of silkscreened paintings. In 1965, he shot a large number of photos documenting trivial goings-on around

仅仅发生在图像层面,更是带来了名声与欲望的最大化复制。

随着"内卷"接踵而至的是,沃霍尔在1964年与1965年迎来事业的顶峰。1964年12月,他登上《艺术论坛》封面,看起来不像任何传统艺术家,而像一个可以与当红影星丹尼斯·霍珀媲美的超级巨星。与此同时,他的新作在新签约的卡斯特利画廊销售一空,买不到画的藏家仍旧在开幕式上涌入画廊,为的就是见这红极一时的波普艺术家一面。[11] 沃霍尔的"Big Time"就这么悄无声息地到来。1964年,他以自己的肖像为主题制作了一批丝网印刷画。1965年,他拍摄了大量记录"工厂"片场琐事的银盐相片,他和绘画助手杰拉德·马兰加、影星莎莉·柯克兰德和名媛伊迪·塞奇威克频繁入镜,成为这批作品的主角。同年,沃霍尔在费城当代艺术中心推出了首个美术馆个展。大批参观者涌入,场面一度失控。最后为了保护画作,艺术中心的工作人员不得不将作品从展墙上取下,安迪本人也在混乱之中被迫从展场屋顶的疏散通道离开。

1960年代的肖像摄影,后来在1970年代发展成了肖像画。1970年代的大部分时间,直到沃霍尔去世之前,受人委托创作肖像画都是他收入的重要来源。沃霍尔的肖像画步骤远比我们想象得要复杂。为他编辑并撰写"口述日记"的作家帕特·哈克特曾在其书中记录下肖像画绘制的全过程:"首先是给绘画对象摆造型,由他(沃霍尔)拍摄大约60张宝丽来一次成像照片。然后,从这60张照片中,他挑选4张,交给一位丝网印刷商,在8英寸×10英寸的醋酸纤维素胶片上制成正片图像。这些胶片送回给他之后,他挑选一张正片图像,决定在哪里剪裁,然后进行修饰、美化,使绘画对象尽可能地漂亮——他会适当加长脖颈,削尖鼻子,扩大嘴唇,处理肤色;简而言之,他会对别人做他希望别人对他做的事情。然后他会请人把经过剪裁、修饰的8英寸×10英寸图像放大到40英寸×40英寸的醋酸纤维素胶片上,然后丝网印刷商会据此制作丝网。"[12]

不管沃霍尔正在为博物馆或画廊筹备什么展览,他公寓的某个角落总是有正在加工的丝网肖像画。这些肖像与1962年的《金色玛丽莲》相比,生产方式更具规模,生产速度更快。为了应对源源不断的肖像画生意,安迪始终让他的助手们预先画好背景:男士肖像画是肉色调,女士肖像画用的则是稍微不同的偏粉红色调。丝网做好之后,精细的图像会与预先画好的彩色区域对齐,然后再将照片的细部通过丝网印刷到油画布上。我们常见到,这些图像与底层颜色对齐方式的细微变化,造成了沃霍尔肖像画一种特别的人物偏移。对于肖像画中的人物形象而言,这显现了存在与现象的分离,以及复制图像与原始图像之间的间隔。[13] 而对于沃霍尔本人而言,这种"偏移"恰恰对应着他创作时既身处其中又置身事外的状态。尤其是在他1978年创作的《自画像》中,三个"沃霍尔"重叠在一起,每一个却都显得心不在焉。

许多人习惯将沃霍尔心理上的"偏移"一路追溯至他在匹兹堡廉价出租公寓里度过的童年。这家来自现今斯洛伐克山区米克瓦的东欧移民,日常可以称为消遣的活动少之又少。安迪·沃霍尔(原名是安德鲁·沃霍拉)是家中最小的儿子。与两个哥哥不同,他虽然聪明伶俐,却自幼害羞怯生。[14] 当哥哥们跟街上的其他小男孩打闹时,安迪却在跟邻家女孩们玩一些安静的游戏。他的母亲朱莉娅·沃霍拉鼓励他拿起画笔,如果安迪画得好,朱莉娅会给他一块好时巧克力棒作为奖励。1949年,沃霍尔从匹兹堡搬往纽约。初来乍到,他曾与别人共用一间公寓。后来他的母亲朱莉娅突然造访纽约,想要留下来照顾他。帕特·哈

the Factory. Warhol, his assistant Gerard Malanga, film star Sally Kirkland, and debutante Edie Sedgwick all posed for his camera, the protagonists of this suite of works. In the same year, Warhol held his first museum solo exhibition at the Institute of Contemporary Art in Philadelphia. Crowds flocked to the show, and the museum lost control. To protect the works, the museum workers had to remove the artworks from the walls, and in the chaos Warhol was forced to flee using the rooftop emergency exit.

Warhol's 1960s portrait photography grew into his portrait paintings of the 1970s. For most of the 1970s until the artist's death, commissioned portraits were a major source of revenue for the artist. The steps involved in Warhol's portrait paintings are far more complicated than one might imagine. Pat Hackett, who edited the artist's oral diaries, recorded the production process in her book: "It began with the subject posing while he took approximately sixty Polaroid photos. (He used Polaroid's Big Shot camera exclusively, and after that model was discontinued he made a special arrangement with the company to buy all the unused stock they had.) Then, from those sixty shots he would choose four and give them to a screen printer (he worked exclusively with one printer at a time – before 1977, his silkscreener was Alex Heinrici; after that, it was Rupert Smith) to make into positive images on 8 × 10 inch acetates. When those came back to him he would choose one image, decide where to crop it, and then doctor it cosmetically in order to make the subject appear as attractive as possible – he'd elongate necks, trim noses, enlarge lips, and clear up complexions as he saw fit; in short, he would do unto others as he would wish others to do unto him. Then he would have the cropped, doctored image on the 8 × 10 inch blown up to a 40 × 40 inch acetate, and from that the screen printer would make a silkscreen."[12]

When he was preparing for a museum or gallery exhibition, a corner of his loft was always producing silkscreen portraits. Compared to the *Gold Marilyn* of 1962, this production method was quicker and more scaled. To meet the demands of his steady stream of portraits commissions, Warhol had his assistants first paint out the background: fleshy tones for men, a variety of subtle pinks for women. Once the screen was ready, the image would align with the prepped color fields, and details of the source photograph were silkscreened onto the canvas. The overlay of the image and the underlayer of color often varied slightly, creating figural deviations in the portrait. Looking at the figural image, this creates a detachment between existence and phenomenon, a break between the reproduced and original images.[13] This sense of deviation perfectly correlates to Warhol's creative position, situated within the moment while also standing outside of it. This is especially true of his *Self-Portrait* from 1978, in which three Warhol heads are superimposed onto one another. All of them appear aloof.

Many trace Warhol's sense of psychological deviation back to his childhood, when he lived in low-cost homes in Pittsburgh. For this Eastern European immigrant family, hailing from the mountain village of Miková in modern-day Slovakia, leisure activities were few and far between. Andy Warhol (née Andrew Warhola) was the youngest son of the family. He was different from his two older brothers: though he had smarts and wit, he was shy and timid from a young age.[14] When his brothers would roughhouse with other boys, Warhol would play quieter games with the neighborhood girls. His mother Julia Warhola would encourage him to draw. If Warhol did well, Julia would reward him with a chocolate bar. Warhol moved from Pittsburgh to New York in 1949. When he first arrived, he shared an apartment with roommates. Not long after, his mother Julia paid a surprise visit to him in New York, and she decided to stay and take care of him. Pat Hackett later recalled that the first time she ever met Julia was in Warhol's Upper East Side home in 1969. Julia greeted her, then, after thinking for a moment, came to the conclusion, "You'd be nice for my Andy – but he's too busy." In 1972, Julia died of a stroke in a nursing home in Pittsburgh. Years after her death, even when close friends would ask how his mother was, Warhol would continue to respond, "Oh, fine."

Warhol completed his last three suites of works in 1986: the series Self-Portrait and Camouflage, and *The Last Supper*. The 1986 self-portrait series comprises what is perhaps the artist's most iconic images of himself. For these works, Warhol's assistant contorted his wig into something akin to Rastafarian dreadlocks, à la Jean-Michel Basquiat. Warhol's face looks skeletal, different from his bold 1960s self-portraits or the mid-life crisis images of 1978. His vacant

克特回忆自己 1969 年第一次在沃霍尔位于曼哈顿上东区的家中见到朱莉娅时,朱莉娅先是跟她打了个招呼,接着思考一秒钟,然后得出结论说:"你对我的安迪会很合适——但是他太忙了。"1972 年,朱莉娅因中风死于匹兹堡的一家养老院。在她死后几年,即便是安迪·沃霍尔最亲密的朋友问起"你母亲还好吗",安迪都会继续说:"哦,她很好。"

安迪·沃霍尔在 1986 年完成了他最后的三个系列:"自画像""迷彩"以及"最后的晚餐"。1986 年的"自画像"系列可能是沃霍尔最具个性的自画像。在这一系列作品中,沃霍尔的助手将他的假发做成了巴斯奎特那样的拉斯特法里式的脏辫发型。沃霍尔在这组肖像画中面容枯槁,已与 1960 年代自画像中表现的年轻气盛以及 1978 年自画像中表现的中年危机大有不同。他用空洞的眼神凝望着观众,一言不发。在深黑色背景的衬托下,他一头银色的假发如圣像的光环一般,令他看起来异常吓人。他不是在戴这顶假发,而是假发——他的名声——在戴着他。这似乎预示着他已经提前获知了自己数月之后将与世长辞。

每次戴起自己的"名声"时,他都会在自己的公寓里打扮自己。他会换上"重量级的夜晚"才用得上的昂贵衣服,然后检查一下他的一次成像相机里是否还有胶卷。不喜欢他的人也忍不住想知道他在做什么,试图通过追随他来拥抱"新"思想。即便是最讨厌他的人,也不得不承认他提前半个多世纪"直播"了他的生活。

艺术评论家彼得·斯杰尔达 1987 年 2 月曾在《美国艺术》写下这样的话:"沃霍尔耸耸肩,转身去了另一个地方,此时我们才恍然顿悟他的才华。他怎么能如此正确呢?!"[15] 如果有人觉得他们厌恶安迪·沃霍尔的艺术理念,很多时候是因为他们知道自己的厌恶并不能影响他的存在。日益碎片化的数码图像时代非但没能解构沃霍尔的图像世界,反而增强了图像消费的趋势。这让沃霍尔如幽灵般久久徘徊在我们身边。他纵使离开了,却依然深嵌于我们"内卷"的现实当中。

周婉京是一位作家及艺术评论人。她毕业于北京大学艺术哲学博士专业,曾任美国布朗大学哲学系访问学者,现在北京第二外国语学院教授美学与艺术理论。她曾出版过五部小说与两部艺术评论文集,获得香港青年文学奖与台湾罗叶文学奖。

gaze aims at the viewer, an expression of silence. Set off against a deep black background, the grey wig sits on his head like a halo, adding to the dread in his face. He's not so much wearing the wig – an icon of his fame – as the wig is wearing him. The painting seems like a premonition, as if he has already learned of his departure from the world just months later.

Every time he wore his famed wig, he was playing the role of himself. On a big night, he would don his most expensive clothes and check to make sure his Polaroid camera was loaded with film. Even those who disliked him wanted to know what he was up to, pursuing him to embrace the new. Even those today who detest him must concede that he "livestreamed" his life more than a half century before anyone else got there.

In the February 1987 edition of *Art in America*, critic Peter Schjeldahl wrote, "One was forever catching onto Warhol's genius at the instants when it shrugged and went elsewhere. *How can he be so right?!*"[15] If there are those who detest Andy Warhol's vision of art, it's because they know that their hatred cannot affect his existence, whatsoever. Our age of increasingly fragmented digital images cannot deconstruct Warhol's world; on the contrary, the trend towards imagistic consumption only grows stronger. Warhol seems like a specter lingering at our side. Though long departed, he is embedded in our involuted world.

Stefanie Yuen King Chow is a writer and art critic. She graduated from Peking University with a PhD in art philosophy, and was a visiting scholar in the Philosophy Department of Brown University. She teaches aesthetics and art theory at Beijing International Studies University. She has published seven books, including five novels and two essays, and has won the Hong Kong Youth Literary Award and the Taiwan Luo Ye Literary Award.

## 注释

1. "太阳底下无新事"原引自《圣经·传道书》第一章第九节，执笔者是大卫的后代所罗门。这里被笔者引述来表明安迪·沃霍尔在不断追逐新鲜事物的同时，已经意识到没有什么是日久弥新的。就像所罗门所说："已有的事，后必再有；已行的事，后必再行。日光之下，并无新事。"这句话后来也在西方哲学史上被引述来形容在柏拉图之后，哲学界没有出现什么新东西，很多所谓"新"的理论都可以被视作对柏拉图思想的解释。
2. 安迪·沃霍尔，《安迪·沃霍尔的哲学（从A到B，再到A）》，纽约：哈科特出版社，1975年，第179页。安迪在与达米安与B的对话中主动引起达米安是如何定义"新艺术"的，但他却抢在达米安回答之前给出了答案："你怎么知道那是新的还是旧的？新艺术一旦做出来就不新了。"
3. 黛博拉·戴维斯：《安迪·沃霍尔的公路旅行》，尹宝莲译，桂林：广西师范大学出版社，2018年，第70页。
4. 同上，第72页。
5. 罗克萨娜·菲利波沃斯卡，《理查·汉密尔顿的造型问题》，《Distillations》2016年第2卷第3期，第34—39页。
6. 安迪·沃霍尔，《安迪·沃霍尔的哲学（从A到B，再到A）》，纽约：哈科特出版社，1975年，第179页。
7. 在安迪看来，"气场"是除本人之外的人能看到的东西。气场的多寡在于，这些看客想要看到多少。这也就揭示了"气场"本身的不实在性。参见同上，第77—78页。
8. 米歇尔·福柯与莫里斯·布朗肖，《福柯/布朗肖》，肖莎等译，郑州：河南大学出版社，2019年，第13页。
9. 同上。
10. 王芊霓、葛诗凡，《专访｜人类学家项飙谈内卷：一种不允许失败和退出的竞争》，澎湃新闻2020年10月22日刊，https://www.thepaper.cn/newsDetail_forward_9648585（查阅于2021年4月1日）。
11. 黛博拉·戴维斯，《安迪·沃霍尔的公路旅行》，尹宝莲译，桂林：广西师范大学出版社，2018年，第263页。
12. 安迪·沃霍尔与帕特·哈克特：《安迪·沃霍尔日记》，金晓宇译，郑州：河南大学出版社，2019年，第10—11页。
13. 同上，第11页。
14. 黛博拉·戴维斯，《安迪·沃霍尔的公路旅行》，尹宝莲译，桂林：广西师范大学出版社，2018年，第5页。
15. 丽贝卡·洛瑞，《沃霍尔效应：一个大事年表》，美国大都会艺术博物馆，https://www.metmuseum.org/exhibitions/listings/2012/steins-collect/~/media/Files/Exhibitions/WarholTimeline.pdf（查阅于2021年4月3日）。

## Notes

1. "There is nothing new under the sun" comes from the Bible in Ecclesiastes 1:9, written by Solomon, descendant of David. Here it is used to describe how even as Warhol was constantly pursuing the new, he was also aware of the fact that nothing stays new forever. The full quotation is, "What has been will be again / what has been done will be done again / there is nothing new under the sun." This phrase was later used in Western philosophy to describe the feeling that after Plato, the philosophical world has not produced anything new – many so-called "new" theories are merely exegesis of Platonic thought.
2. Andy Warhol, *The Philosophy of Andy Warhol (From A to B and Back Again)* (London: Harcourt, 1975), 179. The book documents Warhol's conversations with B and Damian, in which they probe the definition of "new art." Before Damian could respond, Warhol gives his conclusion: "How do you know if it's new or not? New art's never new when it's done."
3. Deborah Davis, *The Trip: Andy Warhol's Plastic Fantastic Cross-Country Adventure* Chinese edition (Guilin: Guangxi Normal University Press), Yin Baolian trans., 70.
4. Ibid, 72.
5. Roksana Filipowska, "Richard Hamilton's Plastic Problem," *Distillations 2*, no. 3 (2016): 34–39.
6. Andy Warhol, *The Philosophy of Andy Warhol (From A to B and Back Again)* (London: Harcourt, 1975), 179.
7. In Warhol's view, one's "aura" is something only other people can see, and they only see as much of it as they want to. This also reveals the insubstantiality of "aura." See ibid, 77–78.
8. Michel Foucault and Maurice Blanchot, *Foucault/Blanchot* Chinese edition (Zhengzhou: Henan University Press, 2019), Xiao Sha trans., 13.
9. Ibid.
10. Wang Qianni and Ge Shifan, "Interview | Anthropologist Xiang Biao on Involution: Competition that Does Not Allow Failure or Retreat," *The Paper*, Oct. 22, 2020, online: https://www.thepaper.cn/newsDetail_forward_9648585, accessed Apr. 1, 2021.
11. Deborah Davis, *The Trip: Andy Warhol's Plastic Fantastic Cross-Country Adventure* Chinese edition (Guilin: Guangxi Normal University Press), Yin Baolian trans., 263.
12. Andy Warhol and Pat Hackett, *The Andy Warhol Diaries* Chinese edition (Zhengzhou: Henan University Press, 2019), Jin Xiaoyu trans., 10-11.
13. Ibid, 11.
14. Deborah Davis, *The Trip: Andy Warhol's Plastic Fantastic Cross-Country Adventure* Chinese edition (Guilin: Guangxi Normal University Press), Yin Baolian trans., 5.
15. Rebecca Lowery, "The Warhol Effect: A Timeline," The Metropolitan Museum of Art, online: https://www.metmuseum.org/exhibitions/listings/2012/steins-collect/~/media/Files/Exhibitions/WarholTimeline.pdf, accessed Apr. 3, 2021.

# 缘起
ORIGINS

# "人们常说时间改变一切，其实是你自己必须去改变一切。"

——安迪·沃霍尔，《安迪·沃霍尔的哲学》

安迪·沃霍尔虽然被看作是纽约的代表人物，但他其实来自宾夕法尼亚州匹兹堡市普通家庭。他的艺术创作与档案资料收藏在当地以其名字命名的美术馆——安迪·沃霍尔美术馆。沃霍尔本名安德鲁·沃霍拉，1928年出生于今属斯洛伐克的宗教氛围浓厚的移民家庭。沃霍尔一家在"大萧条"时期生活困苦，依靠拜占庭礼天主教信仰与东欧社群的支持维持生计。母亲朱莉娅·沃霍拉与沃霍尔一起生活直至1970年代初，她与沃霍尔共同创作，自己也创作了许多作品。尽管生活困窘，沃霍尔依然获得了卡内基理工学院（今卡内基梅隆大学）的图形设计学位，1949年毕业后移居纽约，从此开启了其商业艺术事业。他很快成为顶尖的商业插画师，在经济状况得到改善的同时，也形成了自己标志性的前波普风格。

# "They always say time changes things, but you actually have to change them yourself."

— Andy Warhol, *The Philosophy of Andy Warhol*

Andy Warhol is known as an icon of New York City, but his humble beginnings were in Pittsburgh, Pennsylvania, where his eponymous museum preserves his life and art today. He was born Andrew Warhola in 1928 into a deeply religious, immigrant family from present-day Slovakia. The family struggled during the Great Depression, and they relied on their Byzantine Catholic faith and Eastern European community for support. Warhol's mother, Julia Warhola, would live with the artist until the early 1970s, collaborating on Warhol's works and making many of her own. Despite socioeconomic adversity, Warhol earned a degree in pictorial design from Carnegie Institute of Technology (now Carnegie Mellon University) and launched a commercial art career when he moved to New York City after graduation in 1949. He quickly became a leading commercial illustrator, bringing financial success and development in his signature pre-Pop style.

安德烈·沃霍拉与朱莉娅·沃霍拉夫妇来自喀尔巴阡-卢森尼亚地区，他们一共有三个儿子，安德鲁·沃霍拉是其中最小的一位。与之前的大批移民一样，沃霍拉一家为了追寻更好的生活离开东欧故土。作为虔诚的拜占庭礼天主教徒，他们定期去教堂礼拜，并保留了许多传统习俗。朱莉娅在持家之余会制作复活节彩蛋等传统手工，安德烈则长期在外做搬运等苦力。沃霍尔童年时期常因舞蹈症发作无法上学，这是一种神经紊乱的疾病，通常被称为圣特维斯舞蹈症。在家休息时，沃霍尔喜欢看漫画书、好莱坞杂志以及玩剪纸。他还是一个电影迷，常去当地的电影院或在家看卡通短片。1942 年父亲安德烈去世，同年，沃霍尔升入申利高中。安德烈一直希望沃霍尔能念大学，并在去世前留出专款用于儿子的教育。为了贴补家用，朱莉娅曾做家政清洁，而她的长子保罗、次子约翰经营售卖果蔬的卡车摊，同时还打零工。

Andrew Warhola was the youngest of three sons born to Carpatho-Rusyn parents Andrej and Julia Warhola. Like masses of immigrants before them, the Warholas had left their homeland in Eastern Europe in search of a better life. As devout Byzantine Catholics, the family attended church regularly and continued to observe many customs of their heritage. In addition to managing the home, Julia made traditional handicrafts such as *pysanky*, or decorated Easter eggs, while Andrej worked long hours in manual jobs, such as a building-mover. Growing up, Warhol suffered bouts of chorea, a nervous disorder more commonly known as St. Vitus' Dance, which occasionally kept him from attending school. While at home, Warhol liked to read comics and Hollywood magazines and to play with paper cut-outs. Enraptured by the movies, he often went to local cinemas and watched short cartoons at home. Andrej died in 1942, the same year that Warhol entered Schenley High School. He had always intended for Warhol to attend college, and before he died, he set aside funds for his son's education. In order to support the family, Julia worked as a house cleaner, while her oldest sons Paul and John operated a fruit-and-vegetable truck and worked odd jobs.

《安迪·沃霍尔、朱莉娅·沃霍拉、
乔治·古克和玛丽（扎瓦基）·
普雷斯塔夫人》
作者未知
*Andy Warhol, Julia Warhola, George Guke,
and Mrs. Mary (Zavacky) Preksta*
Unknown
1937

棕褐色原片
Sepia print
16.5 × 11.4 cm

ORIGINS 39

在沃霍尔成长的匹兹堡市奥克兰地区,坐落着匹兹堡大学、卡内基理工学院以及卡内基艺术博物馆。虽然他家的经济状况不佳,但丰富而开放的文化资源和机构为他的艺术实践奠定了基础。在艺术家的童年时期,匹兹堡大学正在奥克兰建造学习大教堂,这座后哥特式的摩天大楼后来成了世界第二高的高校建筑。

Warhol grew up around the Pittsburgh neighborhood of Oakland, home to the University of Pittsburgh, Carnegie Institute of Technology, and the Carnegie Museum of Art. Despite his low economic status, he still had access to rich cultural treasures and institutions, which formed the foundations of his art practice. During the artist's childhood, the University of Pittsburgh was building the Cathedral of Learning in Oakland, a neo-Gothic skyscraper that would become the world's second-tallest building of higher education.

《执行"烟雾控制"政策前，
上午 11 点的匹兹堡市第五大道》
*Looking up Pittsburgh's Fifth Avenue
at 11am before smoke control*
1945

明胶银盐相纸
Gelatin silver print
25.4 × 20.3 cm

《执行"烟雾控制"政策前，
上午 9 点 20 分的匹兹堡市中心》
*Downtown Pittsburgh at 9:20am
before smoke control*
1945

明胶银盐相纸
Gelatin silver print
20.3 × 25.4 cm

《鸟瞰奥克兰》
*Aerial view of Oakland*
1930—1933

明胶银盐相纸
Gelatin silver print
20.3 × 25.4 cm

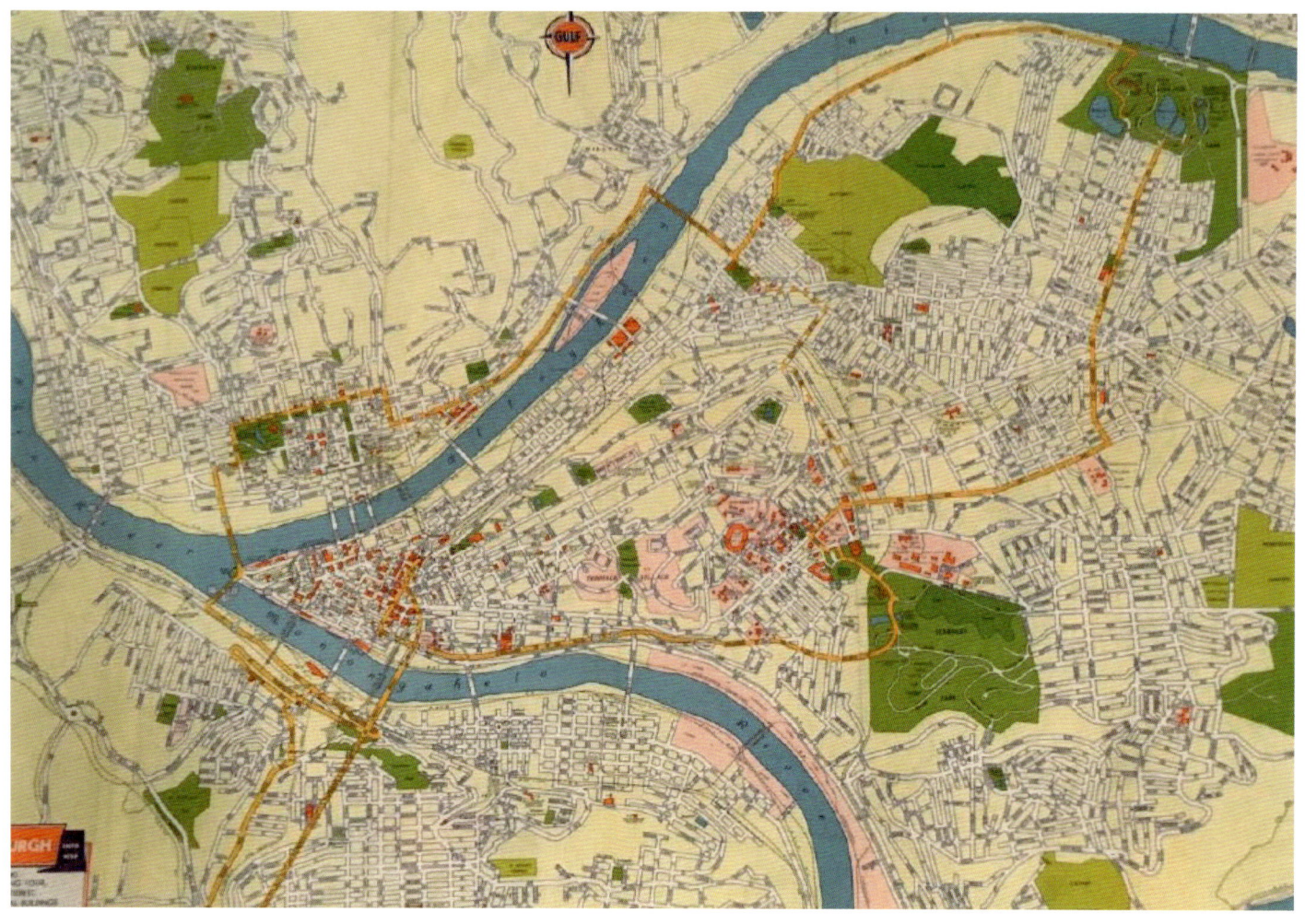

1868年，波士顿作家詹姆斯·帕顿写下名句，形容被新兴工厂与炼钢厂的浓烟滚滚所淹没的匹兹堡是"开盖的地狱"。直至二十世纪三四十年代，这一地区的铝、钢工业都在不断扩张。宾夕法尼亚州在"二战"期间的产钢总量超过了轴心国产量的总和，并因其强大的产能得名"民主兵工厂"。"二战"期间兴盛的工业造成了严重污染，遮天蔽日的浓烟令匹兹堡的街道在正午时分也一片昏黑。为了满足国防生产的需求，战后才开始启用烟雾控制条例。尽管艺术家早年生活在规模很小的移民街区，但热闹的市中心与莫农加希拉河畔林立的熔炉对沃霍尔来说都咫尺可及。作为成长于1940年代的青少年，沃霍尔见证了城市的变迁，高楼大厦与桥梁在他周围不断崛起。这座城市令他得以感受现代生活的奇迹，这其中包括壮观的建筑、大型博物馆、电影院、百货商店以及都市人。

In 1868, Boston writer James Parton famously described Pittsburgh as "hell with the lid taken off" for the thick smoke that poured forth from its burgeoning factories and steel mills. The area's aluminum and steel industries continued to expand throughout the 1930s and 1940s. Pennsylvania produced more steel during World War II than all the Axis powers combined; it was named "the Arsenal of Democracy" for its remarkable production capacity. The robust industry during WWII produced so much pollution that midday streets in Pittsburgh were as dark as night, as smog blotted out the sun. Because of defense production needs, smoke control ordinances were not put into effect until after the war. Although the young artist lived in a small immigrant neighborhood, Warhol was close to both the bustling downtown and the booming furnaces along the Monongahela River. As a teen in the 1940s, Warhol would have seen the city transforming, with ambitious new buildings and bridges springing up all around him. The city allowed him to experience the marvels of modern life, including compelling architecture, major museums, movie theaters, retail centers, and cosmopolitan people.

《匹兹堡湾观光游地图》
*Gulf Pittsburgh Info Map with Sight-seeing Tour*
1940年代 1940s

带框 With frame: 45.7 × 91.4 cm

《福尔摩斯小学》
*Holmes School*
约 ca. 1950—1970

明胶银盐相纸
Gelatin silver print
20.3 × 25.4 cm

《申利高中》
*Schenley High School*
约 ca. 1950—1970

明胶银盐相纸
Gelatin silver print
20.3 × 25.4 cm

《安迪·沃霍尔申利高中班级合照》
Homeroom picture of Andy Warhol's
class at Schenley High School
1944—1945

明胶银盐相纸
Gelatin silver print
12.7 × 18.3 cm

《申利高中毕业纪念册》
匹兹堡申利高中
Schenley Journal
Schenley High School, Pittsburgh
1945

机械装订涂布纸、黑色纸封面
Mechanical bound coated paper
with black paper covers
26.7 × 20.3 × 0.6 cm

《安迪・沃霍尔》
作者未知
*Andy Warhol*
Unknown
约 ca. 1945

棕褐色原片
Sepia print
17.8 × 12.7 cm

ORIGINS

沃霍尔从儿时便受到鼓励发展自己的创意才华。1945年，沃霍尔用家人为他存下的学费进入卡内基理工学院。尽管一开始成绩不佳，需要暑期补习，但从1946年起，沃霍尔充满创意的风格与想法便获得了老师与同学的一致认可。沃霍尔积极参与学校活动，不仅加入卡内基理工美术协会与现代舞俱乐部，还在1948年担任了学生杂志《卡诺》的艺术编辑。

Warhol was encouraged to develop his creative talents from early childhood. With the money the family saved for his college education, Warhol enrolled in Carnegie Institute of Technology in 1945. Although he initially struggled with his coursework and was required to take summer classes, by 1946, Warhol's innovative style and fresh ideas were recognized by faculty and students alike. Warhol was also an active participant in college life. He was a member of Carnegie Institute of Technology's honorary Beaux Arts Society and the Modern Dance Club, and in 1948, he became art editor for the student magazine *Cano*.

《自画像》
*Self-Portrait*
1944

纸板水粉
Gouache on board
40.6 × 27.9 cm

ORIGINS 47

在大一差点被学校劝退后,沃霍尔的老师们建议他先加强绘画功底,再继续学习。这幅速写描绘了顾客从他哥哥保罗的卡车上购买蔬菜水果的场景,这是1946年夏天沃霍尔创作的一系列作品中的一幅。他的绘画水平提升显著,秋季开学时获得了"进步奖"现金奖励。据他的朋友们回忆,这次获奖是他重拾信心的转折点,并为他后来的大胆实验铺平了道路。

After nearly failing his freshman year at college, Warhol was advised by his professors to polish his drawing skills before continuing his studies. This quick sketch of customers purchasing fruits and vegetables from his brother Paul's produce truck is from the series Warhol made over that summer in 1946. His skills improved considerably, and after returning to college in the fall, he received a cash "prize for progress." His friends noted that winning this prize marked a turning point in his confidence and paved the way for bold experiments to come.

《农产品卡车后面的女人和儿童》
*Female and Children Behind Produce Truck*
1946

马尼拉纸上墨水和石墨
Ink and graphite on manila paper
30.5 × 45.7 cm

《女人和农产品卡车》
*Women and Produce Truck*
1946

马尼拉纸上墨水和石墨
Ink and graphite on manila paper
33 × 47.6 cm

ORIGINS

《农产品卡车后面的人》
Figures Behind Produce Truck
1946

马尼拉纸上墨水和石墨
Ink and graphite on manila paper
30.5 × 45.7 cm

《农产品卡车后面的男人》
Male Figure in Back of Produce Truck
1946

马尼拉纸上墨水和石墨
Ink and graphite on manila paper
30.5 × 45.7 cm

《人行道上的四个人》
*Four Figures on Sidewalk*
1946

马尼拉纸上墨水和石墨
Ink and graphite on manila paper
30.5 × 45.7 cm

《断墙前的三个人》
*Three Figures Against Cracked Wall*
1946

马尼拉纸上墨水和石墨
Ink and graphite on manila paper
30.5 × 45.7 cm

ORIGINS 51

《卡内基理工学院学生》
*Unidentified Carnegie Institute
of Technology students*
约 ca. 1948

明胶银盐相纸
Gelatin silver print
7 × 9.5 cm

《卡内基理工学院学生》
*Unidentified Carnegie Institute
of Technology students*
约 ca. 1948

明胶银盐相纸
Gelatin silver print
7 × 9.5 cm

《安迪·沃霍尔（右）
与多萝西·坎托在卡内基
理工学院的艺术工作室》
*Andy Warhol (right) and Dorothy Cantor in an art studio at Carnegie Tech*
约 ca. 1948

明胶银盐相纸
Gelatin silver print
8.9 × 8.9 cm

《安迪·沃霍尔素描像 I》
多萝西·坎托
*Drawing of Andy Warhol I*
Dorothy Cantor
约 ca. 1950—1952

纸上石墨、写生簿
Graphite on paper, sketchbook
27.6 × 21.3 cm

ORIGINS 53

沃霍尔在本科学习期间结识了菲利普·珀尔斯坦。珀尔斯坦也是一位艺术家，他年少成名的经历令沃霍尔着迷。1949年，两人一起搬到纽约发展自己的艺术事业，但很快又分道扬镳，珀尔斯坦与大学时的女友多萝西·坎托成婚，并进入研究生院学习。珀尔斯坦后来成为20世纪最伟大的具象画家之一，专注现代写实主义裸体绘画。

Warhol met Philip Pearlstein during his college years at Carnegie Institute of Technology. Pearlstein was a fellow artist and fascinated Warhol due to his early success in the art world. They moved to New York City together in 1949 to pursue their art careers, but they ended up parting ways after Pearlstein married college sweetheart Dorothy Cantor and started graduate school. Pearlstein would go on to be one the greatest figurative artists of the twentieth century, specializing in Modernist Realist nudes.

《美术课》
菲利普·珀尔斯坦
*Art Class*
Philip Pearlstein
1946—1947

纸板蛋彩
Tempera on board
50.8 × 40.6 cm

ORIGINS 55

1947 年夏天，沃霍尔帮忙为位于匹兹堡市中心的奢侈品商场——约瑟夫·霍恩百货公司设计了橱窗。尽管当时同性恋在匹兹堡尚被视为违法，沃霍尔和几位同性恋同事在霍恩公司可以安心做自己。部门负责人拉里·沃尔默也是一位同性恋者，他曾为纽约的邦威特·特勒百货公司设计橱窗（沃霍尔后来亦工作于此）。沃霍尔称拉里·沃尔默是他大学时期的偶像。

During the summer of 1947, Warhol helped design window displays at Joseph Horne Company, a luxury department store in downtown Pittsburgh. Though homosexuality was illegal in Pittsburgh, Warhol had several gay colleagues, and the workplace at Horne's was a safe space for them to be themselves. Leading the department was Larry Vollmer, a gay man who used to design window displays at the department store Bonwit Teller in New York City (a job which Warhol would do in later years). Warhol described Vollmer as the idol of his university years.

《拉里·沃尔默与安迪·沃霍尔》
作者未知
*Larry Vollmer and Andy Warhol*
Unknown
1947

明胶银盐相纸
Gelatin silver print
9.5 × 11.7 cm

约瑟夫·霍恩百货公司橱窗外景照片
*Exterior view of Joseph Horne Company department store window displays*
1947

明胶银盐相纸
Gelatin silver print
20.3 × 25.4 cm

约瑟夫·霍恩百货公司"送给情人
心之所爱"橱窗照片
*Joseph Horne Company department
store "Give a Valentine that Counts"
window display*
1947

明胶银盐相纸
Gelatin silver print
20.3 × 25.4 cm

约瑟夫·霍恩百货公司旅游服饰橱窗照片
*Joseph Horne Company department store travel attire window display*
1947

明胶银盐相纸
Gelatin silver print
20.3 × 25.4 cm

约瑟夫·霍恩百货公司"男性之选"橱窗照片
*Joseph Horne Company department store "Male-tested Fashions" window display*
1947

明胶银盐相纸
Gelatin silver print
20.3 × 25.4 cm

ORIGINS 59

《安迪·沃霍尔与约瑟夫·霍恩百货商店的同事》
作者未知
*Andy Warhol with unidentified co-workers from Joseph Horne's department store*
Unknown
1947

明胶银盐相纸
Gelatin silver print
9.5 × 12.1 cm

《安迪·沃霍尔与同事》
作者未知
*Andy Warhol and unidentified co-workers*
Unknown
1947

明胶银盐相纸
Gelatin silver print
8.3 × 11.7 cm

《安迪·沃霍尔与同事》
作者未知
*Andy Warhol and unidentified co-workers*
Unknown
1947

明胶银盐相纸
Gelatin silver print
8.3 × 11.7 cm

《安迪·沃霍尔与同事》
作者未知
*Andy Warhol and unidentified co-workers*
Unknown
1947

明胶银盐相纸
Gelatin silver print
8.3 × 11.7 cm

ORIGINS 61

大三结束的暑假,沃霍尔和同班同学租下隶属卡内基理工学院古老宅邸的马车房。年轻的艺术家们称其为"谷仓",并将其改造成前卫艺术工作室,在那里开展抽象创作、现代舞、人物肖像和摄影的实验——多年后的"银色工厂"与此如出一辙。在沃霍尔于此创作的作品中,一系列描绘他用手指挖鼻孔且造型扭曲的自画像给人留下了深刻印象。

In the summer after his junior year, Warhol and his classmates rented the carriage house of an old mansion owned by Carnegie Institute of Technology. The young artists called it The Barn and turned it into an avant-garde studio for experimenting with abstraction, modern dance, portraiture, and photography – much like the Silver Factory in later years. Of the works created here, Warhol's distorted Nosepicker self-portraits, which depict him thrusting his finger into his nose, are the most notable.

《天使》
朱莉娅·沃霍拉
*Angel*
Julia Warhola
1952—1970

丝蒂摩纸上墨水
Ink on Strathmore paper
35.4 × 27.3 cm

《正在祈祷的两名天使》
朱莉娅·沃霍拉
*Two Angels Praying*
Julia Warhola
约 ca. 1957—1960

丝蒂摩纸上墨水
Ink on Strathmore paper
23.5 × 29.8 cm

《三名天使》
朱莉娅·沃霍拉
*Three Angels*
Julia Warhola
1952—1970

丝蒂摩纸上墨水
Ink on Strathmore paper
29.8 × 43.2 cm

ORIGINS

《戴帽子的猫》
朱莉娅·沃霍拉
*Cat with a Hat*
Julia Warhola
约 ca. 1957—1960

纸上墨水
Ink on paper
37.1 × 20.6 cm

《戴帽子的猫》
朱莉娅·沃霍拉
*Cat with a Hat*
Julia Warhola
约 ca. 1957—1960

丝蒂摩纸上墨水
Ink on Strathmore paper
58.4 × 37.5 cm

《戴帽子的猫与"purr"猫叫拟声词》
朱莉娅·沃霍拉
*Cat with a Hat with "Purr" Inscriptions*
Julia Warhola
约 ca. 1957—1961

丝蒂摩纸上墨水
Ink on Strathmore paper
32.1 × 34.6 cm

《猫》
朱莉娅·沃霍拉
*Cat*
Julia Warhola
1952—1970

丝蒂摩纸上墨水
Ink on Strathmore seconds paper
22.9 × 30.8 cm

ORIGINS 71

《戴帽子的猫》
朱莉娅·沃霍拉
Cat with a Hat
Julia Warhola
约 ca. 1957—1961

丝蒂摩纸上墨水
Ink on Strathmore paper
29.8 × 37.5 cm

《猫和小猫咪》
朱莉娅·沃霍拉
Cat with Kittens
Julia Warhola
1952—1970

丝蒂摩纸上墨水
Ink on Strathmore paper
30.2 × 43.2 cm

《两罐金宝汤罐头和两只猫》
朱莉娅·沃霍拉
*Two Campbell's Soup Cans and Two Cats*
Julia Warhola
约 ca. 1953

丝蒂摩纸上墨水
Ink on Strathmore seconds paper
33.3 × 57.5 cm

《五只猫》
朱莉娅·沃霍拉
*Five Cats*
Julia Warhola
约 ca. 1957—1961

丝蒂摩纸上墨水
Ink on Strathmore seconds paper
57.5 × 37.6 cm

ORIGINS 73

《圣诞老人》
朱莉娅·沃霍拉
Santa
Julia Warhola
1952—1970

纸上墨水
Ink on paper
29.7 × 28.1 cm

《手持十字架的两名天使》
朱莉娅·沃霍拉
Two Angels Holding a Cross
Julia Warhola
约 ca. 1960

绿色纸上墨水
Ink on green paper
15.9 × 12.4 cm

《手持十字架的天使》
朱莉娅·沃霍拉
*Angel Holding Cross*
Julia Warhola
约 ca. 1957—1960

金箔纸上墨水
Ink on gold paper
18.4 × 13.7 cm

《手持十字架的天使》
朱莉娅·沃霍拉
*Angel Holding Cross*
Julia Warhola
约 ca. 1957—1960

金箔纸上墨水
Ink on gold paper
18.4 × 13.7 cm

《神圣猫咪》，安迪·沃霍尔母亲绘
朱莉娅·沃霍拉
*Holy Cats by Andy Warhol's Mother*
Julia Warhola
1960

彩色纸上平版印刷、硬麻布封面
Offset lithograph on colored paper
with buckram board cover
书 Book: 23.2 × 14.9 × 0.5 cm

《天使、猫和小天使》
朱莉娅·沃霍拉
*Angels, Cats, and Cherubs*
Julia Warhola
约 ca. 1957—1960

纸上墨水
Ink on paper
76.8 × 57.2 cm

ORIGINS

《手工上色的朱莉娅·沃霍拉照片》
朱莉娅·沃霍拉
*Hand-colored Photograph of Julia Warhola*
Julia Warhola
约 ca. 1959

重磅卡纸和手工上色照片
Heavy weight cardstock and hand-colored photograph
22.9 × 17.8 cm

《二十五只叫山姆的猫和一只蓝色的猫》
*25 Cats Name[d] Sam and One Blue Pussy*
1956

纸上平版印刷和苯胺染料、硬麻布封面
Offset lithograph and Dr. Martin's aniline dye on paper with buckram board cover
23.5 × 15.6 × 1 cm

《爬梯子的女士》
*Females Climbing Ladders*
1949

丝蒂摩纸上墨水、石墨和蛋彩
Ink, graphite, and tempera on Strathmore paper
58.4 × 50.2 cm

ORIGINS  79

1955 至 1958 年，在 I. 米勒制鞋公司担任插画师期间，沃霍尔协助策划了制鞋业最巧妙的市场营销之一。当时 I. 米勒为确立新的公司形象，尝试了各种不同的营销策略，试图通过重复的方式强化产品在消费者脑海中的印象。沃霍尔的涂印技术让他可以针对主题快速创作出一系列插画，并通过作品颜色与构图的替换，为客户提供不同的选择。因沃霍尔在这些插画中所展现出来的精湛技巧，《女装日报》赞誉其为"鞋业达·芬奇"。

From 1955 to 1958, Warhol helped to create one of the shoe industry's most sophisticated marketing campaigns when he worked as an illustrator for the shoe company I. Miller. At the time, I. Miller was attempting to forge a new image for itself by experimenting with marketing strategies, using repetition to imprint their product on the minds of consumers. Warhol's use of the blotted line technique allowed him to quickly create a variety of illustrations along a similar theme. He could alter the color and composition of the artworks, giving his clients a selection from which to choose. Warhol was so skilled with the subject matter that he was even named "the Leonardo da Vinci of the shoe trade" by *Women's Wear Daily*.

《五只鞋和三个女士包》
丝蒂摩纸上墨水、石墨和水粉
*Five Shoes and Three Purses*
1950年代 1950s

Ink, graphite, and gouache on Strathmore seconds paper
36.2 × 57.2 cm

ORIGINS 81

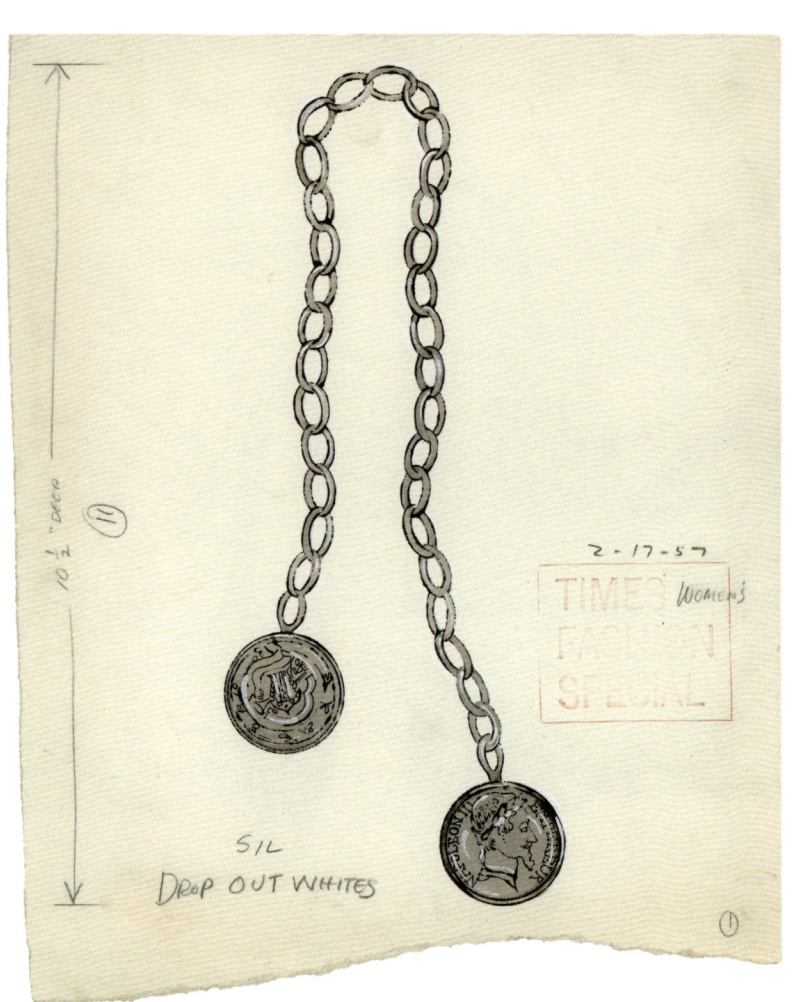

《项链和两枚硬币》
*Necklace and Two Coins*
1957

丝蒂摩纸上墨水
Ink on Strathmore paper
38.7 × 30.5 cm

《高跟鞋》
*High Heel*
1955

丝蒂摩纸上墨水、石墨、蛋彩和拼贴
Ink, graphite, tempera, and printed tape collage on Strathmore paper
19.1 × 24.1 cm

《五只鞋（带印刷套准标记）》
*Five Shoes (with Registration Marks)*
1950 年代 1950s

丝蒂摩纸上墨水、蛋彩和拼贴
Ink, tempera, and collage
on Strathmore paper
44.1 × 29.5 cm

ORIGINS 83

《女士手提包》
*Purse*
1950 年代 1950s

丝蒂摩纸上墨水、石墨和蛋彩
Ink, graphite, and tempera on Strathmore paper
37.5 × 28.3 cm

《服装配饰》
*Multiple Clothing Accessories*
1950 年代 1950s

木板上丝蒂摩纸上墨水
Ink on Strathmore paper on board
55.9 × 37.5 cm

《福恩斯兄弟公司手套广告》
*"Fownes"*
1950 年代 1950s

丝蒂摩纸上墨水、石墨、苯胺染料和拼贴
Ink, graphite, Dr. Martin's aniline dye, and collage on Strathmore paper
39.1 × 28.9 cm

《八个戴着墨镜的女士头像》
*Eight Female Heads Wearing Sunglasses*
1957

丝蒂摩纸上墨水、蛋彩和醋酸盐胶片
Ink and tempera with acetate overlay on Strathmore paper
40 × 58.1 cm

《三个翅膀的人和时尚首饰》
*Three Winged Figures and Fashion Accessories*
1950 年代 1950s

丝蒂摩纸上墨水和苯胺染料
Ink and Dr. Martin's aniline dye on Strathmore paper
43.8 × 57.2 cm

ORIGINS 87

在成为纯艺术家之前,沃霍尔在 1950 年代一直在纽约为《时尚》和《魅力》等杂志绘制时尚广告插图。打造抢眼的品牌图像是沃霍尔商业插画的核心,他不断探索线条与颜色的变化以迎合观众的喜好。可口可乐罐在被沃霍尔搬上画布之前,已经作为绘画元素和其他商品同时出现在他的涂印画里。尽管这段时期的商业经验直接应用在其 1960 年代早期的波普艺术创作中,但这些广告插画却鲜少展出,并且大多被批评家所遗忘。

Before Warhol became a fine artist, he spent the 1950s in New York making illustrations for fashion advertisements in magazines such as *Vogue* and *Glamour*. Cultivating an exciting brand image was central to Warhol's commercial compositions, and he practiced how to present lines and colors in a way that was pleasant to the viewer. Well before Warhol hand-painted Coca-Cola bottles on canvas, they appeared in his blotted line drawings next to other consumer items. Even though he translated his commercial experience directly into his early-1960s Pop art, his commercial works were not exhibited and largely forgotten by critics during his career.

《腿和可口可乐瓶》
*Pair of Legs with Coca-Cola Bottle*
约 ca. 1956

丝蒂摩纸上墨水、水粉和石墨
Ink, gouache, and graphite on Strathmore paper
30.5 × 27.3 cm

ORIGINS

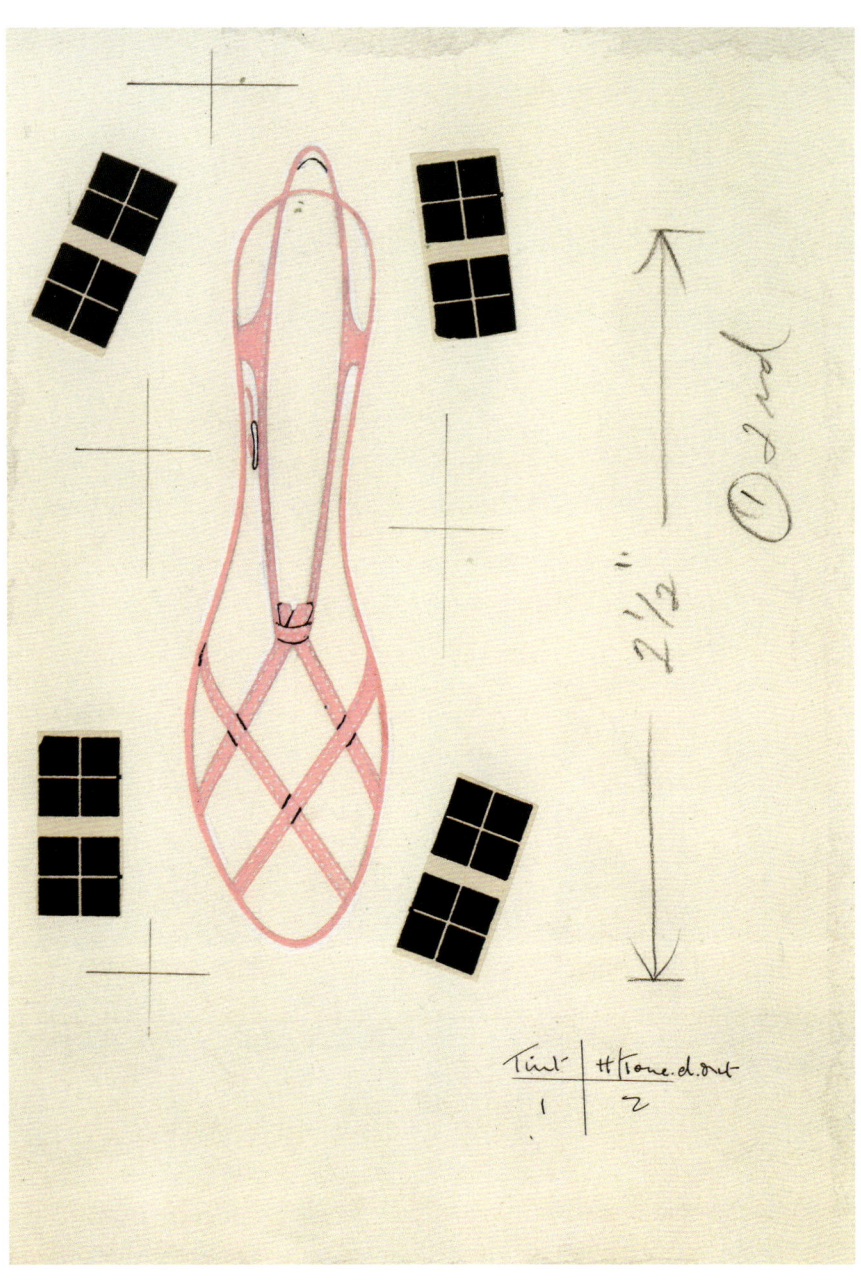

《凉鞋》
*Sandal*
1950 年代 1950s

丝蒂摩纸上墨水蛋彩
Ink and tempera on Strathmore paper
20.6 × 14 cm

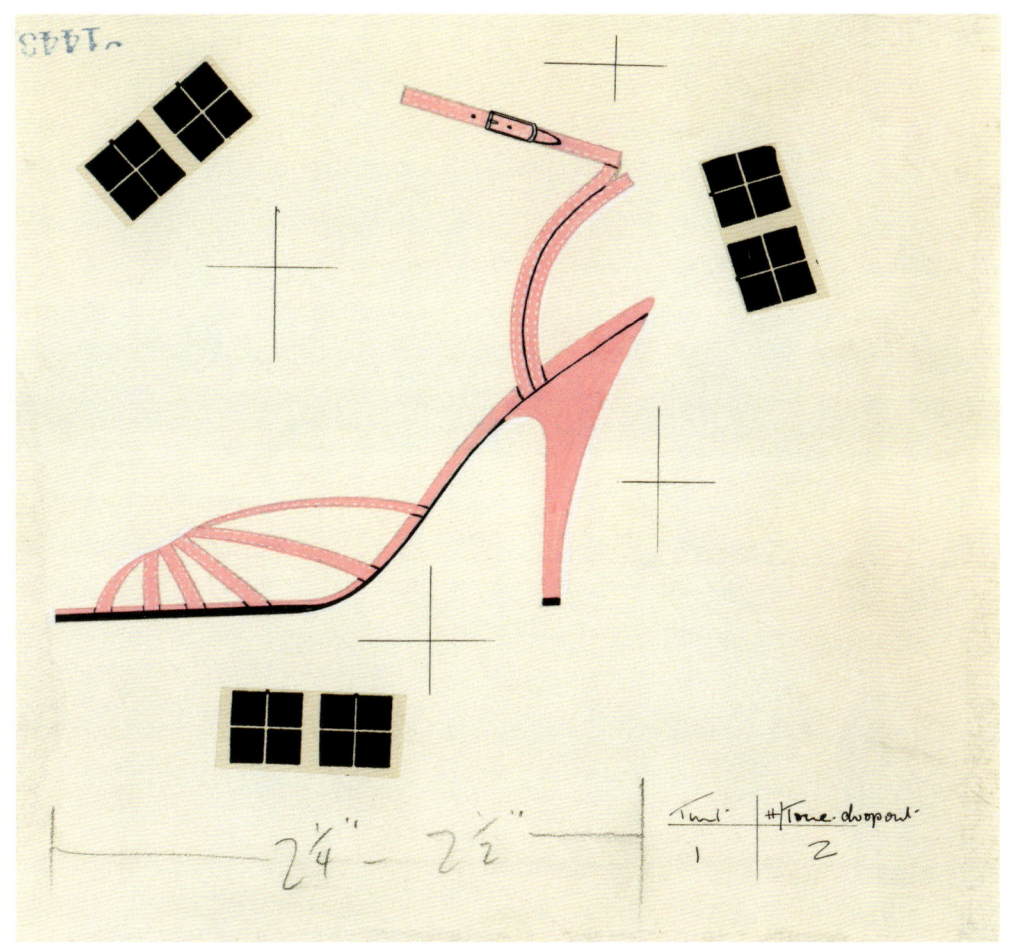

《凉鞋》
*Sandal*
1950 年代 1950s

丝蒂摩纸上墨水、石墨、蛋彩和定位胶带
Ink, graphite, tempera, and registration tape on Strathmore paper
17.5 × 18.1 cm

《鞋（带印刷套准标记）》
*Shoe (with Registration Marks)*
1954

丝蒂摩纸上墨水和蛋彩
Ink and tempera on Strathmore paper
20 × 10.2 cm

ORIGINS 91

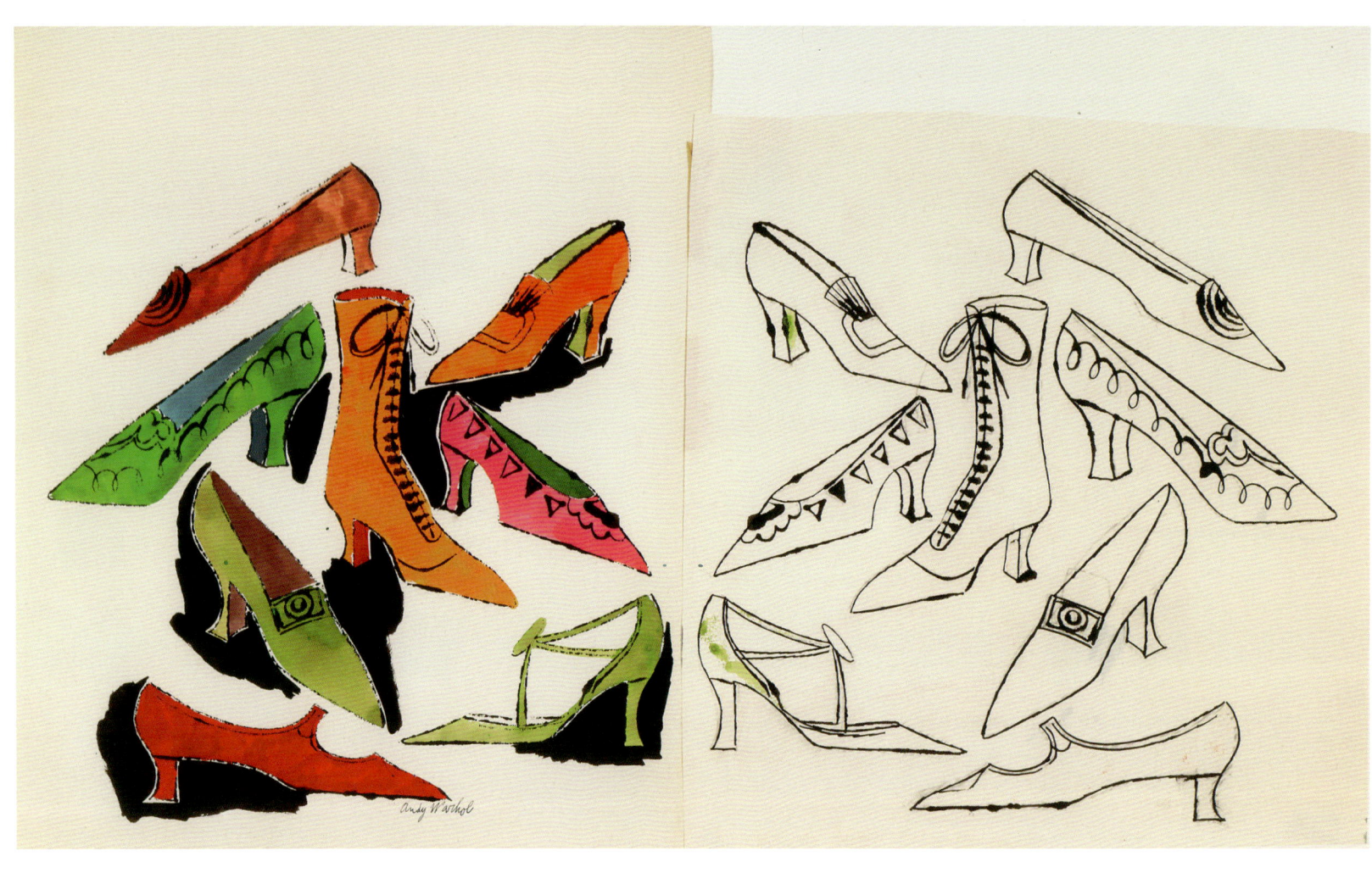

涂印技术是绘画与简易印刷术的结合。沃霍尔先在一张非吸收性纸——例如透写纸上画出线稿,接着将这张纸与另一张吸收性纸两边相接。然后,沃霍尔用钢笔涂描线稿的一小部分,再沿着两张纸的接缝对折并轻压,将墨迹转移(或者说涂印)到第二张纸上。以这一技法得以实现的断续而精致的线条是沃霍尔这一时期插画的特征。

The blotted line combines drawing with a simple printmaking technique. Warhol began by making a line drawing on a piece of non-absorbent paper, such as tracing paper. Next, he hinged this piece of paper to a second sheet of more absorbent paper by taping their edges together on one side. With a fountain pen, Warhol inked over a small section of the drawn lines, then transferred the ink onto the second sheet by folding along the hinge and lightly pressing, or "blotting," the two papers together. The process resulted in the dotted, broken, and delicate lines characteristic of Warhol's illustrations from this period.

《八只鞋》
*Eight Shoes*
1950 年代 1950s

丝蒂摩纸上墨水和苯胺染料
Ink and Dr. Martin's aniline dye on Strathmore paper
41 × 64 cm

《幻想中的鞋》
*Fantasy Shoes*
约 ca. 1956

丝蒂摩纸上墨水和苯胺染料
Ink and Dr. Martin's aniline dye on Strathmore paper
57.5 × 72.7 cm

ORIGINS 93

《高跟鞋》
*High Heel Shoe*
约 ca. 1955

丝蒂摩纸上墨水和苯胺染料
Ink and Dr. Martin's aniline dye on Strathmore paper
22.9 × 27.9 cm

《高跟鞋》
*High Heeled Shoe*
1950 年代 1950s

丝蒂摩纸上墨水、石墨和苯胺染料
Ink, graphite, and Dr. Martin's aniline dye on
Strathmore paper
22.9 × 27.9 cm

ORIGINS

《圣诞鞋》
*Merry Christmas Shoe*
约 ca. 1957

丝蒂摩纸和金箔纸上墨水和苯胺染料
Ink and Dr. Martin's aniline dye on Strathmore and gold paper
23.2 × 31.8 cm

《为蒂芙尼公司设计的圣诞贺卡》
*Christmas Card Design for Tiffany & Co.*
1950 年代 1950s

丝蒂摩纸上墨水、苯胺染料和打印材料
Ink, Dr. Martin's aniline dye, and printed material on Strathmore paper
41.6 × 31.1 cm

《为蒂芙尼公司设计的圣诞贺卡》
*Christmas Card Design for Tiffany & Co.*
1950 年代 1950s

丝蒂摩纸上墨水、苯胺染料和打印材料
Ink, Dr. Martin's aniline dye, and printed material onStrathmore paper
41.6 × 31.1 cm

《为蒂芙尼公司设计的圣诞贺卡》
*Christmas Card Design for Tiffany & Co.*
1950 年代 1950s

丝蒂摩纸上墨水和苯胺染料
Ink and Dr. Martin's aniline dye on Strathmore paper
32.1 × 43.8 cm

ORIGINS

《鸡尾酒时间的星座运势
（"虔诚的摩羯座"）》
Horoscopes for the Cocktail Hour
("Reverent Capricorn")
约 ca. 1961

写生纸上墨水和苯胺染料
Ink and Dr. Martin's aniline dye on sketchbook paper
61 × 45.7 cm

《鸡尾酒时间的星座运势
（"香槟鸡尾酒"）》
*Horoscopes for the Cocktail Hour
("Champagne Cocktail")*
约 ca. 1961

写生纸上墨水、印墨、苯胺染料和拼贴
Ink, stamped ink, Dr. Martin's aniline dye, and collage on sketchbook paper
61 × 45.7 cm

ORIGINS 101

《鸡尾酒时间的星座运势
（"明智的射手座"）》
*Horoscopes for the Cocktail Hour
("Sagacious Sagittarius")*
约 ca. 1961

写生纸上墨水、石墨和苯胺染料
Ink, graphite, and Dr. Martin's aniline
dye on sketchbook paper
61 × 45.7 cm

《"彩绘蛇……弗莱明－约菲公司"（为皮制品商店做的设计）》
*"The Painted Serpent...Fleming Joffe"*
约 ca. 1961

纸上丝网印刷和爬行动物皮拼贴
Screen print and reptile skin collage on paper
57.2 × 43.2 cm

《"人人都爱弗莱明－约菲牌的麂皮产品"》
*"Everybody is in love with Suede at Fleming-Joffe"*
约 ca. 1958—1965

丝蒂摩纸上平版印刷、染色爬行动物皮和麂皮拼贴
Offset lithograph, dyed reptile skin, and suede collage on Strathmore paper
61.3 × 45.4 cm

ORIGINS 103

应蒂芙尼与邦威特·特勒百货公司的橱窗设计总监吉恩·莫尔的邀请，沃霍尔设计了大量的橱窗展示作品。莫尔以乐于雇用新兴艺术家而闻名。除了委托他们围绕特定产品展开设计外，这些艺术家们偶尔也有机会展示自己的作品。包括贾斯珀·约翰斯、罗伯特·劳森伯格和詹姆斯·罗森奎斯特在内的艺术家，都曾为邦威特·特勒百货公司设计过橱窗展示。然而，与沃霍尔不同的是，他们设计橱窗采取匿名的方式，似乎不想玷污他们先锋艺术家的形象。劳森伯格和约翰斯经常以"马特森·约翰斯"的化名进行合作，沃霍尔则毫不在意地在他的橱窗设计上签上大名自我推销，全然无视"纯艺术"与"商业艺术"之间的隔阂。此处展示的是沃霍尔为位于纽约第五大道的邦威特·特勒百货公司香水促销活动设计的两个橱窗，都是依据原始橱窗照片的重制版本。

At the invitation of Gene Moore, a display director for Tiffany & Co and the Bonwit Teller department store, Warhol produced numerous window displays. Moore was well known for hiring emerging artists. In addition to commissioning them to develop designs for specific products, they were occasionally given the opportunity to exhibit their own artwork. Major figures, including Jasper Johns, Robert Rauschenberg, and James Rosenquist, created windows for Bonwit Teller. However, unlike Warhol, they produced their windows anonymously, not wanting to taint their profiles as members of the artistic avant-garde. While Rauschenberg and Johns often collaborated under the pseudonym "Matson Jones," Warhol signed his windows in an act of self-promotion and disregard for the perceived boundaries between "fine" and "commercial" art. The two windows on display here were developed for perfume promotions at Bonwit Teller's Fifth Avenue department store. They have been reconstructed from photographs of the original windows.

邦威特百货Mistigri牌香水橱窗展示
*"Bonwit's Loves Mistigri"*
1955
重制 Reproduction 2021

木板丙烯和蜡笔
Crayon and acrylic on wood
235 × 256.5 × 1.9 cm

邦威特百货Replique牌香水橱窗展示
*"Bonwit's Loves Replique"*
1957
重制 Reproduction 2017

木板丙烯和蜡笔
Crayon and acrylic on wood
235 × 256.5 × 1.9 cm

# 摄影师沃霍尔
**WARHOL THE PHOTOGRAPHER**

> "所有的摄影都是波普，所有的摄影师都是疯子……他们心怀愧疚，因为除了按快门，他们几乎什么都不需要做。"
> ——安迪·沃霍尔

通常被归为画家的安迪·沃霍尔也是一位高产的摄影师，一生之中拍摄了数千幅照片，并且一直采用最新的摄影技术。摄影既是他绘画作品的一部分，也是一种创作媒介。摄影让沃霍尔免于手绘造型之苦，得以专注复制与量产。沃霍尔放大宝丽来照片，利用丝网印刷工艺将图像印在画布之上。随着纽约名流争相订购他的人物肖像作品，这项工艺为他带来了巨大收益。之后，沃霍尔开始尝试黑白照片，尤其是对现成品与自然物体的重复再现。成名后的沃霍尔经常使用美乐时35EL——一种35毫米小型相机记录他的旅行和他参加的上流社会活动。

# "All photography is Pop, and all photographers are crazy […] they feel guilty since they don't have to do very much – just push a button."

— Andy Warhol

While commonly classified as a painter, Andy Warhol was a prolific photographer, shooting thousands of photographs throughout his career and constantly using new camera technology. Photography served both as an aspect of his painting production and as a medium of its own. With photography, Warhol could avoid the difficult process of hand-painting or sketching forms and instead concentrate on replication and mass production. In the silkscreen process, Warhol would enlarge Polaroid photographs and print the image across multiple canvases. This technique proved to be a huge source of income as his portraits became exceedingly popular among the New York elite. Later in his career, Warhol experimented with black-and-white photography, focusing on repetition in found, patterned objects and in nature. After his rise to fame, Warhol documented his travels and high-society events by taking pictures on his Minox 35 EL, a small 35 mm camera.

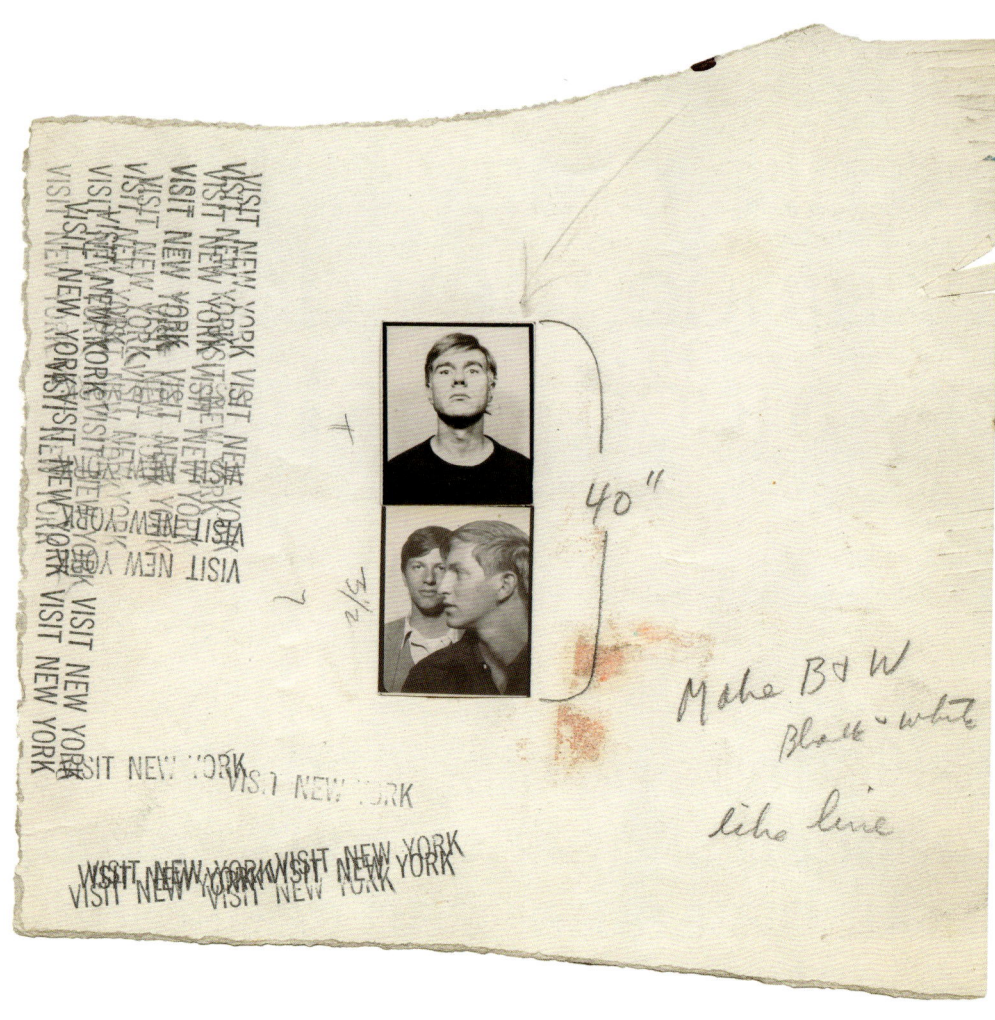

从 1920 年代起,快照亭这种原理简单的自助拍照机器开始流行,并很快在药房、火车站和汽车站都可以找到其身影。快照亭对拍摄对象即时状态的捕捉令沃霍尔很感兴趣,不需要布置复杂的灯光与相机,只需指挥拍摄对象即可。沃霍尔积极拥抱并充分利用这一技术,将连拍的照片用作肖像素材,并作为档案保存。

The photo booth became popular in the 1920s as a simple vending machine to take pictures. Soon these kiosks were located at drugstores, train stations, and bus depots. Warhol was intrigued by the spontaneous results it drew from sitters. Rather than laboring with complicated lighting and cameras, the photo booth freed Warhol to do nothing except stage direct his subjects. Warhol embraced the technology wholeheartedly, using the strips of stacked photos as source material for portraits and collecting them as documents.

《机械感（安迪·沃霍尔快照亭自拍与迈克和鲍勃·艾布拉姆斯快照亭照片）》
*Mechanical (Andy Warhol photobooth self-portrait with Mike and Bob Abrams photobooth portraits)*
约 ca. 1964

重磅纸上快照亭照片、石墨和墨水
Photobooth photographs, graphite, and ink on heavyweight paper
25.4 × 25.7 cm

《自画像》
*Self-Portrait*
1964

布上丙烯、金属漆和丝网印刷
Acrylic, metallic paint, and silkscreen ink on linen
51.1 × 41 × 1.9 cm

WARHOL THE PHOTOGRAPHER　111

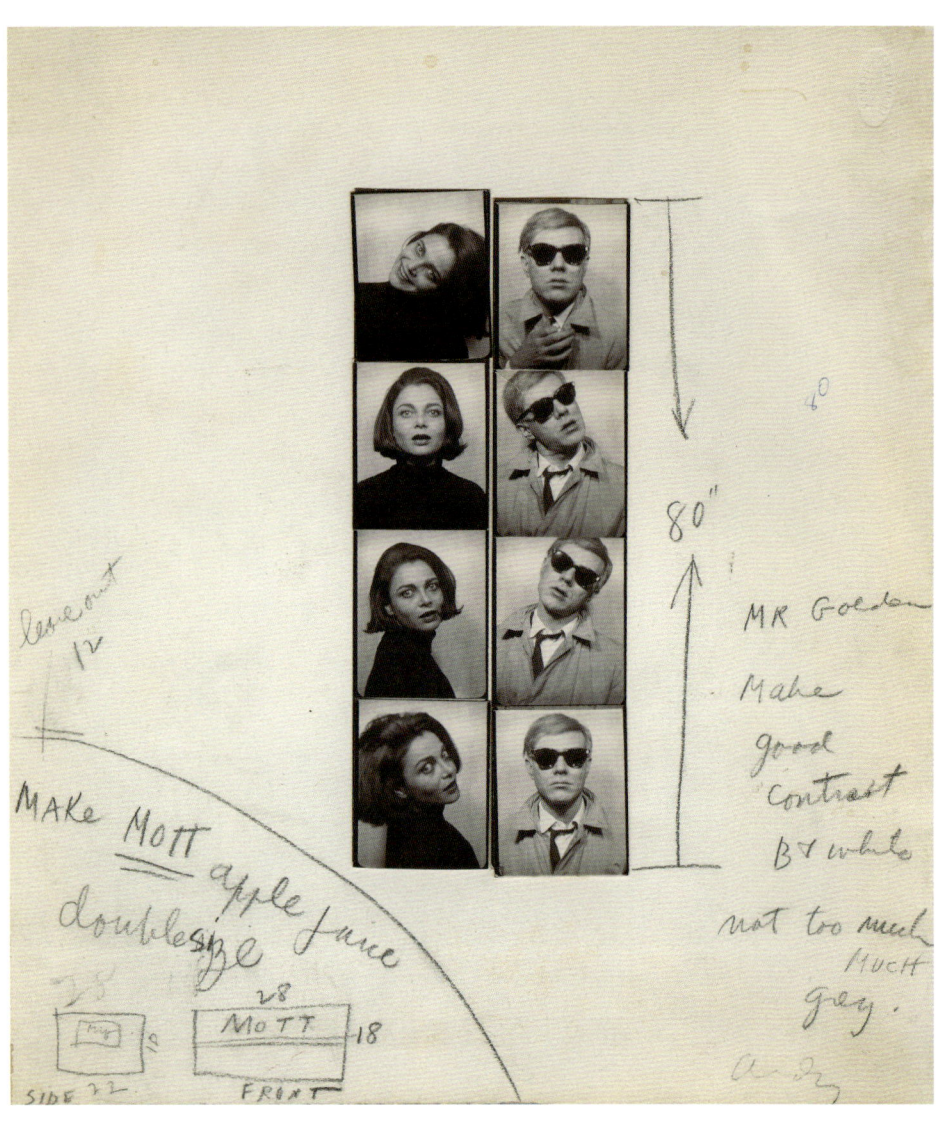

《机械感（安迪·沃霍尔快照亭自拍与
朱迪丝·格林的快照亭照片）》
*Mechanical (Andy Warhol photobooth
self-portrait with Judith Green photobooth
portrait)*
约 ca. 1963

重磅纸上快照亭照片和石墨
Photobooth photographs and graphite
onheavyweight paper
32.4 × 27.9 cm

《自画像》
*Self-Portrait*
1963—1964

布上丙烯和丝印油墨
Acrylic and silkscreen ink on linen
50.8 × 40.6 cm

WARHOL THE PHOTOGRAPHER

1965年，摄影师帕特西亚·考菲尔德经过曼哈顿一家书店橱窗，看到里面挂着一幅沃霍尔的海报《花》。她认出了那是自己的作品，并联系了律师。她拍摄的木槿花照片原本刊登在1964年6月号的《现代摄影》杂志上，但沃霍尔未经许可便加以使用。沃霍尔复制、剪切、平面化了考菲尔德的照片，加强对比度并添加了明亮的颜色。他在那一年售出了几百幅作品，且均未提及照片出自考菲尔德之手。和许多起诉沃霍尔的侵权案一样，这起诉讼最终也达成了庭外和解。

In 1965, photographer Patricia Caulfield walked by a poster of Warhol's *Flowers* displayed in a Manhattan bookstore window. She recognized her own work and contacted a lawyer. Her photograph of hibiscus blooms, originally printed in the June 1964 issue of *Modern Photography*, had been appropriated by Warhol without permission or attribution. Warhol copied, cropped, and flattened Caulfield's image, enhancing the contrast and adding vibrant color. He sold hundreds of paintings that year without crediting Caulfield for her work. Like earlier copyright infringement claims against Warhol, the lawsuit was eventually settled out of court.

《花》
*Flowers*
1964

布上丙烯、铅笔和丝网印刷
Acrylic, silkscreen ink,
and pencil on linen
121.9 × 121.9 cm

《花》
*Flowers*
1964

布上丙烯、铅笔和丝网印刷
Acrylic, silkscreen ink,
and pencil on linen
121.9 × 121.9 cm

传言沃霍尔在他生命最后十年里拍摄了 15 万张照片。在 1970 年代末，35 毫米胶片相机在市场上已经很容易买到。这些小巧的傻瓜相机价格低廉，沃霍尔带着它参加各种各样的社交活动，包括慈善晚会、时装秀、生日派对和艺术机构开幕式，等等。沃霍尔几乎会拍摄任何人，无论是在私人场合还是在公共领域。他还会用相机记录街景、建筑与窗外的景色———一切能吸引艺术家之眼的事物。与他用宝丽来拍摄的照片有很大不同，这些照片捕捉到被拍摄者并未意识到的真实瞬间。

According to some accounts, Warhol took 150,000 photographs in the last decade of his life. In the late 1970s, 35mm cameras became readily available on the market. These small, "point and shoot" models were inexpensive, and Warhol could carry one with him to every social function he attended, including benefits, fashion shows, birthday parties, and art openings. Warhol photographed almost everyone who was anyone, in both private and public settings. He also used the camera to document street scenes, buildings, and the views out his window – anything and everything that caught his experienced eye. These photographs differ greatly from his Polaroids, as they capture candid moments with the subjects less aware of the camera.

《安迪·沃霍尔给一对情侣拍照》
罗伯特·肖
*Andy Warhol photographing an unidentified couple*
Robert Shaw
1972

明胶银盐相纸
Gelatin silver print
27.9 × 35.6 cm

《安迪·沃霍尔与一位男士》
罗伯特·肖
*Andy Warhol with unidentified man*
Robert Shaw
1972

明胶银盐相纸
Gelatin silver print
27.9 × 35.6 cm

1971 年 5 月，宝丽来推出 Big Shot 相机，这种廉价、笨拙、塑料外壳的设备专为拍摄肖像照片而制。仅需二十美元就可以得到"仿摄影棚"质量的光鲜照片，这种照片中绝大多数面孔都不再有皱纹与阴影。沃霍尔对 Big Shot 青睐有加并大量购入，他在 1970 年代创作的名人肖像几乎都是用这种相机拍摄而成。拍摄完成后，他把照片送到丝网印刷厂进行进一步的美化处理，然后用丝网印到画布上。

In May of 1971, Polaroid released the Big Shot camera – a cheap, clunky, plastic device made specifically for portrait photographs. For only USD 20, it could provide flattering "faux-studio"-quality pictures that could dissolve most wrinkles and leave almost any face shadowless. Warhol fell in love with the Big Shot, collecting them en masse and using them for the majority of his celebrity portraits in the 1970s. After the shoots, he would send them off to his screen printer for more flattering edits, then silkscreen the image onto painted canvas.

宝丽来 Big Shot 照相机
*Polaroid Big Shot*
约 ca. 1972

模压塑料、金属零件
Molded plastic with metal parts
26 × 15.2 × 17.1 cm

宝丽来 Big Shot 照相机
*Polaroid Big Shot*
约 ca. 1972

模压塑料、金属零件
Molded plastic with metal parts
26 × 15.2 × 17.1 cm

《安迪·沃霍尔与一位女士》
罗伯特·肖
*Andy Warhol with unidentified woman*
Robert Shaw
1972

明胶银盐相纸
Gelatin silver print
35.6 × 27.9 cm

WARHOL THE PHOTOGRAPHER  119

沃霍尔的拍摄地点包括工作室、酒店房间和拍摄对象的公寓。他在 1970 年代常用宝丽来 Big Shot 立拍得相机，每次都拍摄成卷的照片，直到能选出五张得意之作。与 1960 年代照相亭拍摄的肖像类似，高对比度的宝丽来照片可以掩盖瑕疵，美化拍摄对象，正好适合转成丝网印刷。他所拍摄的女性肖像都是半身像或是头像，男性肖像则经常有手进入画面，照片中人手举雪茄或其他能体现主人公个性的物品。

Warhol set up portrait sessions in his studio, hotel rooms, and sitter's apartments. In the 1970s, he used a Polaroid Big Shot, taking several rolls of pictures until he had at least five he liked. Similar to the photo booth portraits in the 1960s, the Polaroid yielded a high-contrast image that flattered the sitter by leaving out blemishes and imperfections – perfect for transforming into silkscreen paintings. Women posed with bare shoulders or from the neck up, and men's hands often came into play, holding cigars or other objects used to reveal an aspect of the sitter's personality.

《简·方达》
*Jane Fonda*
1982

宝丽来 Polacolor 2 彩色胶片
Polaroid™ Polacolor 2
10.8 × 8.6 cm

《大幅投影胶片（简·方达）》
*Large acetate (Jane Fonda)*
1982

聚酯膜上感光乳剂
Photo emulsion on
polyester film base
137.2 × 106.7 cm

《简·方达》
*Jane Fonda*
1982

布上丙烯和丝印油墨
Acrylic and silkscreen ink on linen
121.9 × 111.8 cm

《简·方达》
*Jane Fonda*
1982

布上丙烯和丝印油墨
Acrylic and silkscreen ink on linen
121.9 × 111.8 cm

《大幅描摹（简·方达）》
*Large tracing (Jane Fonda)*
1982

不透明聚酯板上石墨
Graphite on opaque polyester sheet
114.3 × 88.9 cm

《简·方达》
*Jane Fonda*
1982

莱诺克斯博物馆纸板上丝网印刷
Screen print on Lenox Museum Board
101 × 80.3 cm

身兼演员、舞者、歌手的皮娅·扎多拉是百老汇童星出身，不过她的演员生涯一直未见起色。1977年，她嫁给百万富翁梅苏莱姆·里克里斯，并聘请沃霍尔为她创作肖像，以装饰他们在洛杉矶的豪宅。沃霍尔在日记中记述了最初的定制问询："她到了，很可爱的女孩。她的丈夫里克里斯过来给我展示了一些照片。她很和善，我觉得她以后会成为大明星。她皮肤很好。"但后来扎多拉只选了十二幅肖像中的两幅，这让沃霍尔倍感失望。

Actress, dancer, and singer Pia Zadora began her career as a child star on Broadway, but her film career never materialized. In 1977, she married corporate millionaire Meshulam Riklis and later hired Warhol to do her portrait for their Los Angeles mansion. Warhol wrote in his diary about the initial portrait consultation: "She arrived and was so cute. Her husband, Riklis, came and showed pictures. She's so sweet and I think she's going to be a big star. Her skin is beautiful." He was later disappointed when she picked out only two of the twelve versions of her portrait.

《皮娅·扎多拉》
Pia Zadora
1983

宝丽来 Polacolor ER 彩色胶片
Polaroid™ Polacolor ER
10.8 × 8.6 cm

《皮娅·扎多拉》
Pia Zadora
1983

宝丽来 Polacolor ER 彩色胶片
Polaroid™ Polacolor ER
10.8 × 8.6 cm

《安迪·沃霍尔 给 皮娅·扎多拉拍照》
戴维·麦高夫
Andy Warhol photographing Pia Zadora
David McGough
1983

明胶银盐相纸
Gelatin silver print
20.3 × 25.4 cm

1960年代初，沃霍尔开始创作定制肖像，这后来成为他主要的收入来源。画中人多是国际社交界、艺术界和娱乐界的名流。1980年代初，沃霍尔每年约创作50幅肖像，一对双联肖像定价4万美元，私人订制为他增加了200万美元的年收入。这些肖像尺寸基本相同（101.6 × 101.6 cm），沃霍尔希望藏家尽可能多地购买这些肖像，以用这些作品拼成一面耀眼的肖像墙。

Warhol started painting portrait commissions in the early 1960s and this developed into his main source of income. Many of his subjects were well-known in international social circles, the art world, and the entertainment industry. In the early 1980s, Andy was painting about 50 clients a year; at USD 40,000 for a two-panel portrait, the private commissions added another two million to his annual profits. They typically came in one size (101.6 × 101.6 cm) and Warhol preferred that clients buy as many as possible to create a dazzling grid of portraits.

《皮娅·扎多拉》
*Pia Zadora*
1983

布上丙烯和丝印油墨
Acrylic and silkscreen ink on linen
101.6 × 101.6 cm

《皮娅·扎多拉》
*Pia Zadora*
1983

布上丙烯和丝印油墨
Acrylic and silkscreen ink on linen
101.6 × 101.6 cm

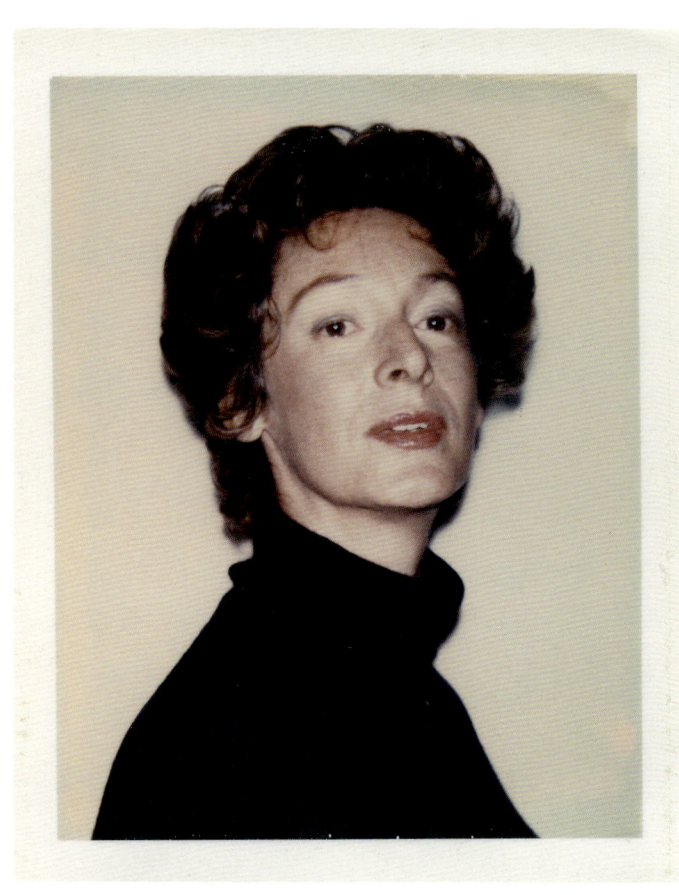

《马雷拉·阿涅利》
*Marella Agnelli*
1972

宝丽来 Polacolor (108) 彩色胶片
Polaroid™ Polacolor type 108
10.8 × 8.6 cm

《马雷拉·阿涅利》
*Marella Agnelli*
1973

布上丙烯和丝印油墨
Acrylic and silkscreen ink on linen
101.6 × 101.6 cm

《马雷拉·阿涅利》
*Marella Agnelli*
1973

布上丙烯和丝印油墨
Acrylic and silkscreen ink on linen
101.6 × 101.6 cm

WARHOL THE PHOTOGRAPHER 129

《维塔斯·格鲁莱蒂斯》
*Vitas Gerulitas*
1977

宝丽来 Polacolor (108) 彩色胶片
Polaroid™ Polacolor type 108
10.8 × 8.6 cm

《维塔斯·格鲁莱蒂斯》
*Vitas Gerulitas*
1977

布上丙烯和丝印油墨
Acrylic and silkscreen ink on linen
101.6 × 101.6 cm

《维塔斯·格鲁莱蒂斯》
*Vitas Gerulitas*
1977

布上丙烯和丝印油墨
Acrylic and silkscreen ink on linen
101.6 × 101.6 cm

WARHOL THE PHOTOGRAPHER 131

丽莎·明尼里是沃霍尔二十世纪七八十年代密友圈的核心人物。她是好莱坞名流朱迪·加兰和导演文森特·明尼里的爱女,自蹒跚学步时就登上了大荧幕,并因参演音乐电影《歌厅》(1972)广受好评。沃霍尔为她创作的肖像展示了这位迷人明星深邃的目光与令人难忘的面庞。作为沃霍尔的挚友,她的肖像拍摄如同一场盛会,甚至连披头士乐队的约翰·列侬也作为惊喜嘉宾出场。

Liza Minnelli was an important part of Warhol's inner circle in the 1970s and 1980s. Daughter to Hollywood royalty, Judy Garland and director Vincente Minnelli, she first appeared onscreen as a toddler and gained critical acclaim for her role in the musical film *Cabaret* (1972). Warhol's portraits of her present an alluring celebrity with a powerful glance and unforgettable face. As a dear friend to Warhol, her photoshoot involved particular pageantry and even a surprise visit from John Lennon of The Beatles.

安迪·沃霍尔
《丽莎·明尼里》
*Liza Minnelli*
1977

宝丽来 Polacolor (108) 彩色胶片
Polaroid™ Polacolor type 108
10.8 × 8.6 cm

《丽莎·明尼里：卡内基音乐厅演唱会》
丽莎·明尼里
*Liza Minnelli: Live at Carnegie Hall*
Liza Minnelli
1981

涂层唱片封套上平版印刷
Offset lithograph on coated record cover stock
31.4 × 31.1 cm

《丽莎·明尼里》
*Liza Minnelli*
约 ca. 1978

碎布纸上丝网印刷
Screen print on Curtis rag paper
114.3 × 88.9 cm

《丽莎·明尼里》
*Liza Minnelli*
约 ca. 1978

碎布纸上丝网印刷
Screen print on Curtis rag paper
114.3 × 88.9 cm

WARHOL THE PHOTOGRAPHER

《小幅投影胶片（丽莎·明尼里）》
*Small acetate (Liza Minnelli)*
1978

聚酯膜上感光乳剂
Photo emulsion on polyester film base
31.1 × 25.4 cm

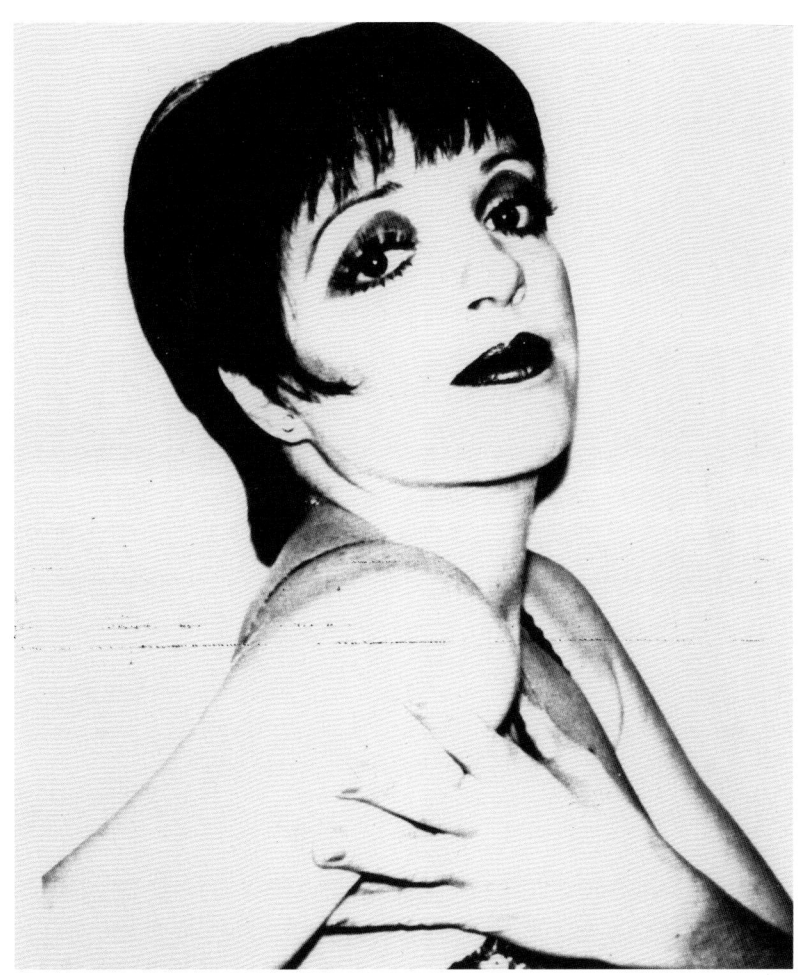

《小幅投影胶片（丽莎·明尼里）》
*Small acetate (Liza Minnelli)*
1978

聚酯膜上感光乳剂
Photo emulsion on polyester film base
30.5 × 25.4 cm

《小幅投影胶片（丽莎·明尼里）》
*Small acetate (Liza Minnelli)*
1978

聚酯膜上感光乳剂
Photo emulsion on polyester film base
30.5 × 25.4 cm

WARHOL THE PHOTOGRAPHER 135

《丽莎·明尼里》
*Liza Minnelli*
1979

布上丙烯和丝印油墨
Acrylic and silkscreen ink on linen
101.6 × 101.6 cm

《丽莎·明尼里》
*Liza Minnelli*
1979

布上丙烯和丝印油墨
Acrylic and silkscreen ink on linen
101.6 × 101.6 cm

1940年代末，沃霍尔在念大学时就开始痴迷现代舞。他上过舞蹈课，并以现代舞动作为灵感创作作品。当时最出色的现代舞舞者与编舞之一玛莎·葛兰姆也是匹兹堡人。据说沃霍尔在大学期间，曾看过葛兰姆在匹兹堡巡演时表演的阿伦·科普兰的《阿巴拉契亚之春》(1944)。1970年代，沃霍尔在为玛莎·葛兰姆创作肖像时，曾向她表达自己的艺术创作深受其作品影响。

Warhol became fascinated with modern dance during his college years in the late 1940s. He took dance classes and created art inspired by modern dance movements. Martha Graham was one of the biggest modern dancers and choreographers at the time and was also from Pittsburgh. Warhol reportedly saw Graham perform a dance to Aaron Copland's *Appalachian Spring* (1944) musical composition during college while she was touring in Pittsburgh. Later, when the artist did her portrait in the 1970s, he told her how deeply moved he was by her work.

《玛莎·葛兰姆》
*Martha Graham*
1980

布上丙烯和丝印油墨
Acrylic and silkscreen ink on linen
101.6 × 101.6 cm

《玛莎·葛兰姆》
*Martha Graham*
1980

布上丙烯和丝印油墨
Acrylic and silkscreen ink on linen
101.6 × 101.6 cm

WARHOL THE PHOTOGRAPHER

《马里莎·贝伦森》
*Marisa Berenson*
1982
宝丽来 Polacolor ER 彩色胶片
Polaroid™ Polacolor ER
10.8 × 8.6 cm

《马里莎·贝伦森》
*Marisa Berenson*
1983—1984
布上丙烯和丝印油墨
Acrylic and silkscreen ink on linen
101.6 × 101.6 cm

《马里莎·贝伦森》
*Marisa Berenson*
1983—1984
布上丙烯和丝印油墨
Acrylic and silkscreen ink on linen
101.6 × 101.6 cm

WARHOL THE PHOTOGRAPHER   141

《米盖尔·波塞》
*Miguel Bosé*
1983

莱诺克斯博物馆纸板上丝网印刷
Screen print on Lenox Museum Board
109.9 × 77.5 cm

《摩纳哥卡罗琳公主》
*Princess Caroline of Monaco*
1983

莱诺克斯博物馆纸板上丝网印刷
Screen print on Lenox Museum Board
102.6 × 102.2 cm

《米盖尔·波塞》
*Miguel Bosé*
1983

宝丽来 Polacolor ER 彩色胶片
Polaroid™ Polacolor ER
10.8 × 8.6 cm

《米盖尔·波塞》
*Miguel Bosé*
1983

布上丙烯和丝印油墨
Acrylic and silkscreen ink on linen
91.4 × 91.4 cm

《米盖尔·波塞》
*Miguel Bosé*
1983

布上丙烯和丝印油墨
Acrylic and silkscreen ink on linen
91.4 × 91.4 cm

WARHOL THE PHOTOGRAPHER 145

《谢丽尔·提格丝》
*Cheryl Tiegs*
1984

宝丽来 Polacolor ER 彩色胶片
Polaroid™ Polacolor ER
10.8 × 8.6 cm

《谢丽尔·提格丝》
*Cheryl Tiegs*
约 ca. 1984

布上丙烯和丝印油墨
Acrylic and silkscreen ink on canvas
101.6 × 101.6 cm

《谢丽尔·提格丝》
*Cheryl Tiegs*
约 ca. 1984

布上丙烯和丝印油墨
Acrylic and silkscreen ink on canvas
101.6 × 101.6 cm

WARHOL THE PHOTOGRAPHER     147

《乌尔里克·特罗亚堡》
*Ulrik Trojaborg*
1986

宝丽来 Polacolor ER 彩色胶片
Polaroid™ Polacolor ER
10.8 × 8.6 cm

《乌尔里克·特罗亚堡》
*Ulrik Trojaborg*
1986

布上丙烯和丝印油墨
Acrylic and silkscreen ink on linen
101.6 × 101.6 cm

《乌尔里克·特罗亚堡》
*Ulrik Trojaborg*
1986

布上丙烯和丝印油墨
Acrylic and silkscreen ink on linen
101.6 × 101.6 cm

将近 40 年间，沃霍尔的纽约夜生活都是在俱乐部和酒吧里度过的，社交活动从不间断。1950 年代，他的据点是一家由同性恋者开设的名为"缘分 3 号"的咖啡馆，他也在此制作、展示和销售自己的作品。1965 年，沃霍尔及其友人的聚会则转移到位于联合广场的餐吧——"麦克斯的堪萨斯城"。而当 1970 年代迪斯科风靡纽约时，沃霍尔常常出没于史蒂夫·鲁贝尔开设的最负盛名的 54 俱乐部。尽管准入政策非常严苛，但一旦进了舞池，无论来自上流社会还是出身下层，所有人全都在此纵情摇摆，沃霍尔对此一言以蔽之："门前上演专政，舞池里纵情民主。"

For nearly 40 years, Warhol's nights in New York were spent in clubs and bars where socializing was a constant. In the 1950s, he was a regular at Serendipity 3, a gay-owned cafe where he created, showed, and sold his work. In 1965, Max's Kansas City, a bar and restaurant in Union Square, became a hangout for Warhol and his entourage. Disco burst onto the New York scene in the 1970s, and its famous epicenter was Studio 54, founded by Steve Rubell and frequented by Warhol. High society mingled with low on its dance floor, even though getting past the doorman was difficult – as Warhol succinctly put it, it was "a dictatorship at the door, a democracy on the floor."

《瑞莉·霍尔》
*Jerry Hall*
约 ca. 1981

明胶银盐相纸
Gelatin silver print
20.3 × 25.4 cm

《瑞莉・霍尔》
*Jerry Hall*
1979

明胶银盐相纸
Gelatin silver print
20.3 × 25.4 cm

《瑞莉・霍尔与生日蛋糕》
*Jerry Hall with Birthday Cake*
1980

明胶银盐相纸
Gelatin silver print
25.4 × 20.3 cm

《瑞莉·霍尔》
*Jerry Hall*
约 ca. 1981

明胶银盐相纸
Gelatin silver print
20.3 × 25.4 cm

西班牙艺术家萨尔瓦多·达利在纽约期间，沃霍尔与其交往甚密。两人初次见面是在 1965 年，达利将沃霍尔叫到他的酒店房间，为沃霍尔戴上一顶印加头饰。沃霍尔在匹兹堡上大学时接触到达利的超现实主义艺术，一直对其十分仰慕。沃霍尔的"超级明星"之一伊莎贝尔·C. 迪弗雷纳（艺名乌尔特拉·维奥莱特）曾是达利的门徒与缪斯，她利用与两位艺术名家的关系推广自己。达利出演了沃霍尔 1966 年的《试镜》，两人在 1970 年代也有过数次往来。

Warhol crossed paths with Spanish artist Salvador Dalí frequently while in New York City. The two first met in 1965 when Dalí summoned Warhol to his hotel room and proceeded to put an Incan headdress on the artist. Warhol was a long admirer of Dalí's Surrealist art, seeing it first during his college years in Pittsburgh. Ultra Violet, one of Warhol's Superstars, was a former mentee and muse of Dalí, and she used her connection to the two popular artists for her own self-promotion. Dalí sat for a Warhol Screen Test in 1966 and the two shared several other recorded interactions throughout the 1970s.

《萨尔瓦多·达利与乌尔特拉·维奥莱特,纽约》
*Salvador Dali and Ultra Violet, New York*
1970 年代 1970s

明胶银盐相纸
Gelatin silver print
41 × 50.2 cm

《丽莎·明尼里》
*Liza Minnelli*
1978

明胶银盐相纸
Gelatin silver print
20.3 × 25.1 cm

《安迪·沃霍尔、玛莎·葛兰姆和生日蛋糕》
*Andy Warhol, Martha Graham, and a birthday cake*
1981

明胶银盐相纸
Gelatin silver print
20.3 × 25.4 cm

《无题（周天娜与香奈儿包装盒）》
*Untitled (Tina Chow with CHANEL box)*
约 ca. 1985

明胶银盐相纸
Gelatin silver print
20.3 × 25.4 cm

《约翰·贝尼特斯、黛比·哈里和卡尔文·克莱因》
*Jellybean Benitez, Debbie Harry, and Calvin Klein*
约 ca. 1983

明胶银盐相纸
Gelatin silver print
20.3 × 25.4 cm

WARHOL THE PHOTOGRAPHER    157

葛蕾斯·琼斯是一位出众的音乐家、模特、演员和表演者。1948 年（或琼斯自称的 1951 年）出生于牙买加，她从 1970 年代早期开始模特事业，并发布了自己的首张专辑。到了 1980 年代，琼斯已成为炙手可热的歌手与好莱坞女演员。她是一位大胆无畏的跨界艺人，毫不掩饰自己中性化和戏剧性的特征，并且也享受人们对此的关注。沃霍尔和琼斯于 1970 年代中期因拥有许多共同朋友和兴趣而相识。

Grace Jones is a groundbreaking musician, model, actress, and performer. Born in Jamaica in 1948 (or 1951, according to Jones), she began modeling in the early 1970s and released her first album that same decade. By the 1980s, Jones became an in-demand vocalist and Hollywood actress. Jones was a fearless, multidisciplinary entertainer who relished attention – unapologetically androgynous and theatrical. Warhol and Jones met in the mid-1970s, drawn together by mutual friends and many shared interests.

《葛蕾丝·琼斯》
*Grace Jones*
约 ca. 1985

明胶银盐相纸
Gelatin silver print
20.3 × 25.4 cm

《比安卡·贾格尔、丽莎·明尼里和杰奎琳·奥纳西斯在丽莎·明尼里的更衣室,纽约》
*Bianca Jagger, Liza Minnelli, and Jackie Onassis in Liza's Dressing Room, New York*
1970 年代 1970s

明胶银盐相纸
Gelatin silver print
41 × 50.5 cm

《丽莎·明尼里和约翰·列侬在沃霍尔的"工厂",纽约》
*Liza Minnelli and John Lennon at Warhol's Factory, New York*
1970 年代 1970s

明胶银盐相纸
Gelatin silver print
40.6 × 50.5 cm

鲍勃·科拉切洛从 1969 年开始为《村声》杂志撰写影评，由此开启了他的写作生涯。1970 年，沃霍尔和合作伙伴保罗·莫里西在读到他对两人的电影《垃圾》(1970) 的评论后认识了这位作家。沃霍尔邀请科拉切洛为他新创的《访问》杂志撰稿，并随后聘任他为杂志编辑。这家杂志社运营至今，目前专注流行文化的报道。科拉切洛从 1970 年代直到 1980 年代初一直担任该杂志编辑，他也成为沃霍尔事业上关系紧密的合作伙伴。科拉切洛著有《神圣恐惧》(1990) 一书，在此书中回顾了其与沃霍尔的工作经历。

Bob Colacello began his writing career in 1969 penning film reviews for the *The Village Voice*. In 1970, Warhol and colleague Paul Morrissey were drawn to him through his review of their film *Trash* (1970). Warhol asked Colacello to write for his startup magazine, titled Interview. Colacello was soon promoted to editor of the magazine, now dedicated to popular culture. He stayed on throughout the 1970s and early 1980s, becoming a confidante closely involved with the business side of Warhol's commissions. Colacello is also the author of the memoir *Holy Terror* (1990), which describes his time working for Warhol.

《莫妮克·范·盖德林、鲍勃·科拉切洛和托马斯·安曼》
*Monique van Vooren, Bob Colacello, and Thomas Ammann*
年份未知 n.d.

明胶银盐相纸
Gelatin silver print
20.3 × 25.4 cm

WARHOL THE PHOTOGRAPHER 163

《朱迪·福斯特与鲍勃·科拉切洛》
*Jodie Foster and Bob Colacello*
年份未知 n.d.

明胶银盐相纸
Gelatin silver print
20.3 × 25.4 cm

《周天娜、弗兰·勒博维茨和一位男士》
*Tina Chow, Fran Lebowitz, and Unidentified Men*
1980

明胶银盐相纸
Gelatin silver print
20.3 × 25.4 cm

《杰奎琳·肯尼迪·奥纳西斯与
查尔斯·亚当斯》
*Jackie Kennedy Onassis
and Charles Addams*
约 ca. 1980

明胶银盐相纸
Gelatin silver print
25.4 × 20.3 cm

《亨利·基辛格与伊丽莎白·
泰勒·华纳,华盛顿特区》
*Henry Kissinger and Elizabeth
Taylor Warner, Washington, DC*
1970 年代 1970s

明胶银盐相纸
Gelatin silver print
41 × 50.5 cm

WARHOL THE PHOTOGRAPHER 165

罗伯特·梅普尔索普是美国酷儿摄影师。他比沃霍尔小18岁,是将沃霍尔视为波普艺术前辈的年轻一代美国艺术家。尽管两位艺术家交往频繁,且为对方创作了肖像,沃霍尔却从未将梅普尔索普与自己相提并论。此外,他们的摄影风格有许多共同之处,并都探索男同性恋题材,尤其是身体与面部轮廓的性别特征。

Robert Mapplethorpe was a queer American photographer, eighteen years younger than Warhol and part of a generation of New York artists who looked up to him as a pioneer of Pop Art. Although both artists crossed paths many times and did portraits of one another, Warhol never saw Mapplethorpe as an equal. Despite this, they shared similar styles in photography and experimented with gay erotica, focusing on the contours of the body and face in a sexualized way.

《罗伯特・梅普尔索普》
*Robert Mapplethorpe*
约 ca. 1978

明胶银盐相纸
Gelatin silver print
25.4 × 20.3 cm

WARHOL THE PHOTOGRAPHER 167

《史蒂夫·鲁贝尔》  
*Steve Rubell*  
1985  

明胶银盐相纸  
Gelatin silver print  
25.4 × 20.3 cm

《西尔维斯特·史泰龙》  
*Sylvester Stallone*  
约 ca. 1977  

明胶银盐相纸  
Gelatin silver print  
25.4 × 20.3 cm

《维克多·雨果》
*Victor Hugo*
年份未知 n.d.

明胶银盐相纸
Gelatin silver print
25.4 × 20.3 cm

《送货员》
*Unidentified Delivery Man*
1980

明胶银盐相纸
Gelatin silver print
25.4 × 20.3 cm

WARHOL THE PHOTOGRAPHER 169

比安卡·佩雷兹-莫拉·玛西亚出生于尼加拉瓜，在得到一笔奖学金后移居法国，她与米克·贾格尔相遇于他的音乐会。1970年代她身兼模特和演员两职，既是一位时尚偶像，也是一位母亲。她长期致力于人道主义事业，直至今日仍然如此。沃霍尔和比安卡·贾格尔相识于1971年她与米克·贾格尔结婚后不久。他很欣赏她的风格与智慧。即使在她与米克离婚后，沃霍尔与比安卡也一直是挚友。

Bianca Pérez-Mora Macias was born in Nicaragua and moved to France after receiving a scholarship, where she would meet Mick Jagger after one of his concerts. Working as a model and actress in the 1970s, she became a fashion icon as well as a mother. She has had a long-term interest in humanitarian causes and continues in these efforts today. Warhol met Bianca Jagger in 1971, shortly after her marriage to Mick Jagger, and became fond of her style and intelligence. Warhol and Bianca remained great friends even after her divorce from Mick.

《比安卡·贾格尔与克丽丝·罗耶》
*Bianca Jagger and Chris Royer*
1981

明胶银盐相纸
Gelatin silver print
25.4 × 20.3 cm

 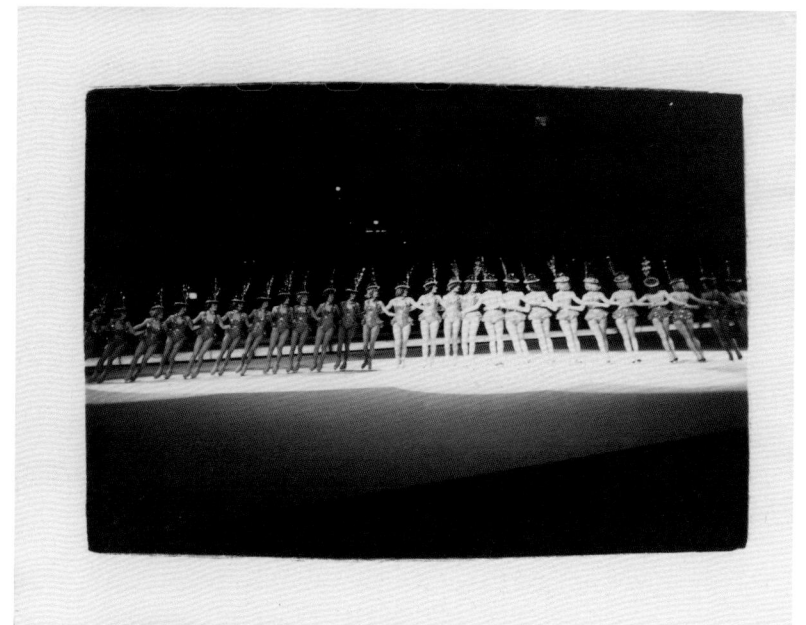

《约翰·特拉沃尔塔与一位女士》
*John Travolta and Unidentified Woman*
1980

明胶银盐相纸
Gelatin silver print
20.3 × 25.4 cm

《多萝西·哈蜜尔与白雪溜冰团》
*Dorothy Hamill and Ice Capades*
年份未知 n.d.

明胶银盐相纸
Gelatin silver print
20.3 × 25.4 cm

《卢·里德》
*Lou Reed*
1976—1986

明胶银盐相纸
Gelatin silver print
25.4 × 20.3 cm

《克里斯·斯泰因与黛比·哈里》
*Chris Stein and Debbie Harry*
1982

明胶银盐相纸
Gelatin silver print
25.4 × 20.3 cm

1964 年，在年轻的社交名媛、"工厂"超级明星、"宝贝"简·霍尔泽举办的晚宴上，沃霍尔认识了滚石乐队的米克·贾格尔。这次相遇标志着一段持续 20 多年友谊的开始，两人的友谊以各种方式得到了印证。1969 年，沃霍尔曾用贾格尔作为《访问》杂志第二期的封面。之后，贾格尔将滚石乐队的三张专辑封面设计交到了沃霍尔手上。虽然 1969 年的第一次设计最终并未采用，另外两张专辑封面设计则被公认为沃霍尔唱片封面设计的顶尖杰作。他为滚石乐队专辑《小偷小摸》（1971）设计的专辑封面荣获格莱美奖提名，使其很早便成为永恒的经典。为滚石乐队设计的第三张专辑《爱你一世》（1977）的封面则展示了乐队成员互相撕咬的情景，这是对专辑名同类相食双关语的戏仿，同时散发着令人吃惊的新朋克感。随着友谊的发展，当滚石乐队在 1972 年和 1975 年进行北美巡演时，沃霍尔被允许进入演唱会后台。1975 年，滚石乐队还租用了沃霍尔在蒙托克长岛的住宅作为排练场所。贾格尔一家（米克、比安卡和他们的女儿洁德）也都曾在那里度假。

In 1964, Warhol met Mick Jagger of the Rolling Stones at a dinner party thrown by Baby Jane Holzer, young socialite and Factory Superstar. The occasion marked the start of a friendship that was to last for more than twenty years, and that manifested itself in numerous ways. In 1969, Warhol placed Jagger on the cover of the second issue of *Interview* magazine. Eventually, Jagger entrusted Warhol with the cover design for three Rolling Stones albums. Although the first commission (1969) was not realized, the others are regarded as two of Warhol's masterpieces in the field. His concept for *Sticky Fingers* (1971) was nominated for a Grammy award, giving it early stature as an enduring classic. His third design, for *Love You Live* (1977), shows the band members biting each other in a parody of the cannibalistic double entendre of the title while also evoking a shocking new punk sensibility. As their friendship developed, Warhol was granted backstage access to their North American tours in 1972 and 1975, and in the latter year, they rented Warhol's Long Island home in Montauk as a rehearsal space. The Jaggers (Mick, Bianca, and their daughter Jade) also vacationed there.

《米克·贾格尔》
*Mick Jagger*
1982

明胶银盐相纸
Gelatin silver print
20.3 × 25.4 cm

WARHOL THE PHOTOGRAPHER 175

《马里莎·贝伦森》
*Marisa Berenson*
1981

明胶银盐相纸
Gelatin silver print
25.4 × 20.3 cm

《马里莎·贝伦森》
*Marisa Berenson*
约 ca. 1980

明胶银盐相纸
Gelatin silver print
25.4 × 20.3 cm

《多莉·帕顿与奥莉维亚·纽顿－约翰》
*Dolly Parton and Olivia Newton-John*
年份未知 n.d.

明胶银盐相纸
Gelatin silver print
20.3 × 25.4 cm

《伊恩·麦克莱恩与一位男士》
*Ian McKellen and Unidentified* Man
1980 年代 1980s

明胶银盐相纸
Gelatin silver print
25.4 × 20.3 cm

WARHOL THE PHOTOGRAPHER

《雪儿》
*Cher*
1984—1985

明胶银盐相纸
Gelatin silver print
20.3 × 25.4 cm

音乐剧《修女》派对现场
*Nunsense party*
1986

明胶银盐相纸
Gelatin silver print
25.4 × 20.3 cm

《大卫·斯帕达、葛蕾丝·琼斯和凯斯·哈林》
*David Spada, Grace Jones, and Keith Haring*
1984

明胶银盐相纸
Gelatin silver print
25.4 × 20.3 cm

WARHOL THE PHOTOGRAPHER 179

沃霍尔并不热衷户外活动，但他去过很多风景优美的地方拍摄自然景观。他在长岛蒙托克的海滨别墅度假时，常用相机记录海滨的纹理与质感。一张从飞机舷窗拍摄的照片展示了河流支流的蜿蜒曲线。拍摄自然风光并不属于波普艺术的范畴，但沃霍尔一直在尝试新的主题与材料。他在 1960 年代曾尝试用日落的照片创作风景电影，可见海滨和自然也是他所熟悉的主题。

Although he was not outdoorsy, Warhol traveled to many picturesque locations and photographed natural beauty. During vacations at his beach house in Montauk on Long Island, Warhol liked to photograph the textures of the shoreline. One photograph, taken from an airplane window, depicts the meandering curves of a tributary. Shooting natural landscapes was not within the realm of Pop Art, but Warhol was constantly trying new subjects and materials. He had experimented with landscape film in the 1960s with shots of sunsets, so the subject matter of shorelines and nature was familiar to the artist.

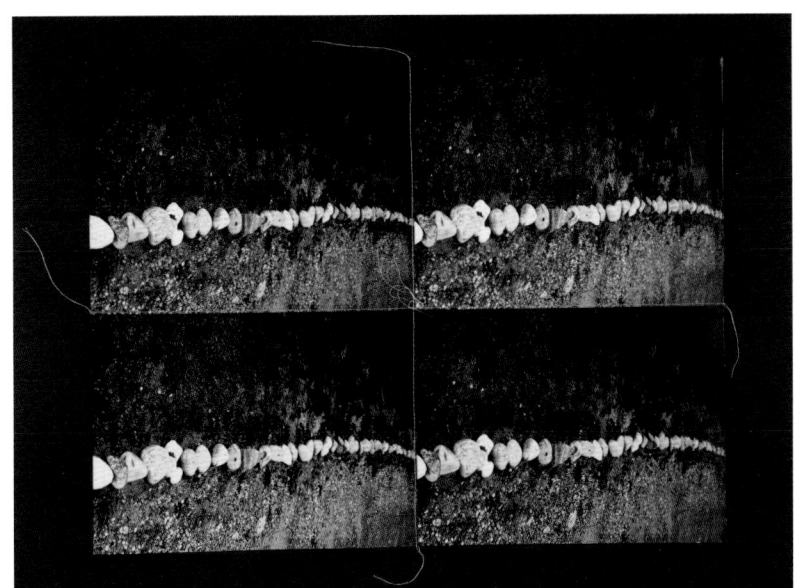
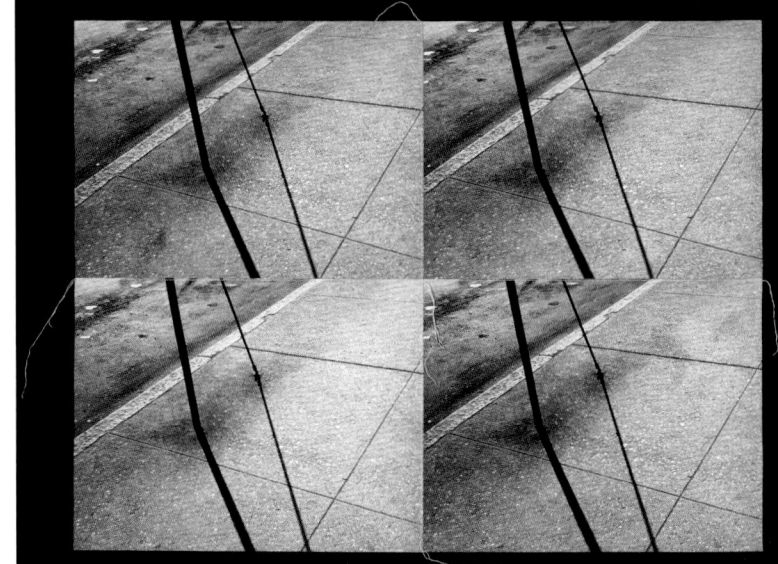

《支流（鸟瞰），1976—1986》
*Tributary (Aerial View), 1976-1986*
1986

线缝明胶银盐相纸
Gelatin silver prints sewn with thread
54.3 × 69.9 cm

《岩石海岸线，1976—1986 年》
*Rocky Shoreline, 1976-1986*
1986

线缝明胶银盐相纸
Gelatin silver prints sewn with thread
54.6 × 69.9 cm

《缝制照片（蒙托克，火岛夏天）》
*Sewn Photograph (Montauk, Fire Island Summer)*
1976—1986

线缝明胶银盐相纸
Gelatin silver prints sewn with thread
69.9 × 54.3 cm

《人行道，1976—1986》
*Sidewalk, 1976-1986*
1986

线缝明胶银盐相纸
Gelatin silver prints sewn with thread
54 × 69.9 cm

《霍尔斯顿的书架,约 1978》
*Halston's Bookshelves, ca. 1978*
1986

线缝明胶银盐相纸
Gelatin silver prints sewn with thread
54.6 × 69.5 cm

《石滩,1976 — 1986》
*Beach with Stones, 1976-1986*
1986

线缝明胶银盐相纸
Gelatin silver prints sewn with thread
54.6 × 69.5 cm

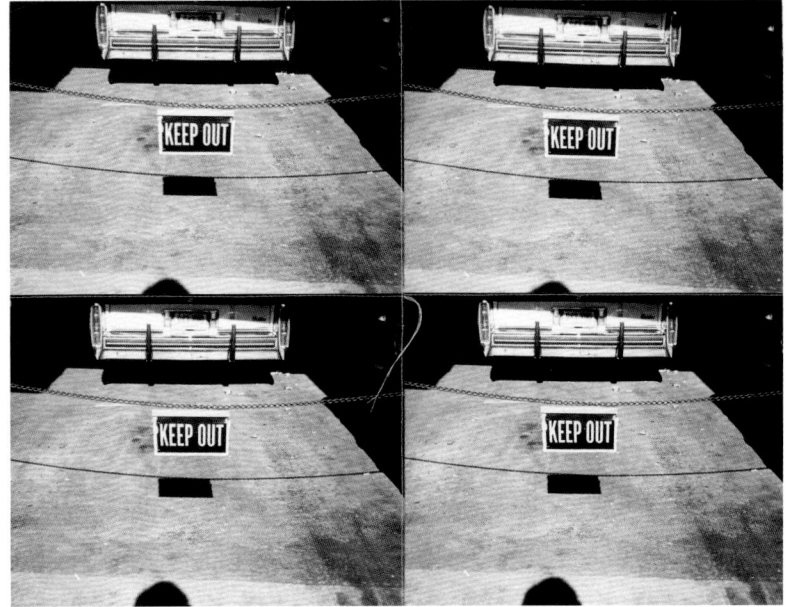

《向后倾斜的大楼，1976—1986》
*Receding Building, 1976-1986*
1986

线缝明胶银盐相纸
Gelatin silver prints sewn with thread
69.9 × 54.3 cm

《标志（"禁止入内"），
1976—1986》
*Sign ("Keep Out"), 1976-1986*
1986

线缝明胶银盐相纸
Gelatin silver prints sewn with thread
54.6 × 69.1 cm

WARHOL THE PHOTOGRAPHER 183

《米克·贾格尔，约 1978》
*Mick Jagger, ca. 1978*
1986

线缝明胶银盐相纸
Gelatin silver prints sewn with thread
54.3 × 70.2 cm

《多莉·帕顿和凯斯·哈林,1985》
*Dolly Parton and Keith Haring, 1985*
1986

线缝明胶银盐相纸
Gelatin silver prints sewn with thread
70.5 × 80.3 cm

WARHOL THE PHOTOGRAPHER

1982 年 10 月，沃霍尔应年轻的企业家萧永丰邀请前往香港旅行，沃霍尔受其委托为一家私人俱乐部创作查尔斯王子与黛安娜王妃的肖像。沃霍尔抵达后，萧永丰为他准备了一次为期三天的惊喜之旅，前往当时外国游客罕至的北京。沃霍尔在萧永丰和摄影师克里斯托弗·马科斯的陪伴下，游览了长城和天安门广场。马科斯和沃霍尔拍摄了大量游客照记录他们的旅行，包括一张以毛泽东像为背景的照片，而这幅肖像正是沃霍尔十年前创作的"毛"系列的原型。

In October 1982, Warhol traveled to Hong Kong at the invitation of Alfred Siu, a young entrepreneur who commissioned Warhol to do portraits of Prince Charles and Lady Diana for an exclusive nightclub. Upon Warhol's arrival, Siu surprised him with a three-day trip to Beijing, which did not receive many foreign visitors at the time. Warhol visited the Great Wall and Tiananmen Square, accompanied by Siu and photographer Christopher Makos. Makos and Warhol took extensive "tourist" photographs to document their trip, including a shot with Mao Zedong in the background – the image replicated ten years earlier in Warhol's Mao series.

《安迪・沃霍尔与克里斯・马科斯》
*Andy Warhol and Chris Makos*
1982

手工上色照片
Handcolored photograph
17.1 × 15.9 cm

WARHOL THE PHOTOGRAPHER

《缝制照片（中国），1982》
*Sewn Photograph (China), 1982*
1986

线缝明胶银盐相纸
Gelatin silver prints sewn with thread
69.9 × 54.6 cm

《中国，1982》
*China, 1982*
1986

线缝明胶银盐相纸
Gelatin silver prints sewn with thread
54.6 × 69.9 cm

《中国（电影海报），1982》
*China (Movie Poster), 1982*
1986

线缝明胶银盐相纸
Gelatin silver prints sewn with thread
55.2 × 69.9 cm

WARHOL THE PHOTOGRAPHER   189

《天窗与建筑》
*Skylight and Building*
1980

明胶银盐相纸
Gelatin silver print
20.3 × 25.4 cm

《台阶》
*Steps*
1982

明胶银盐相纸
Gelatin silver print
20.3 × 25.4 cm

《海报》
*Posters*
1980

明胶银盐相纸
Gelatin silver print
20.3 × 25.4 cm

《苏维埃战争纪念碑》
*Soviet War Memorial*
约 ca. 1982

明胶银盐相纸
Gelatin silver print
25.4 × 20.3 cm

WARHOL THE PHOTOGRAPHER

《结构》
*Structure*
年份未知 n.d.

明胶银盐相纸
Gelatin silver print
20 × 25.4 cm

《结构》
*Structure*
年份未知 n.d.

明胶银盐相纸
Gelatin silver print
20 × 25.4 cm

《建筑》
*Buildings*
年份未知 n.d.

明胶银盐相纸
Gelatin silver print
20 × 25.4 cm

《建筑（阳台）》
*Building (Balconies)*
年份未知 n.d.

明胶银盐相纸
Gelatin silver print
20 × 25.4 cm

《盥洗室》
*Bathroom*
年份未知 n.d.

明胶银盐相纸
Gelatin silver print
20.3 × 25.4 cm

《佛罗里达州棕榈沙滩上的脚》
*Feet in the sand in Palm Beach, Florida*
约 ca. 1982

明胶银盐相纸
Gelatin silver print
20.3 × 25.4 cm

《沙滩上的脚印》
*Footprints on a beach*
约 ca. 1982

明胶银盐相纸
Gelatin silver print
20.3 × 25.4 cm

《佛罗里达州棕榈滩上方的飞机》
*Airplane over Palm Beach, Florida*
约 ca. 1982

明胶银盐相纸
Gelatin silver print
20.3 × 25.4 cm

《成排的明胶银盐相纸相片》
*Rows of Gelatin Silver Prints*
约 ca. 1980—1984

明胶银盐相纸
Gelatin silver print
20.3 × 25.4 cm

《纪念碑上的树》
*Trees at an undetermined* monument
约 ca. 1980—1984

明胶银盐相纸
Gelatin silver print
25.4 × 20.3 cm

《树》
*Tree*
约 ca. 1980—1984

明胶银盐相纸
Gelatin silver print
20.3 × 25.4 cm

 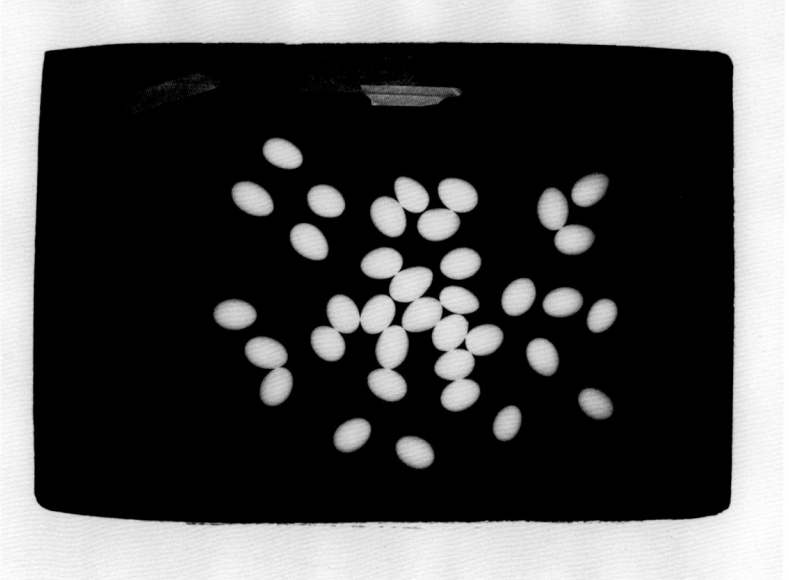

《跳蚤市场（鸡蛋盒中的高尔夫球）》
*Flea market (golf balls in egg cartons)*
年份未知 n.d.

明胶银盐相纸
Gelatin silver print
20.3 × 25.2 cm

《蛋》
*Eggs*
1982

明胶银盐相纸
Gelatin silver print
20.3 × 25.4 cm

《成排的相片》
*Rows of Prints*
约 ca. 1980–1984

明胶银盐相纸
Gelatin silver print
25.4 × 20.3 cm

《框》
*Frames*
1982

明胶银盐相纸
Gelatin silver print
25.4 × 20.3 cm

WARHOL THE PHOTOGRAPHER

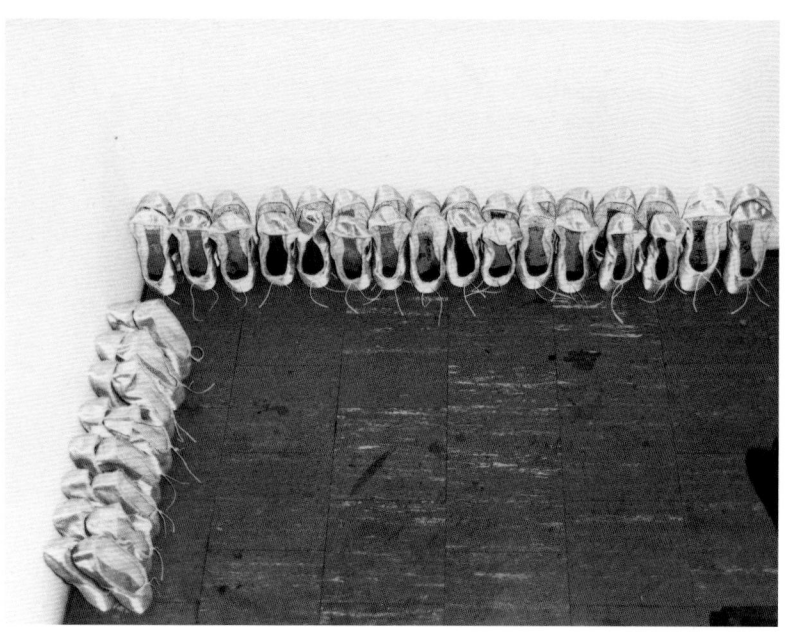 

《芭蕾舞鞋》  
*Ballet Slippers*  
年份未知 n.d.

明胶银盐相纸  
Gelatin silver print  
20.3 × 25.4 cm

《静物（可口可乐产品）》  
*Still-life (Coca-Cola merchandise)*  
1980 年代 1980s

明胶银盐相纸  
Gelatin silver print  
20.3 × 25.4 cm

《鞋》
*Shoes*
约 ca. 1980

明胶银盐相纸
Gelatin silver print
25.4 × 20.3 cm

《成排的物体》
*Serial Objects*
1980 年代 1980s

明胶银盐相纸
Gelatin silver print
25.4 × 20.3 cm

《头骨》
*Skulls*
1986

明胶银盐相纸
Gelatin silver print
20 × 25.2 cm

《鸟瞰》
*Aerial view*
1984

明胶银盐相纸
Gelatin silver print
20.3 × 25.4 cm

《中国（可口可乐瓶）》
*China (Coca-Cola Bottles)*
1982

明胶银盐相纸
Gelatin silver print
20.2 × 25.4 cm

《雕塑模型》
*Sculpture Models*
1984

明胶银盐相纸
Gelatin silver print
25.4 × 20.3 cm

《毛线》
*Italian yarn*
1982—1983

宝丽来 Polacolor ER 彩色胶片
Polaroid™ Polacolor ER
10.8 × 8.6 cm

《灯泡》
*Light bulbs*
1980

宝丽来 Polacolor ER 彩色胶片
Polaroid™ Polacolor ER
10.8 × 8.6 cm

《葡萄》
*Grapes*
1981

宝丽来 Polacolor 2 彩色胶片
Polaroid™ Polacolor 2
10.8 × 8.6 cm

《葡萄》
*Grapes*
1981

宝丽来 Polacolor 2 彩色胶片
Polaroid™ Polacolor 2
10.8 × 8.6 cm

WARHOL THE PHOTOGRAPHER     205

 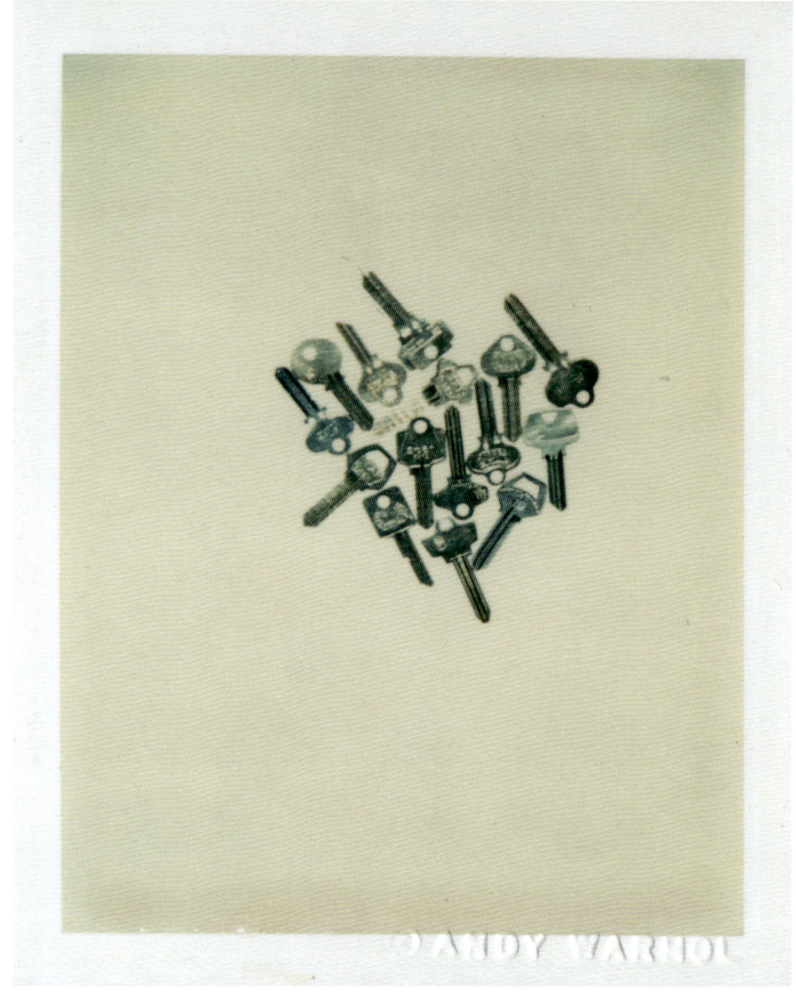

《鞋》
*Shoes*
1980

宝丽来 Polacolor 2 彩色胶片
Polaroid™ Polacolor 2
38.1 × 35.6 cm

《钥匙》
*Keys*
1980

宝丽来 Polacolor 2 彩色胶片
Polaroid™ Polacolor 2
10.8 × 8.6 cm

《鞋（女式）》
*Shoes (Women's group)*
1980

宝丽来 Polacolor 2 彩色胶片
Polaroid™ Polacolor 2
38.1 × 35.6 cm

《布里洛盒子》
*Brillo boxes*
1979

宝丽来 Polacolor 2 彩色胶片
Polaroid™ Polacolor 2
38.1 × 35.6 cm

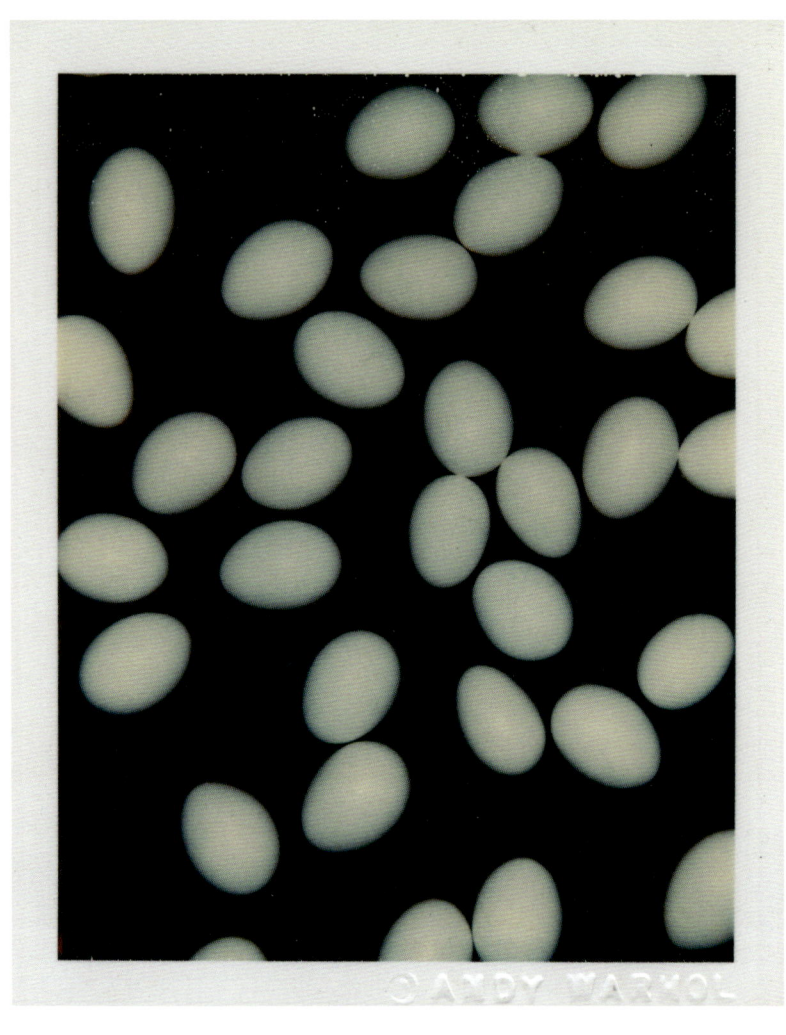

《复活节彩蛋》
*Easter Eggs*
1982

宝丽来 Polacolor 2 彩色胶片
Polaroid™ Polacolor 2
10.8 × 8.6 cm

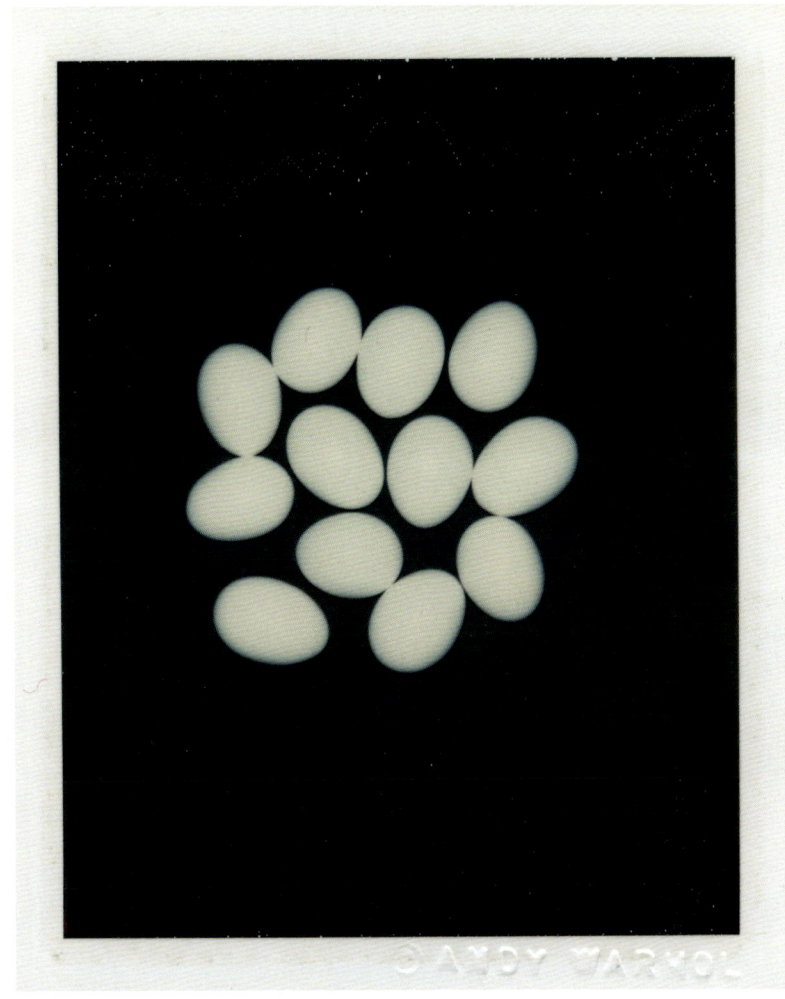
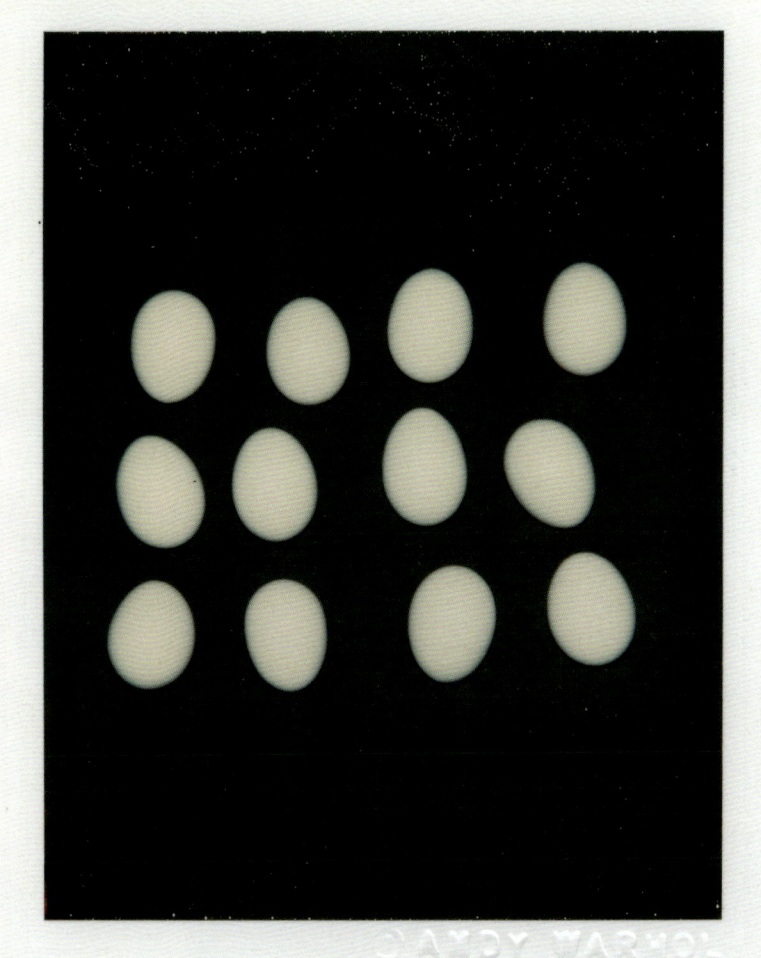

《复活节彩蛋》
*Easter Eggs*
1982

宝丽来 Polacolor 2 彩色胶片
Polaroid™ Polacolor 2
10.8 × 8.6 cm

《复活节彩蛋》
*Easter Eggs*
1982

宝丽来 Polacolor 2 彩色胶片
Polaroid™ Polacolor 2
10.8 × 8.6 cm

WARHOL THE PHOTOGRAPHER

# 电影作为客体
CINEMA AS OBJECT

> "当时非常有趣，我们都很高兴参与其中……安迪有这种本领：他让你出现在电影里，然后把你变成超级明星。这迎合了人们的虚荣心，大家都想出演电影，然后变成超级明星。"
> ——杰拉德·马兰加，沃霍尔的助手

沃霍尔自童年时就痴迷电影，一直以秀兰·邓波儿、伊丽莎白·泰勒、朱迪·加兰等好莱坞明星为偶像。1960年代初，沃霍尔的波普事业刚起步不久，就开始着手拍摄电影。他著名的名为"银色工厂"的工作室——或简称"工厂"——成了他的影棚，他把所有走进"工厂"的人都打造成了明星。"超级明星"是沃霍尔影片中的常驻角色，表演者在摄影机前本色出演各种怪异角色。整个二十世纪六七十年代，作为艺术家与导演的沃霍尔拍摄了一系列前卫影像，其中既有叙事松散的电影，也有长达五小时的静帧镜头，甚至还有一些被联邦调查局认定为色情的作品。这些作品在沃霍尔生前很少展出，直到近年数字修复工作重新赋予这些胶片电影以活力，也让我们得以进一步了解作为波普艺术的影像。1980年代，沃霍尔的创作转向更为传统的波普影像，拍摄了肥皂剧、电视节目以及音乐短片。

> "It was all fun and games and we were all willing to participate [...] Andy had this knack: he'd put you in this movie, and he'd make you a Superstar. It was hitting on people's vanities. People wanted to be in the movies and be a superstar."

— Gerard Malanga, Warhol's assistant

Film had enchanted Warhol since he was a child, and he grew up idolizing Hollywood stars like Shirley Temple, Elizabeth Taylor, and Judy Garland. When Warhol's Pop career took off in the early 1960s, it did not take long until Warhol started filming. His famed studio called the Silver Factory, or simply the Factory, became his film set, and he made a star of all the characters who walked through his doors. The Superstars were Warhol's in-house acting crew, performing their roles by acting like their eccentric selves on camera. Throughout the 1960s and 1970s, the artist/filmmaker made a range of avant-garde cinema, from loose narrative films to five-hour still shots and even what the Federal Bureau of Investigation considered pornography. Many of these were only briefly shown during Warhol's lifetime until recent efforts to restore them, creating vivid digital files and enhancing our understanding of film as Pop. In the 1980s, he turned to more traditional Pop filming, creating video soap operas, a cable television series, and music videos.

《安迪·沃霍尔用宝莱克斯电影摄像机拍摄》
弗雷德·麦克达拉
*Andy Warhol filming with Bolex movie camera*
Fred McDarrah
1964

明胶银盐相纸
Gelatin silver print
30 × 40 cm

奥瑞康 CM-72A 摄像机
*Auricon CM-72A*
约 ca. 1964

混合档案材料
胶片盒:33 × 63.5 cm
Mixed archival material
Film cannister: 33 × 63.5 cm

三脚架
*Tripod*
约 ca. 1964

木材、金属、塑料
高度:116.8 cm
Wood, metal, and plastic
Folded: 116.8 cm

《安迪·沃霍尔正在拍摄电影
＜泰勒·米德之臀＞》
弗雷德·麦克达拉
*Andy Warhol Filming Taylor Mead's Ass*
Fred McDarrah
1964

明胶银盐相纸
Gelatin silver print
40 × 30 cm

CINEMA AS OBJECT

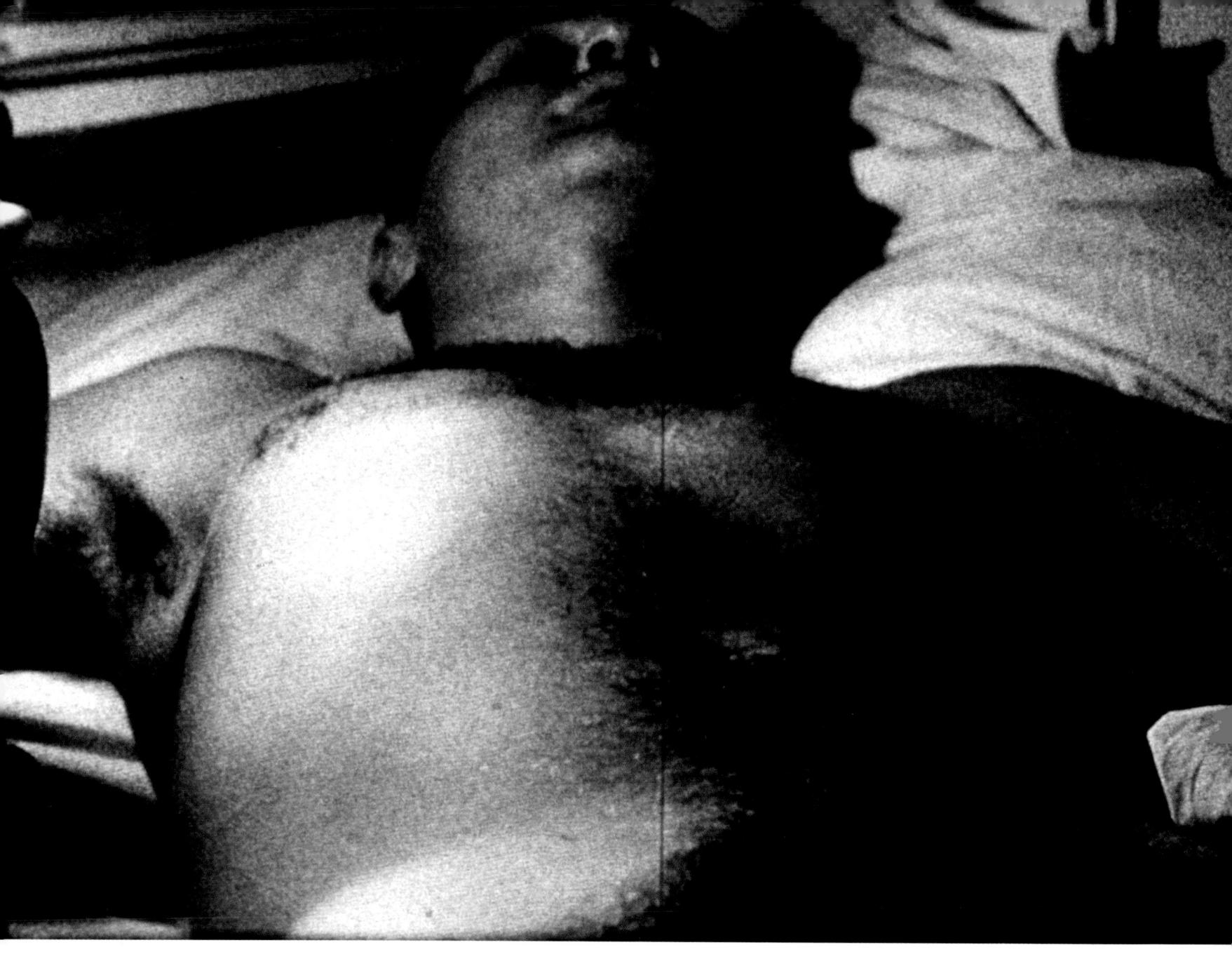

1963 年，沃霍尔开始和约翰·焦尔诺约会，这位兼做股票交易员的诗人很快就成为波普艺术家眼中的灵感缪斯。有吸食安非他命习惯的沃霍尔常常失眠，而焦尔诺则因为酗酒而能迅速入眠。沃霍尔因此用宝来克斯相机记录了焦尔诺睡眠的画面，略带倾斜的拍摄角度凸显了伴侣的身体轮廓。沃霍尔用这些胶卷制作了长达五小时的电影《沉睡》，这也是他首部真正意义上的电影。

Warhol began dating poet-turned-stockbroker John Giorno in 1963, and he quickly became a subject of the Pop artist's work. Giorno was a heavy drinker, and Warhol was a user of amphetamines, so there were many nights when Warhol was awake while Giorno was fast asleep. Warhol began filming Giorno sleeping on his Bolex camera, angling the shot to emphasize the contours of his lover's body. The reels were edited to make the five-hour film *Sleep*, Warhol's first real movie.

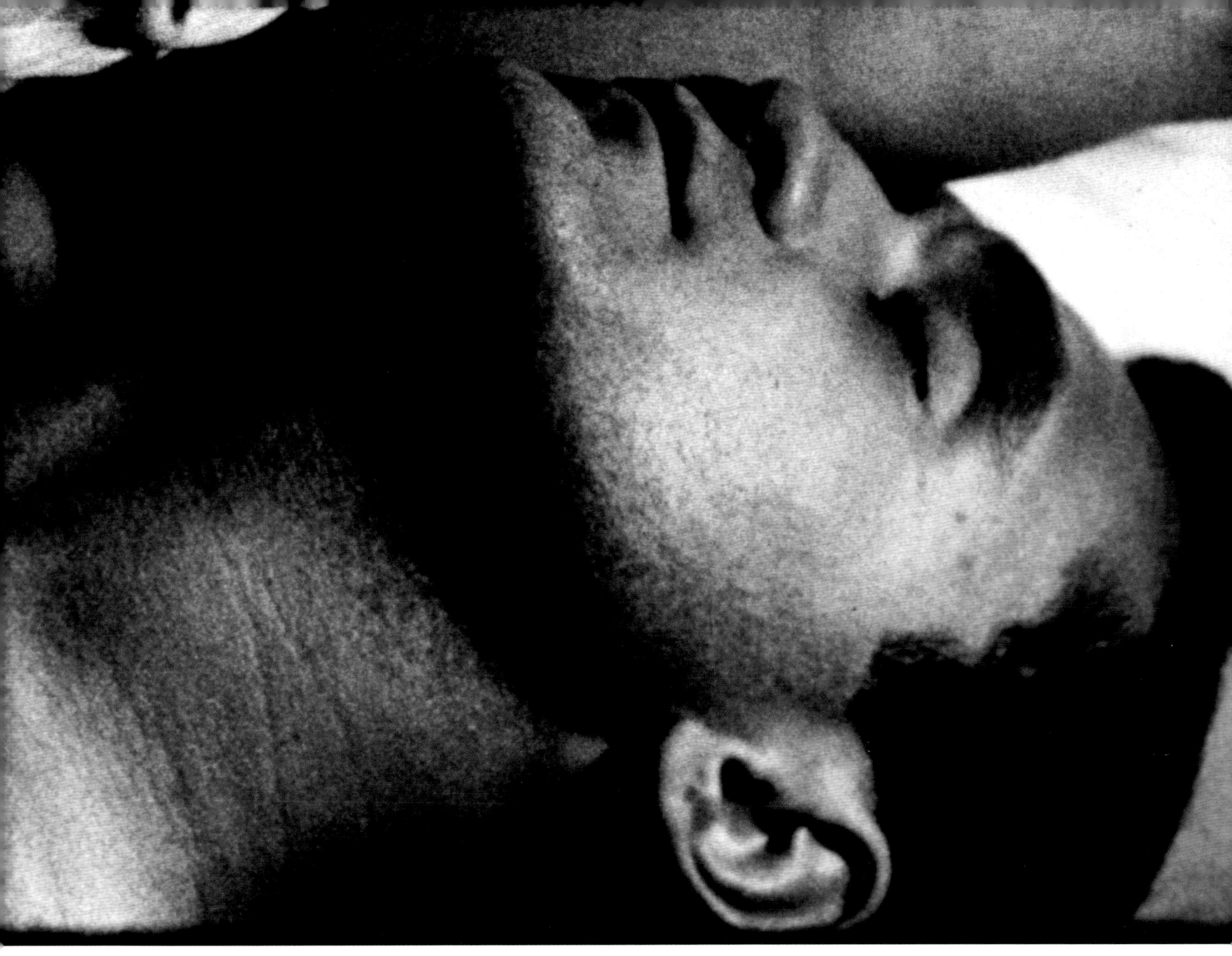

《沉睡》
*Sleep*
1964

16 毫米黑白无声电影，16fps
5 小时 21 分
16 mm film, black and white, silent, 16fps
321'

《泰勒·米德》
*Taylor Mead*
1963—1964

快照亭照片
Photobooth photograph
20 × 4.1 cm

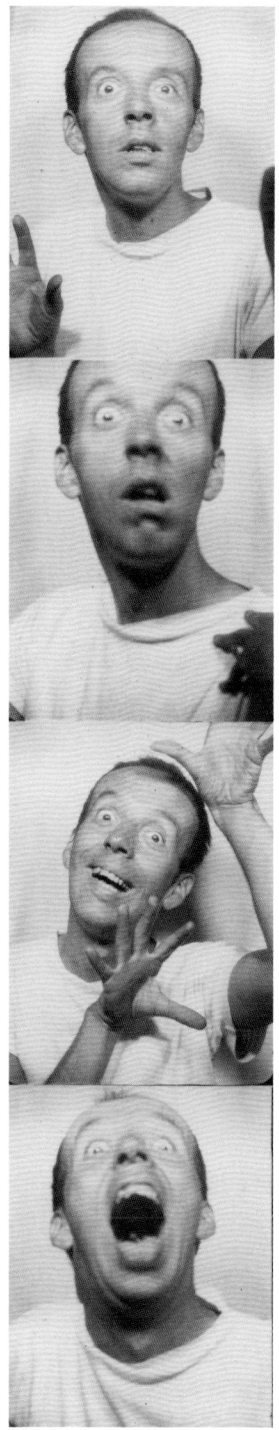

1963 年夏，泰勒·米德遇到沃霍尔时，已经因出演罗恩·赖斯的《花贼》（1960）成为著名的地下电影演员。10 月，米德与沃霍尔一起驾车横跨美国前往洛杉矶，拍摄了无政府主义电影《泰山和珍妮某种意义上的回归》（1964）。应《村声》杂志发起的挑战，沃霍尔拍摄了 90 分钟的电影《泰勒·米德之臀》（1964），随后在 1968 年他所拍摄的《圣地亚哥冲浪者》中，捕捉下米德最为精彩的表演。米德同时也是一位诗人、画家与作家，2013 年去世前一直生活在纽约。

When Taylor Mead met Warhol in the summer of 1963, he was already a well-known underground actor, starring in Ron Rice's Beat film *The Flower Thief* (1960). In October, Mead drove across the country with Warhol to Los Angeles, where they shot the anarchic *Tarzan & Jane Regained... Sort Of* (1964). In response to a challenge in *The Village Voice*, Warhol made the 90-minute film *Taylor Mead's Ass* (1964), and in 1968, he captured one of Mead's best performances in his feature *San Diego Surf*. Mead was also a poet, painter, and writer in New York City until his death in 2013.

《约翰·焦尔诺》
*John Giorno*
约 ca. 1963

快照亭照片
Photobooth photograph
20 × 4.1 cm

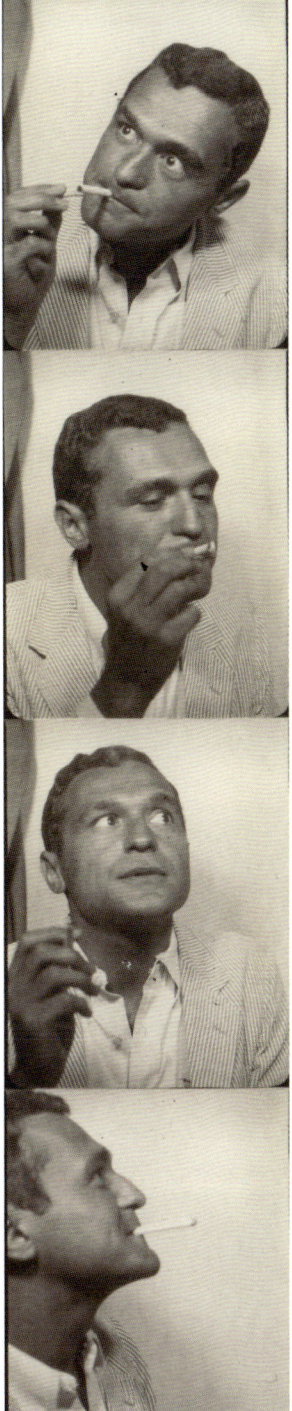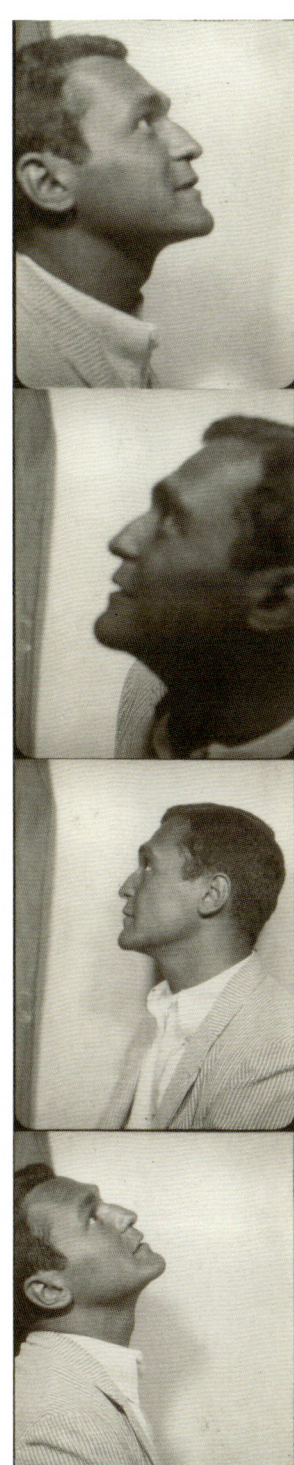

约翰·焦尔诺与沃霍尔相识于 1960 年代初,并出演了他的首部电影《沉睡》(1963)。两人在他们共同好友温·张伯伦的乡间住宅首次见面之后,很快开始交往并发展了持续大约两年的恋情。到了 1960 年代中期,焦尔诺已经成为极具创新和实验精神的诗人与艺术家。在艾滋病大流行期间,他积极奔走发声,筹款帮助患病的弱势群体。 直到 2019 年去世前,焦尔诺一直都在从事诗歌与艺术创作。

John Giorno met Warhol in the early 1960s and starred in his first film, *Sleep* (1963). The two first met at the country home of their mutual friend Wynn Chamberlain. Soon thereafter, they began a romantic relationship that lasted for roughly two years. By the mid-1960s, he had established himself as an innovative and experimental poet and artist. With the onslaught of the AIDS epidemic, Giorno became an outspoken, tireless activist and fundraiser to assist those living with the illness. Giorno continued making art and writing poetry until his death in 2019.

CINEMA AS OBJECT

《自画像》
*Self-Portrait*
约 ca. 1963

明胶银盐相纸
Gelatin silver print
19.8 × 4.1 cm

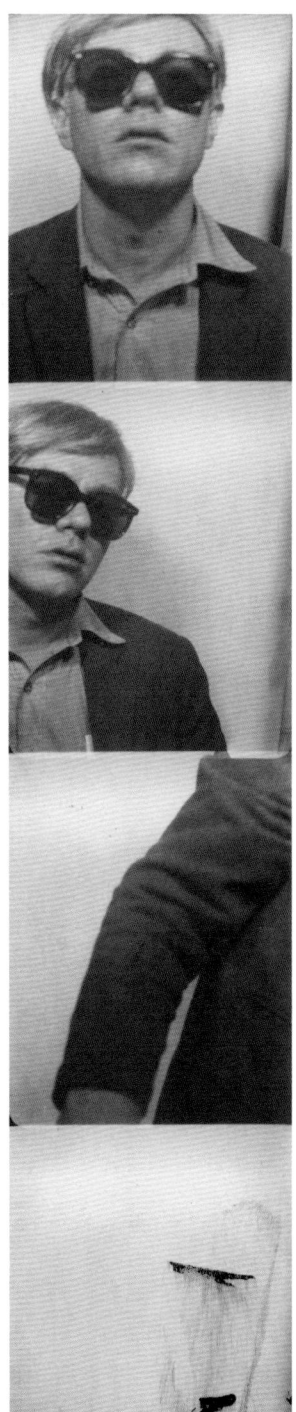

《杰拉德·马兰加》
*Gerard Malanga*
约 ca. 1965

快照亭照片
Photobooth photograph
19.4 × 3.8 cm

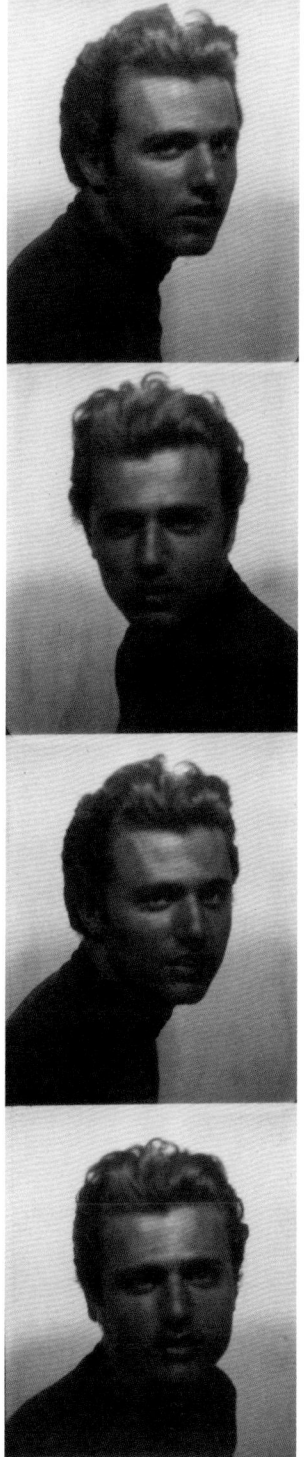

《伊迪·塞奇威克》
*Edie Sedgwick*
约 ca. 1965

快照亭照片
Photobooth photograph
20 × 4.1 cm

伊迪丝（昵称伊迪）·明特恩·塞奇威克出身于新英格兰富裕家庭，童年和青少年生活问题不断。1965年初，认识沃霍尔之前，伊迪便已患有精神疾病，并且饱受进食障碍和药物滥用的折磨。沃霍尔和她在一场聚会上初遇，立刻就被她的美丽和魅力所吸引。因其极具标志性和感染力的时尚风格，《Vogue》杂志将她评为1965年的"潮流女孩"（It Girl）。接下来的几年间，他们出双入对，沃霍尔也在此期间拍摄了多达20余部电影，其中多部作品都以这位问题缠身的明星为主角，两人也时常成为报纸头版的话题人物。

Born into a wealthy New England family, Edith (Edie) Minturn Sedgwick had a troubled childhood and adolescence. Before meeting Warhol in early 1965, she had already struggled with mental illness, an eating disorder, and drug abuse. When Warhol met her at a party, he was immediately mesmerized by her beauty and charm. Sedgwick was named the 1965 "It Girl" by *Vogue* magazine for her iconic and influential fashion. For a few years, Warhol and Sedgwick were inseparable, during which time Warhol shot more than twenty films featuring the troubled star and the two made headline news together.

1964年7月25日至26日，沃霍尔将镜头对准纽约市著名地标，拍下了《帝国大厦》一片。他将摄像头架在时代生活大厦高层办公室的窗台上，对准帝国大厦，从晚上8点开始定格拍摄暮色6小时，直到凌晨2点半。沃霍尔的电影拍摄没有遵循好莱坞的既定规则，整部影片只有一个镜头，且影片时长与真实拍摄时间相同，毫无缩减。不仅所有镜头没有经过剪辑，在电影首映时他更以慢速播放全片，让播放时长达到8小时有余，凸显了这部电影肖像的史诗气质。

Warhol shot *Empire*, a portrait of New York City's famous landmark, on July 25–26, 1964. By aiming his camera out a window of the Time-Life Building, he recorded the Empire State Building for six hours, from the twilight of 8 pm through darkness until 2:30 am. Ignoring Hollywood conventions, Warhol's film contains only one image and extends – rather than condenses – real time. Not only did he use all of the footage he shot, unedited, he also projected it in slow motion at the film's premiere, bringing the final running time to slightly over eight hours – a truly epic film portrait.

《帝国大厦》
*Empire*
1964

16 毫米黑白无声电影，16fps
8 小时 5 分
16 mm film, black and white, silent, 16fps
485'

1964 年初，看到朋友比利·内姆（原名威廉·林力希）装修成全银色的公寓后，沃霍尔便动念请他帮忙将新搬进的挑高工作室改造成同样颜色。内姆花了几个月时间粉刷墙面和挑高的房顶，贴上锡纸，让整个房间闪耀着如同宇宙深空的质感。沃霍尔在这个"银色工厂"与杰拉德·马兰加等助手共同制作各种大型绘画、雕塑和电影。"银色工厂"也几乎成了 1960 年代所有去纽约的人最想到访的地方。这里夸张奔放和充满创造力的气氛扭转了人们对艺术家工作室的印象，整个空间也可被看作是一场不散的狂欢宴席，有着开放的精神，永不间断的实验性与戏剧性。

In early 1964, Warhol asked his friend Billy Name (William Linich) to decorate his new loft studio in silver after seeing Name's apartment painted in the same color. It took Name several months to paint and foil the walls and high ceilings of the space, but when it was finished, the room glistened with a cosmic aura. At the Silver Factory, Warhol made larger paintings, sculptures, and films with Gerard Malanga and other assistants. It seems nearly everyone who came to New York in the 1960s claimed to have visited the Silver Factory. The atmosphere of excess and creativity transformed the traditional notion of an artist's studio into a vision of a permanent carnival, marked by openness, continuous experimentation, and drama.

《比利·内姆给安迪·沃霍尔拍照》
斯蒂芬·肖尔
*Billy Name Photographing Andy Warhol*
Stephen Shore
1965

明胶银盐相纸
Gelatin silver print
12.7 × 20 cm

17岁时，年少有志的摄影师斯蒂芬·肖尔结识了沃霍尔，当即问他能否拍摄"银色工厂"，为其记录日常点滴，并得到了沃霍尔的应允。于是在沃霍尔拍摄电影的巅峰期——1965年到1966年期间，肖尔便化身为"银色工厂"的记录者，拍摄进出这里的"超级明星"以及工作室的帮手如莎莉·柯克兰德、艾薇·尼科尔森和比利·内姆等人。肖尔也成了这个时代最重要的美国摄影师之一，他对沃霍尔生活的摄影记录，为我们深入了解艺术家的创作过程提供了重要的内部视角。

At the age of seventeen, an aspiring young photographer named Stephen Shore befriended Warhol and asked if he could photograph the goings-on around the Silver Factory. Warhol accepted. From 1965 to 1966, Shore became the Factory's de facto photographer during the pinnacle of Warhol's filmmaking, capturing Superstars and studio helpers such as Sally Kirkland, Ivy Nicholson, and Billy Name. Shore would become one of the most significant American photographers of our time, and his photographs of Warhol's life provide an essential insider's perspective on the creative process of the artist.

《安迪·沃霍尔与杰拉德·马兰加》
斯蒂芬·肖尔
*Andy Warhol and Gerard Malanga*
Stephen Shore
1965

明胶银盐相纸
Gelatin silver print
12.7 × 20.3 cm

《莎莉·柯克兰德》
斯蒂芬·肖尔
*Sally Kirkland*
Stephen Shore
1965

明胶银盐相纸
Gelatin silver print
12.7 × 20.3 cm

《莎莉·柯克兰德》
斯蒂芬·肖尔
*Sally Kirkland*
Stephen Shore
1965

明胶银盐相纸
Gelatin silver print
12.7 × 20.3 cm

《伊迪·塞奇威克与莎莉·柯克兰德》
斯蒂芬·肖尔
*Edie Sedgwick and Sally Kirkland*
Stephen Shore
1965

明胶银盐相纸
Gelatin silver print
12.7 × 20.3 cm

《伊迪·塞奇威克》
斯蒂芬·肖尔
*Edie Sedgwick*
Stephen Shore
1965

明胶银盐相纸
Gelatin silver print
12.7 × 20.3 cm

《莎莉·柯克兰德》
斯蒂芬·肖尔
*Sally Kirkland*
Stephen Shore
1965

明胶银盐相纸
Gelatin silver print
12.7 × 20.3 cm

《杰拉德·马兰加与艾薇·尼科尔森》
斯蒂芬·肖尔
*Gerard Malanga and Ivy Nicholson*
Stephen Shore
1965

明胶银盐相纸
Gelatin silver print
12.7 × 20.3 cm

《贝弗利·格兰特和杰克·史密斯在安迪·沃霍尔的电影＜蝙蝠侠 德古拉＞中（1964）》
丹尼斯·霍珀
*Beverly Grant and Jack Smith on the set of Andy Warhol's film Batman Dracula (1964)*
Dennis Hopper
1964

明胶银盐相纸
Gelatin silver print
17.5 × 25.2 cm

《1965年，安迪·沃霍尔和保罗·莫里西等人正在拍摄电影＜我的小白脸＞》
斯蒂芬·肖尔
*Andy Warhol, Paul Morrissey, and others during the filming of My Hustler, 1965*
Stephen Shore
重印 Reprint 1997

明胶银盐相纸
Gelatin silver print
25.4 × 20.3 cm

《安迪·沃霍尔、查克·魏因、杰拉德·马兰加和伊迪·塞奇威克在戴维·麦凯布工作室内摆出波普造型,纽约市,1965年春》
戴维·麦凯布
*Andy Warhol, Chuck Wein, Gerard Malanga and Edie Sedgwick as composite Pop creature at David McCabe's studio, New York City, spring 1965*
David McCabe

明胶银盐相纸
Gelatin silver print
50.5 × 40.6 cm

1964年,沃霍尔雇请英国摄影师戴维·麦凯布记录他一整年的工作和生活。这段时间,麦凯布在"银色工厂"拍下了沃霍尔最具代表性的系列工作照,以及"超级明星"伊迪·塞奇威克和助手杰拉德·马兰加等人的身影。麦凯布的照片见证了沃霍尔职业生涯的关键时刻,当时他创立了"工厂",着手创作具有突破性的作品,如"死亡与灾难"、"布里洛盒子"和"花朵"等系列作品,同时还拍摄了"试镜"系列和《帝国大厦》(1964)等影像作品。

British photographer David McCabe was contracted by Warhol in 1964 to document the artist's life and work for an entire year. During that time, the photographer captured iconic shots of Warhol at work in the Silver Factory, Superstars such as Edie Sedgwick, and assistant Gerard Malanga. McCabe's photographs recorded a pivotal period of Warhol's career, when he founded the Factory and worked on ground-breaking pieces like the Death and Disaster series, the Brillo Boxes, and the Flowers series, along with films such as the Screen Tests and *Empire* (1964).

CINEMA AS OBJECT 237

《安迪·沃霍尔和奥瑞康摄像机在
"工厂"的<乙烯>片场,纽约市,
1965年4月初》
戴维·麦凯布
*Andy Warhol and the Auricon
newsreel camera on the set of VINYL
at the Factory, New York City, early
April 1965*
David McCabe
重印 Reprint 1996

明胶银盐相纸
Gelatin silver print
27.9 × 35.2 cm

《伊迪·塞奇威克、罗杰·特鲁多和勒内·里卡德(远端)在《厨房》片场(巴德·维特沙夫特公寓内),纽约市,1965年5月》
戴维·麦凯布
*Edie Sedgwick, Roger Trudeau and Rene Ricard (in background) on the set of KITCHEN (in the apartment of Bud Wirtschafter, New York City, May 1965*
David McCabe
重印 Reprint 1996

明胶银盐相纸
Gelatin silver print
35.6 × 27.9 cm

CINEMA AS OBJECT 239

《艾薇·尼科尔森试镜，1966》
比利·内姆
*Ivy Nicholson's Screen Test, 1966*
Billy Name
重印 Reprint 1996

明胶银盐相纸
Gelatin silver print
27.9 × 35.6 cm

沃霍尔创作了约 500 部华丽动人的动态肖像作品，即"试镜"系列。1964 至 196 年间，有数百位知名或不知名的"银色工厂"访客参与了拍摄，其中包括艺术家萨尔瓦多·达利、音乐家鲍勃·迪伦、潮流女孩伊迪·塞奇威克。拍摄时，沃霍尔要求访客尽量保持姿势不动，先用强光打亮拍摄对象，再用 16 毫米的宝莱克斯摄影机和 100 英尺黑白胶片拍摄影像。每一部无声"试镜"都只拍一卷胶片的长度。最终将 2 分 45 秒的动态肖像以慢速播放变成 4 分钟的影片，从而营造出梦幻而引人遐想的效果。

Warhol created approximately 500 beautiful and revealing film portraits called Screen Tests. The subjects — hundreds of different individuals shot between 1964 and 1966 — were visitors, both familiar and anonymous, to the Silver Factory, including artist Salvador Dalí, musician Bob Dylan, and "It Girl" Edie Sedgwick. To make the Screen Tests, Warhol asked visitors to pose and remain as still as possible. Warhol lit his subjects with a strong light and recorded them with his stationary 16mm Bolex camera on 100-foot rolls of black-and-white film. Each silent Screen Test lasted only as long as the film roll. The resulting 2:45 min portraits were projected in slow motion so that each ran for approximately 4 minutes, producing a dreamy and contemplative effect.

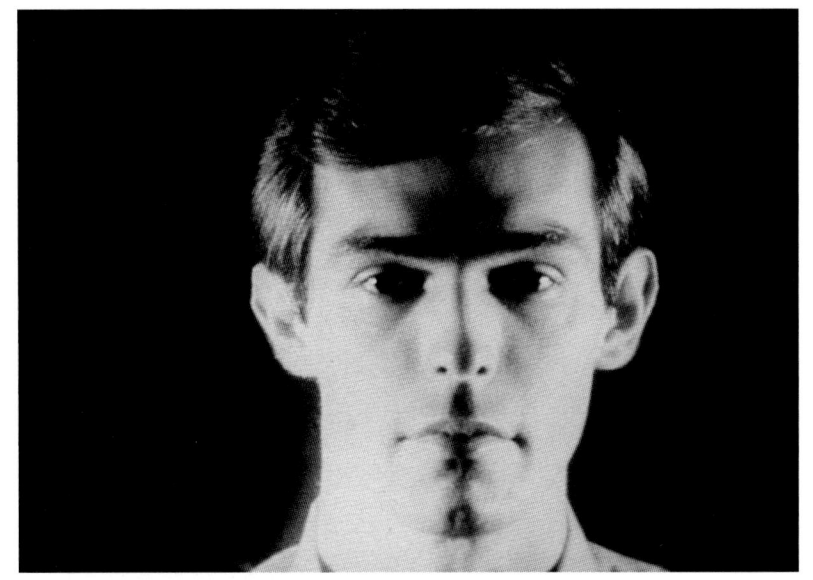

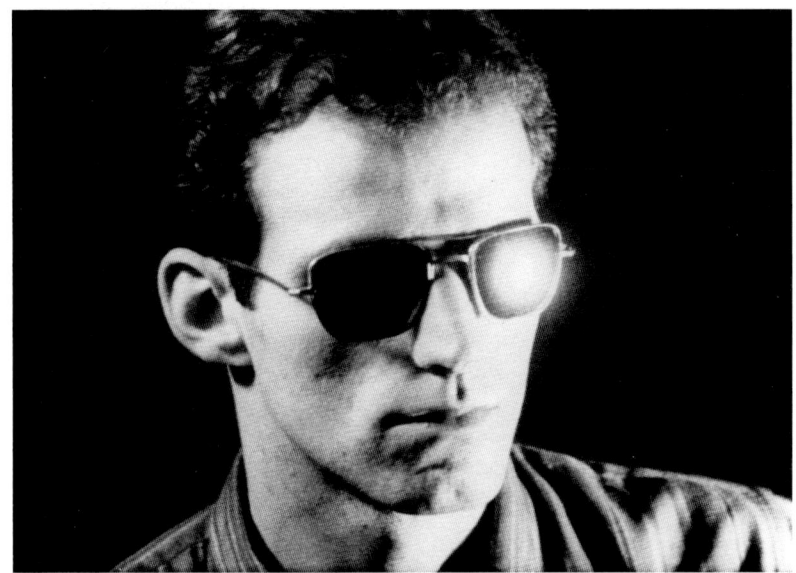
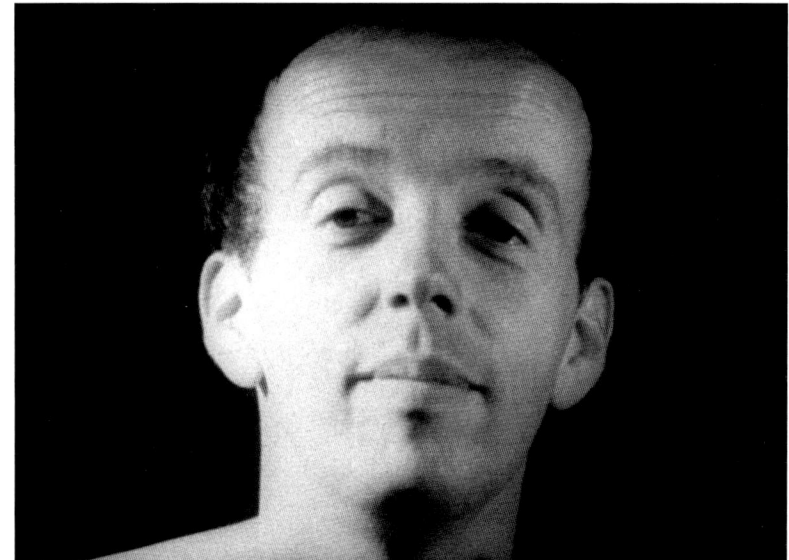

《彼得・于亚尔》[ST157]
*Peter Hujar* [ST157]
1964

16 毫米黑白无声电影，16fps
16 mm film, black and white, silent, 16fps
4'24"

《鲁弗斯・科林斯》[ST61]
*Rufus Collins* [ST61]
1964

16 毫米黑白无声电影，16fps
16 mm film, black and white, silent, 16fps
4'30"

《比利・林奇》[ST194]
*Billy Linich* [ST194]
1964

16 毫米黑白无声电影，16fps
16 mm film, black and white, silent, 16fps
4'24"

《泰勒・米德》[ST209]
*Taylor Mead* [ST209]
1964

16 毫米黑白无声电影，16fps
16 mm film, black and white, silent, 16fps
4'24"

CINEMA AS OBJECT 241

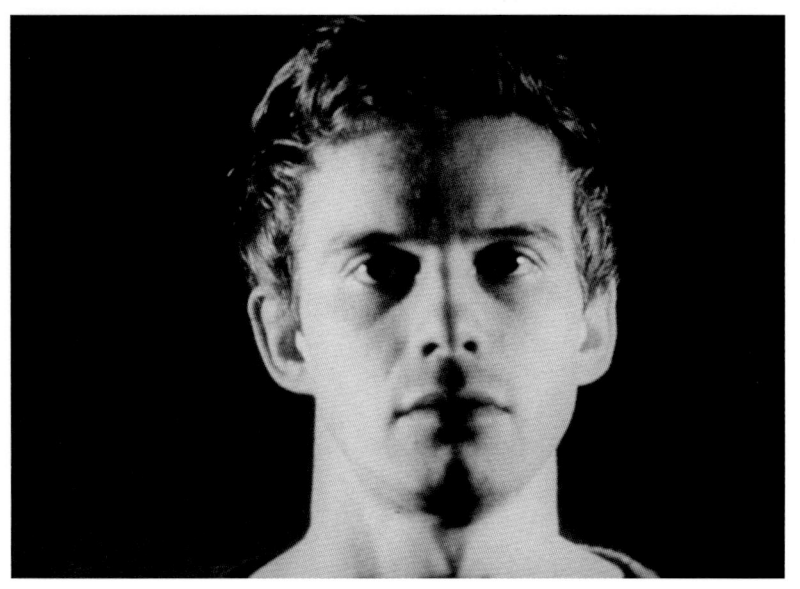
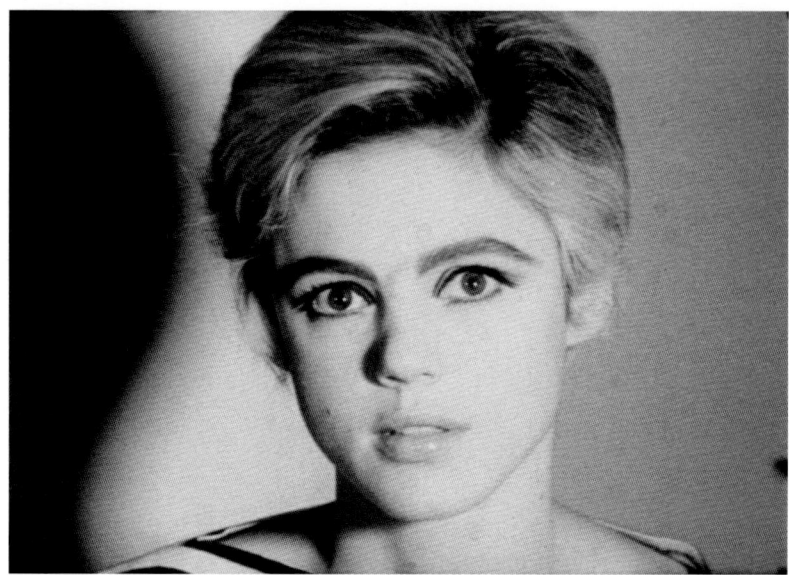

《沃尔特·戴恩伍德》[ST65]
*Walter Dainwood* [ST65]
1964

16 毫米黑白无声电影，16fps
16 mm film, black and white, silent, 16fps
4'24"

《伊迪·塞奇威克》[ST308]
*Edie Sedgwick* [ST308]
1965

16 毫米黑白无声电影，16fps
16 mm film, black and white, silent, 16fps
4'36"

《男孩》[ST31]
*Boy* [ST31]
1964

16 毫米黑白无声电影，16fps
16 mm film, black and white, silent, 16fps
4'30"

《埃米·托宾》[ST335]
*Amy Taubin* [ST335]
1964

16 毫米黑白无声电影，16fps
16 mm film, black and white, silent, 16fps
4'24"

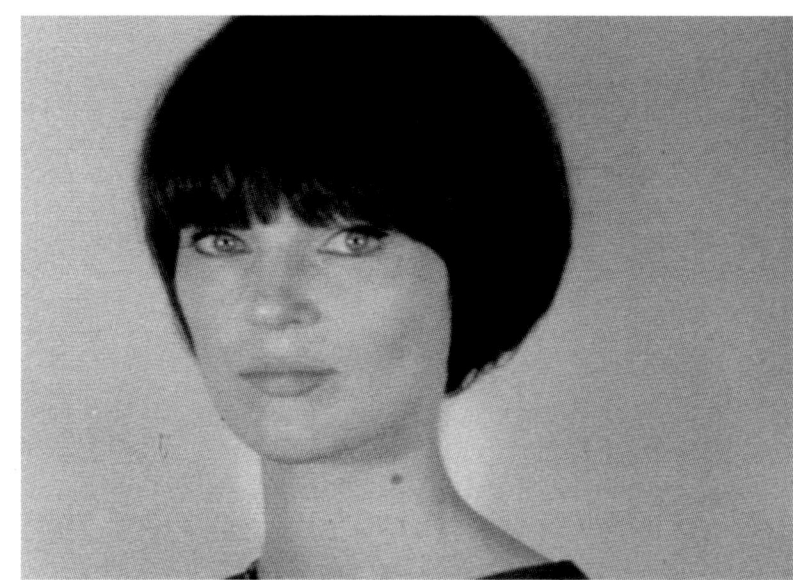

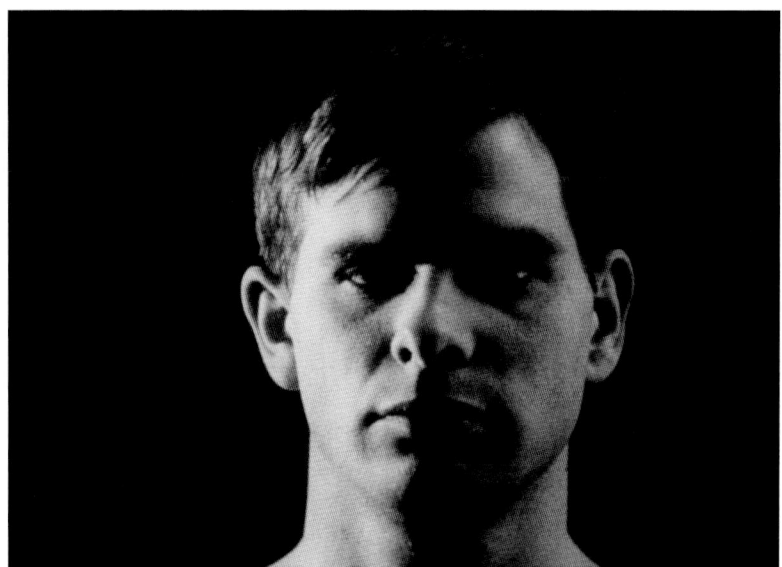

《弗朗索瓦·德梅尼尔》[ST212]
*Francois de Menil* [ST212]
1965

16 毫米黑白无声电影，16fps
16 mm film, black and white, silent, 16fps
4'30"

《艾薇·尼科尔森》[ST230]
*Ivy Nicholson* [ST230]
1964

16 毫米黑白无声电影，16fps
16 mm film, black and white, silent, 16fps
4'30"

《简·霍尔泽》[ST142]
*Jane Holzer* [ST142]
1964

16 毫米黑白无声电影，16fps
16 mm film, black and white, silent, 16fps
4'30"

《凯莉·埃迪》[ST89]
*Kelly Edey* [ST89]
1964

16 毫米黑白无声电影，16fps
16 mm film, black and white, silent, 16fps
4'30"

CINEMA AS OBJECT 243

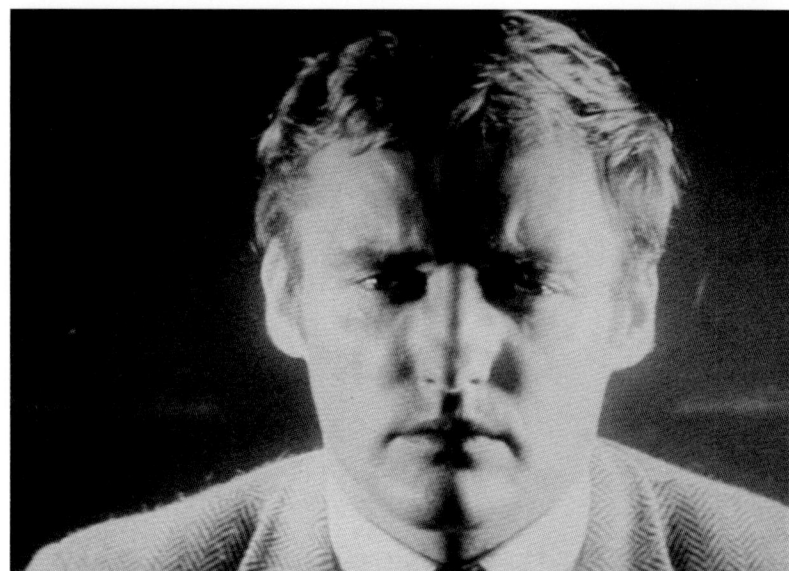

《布鲁克·海沃德》[ST132]
*Brooke Hayward* [ST132]
1964

16 毫米黑白无声电影，16fps
16 mm film, black and white, silent, 16fps
4'30"

《丹尼斯·霍珀》[ST154]
*Dennis Hopper* [ST154]
1964

16 毫米黑白无声电影，16fps
16 mm film, black and white, silent, 16fps
4'24"

《多尼尔·卢纳》[ST195]
*Donyale Luna* [ST195]
1965

16 毫米黑白无声电影，16fps
16 mm film, black and white, silent, 16fps
4'30"

《弗雷迪·赫科》[ST137]
*Freddy Herko* [ST137]
1964

16 毫米黑白无声电影，16fps
16 mm film, black and white, silent, 16fps
4'36"

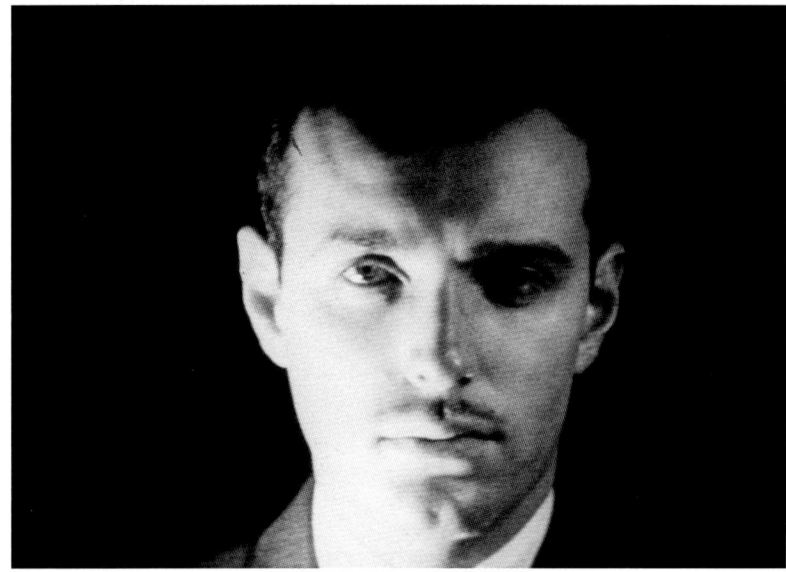

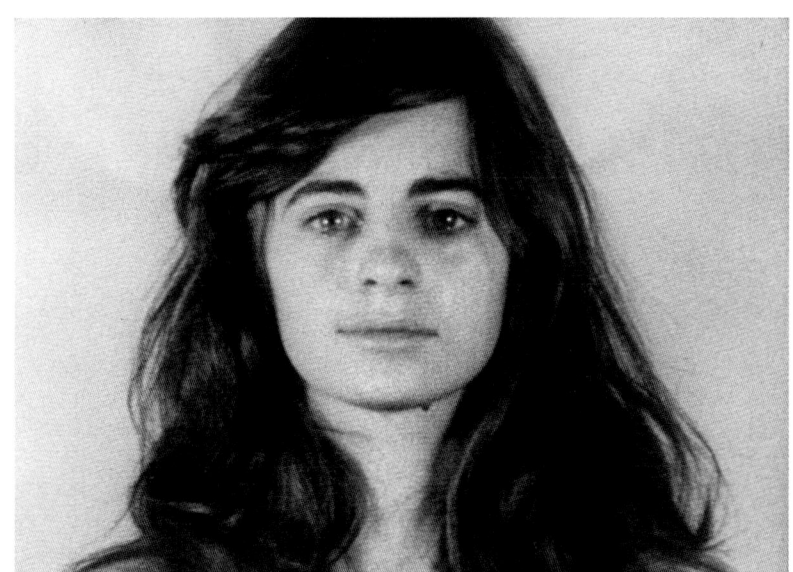

《杰拉德·马兰加》[ST198]
*Gerard Malanga* [ST198]
1964

16 毫米黑白无声电影，16fps
16 mm film, black and white, silent, 16fps
4'36"

《格雷戈里·巴特库克》[ST18]
*Gregory Battcock* [ST18]
1964

16 毫米黑白无声电影，16fps
16 mm film, black and white, silent, 16fps
4'30"

《莎莉·柯克兰德》[ST181]
*Sally Kirkland* [ST181]
1964

16 毫米黑白无声电影，16fps
16 mm film, black and white, silent, 16fps
4'30"

《安妮·布坎南》[ST33]
*Ann Buchanan* [ST33]
1964

16 毫米黑白无声电影，16fps
16 mm film, black and white, silent, 16fps
4'30"

# 沃霍尔重塑
## WARHOL REMIXED

沃霍尔不但拥有惊人的创造力，还是一名商业艺术家，永远都在思考如何为自己的艺术事业增加收入。在职业生涯晚期，他构思了一些类似市场营销的艺术项目，例如对1960年代的流行元素进行混搭，加入风格变化以适应新的时代潮流。另外，诸如金宝汤罐头和可口可乐瓶等商业主题也随着1980年代的品牌更新进行了调整，一些新品牌如巴黎水、苹果电脑和绝对伏特加等公司也纷纷与沃霍尔展开合作。1960年代，随着沃霍尔绘制的玛丽莲·梦露原作市场价格的上涨，沃霍尔再次回归该主题的创作。但不再使用1960年代强调运笔的手绘创作，而是变成光滑的平涂——典型的1980年代美国视觉风格。沃霍尔晚年也曾重返影像创作，为MTV电视台制作了《安迪·沃霍尔十五分钟访谈》系列节目，于1985年至1987年播出。

In addition to being a revolutionary creative, Warhol was a business artist, constantly looking for ways to increase revenue for his enterprise. Later in his career, he made artistic decisions like a marketing firm by taking subjects that had been popular in the 1960s and remixing them, adding stylistic twists to fit the new decade. Commercial subjects like the Campbell's soup cans and the Coca-Cola bottles were updated with the new branding of the 1980s, and new brands were introduced to his repertoire thanks to corporate commissions from companies like Perrier bottled water, Macintosh computers, and Absolut vodka. Warhol also revisited subjects such as Marilyn Monroe after his original 1960s works rose in price on the art market. In the later canvases, Warhol abandoned the gestural, hand-painted nature of the 1960s works and adopted a slick flatness that was emblematic of American visual style in the 1980s. Warhol also revisited film at the end of his life, starting an MTV series called *Andy Warhol's Fifteen Minutes*, which ran from 1985–1987.

1974年，沃霍尔将位于德克大楼六年之久的曼哈顿中城工作室迁到联合广场对面的大楼。新的办公及工作空间更加宽敞，这意味着"银色工厂"所代表的1960年代狂野不羁精神的退位，自此转向企业经营的沃霍尔开始专注于各种委托创作以及名人肖像的制作。新工作室设置有全木装修的会议室、《访问》杂志办公室和放映厅。而配置的摄像头和防弹门则反映了自1968年在自己工作室遭瓦莱丽·索拉纳斯枪击之后，沃霍尔依然还心有余悸。

In 1974, after six years at the Decker Building in Midtown Manhattan, Warhol and his helpers moved across Union Square to a larger space. The new offices and studio signaled a shift from the wild days of the 1960s Silver Factory to entrepreneurial ventures such as commissions and celebrity portraits. The new studio had a wood-paneled conference room, offices for Interview magazine, a screening room, security cameras, and a bulletproof door to protect against armed intruders, whom Warhol feared after Valerie Solanas shot him at his studio in 1968.

《1982年9月21日,安迪·沃霍尔在纽约市百老汇大道860号"工厂"的办公室打电话。》
马克·辛克
*Andy Warhol on the phone in his personal office at the Factory, 860 Broadway, on September 21, 1982 in New York City, New York.*
Mark Sink
1982

Vu-Lyte II 投影仪由查尔斯·贝泽勒公司出品，是 1950 年代利用实物投影技术反射不透明打印材料进行投屏的一种投影仪。沃霍尔通过投影仪可以快速准确地为选定的流行文化主题绘制轮廓线稿，然后再进行手工涂色。简洁的绘画和精准的线条是建构沃霍尔波普美学的关键，这在 1960 年代早期沃霍尔选择了与抽象表现主义截然不同的创作道路之后变得尤为重要。投影设备也让沃霍尔可以对其创作进行大规模生产。自 15 世纪达·芬奇发明通过暗箱投射上下颠倒的影像，从而可以准确勾勒物体的轮廓的方法以来，艺术家便一直采用这种设备作为艺术创作的工具。

The Charles Beseler Vu-Lyte II is a 1950s opaque projector that reflects non-transparent print materials and enlarges them onto a screen. The Vu-Lyte allowed Warhol to quickly and accurately draw outlines of his pop-culture subjects, which he would then hand-paint. Precision drawings with clean lines were crucial to Warhol's Pop aesthetic, especially when Warhol broke from his Abstract Expressionist peers in the early 1960s. Such devices also enabled him to produce on a mass scale. Projectors have been used by artists since the fifteenth century, when Da Vinci invented the camera obscura to screen images upside down and sketch accurate outlines of subjects.

贝泽勒 Vu-Lyte 反射式放映机
Beseler Vu-Lyte
约 ca. 1960

混合档案材料
Mixed archival material
66.7 × 38.7 × 51.4 cm

豪华汽车品牌凯迪拉克成立于 1902 年。沃霍尔十分熟悉这家公司，并热衷于描绘凯迪拉克汽车。观众可以在此次展出的 1950 年代的商业插画与 1960 年代早期的波普绘画中体味沃霍尔在职业生涯不同阶段与这一标志性品牌的不解之缘。沃霍尔曾受《时尚芭莎》杂志之托，以 1958 年的凯迪拉克 Coupe de Ville 系列轿跑车为蓝本，创作了《四名着戏装的男士全身像》与《车》，呈现出"对美国轿车流行现象的视觉评论"。《七辆凯迪拉克》是一幅早期的波普作品，画布上黑色油墨丝网印刷的汽车似为 1963 年 Fleetwood（特别版）四门硬顶车，这是凯迪拉克在 1962 年与 1963 年间发布的限量车型，该车的后悬更短，便于停车，专门为拥有高层公寓和地下车库的纽约车主设计。沃霍尔选择了这款充满魅力的车型，并通过丝网印刷技术复制汽车图像，突出"机械制造"的视觉效果，展露出他对消费文化和物质欲望的敏锐观察。

The luxury automobile brand Cadillac was founded in 1902. Warhol was familiar with the company and enjoyed depicting their vehicles. Through the works in this exhibition, one can see how the artist engaged with the iconic brand in different stages of his career, both in his commercial illustrations of the 1950s and in his initial Pop Art paintings of the early 1960s. Four Male Costumed Full Figures and Car were both created as commissions for Harper's Bazaar, which requested that he "make a visual comment on the phenomenon of the American motorcar." The works illustrate a 1958 Cadillac Coupe de Ville. Seven Cadillacs is an early Pop work featuring what is likely a 1963 Fleetwood (Special) four-door hardtop in black silkscreen ink on linen. This was a limited production model from 1962 and 1963 designed specifically for Cadillac owners who lived in New York City high-rise apartments with underground garages, as the car had a shorter deck for easier parking. By selecting this glamourous vehicle and repeating the image to look "machine made" through his silkscreen technique, Warhol reveals a sharp eye for consumer culture and desire.

《车》
*Car*
1950 年代 1950s

丝蒂摩纸上墨水和苯胺染料
Ink and Dr. Martin's aniline dye on Strathmore paper
33.7 × 65.1 cm

《四名着戏装的男士全身像》
*Four Male Costumed Full Figures*
1950 年代 1950s

丝蒂摩纸上墨水和苯胺染料
Ink and Dr. Martin's aniline dye on Strathmore Seconds paper
57.2 × 72.4 cm

《凯迪拉克》
*Cadillac*
1962

写生纸上石墨
Graphite on sketchbook paper
61 × 45.7 cm

《七辆凯迪拉克》
*Seven Cadillacs*
1962

布上丝网印刷
Silkscreen ink on linen
142.2 × 48.3 cm

WARHOL REMIXED  255

1961年,沃霍尔首次尝试将可口可乐瓶纳入创作主题,自此迎来了他职业生涯的关键转变。绘画所用底图来自他母亲订阅的《拜占庭天主世界报》的广告版。艺术家有意使用强调手势运笔的灰色和黑色笔触,放大消费品的尺寸以获得宏伟的效果,其构图明显带有抽象表现主义绘画的影子。此外,这件作品也证明沃霍尔的丝网印刷作品实际上是从手绘逐渐过渡发展而来。画布的细节体现了艺术家首先用蜡笔构图,再用笔刷上色的创作过程。

The 1961 Coca-Cola bottle, one of Warhol's first attempts at the subject, marks a crucial point in his career. The source for the image was an ad from his mother's *Byzantine Catholic World* newspaper. With its heroic scaling of the consumer product rendered in gestural black and gray strokes, Warhol's composition might be easily compared with Abstract Expressionist paintings. In addition, this work provides evidence that Warhol's transition from hand-painted works to silkscreened ones did not happen overnight. Close scrutiny of the canvas reveals that he first sketched out the composition in crayon and then painted over it with a brush.

《可口可乐瓶》
*Coca-Cola Bottles*
约 ca. 1982

明胶银盐相纸
Gelatin silver print
20.3 × 25.4 cm

《可口可乐 2》
*Coca-Cola 2*
1961

布上酪蛋白颜料和蜡笔
Casein and crayon on linen
176.5 × 132.7 cm

WARHOL REMIXED 257

1950年代末,沃霍尔将更多精力投入到绘画上。受1950年代中期席卷英国的波普艺术运动吸引,1961年,沃霍尔基于漫画和广告创作了其第一批波普绘画。早期的这些作品多为沃霍尔先运用投影仪将杂志上的图像和照片放大,再手工将投影轮廓转绘至画布上。再后来,借助可完美复制商业广告样貌的丝网印刷技术,沃霍尔在可以忠实复刻挪用原图的同时,还可以对无穷无尽的色彩组合、多层套印和套准偏移工艺展开实验。

By the end of the 1950s, Warhol began to devote more energy to painting. He was drawn to the Pop Art movement, which began in Britain in the mid-1950s. In 1961, Warhol created his first Pop paintings based on comics and ads. Warhol made many of these early works by enlarging images from magazines and photographs with an opaque projector and then hand painting the projections on canvas. Later, photographic silkscreen printing replicated the look of commercial advertising, giving Warhol a faithful duplication of his appropriated source images while allowing him to experiment with over-printing, off-registration, and endless color combinations.

《金宝汤罐头》
*Campbell's Soup Can*
1962

布上酪蛋白颜料、纸胶带和石墨
Casein, masking tape, and graphite on linen
181 × 135.9 cm

电视、电子通讯和大众广告的影响力在1960年代初刚刚萌芽。大众不仅能一眼认出金宝汤罐头上红白相间的标签,对该产品所带来的日常饮食体验也可说是再熟悉不过了。金宝汤罐头是沃霍尔在1960年代创作的第一批波普绘画系列的一部分。到了1970年代中期,艺术家又将该图像用在"反转与回顾"系列作品中。终于在1985年,沃霍尔创作了一系列以金宝汤盒为主题的小幅丝网印刷作品。

The early 1960s saw the beginning of the pervasive influence of television, instant communications, and mass advertising. The familiar red-and-white label of a Campbell's soup can was immediately recognizable to most Americans, and eating Campbell's soup was a widely shared experience. The Campbell's soup cans were one of Warhol's first Pop paintings in the 1960s, and then he featured them again in the mid-1970s as part of his Reversals and Retrospectives series. Finally, in 1985, he used the soup's cardboard box packaging for a series of small silkscreen paintings.

《标签撕开的大金宝汤罐头
（胡椒浓汤味）》
*Big Torn Campbell's Soup Can
(Pepper Pot)*
1962

布上酪蛋白颜料和石墨
Casein and graphite on canvas
181.9 × 132.1 cm

《挤压过的金宝汤罐头（牛肉面味）》
*Crushed Campbell's Soup Can
(Beef Noodle)*
1962

棉布上酪蛋白颜料和石墨
Casein and graphite on cotton canvas
182.6 × 132.1 cm

《金宝汤罐头 II：传统蔬菜味》
Campbell's Soup II: Old Fashioned Vegetable
1969

纸上丝网印刷
Screen print on paper
88.9 × 58.4 cm

《金宝汤罐头 II：苏格兰浓汤味》
Campbell's Soup II: Scotch Broth
1969

纸上丝网印刷
Screen print on paper
88.9 × 58.4 cm

《金宝汤罐头 II：切达奶酪味》
Campbell's Soup II: Cheddar Cheese
1969

纸上丝网印刷
Screen print on paper
88.9 × 58.4 cm

《金宝汤罐头 II：素食蔬菜味》
Campbell's Soup II: Vegetarian Vegetable
1969

纸上丝网印刷
Screen print on paper
88.9 × 58.4 cm

《金宝汤罐头 II：番茄牛肉圈形面味》
Campbell's Soup II: Tomato - Beef Noodle O's
1969

纸上丝网印刷
Screen print on paper
88.9 × 58.4 cm

《金宝汤罐头 II：黄金蘑菇味》
Campbell's Soup II: Golden Mushroom
1969

纸上丝网印刷
Screen print on paper
88.9 × 58.4 cm

《金宝汤罐头 II：新英格兰蛤蜊浓汤味》
Campbell's Soup II: New England Clam Chowder
1969

纸上丝网印刷
Screen print on paper
88.9 × 58.4 cm

《金宝汤罐头 II：热狗豆味》
Campbell's Soup II: Hot Dog Bean
1969

纸上丝网印刷
Screen print on paper
88.9 × 58.4 cm

《金宝汤罐头 II：鸡肉面糊味》
Campbell's Soup II: Chicken 'n Dumplings
1969

纸上丝网印刷
Screen print on paper
88.9 × 58.4 cm

《金宝汤罐头 II：生蚝浓汤味》
Campbell's Soup II: Oyster Stew
1969

纸上丝网印刷
Screen print on paper
88.9 × 58.4 cm

WARHOL REMIXED 263

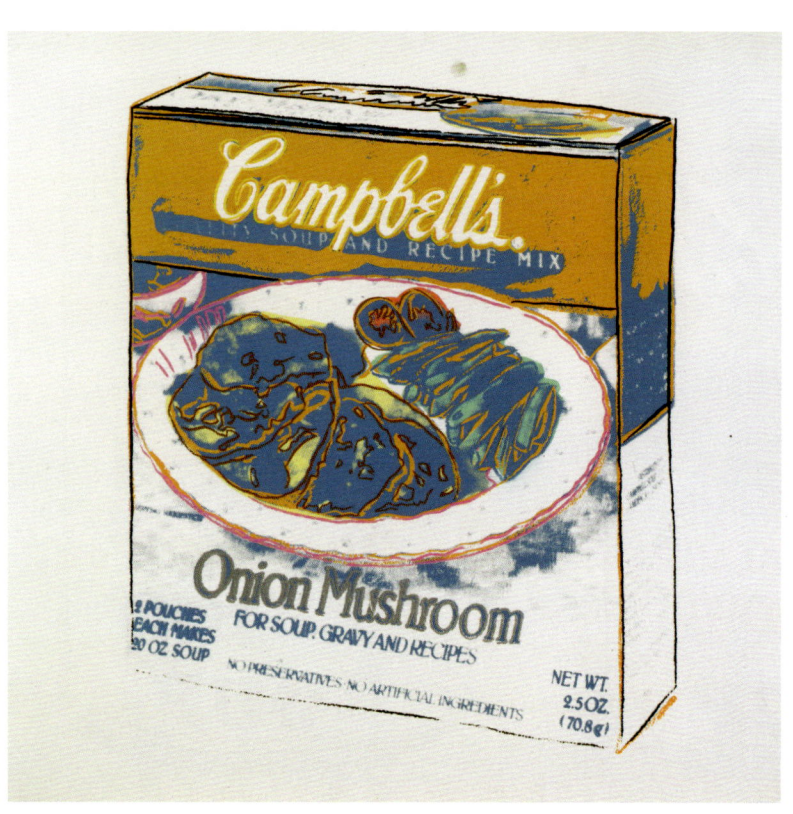

《金宝汤盒（洋葱蘑菇味）》
*Campbell's Onion Mushroom Soup Box*
1986

布上丙烯和丝印油墨
Acrylic and silkscreen ink on linen
50.8 × 50.8 cm

《金宝汤盒》
*Campbell's Noodle Soup Box*
1986

布上丙烯和丝印油墨
Acrylic and silkscreen ink on linen
50.8 × 50.8 cm

《金宝汤盒》
*Campbell's Noodle Soup Box*
1986

布上丙烯和丝印油墨
Acrylic and silkscreen ink on linen
50.8 × 50.8 cm

《金宝汤盒（鸡肉米汤味）》
*Campbell's Chicken Rice Soup Box*
1986

布上丙烯和丝印油墨
Acrylic and silkscreen ink on linen
50.8 × 50.8 cm

《金宝汤盒（洋葱蘑菇味）》
*Campbell's Onion Mushroom Soup Box*
1986

《金宝汤盒》
*Campbell's Noodle Soup Box*
1986

布上丙烯和丝印油墨
Acrylic and silkscreen ink on linen
50.8 × 50.8 cm

布上丙烯和丝印油墨
Acrylic and silkscreen ink on linen
50.8 × 50.8 cm

《金宝汤盒》
*Campbell's Noodle Soup Box*
1986

布上丙烯和丝印油墨
Acrylic and silkscreen ink on linen
50.8 × 50.8 cm

《金宝汤盒》
*Campbell's Noodle Soup Box*
1986

布上丙烯和丝印油墨
Acrylic and silkscreen ink on linen
50.8 × 50.8 cm

《金宝汤盒（鸡肉面味）》
*Campbell's Soup Box (Chicken Noodle)*
1986

手工纸上石墨
Graphite on HMP paper
80 × 60.3 cm

《金宝汤罐头（云吞）》
*Campbell's Soup Can (Wonton)*
约 ca. 1981

手工纸上石墨
Graphite on HMP paper
80 × 62.2 cm

WARHOL REMIXED

自1963年起，沃霍尔开始制作包括布里洛盒子、亨氏番茄酱在内的一系列纸盒雕塑。沃霍尔的作品和这些商品原本的纸盒包装几乎没有任何外观差异，这些创作进一步深化了杜尚现成品的概念。马塞尔·杜尚将小便池和铲雪锹等真实的日常用品当作艺术品，而沃霍尔的纸盒看似机械生产，实际上却是通过制作、涂色、丝网印刷等步骤手工制作完成的。1964年，当这些布里洛纸盒首次展出时，盒子紧密地高高垒起，观众感觉仿佛置身于杂货店的仓库之中。

Warhol began making Brillo, Heinz ketchup, and other box sculptures in 1963. The finished artworks very closely resembled their cardboard models, a method of art-making that teetered on the Duchampian concept of the readymade. Unlike Marcel Duchamp, who employed actual objects like a urinal and a snow shovel as artworks, Warhol made, painted, and silkscreened these boxes by hand in a machine-like process. The Brillo boxes were first exhibited in 1964, when they were tightly packed and piled high, recalling a grocery warehouse.

《布里洛含皂钢丝棉包装盒》
*Brillo Soap Pads Box*
1964

胶合板上丝网油墨和建筑漆
Silkscreen ink and house paint on plywood
43.2 × 43.2 × 35.6 cm

《金宝汤番茄汁包装箱》
*Campbell's Tomato Juice Box*
1964

胶合板上丝网油墨和建筑漆
Silkscreen ink and house paint on plywood
25.4 × 48.3 × 24.1 cm

《亨氏番茄酱包装箱》
*Heinz Tomato Ketchup Box*
1964

胶合板上丝网油墨和建筑漆
Silkscreen ink and house paint on plywood
21.6 × 39.4 × 26.7 cm

《德尔蒙桃罐头包装箱》
*Del Monte Peach Halves Box*
1964

胶合板上丝网油墨和建筑漆
Silkscreen ink and house paint on plywood
30.5 × 38.1 × 24.1 cm

沃霍尔从小就深受好莱坞电影明星的影响。玛丽莲·梦露银幕女神的地位以及她在 1962 年 8 月意外离世的消息,促使沃霍尔采用最新的照相丝网印刷技术创作了著名的梦露肖像。沃霍尔利用电影《飞瀑怒潮》(1953)的宣传照为底本,制作了约 50 幅画作,其中的《玛丽莲·梦露之唇》(1962)反复展现了这位女明星诱人的招牌微笑,仿佛要将她的形象铭刻在美国的文化记忆之中。

Since childhood, Warhol had been greatly influenced by Hollywood movie stars. Marilyn Monroe's status as a screen goddess and her unexpected and tragic death in August 1962 inspired Warhol to utilize his newest technique, the photo-silkscreen, to create his famous portraits of her. Warhol used a cropped publicity still from the film *Niagara* (1953) as the basis for about 50 paintings, including *Marilyn Monroe's Lips* (1962), in which her beckoning smile is repeated again and again, searing Monroe's image into American cultural memory.

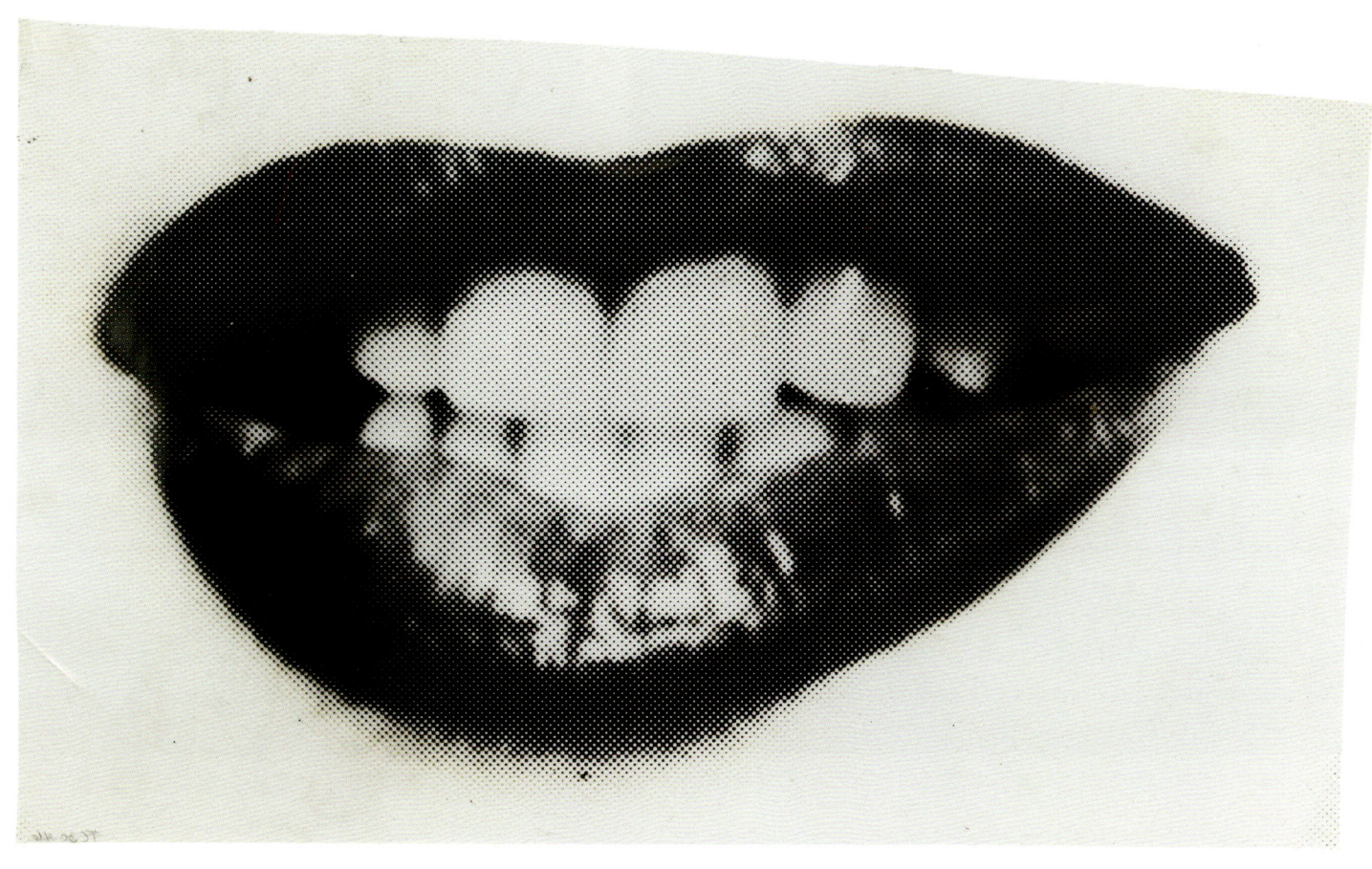

《玛丽莲·梦露：玛丽莲（"反转"系列）》
Marilyn Monroe: Marilyn (Reversal series)
约 ca. 1978

碎布纸上丝网印刷
Screen print on Curtis rag paper
57.2 × 44.5 cm

《投影胶片（玛丽莲·梦露的嘴唇）》
玛丽莲·梦露
Acetate (Marilyn Monroe's lips)
Marilyn Monroe
1962—1964

聚酯膜上感光乳剂
Photo emulsion on polyester film base
17.8 × 28.9 cm

1962 年，玛丽莲·梦露去世后不久，沃霍尔便创作了一系列丝网印刷作品，将这位女明星的形象重复排列在多个版面上。1967 年，他再次回访这个主题，采用和 1962 年相同的图像，但使用多种迷幻色彩制作了数百幅版画。1960 年代后期，沃霍尔的电影事业耗费了大量资金却少有回报，沃霍尔之所以创作本系列作品，有可能是为了他的电影事业筹款。此系列多数作品都被沃霍尔外包给一家丝网印刷公司制作。

Shortly after Marilyn Monroe's death in 1962, Warhol created a series of silk-screen works depicting the actress's face replicated on multiple panels. In 1967, he revisited the subject and created hundreds of prints using the same image as in 1962, altering them with a variety of psychedelic colors. This project was likely used to source funds for Warhol's film enterprises, which consumed him in the late 1960s but yielded little money. Warhol outsourced the labor for the majority of this project, allowing an external silkscreening firm to do most of the work.

《玛丽莲·梦露（玛丽莲）》
*Marilyn Monroe (Marilyn)*
1967

纸上丝网印刷
Screen print on paper
91.4 × 91.4 cm

《玛丽莲·梦露（玛丽莲）》
*Marilyn Monroe (Marilyn)*
1967

纸上丝网印刷
Screen print on paper
91.4 × 91.4 cm

《玛丽莲·梦露（玛丽莲）》
*Marilyn Monroe (Marilyn)*
1967

纸上丝网印刷
Screen print on paper
91.4 × 91.8 cm

《玛丽莲·梦露（玛丽莲）》
*Marilyn Monroe (Marilyn)*
1967

纸上丝网印刷
Screen print on paper
91.4 × 91.4 cm

《玛丽莲·梦露（玛丽莲）》
*Marilyn Monroe (Marilyn)*
1967

纸上丝网印刷
Screen print on paper
91.4 × 91.4 cm

《玛丽莲·梦露（玛丽莲）》
*Marilyn Monroe (Marilyn)*
1967

纸上丝网印刷
Screen print on paper
91.4 × 91.4 cm

《玛丽莲·梦露书本设计小样》
*Marilyn Monroe Book Maquette*
约 ca. 1968

综合媒介
Mixed media
15.2 × 24.1 × 1.9 cm

WARHOL REMIXED

《牛》壁纸
*Cow Wallpaper*
1966

纸上丝网印刷
Screenprint on paper

《牛》壁纸是沃霍尔在20世纪60至80年代所设计的壁纸系列的第一件作品。这件作品在当时被认为极富创新和波普精神,也让人回想起传统装饰艺术中的家装壁纸。19世纪至20世纪初,美国家庭流行使用设计复杂的壁纸覆盖起居室的墙面,然后将画作悬挂其上。艺术家设计壁纸的传统由来已久:从16世纪的阿尔布雷特·丢勒到20世纪的亚历山大·考尔德,这很可能启发了沃霍尔的创作。在1970年于惠特尼美术馆举办的个人回顾展上,沃霍尔将自己的画作挂在《牛》壁纸上。那次展览同时还展出了沃霍尔设计的其他壁纸,其中包括《毛》《自画像》《华盛顿纪念碑》和《鱼》。

Warhol created *Cow Wallpaper* as the first in a series of wallpaper designs he made from the 1960s to the 1980s. At the time, *Cow Wallpaper* seemed to be something totally new and totally Pop; however, it also recalled the traditional decorative art of domestic wallpaper design. Between the nineteenth and early twentieth centuries, intricately designed wallpaper often covered sitting room walls, upon which paintings were also hung. The long history of artist-designed wallpaper – from Albrecht Dürer in the sixteenth century to Alexander Calder in the twentieth century – also likely inspired Warhol. For his 1970 retrospective at the Whitney Museum of American Art, Warhol hung his own paintings on *Cow Wallpaper*. Other Warhol-designed wallpapers in that exhibition included *Mao*, *Self-Portrait*, *Washington Monument*, and *Fish*.

《华盛顿纪念碑》壁纸
*Washington Monument Wallpaper*
1974

纸上丝网印刷
Screenprint on paper

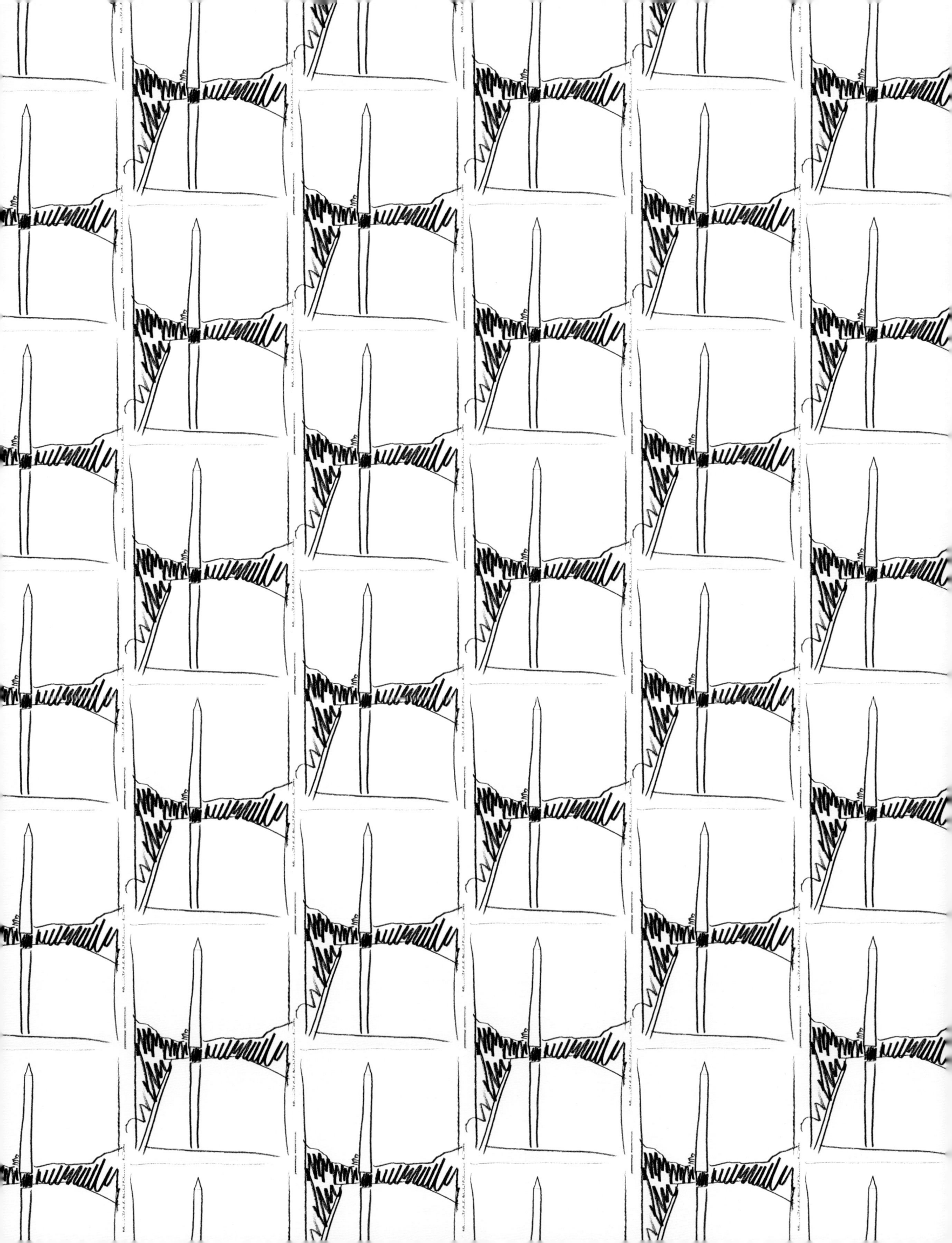

《自画像》壁纸
*Self-Portrait Wallpaper*
1978

纸上丝网印刷
Screenprint on paper

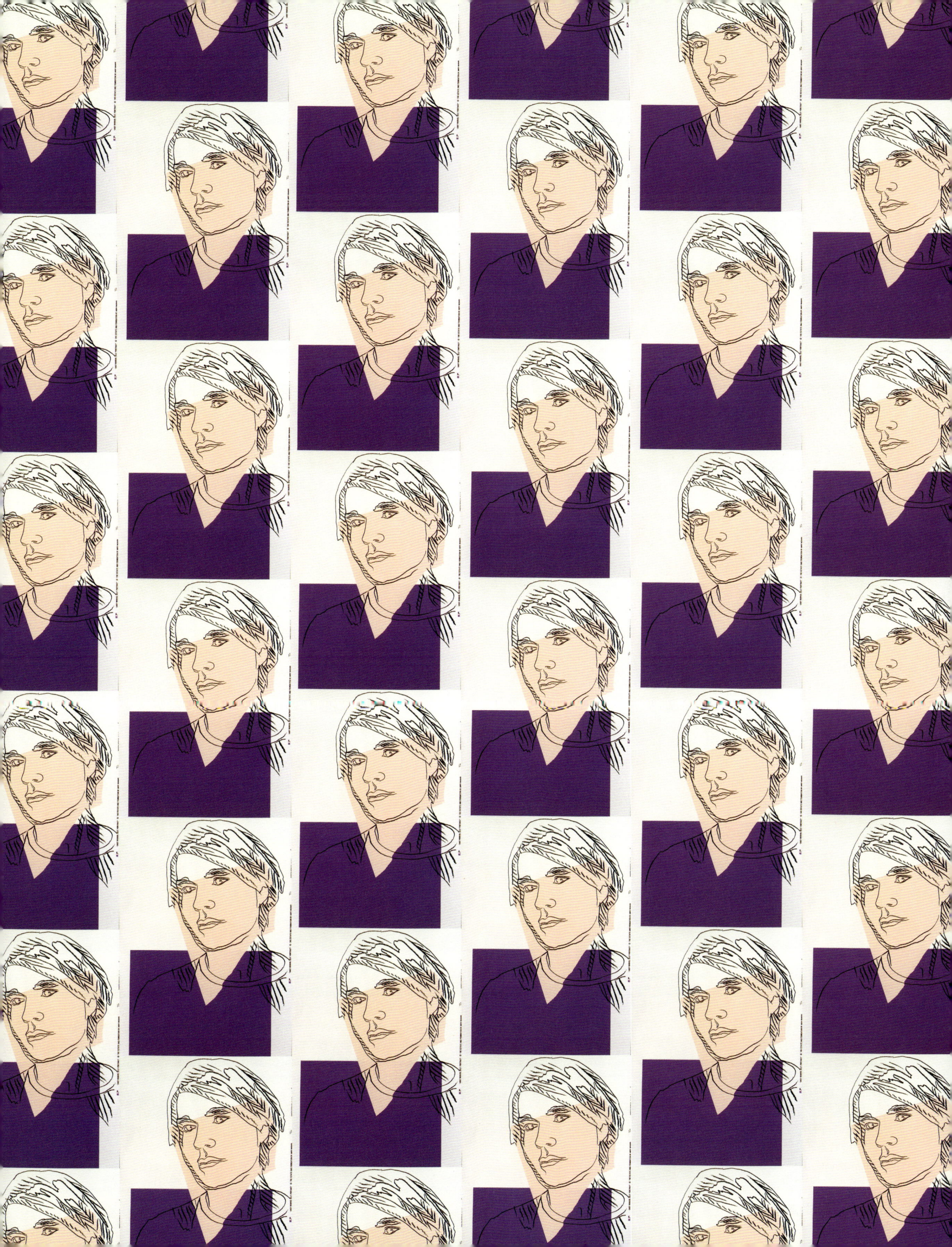

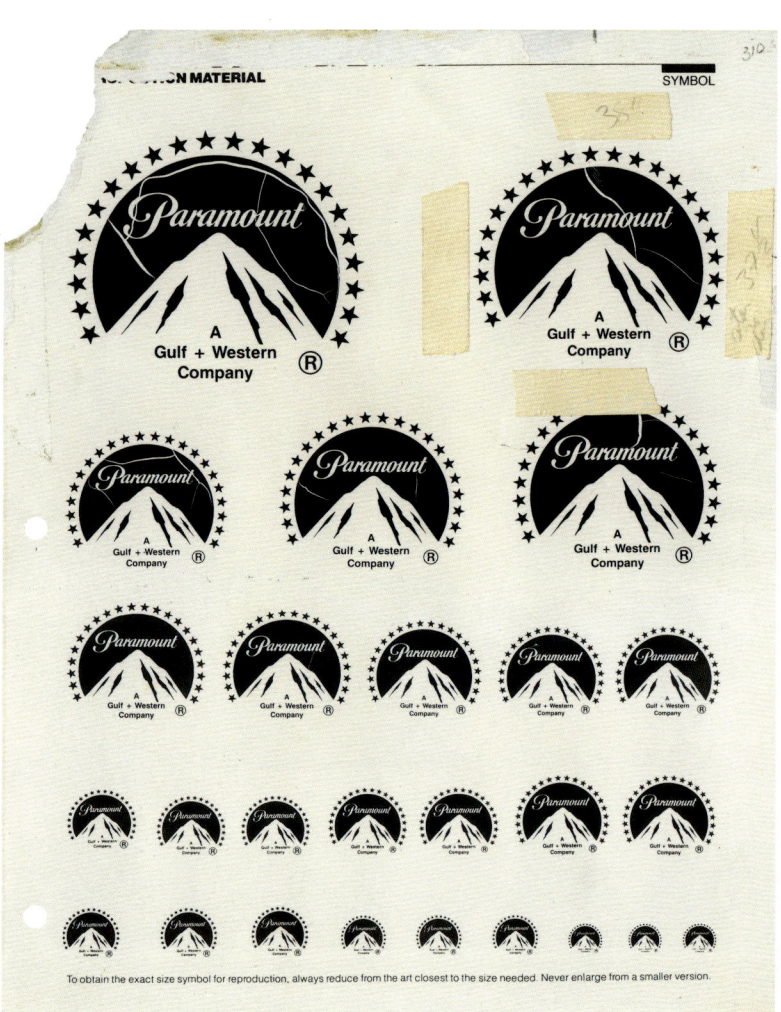

乔恩·古尔德出身于新英格兰的富裕家庭,曾在洛杉矶的派拉蒙影业担任执行制片人。1980 年,沃霍尔经由两人的共同朋友与古尔德相识。沃霍尔当时 52 岁,古尔德只有 27 岁。认识一年后,古尔德搬进了沃霍尔在纽约的联排别墅。在接下来的两年里,他们几乎形影不离,乘坐私人飞机四处旅行,在国际大都市的圈子中如鱼得水。古尔德是沃霍尔最后一位亲密伴侣,但作为一个并未公开出柜的艾滋病患者,古尔德最终与沃霍尔分开,搬回了加利福尼亚。古尔德于 1986 年 9 月 18 日去世。沃霍尔在日记中并没有提及此事,但在几天后他写道:"那些洛杉矶的新闻报道不言自明,我不想谈论它们。"

Jon Gould came from a wealthy New England family and worked as an executive at Paramount Pictures in Los Angeles. In 1980, Gould was introduced to Warhol through a mutual friend. Warhol was 52 years old at the time, and Gould was 27. A year after meeting, Gould moved into Warhol's townhouse in New York. For the next two years, they were nearly inseparable companions, traveling to jet-set locations and mingling in cosmopolitan circles. Gould was Warhol's last romantic partner, but as a closeted gay man diagnosed with AIDS, Gould eventually distanced himself from Warhol and moved back to California. Gould passed away on September 18, 1986. Warhol left this out of his diary, noting a few days later, "And the Diary can write itself on the other news from L.A., which I don't want to talk about."

《派拉蒙影业公司商标标志》
作者未知
*Paramount Pictures trademark symbols*
Unknown
1980s

涂布纸上油墨印刷、纸胶带、石墨标记
Printed ink on coated paper with masking tape and graphite markings
27.8 × 21.4 cm

《广告：派拉蒙影业》
*Ads: Paramount*
1985

布上丙烯和丝印油墨
Acrylic and silkscreen ink on linen
55.9 × 55.9 cm

《广告：派拉蒙影业》
*Ads: Paramount*
1985

莱诺克斯博物馆纸板上丝网印刷
Screen print on Lenox Museum Board
96.5 × 96.5 cm

《免税》
*Duty Free*
约 ca. 1982 年

布上丙烯和丝印油墨
Acrylic and silkscreen ink on canvas
101.6 × 101.6 cm

《李维斯牛仔裤（四幅）》
*Levi's (Four Images)*
1984

布上丙烯和丝印油墨
Acrylic and silkscreen ink on linen
101.6 × 101.6 cm

WARHOL REMIXED 287

《绝对伏特加》
*Absolut Vodka*
1985

手工纸上丙烯
Acrylic on HMP paper
80.6 × 61 cm

《绝对伏特加》
*Absolut*
年份未知 n.d.

明胶银盐相纸
Gelatin silver print
20.3 × 25.4 cm

《绝对伏特加》
*Absolut Vodka*
1985

布上丙烯和丝印油墨
Acrylic and silkscreen ink on linen
101.6 × 101.6 cm

自1980年代起,沃霍尔回归始于50年代的商业艺术,开始承接各种委托创作以支持自己公司的运营。法国瓶装水品牌巴黎水委托他运用品牌经典的泪珠瓶形象制作一系列丝网印刷作品,这次合作造就了巴黎水的销售热潮。"巴黎水"系列作品是对沃霍尔波普生涯开始时创作的可口可乐瓶和金宝汤罐头作品的延续,同时也体现了美国文化品味的不断变化。

By the 1980s, Warhol began doing commission work to support his business, Andy Warhol Enterprises, returning to the field of commercial art where he began in the 1950s. Perrier, a French bottled water brand, commissioned the artist to do a series of vibrant silkscreen prints of their classic teardrop bottles, which became a huge promotional success for the company. The Perrier bottles recalled the Coca-Cola bottles and Campbell's soup cans that Warhol mass produced at the beginning of his Pop career, reflecting the changing tastes of American culture.

《巴黎水包装瓶》
*Perrier Bottles*
1983

布上丙烯和丝印油墨
Acrylic and silkscreen ink on linen
50.8 × 76.2 cm

《巴黎水包装瓶》
*Perrier Bottles*
1983

布上丙烯和丝印油墨
Acrylic and silkscreen ink on linen
76.2 × 50.8 cm

《巴黎水包装瓶》
*Perrier Bottles*
1983

布上丙烯和丝印油墨
Acrylic and silkscreen ink on linen
76.2 × 50.8 cm

《巴黎水包装瓶》
*Perrier Bottles*
1983

布上丙烯和丝印油墨
Acrylic and silkscreen ink on linen
76.2 × 50.8 cm

沃霍尔善于选用大众熟知的品牌商标作为创作对象，这成就了他的艺术生涯，也让他成为波普艺术的引领者。沃霍尔深知广告对消费者的强大影响力，并在作品中采用类似广告的方式吸引观众的注意力。他选择描绘广受大众欢迎的产品，这就意味着作品能引起观众广泛的共鸣；并且这平民化的食品消除了消费者的阶层门槛。此外，沃霍尔的创作通常以印刷广告上的商品形象为底本，而非商品自身。例如，《新可口可乐》就是以一系列可乐飞溅出罐外的图片绘制而成。这幅作品原是一件委任作品，拟作为《时代》杂志一篇文章的配图，该文章报道了1985年可口可乐更改原始配方所引发的公众热议，但这幅作品最后并没有发表。

Warhol's use of familiar brands and logos helped launch his career and establish him as a leading Pop artist. Warhol understood that advertisements have a powerful influence over consumers and used similar methods to capture viewers' attentions in his artwork. The beloved, popular products he depicted represented widely shared experiences; regardless of social or economic status, these consumables were consistent in price and flavor. Warhol often based his images of products on photographs and print advertisements, rather than the actual objects themselves. The imagery in *New Coke* was taken from pictures of a spilled can of soda. The commission was originally meant to accompany a *Time* magazine article about the public uproar caused when Coca-Cola changed their original recipe in 1985, but the artwork went unpublished.

《新可口可乐》
*New Coke*
约 ca. 1985

手工纸上丝网印刷
Screen print on HMP paper
80.6 × 62.2 cm

《新可口可乐》
*New Coke*
约 ca. 1985

粘贴彩色美术纸上丝网印刷
Screen print on taped sheets of colored graphic art paper
90.5 × 60.6 cm

沃霍尔是一个热爱新技术的人。1985年夏天,康懋达国际公司赠予沃霍尔人生中第一台家用电脑Amiga 1000,他欣然签约成为这家公司的品牌大使。当年稍晚,沃霍尔在日记中记下他参加约翰·列侬之子肖恩·列侬和小野洋子生日聚会的经历:"当时有一个年轻人在帮肖恩设置他收到的礼物,一台苹果电脑。我对他说,之前有人不停打电话给我,说要送我一台苹果电脑,但我没搭理他。那个年轻人居然抬头说道:'对,那就是我。我叫史蒂夫·乔布斯。'"沃霍尔在那天晚上学会了用苹果电脑,并且承认道:"在发明这台电脑的聪明小伙子面前,我突然感觉自己老了,而且落伍了。"

Warhol loved technology. In the summer of 1985, he was given his first Amiga 1000 home computer by Commodore International and enthusiastically signed on with the company as a brand ambassador. Later that year, while visiting Sean Lennon and Yoko Ono for a birthday party, Warhol wrote in his diary about "a kid there setting up the Apple computer that Sean had gotten as a present, the Macintosh model. I said that once some man had been calling me a lot wanting to give me one, but that I'd never called him back or something, and then the kid looked up and said, 'Yeah, that was me. I'm Steve Jobs.'" That evening, Warhol learned to use the Apple computer and confessed, "I felt so old and out of it with this young whiz guy right there who helped invent it."

《广告：苹果》
*Ads: Apple*
1985

布上丙烯和丝印油墨
Acrylic and silkscreen ink on linen
55.9 × 55.9 cm

在 1985 年创作的系列作品中，沃霍尔以标志性的商业广告为主题，涵盖了从皮草大衣到好莱坞电影等广告。自 1950 年代起，沃霍尔就深谙广告的重要性，并对女性时装和配饰的流行趋势了如指掌。在这幅画作中，沃霍尔为可可·香奈儿（Coco Chanel）广受欢迎的香奈儿 5 号香水瓶重新配上鲜艳的色彩，赋予这款经典产品极具当代性的造型与神韵。香奈儿公司非常喜欢这件作品，最终选择用这件作品为香水做市场宣传。

For a 1985 series, Warhol selected several iconic commercial advertisements, ranging from ads for fur coats to Hollywood motion pictures. Warhol had understood the importance of advertising since the 1950s and was skilled in illustrating the latest trends in women's fashion and accessories. In this painting, Warhol reconfigures the bottle of Coco Chanel's hugely popular fragrance CHANEL N°5 in bright colors, giving this classic product a contemporary look and feel. CHANEL liked it so much that they eventually used the image to market the perfume.

纽约 Esquire 公司
Esquire, Inc., New York
《杂志广告（香奈儿 5 号香水，
〈Esquire〉杂志，1955 年 1 月刊）》
*Magazine Advertisement (CHANEL
N°5, Esquire magazine, January 1955)*
1955

涂布纸上油墨印刷
Printed ink on coated paper
33.5 × 25.7 cm

《广告：香奈儿》
*Ads: CHANEL*
1985

布上丙烯和丝印油墨
Acrylic and silkscreen ink on linen
55.9 × 55.9 cm

WARHOL REMIXED   297

1985年，沃霍尔新成立的安迪·沃霍尔电视制作公司，出品了《安迪·沃霍尔十五分钟访谈》访谈节目。这个节奏轻快的节目是他与刚成立几年的 MTV 全球音乐电视台合作的成果，其中心思想是"今天每个人只有 15 秒的机会，所以要抓紧了"。每期节目都围绕着纽约的音乐、视觉艺术、时尚与夜生活展开，探索属于这个时代的文化。沃霍尔对自己多年来打造的荧幕形象充满自信，他不仅作为节目的嘉宾，更担纲主持人大梁。沃霍尔每集会邀请他的友人轮流出镜，例如歌星黛比·哈里和模特瑞莉·霍尔。令人遗憾的是，《安迪·沃霍尔十五分钟访谈》总共只播出了 5 集，随着沃霍尔 1987 年的意外去世，该节目最后一集以对沃霍尔的特别致敬画下了句点。

In 1985, Warhol's new company, Andy Warhol T.V. Productions, developed *Andy Warhol's Fifteen Minutes*. A fast-paced show co-produced with the young music video cable network MTV, its guiding philosophy was "Today you only get fifteen seconds. So make it good." Through each episode's theme, the show collaged music, visual arts, fashion, nightlife, and New York City to explore the cultural zeitgeist. Confident in the onscreen persona he had cultivated over the years, Warhol did not just feature as a guest on the show, but embraced his role as host. Warhol appeared in every episode alongside friends such as singer Debbie Harry and model Jerry Hall. Sadly, *Andy Warhol's Fifteen Minutes* only lasted five episodes. The final episode paid special tribute to the artist after his unexpected death in 1987.

《安迪·沃霍尔十五分钟访谈
（第 4 集）》
*Andy Warhol's Fifteen Minutes
(episode 4)*
1987

1 英寸彩色有声录像带
1-inch videotape, color, sound
30'

《安迪·沃霍尔十五分钟访谈
（第 4 集）》
*Andy Warhol's Fifteen Minutes
(episode 4)*
1987

1 英寸彩色有声录像带
1-inch videotape, color, sound
30'

《安迪·沃霍尔电视秀
（第 1 季，第 10 集）》
*Andy Warhol's T.V.
(season 1, episode 10)*
1981

¾ 英寸彩色有声录像带
¾-inch videotape, color, sound
30'

# 非物质
## THE IMMATERIAL

直到去世之前，沃霍尔始终坚持经典波普主题的创作，在艺术生涯晚期亦涉足抽象和概念艺术。"氧化""迷彩"和"罗夏墨迹测验"等系列作品体现了沃霍尔对全新非具象美学的零星探索，以及他对"崇高性"这种超越自然的宏伟力量的兴趣。神秘主义对沃霍尔来说并不是陌生的主题，毕竟他成长于虔诚的拜占庭礼天主教家庭，且终其一生都保持着去教堂礼拜的习惯。1968年，遭瓦莱丽·索拉纳斯枪击几乎殒命之后，沃霍尔作品中的精神性以及惧怕死亡的线索变得越发清晰。《无形的雕塑》（1985）是沃霍尔晚期愈趋概念化的表演作品，在实行此项目的一个月内，他每晚都在空无一物的雕塑台座旁呆立不动。这件作品也体现了沃霍尔艺术中非物质性的"灵韵"，嘲讽了艺术与艺术家之间看似不可分割的联系。与上述抽象作品形成鲜明对比的则是沃霍尔的"神话"系列和自画像系列，这些作品将沃霍尔升华为美国的神话或圣人，随着其1987年的突然离世，沃霍尔也的确变成了美国的传奇人物。

While Warhol continued to represent traditional Pop subjects until his death, the artist also turned towards abstraction and conceptual art at the end of his career. Series such as Oxidation, Camouflage, and Rorschach show Warhol toying with new types of nonfigurative beauty that hint at the sublime — a term sometimes used to describe the vastness of the supernatural. No stranger to the mystical, Warhol was raised in a deeply religious Byzantine Catholic home and remained a church-goer his entire life. After the artist was shot by Valerie Solanas and nearly died in 1968, his spirituality and fear of death grew more apparent in his art. In a late work of conceptual nature, he performed his *Invisible Sculpture* (1985), during which he stood motionless next to an empty pedestal every night for a month. This work commented on the immaterial aura of Warhol's art, poking fun at the inseparable association between art and artist. In contrast to these abstract works, Warhol's Myths series and self-portraits elevate him as an American myth or saint, which he would later become after his unexpected passing in 1987.

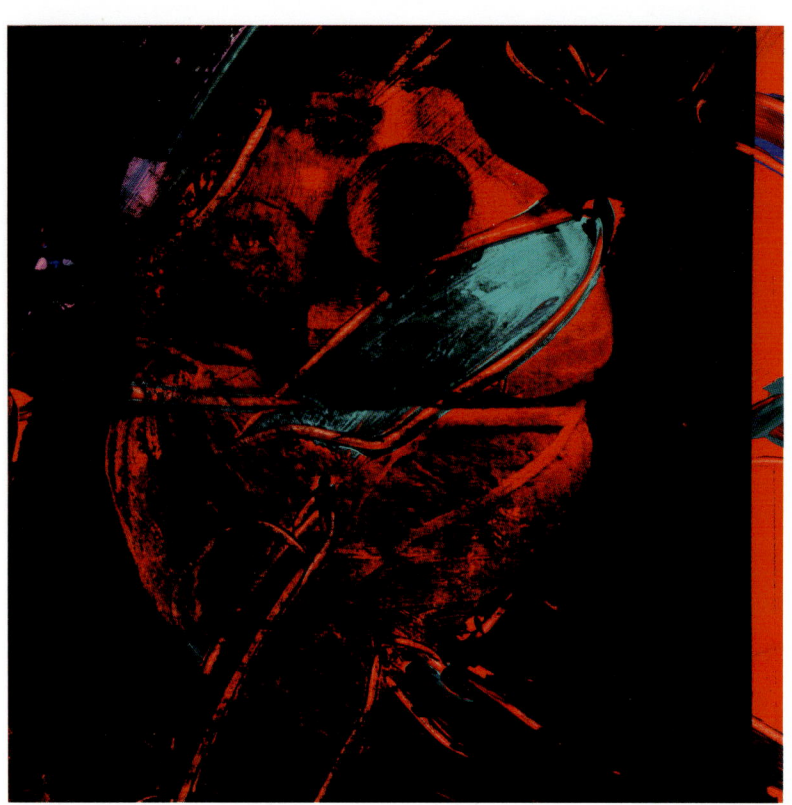 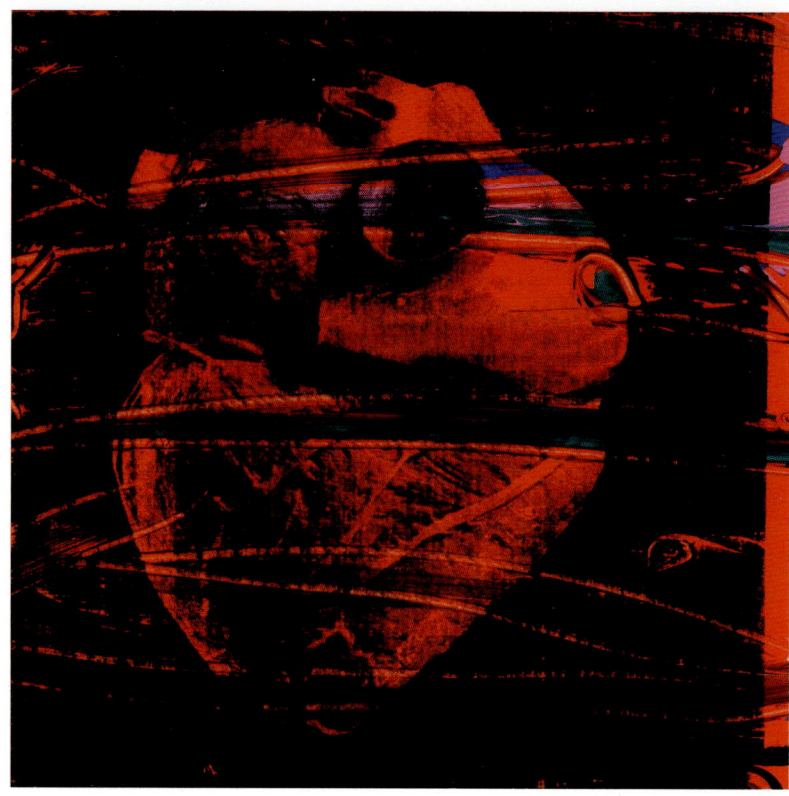

《人类心脏》
*Human Heart*
约 ca. 1979

布上丙烯和丝印油墨
Acrylic and silkscreen ink on canvas
55.9 × 55.9 cm

《人类心脏》
*Human Heart*
约 ca. 1979

布上丙烯和丝印油墨
Acrylic and silkscreen ink on canvas
55.9 × 55.9 cm

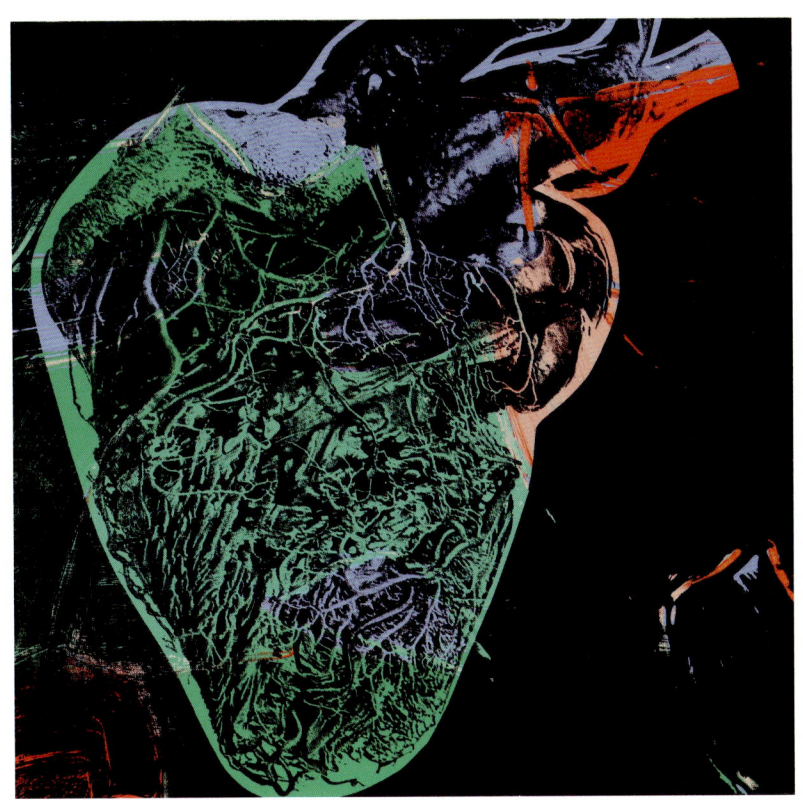
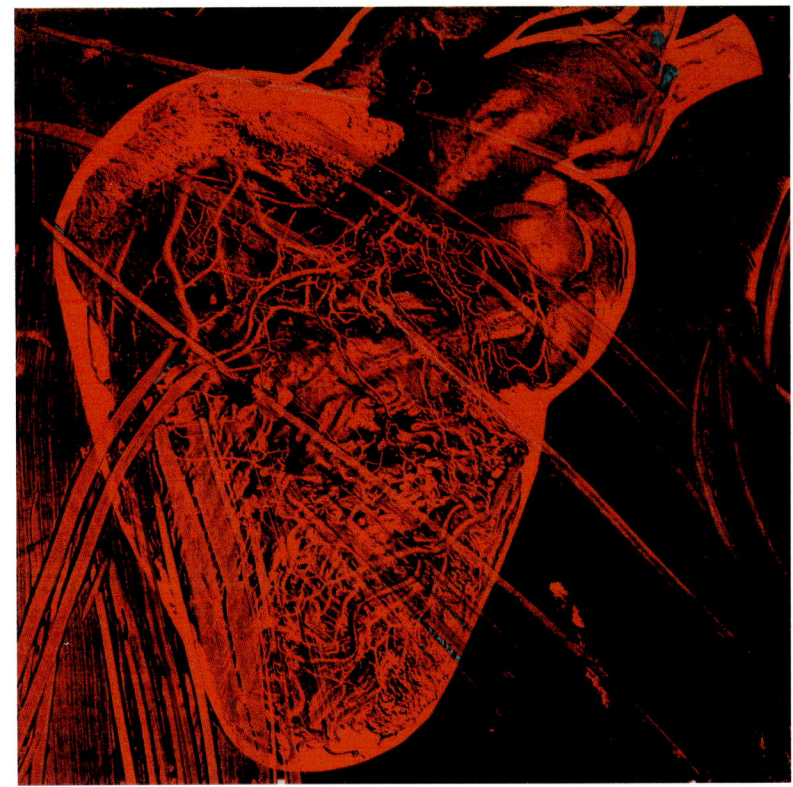

《人类心脏》
*Human Heart*
约 ca. 1979

布上丙烯和丝印油墨
Acrylic and silkscreen ink on canvas
55.9 × 55.9 cm

《人类心脏》
*Human Heart*
约 ca. 1979

布上丙烯和丝印油墨
Acrylic and silkscreen ink on canvas
55.9 × 55.9 cm

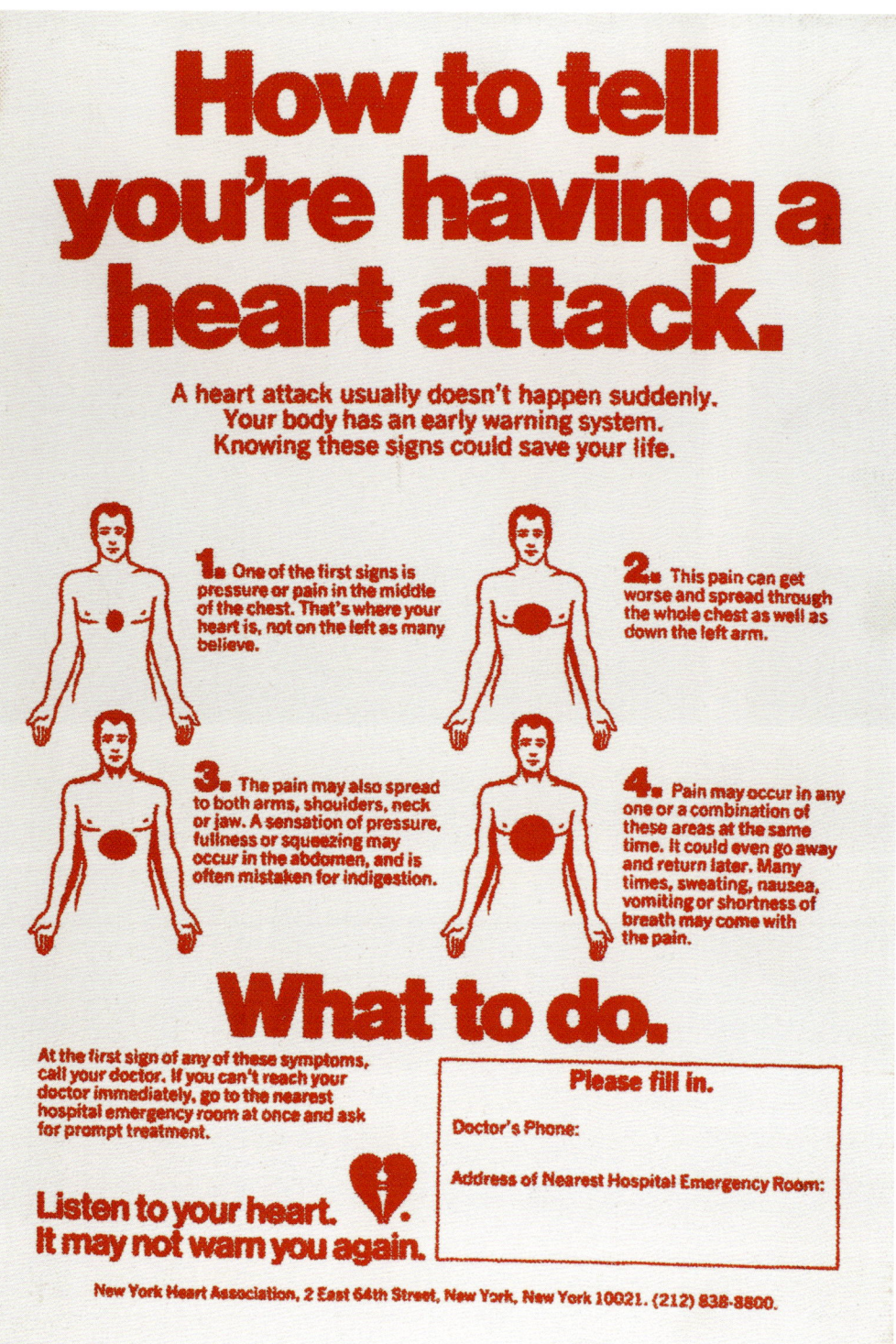

1968 年，差点命丧瓦莱丽·索拉纳斯之手后，沃霍尔余生都受到恐惧与偏执的困扰。子弹损伤了他的肺、脾、胃、肝和食道，在此后的岁月里，沃霍尔始终对自己的身体状况忧心忡忡，依靠私人教练、疗愈水晶和教堂祷告维持健康。在这些人类心脏的丝网印刷作品中，沃霍尔随性挥洒颜料，使它们充满活力，或许同时也是在暗示天主教忠诚的圣心。1980 年代，他还创作了一些小幅心形糖果盒绘画作品作为情人节礼物，其中还包括一个令人"心悸"的版本以提高大家对心脏病的认知。1987 年，沃霍尔因胆囊手术失败意外去世。

After nearly being killed in 1968 by Valerie Solanas, Warhol was plagued by fear and paranoia for the rest of his life. The gun's bullet had damaged his lungs, spleen, stomach, liver, and esophagus. For the rest of his life, Warhol's health remained a concern, and he relied on a personal trainer, healing crystals, and visits to church to preserve his fitness. Warhol created these silkscreens of human hearts with a gestural application of paint, giving them vibrancy and perhaps alluding to the Sacred Heart, a symbol of devotion among Catholics. In the 1980s, he made smaller paintings of heart-shaped candy boxes as Valentine's Day gifts, including a more chilling version related to heart attack awareness. In 1987, Warhol would die unexpectedly from a failed gallbladder procedure.

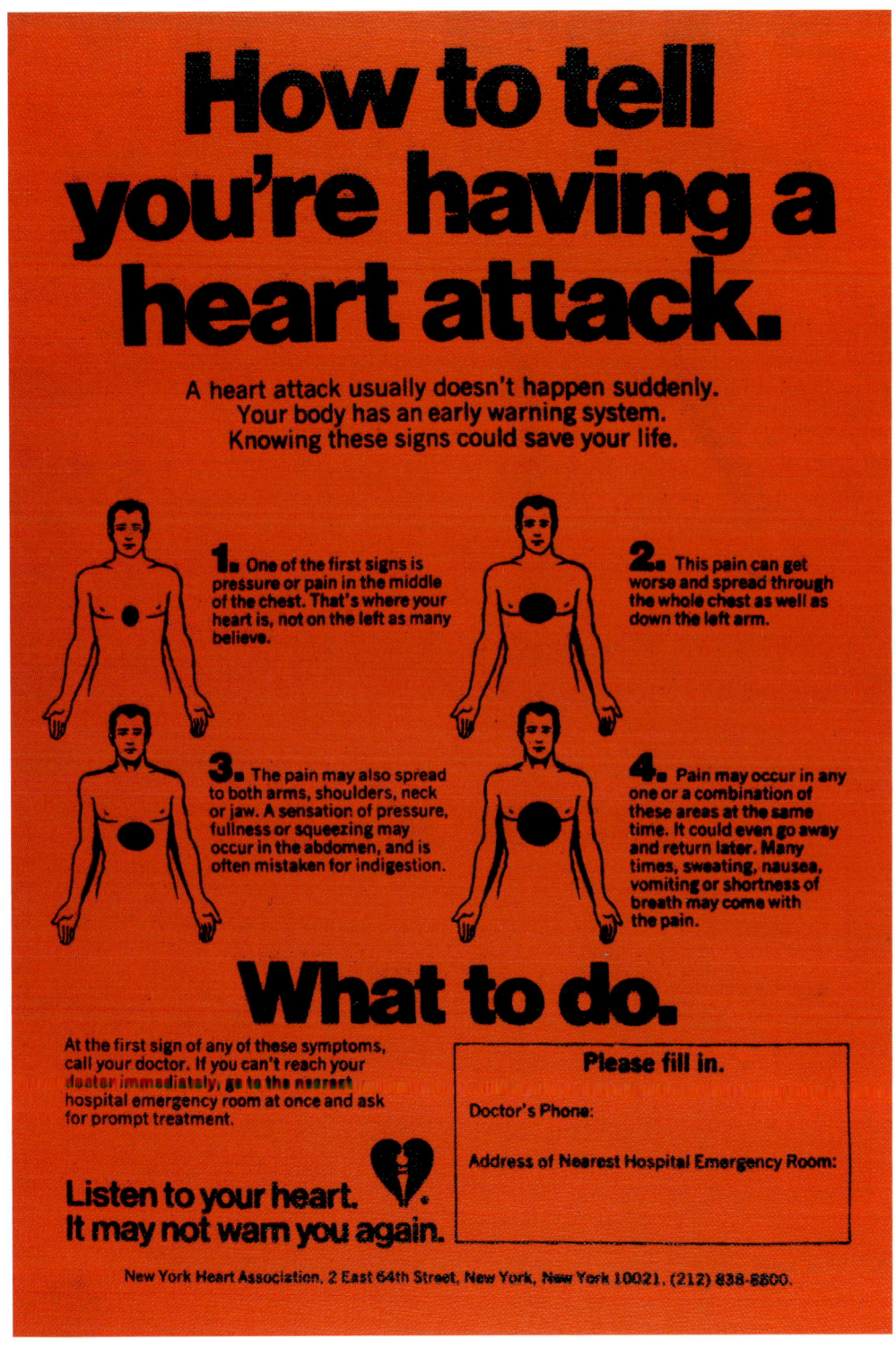

《情人节心脏健康宣传广告
（……"心动"的感觉）》
Valentine's Hearts Ads (...Having a
Heart Attack)
1982—1983

布上丙烯和丝印油墨
Acrylic and silkscreen ink on linen
38.1 × 25.4 cm

《情人节心脏健康宣传广告
（……"心动"的感觉）》
Valentine's Hearts Ads (...Having a
Heart Attack)
1982—1983

布上丙烯和丝印油墨
Acrylic and silkscreen ink on linen
38.1 × 25.4 cm

THE IMMATERIAL

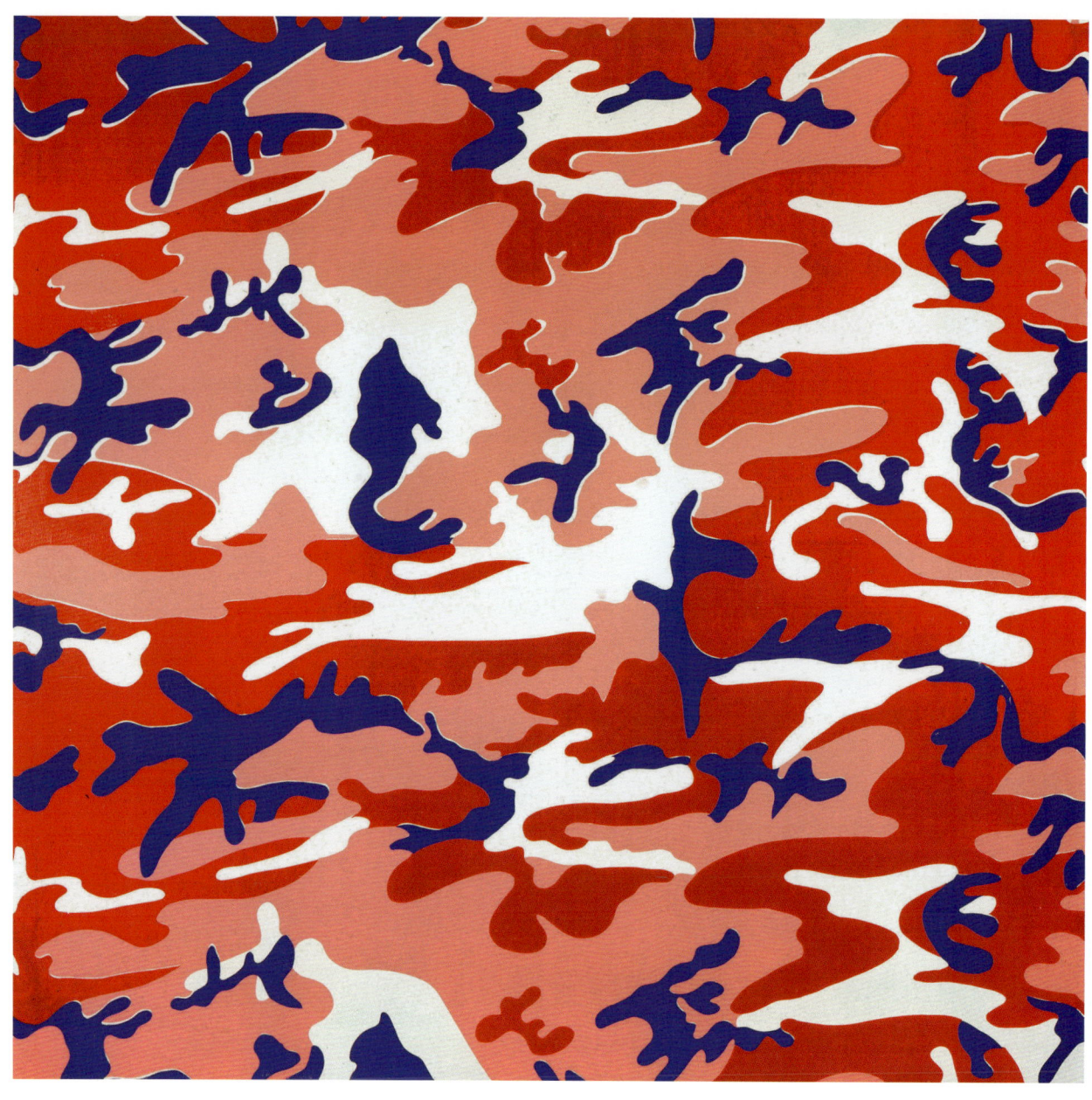

据称,沃霍尔曾询问他的工作室助手:"我该如何画得抽象,却又不完全抽象?"迷彩对于沃霍尔来说既是一种抽象图样,同时又易于识别且能引发丰富的联想。迷彩图案原是艺术家在 20 世纪初出于军事用途而发明的,最初用来隐藏装备,后用于设计军装。沃霍尔一开始将迷彩面料用作丝网印刷的承印材质。至于绘画作品,他常选择亮眼的色彩来与标准的军用色调形成鲜明的对比。它们既能够隐藏事物,也能揭露事物。沃霍尔将迷彩作为他许多作品的背景或是覆盖层,其中包括自画像和"最后的晚餐"系列中的作品。

Warhol reportedly asked his studio assistants, "What can I do that would be abstract but not really abstract?" The camouflage pattern allowed Warhol to work with both an abstract pattern and an immediately recognizable image that drew rich associations. Camouflage was originally created by artists for military use at the beginning of the twentieth century, first for concealing equipment and later for uniform design. Warhol began this project with actual camouflage fabric as the basis for his silkscreens. For the paintings, he often chose lush colors, which contrasted immensely with the standard military print. They had the power to conceal and reveal. Warhol used camouflage as the background and overlay for many of his works, including self-portraits and paintings from The Last Supper series.

《迷彩》
*Camouflage*
1986

布上丙烯和丝印油墨
Acrylic and silkscreen ink on linen
203.2 × 203.2 cm

《迷彩》
*Camouflage*
1986

布上丙烯和丝印油墨
Acrylic and silkscreen ink on linen
203.8 × 193.7 cm

沃霍尔先在一半画布上用颜料作画，再将另一半折叠于上，通过这样的方式得到如同镜像一般的画面。与他同时期的其他作品类似，《罗夏墨迹测验》对抽象和具象主义进行了嫁接。沃霍尔的灵感来自瑞士精神科医生赫尔曼·罗夏提出的著名的人格测试实验。最原始的"罗夏测验"由十个标准化墨迹组成。医生通过患者对于标准墨迹的不同反应对其人格进行心理评估。沃霍尔的《罗夏墨迹测验》在比例和设计上都与原始的墨迹图样有所不同，它们既是对罗夏墨迹图样的再次创作，亦是激发观众解读的抽象表达。

By applying paint to one half of his canvas and then folding the other half over it, Warhol printed a mirror image. Like other works of the same period, the Rorschach works bridge abstraction and representation. Warhol was inspired by the famous personality test developed by Swiss psychiatrist Hermann Rorschach. The original Rorschach test consisted of ten standardized inkblots. Individual responses to the standardized blots led to psychological assessments about a patient's personality. Warhol's paintings differ from the originals in both scale and design. When exhibited, these works become both reworkings of Rorschach's originals as well as abstract forms that invite interpretation.

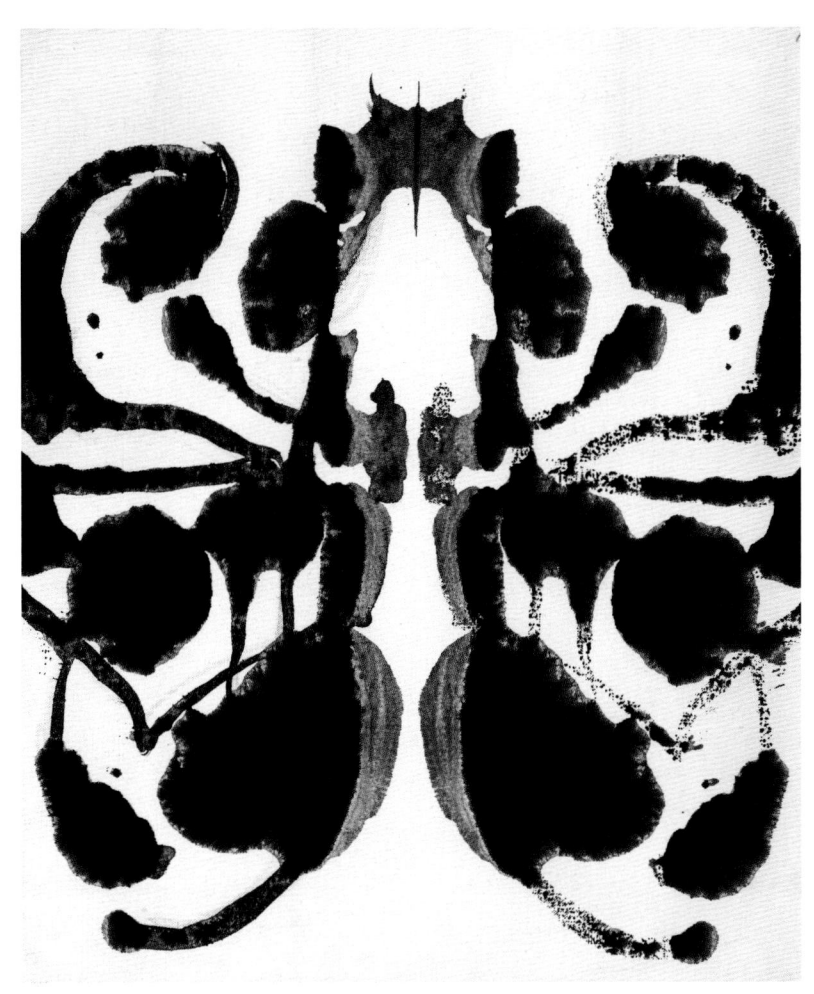

《罗夏墨迹测验》
*Rorschach*
1984

布上丙烯和丝印油墨
Acrylic and silkscreen ink on linen
50.8 × 40.6 cm

《罗夏墨迹测验》
*Rorschach*
1984

布上丙烯和丝印油墨
Acrylic and silkscreen ink on linen
50.8 × 40.6 cm

THE IMMATERIAL 311

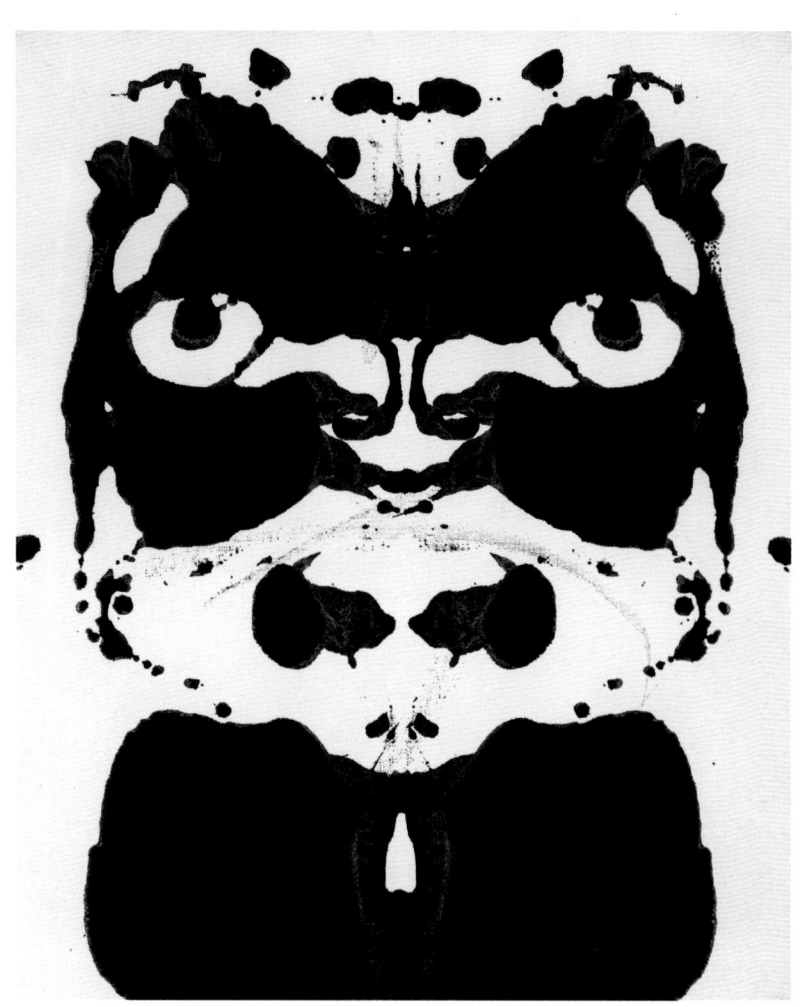

《罗夏墨迹测验》  　　　　　《罗夏墨迹测验》
*Rorschach*　　　　　　　　　*Rorschach*
1984　　　　　　　　　　　　1984

布上丙烯和丝印油墨　　　　　布上丙烯和丝印油墨
Acrylic and silkscreen ink on linen　Acrylic and silkscreen ink on linen
50.8 × 40.6 cm　　　　　　　50.8 × 40.6 cm

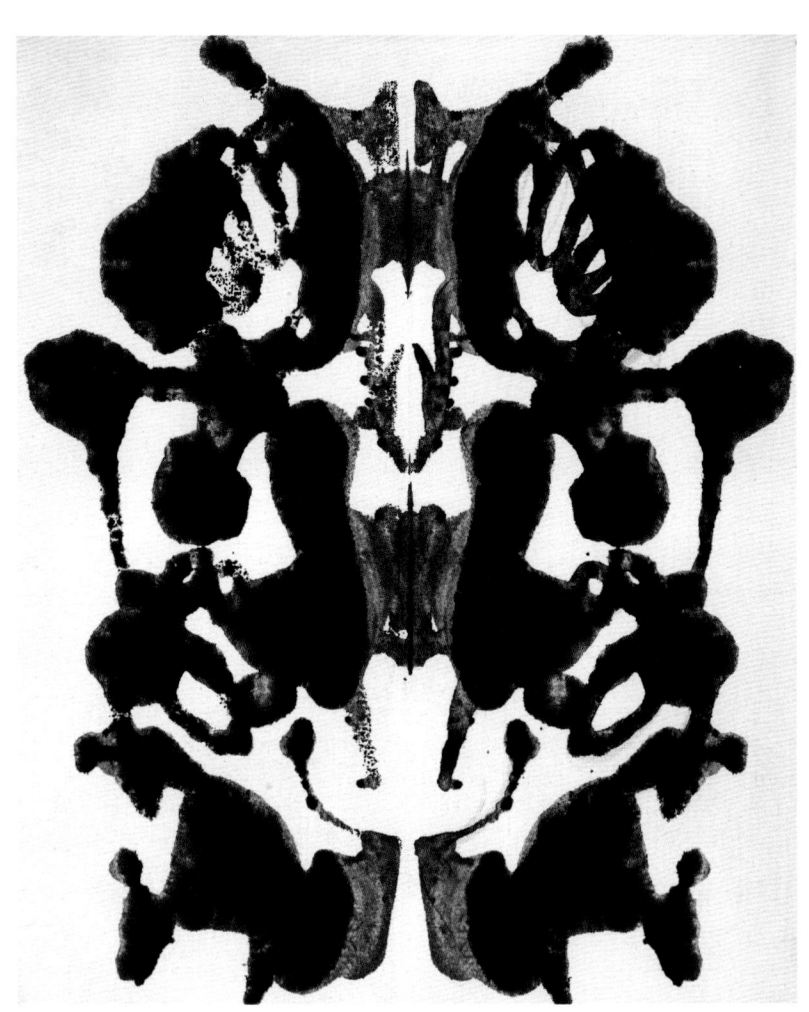

《罗夏墨迹测验》
*Rorschach*
1984

布上丙烯和丝印油墨
Acrylic and silkscreen ink on linen
50.8 × 40.6 cm

《罗夏墨迹测验》
*Rorschach*
1984

布上丙烯和丝印油墨
Acrylic and silkscreen ink on linen
50.8 × 40.6 cm

沃霍尔在"商业艺术"上成功的若干最佳例证，都可以在他1981年春天创作的"神话"系列中找到。采用丝网印刷的想法最早由艺术品经纪人罗纳德·费尔德曼提出，沃霍尔创作所采用的多数素材都由他提供，他还希望将备受欢迎的作品卖给那些有意要购买家庭装饰的赞助人。此系列作品基本重复采用了沃霍尔1960年代一些作品的主题，比如梦露和猫王，但缺乏与原作同样的创造性、强烈的感情和严肃性。该系列中的一幅自画像《阴影》将美国传奇人物与他个人的形象并置，同时也从他的偶像马塞尔·杜尚类似的自画像中汲取了灵感。

Some of the best examples of Warhol's "business art" are found in the Myths series, made in the spring of 1981. The screen prints were initiated by art dealer Ronald Feldman, who found most of the images for Warhol and intended the popular works to be sold to patrons looking for décor. The subject matter is essentially reused from 1960s Warhol works, such as the Marilyns and Elvises, but they lack the same creativity, intensity, and seriousness. A self-portrait in this series, *The Shadow*, places the legend of Warhol alongside these American myths and references similar self-portraits by Warhol's hero Marcel Duchamp.

《神话：阴影》
*Myths: The Shadow*
1981

莱诺克斯博物馆纸板上丝网印刷和钻石粉末
Screen print with diamond dust on Lenox Museum Board
96.5 × 96.7 cm

《神话：明星》
*Myths: The Star*
1981

莱诺克斯博物馆纸板上丝网印刷和钻石粉末
Screen print with diamond dust on Lenox Museum Board
96.5 × 96.7 cm

THE IMMATERIAL

《神话:山姆大叔》
*Myths: Uncle Sam*
1981

莱诺克斯博物馆纸板上丝网印刷和钻石粉末
Screen print with diamond dust on Lenox Museum Board
96.5 × 96.7 cm

《神话:超人》
*Myths: Superman*
1981

莱诺克斯博物馆纸板上丝网印刷和钻石粉末
Screen print with diamond dust on Lenox Museum Board
96.5 × 96.7 cm

《神话:女巫》
*Myths: The Witch*
1981

莱诺克斯博物馆纸板上丝网印刷和钻石粉末
Screen print with diamond dust on Lenox Museum Board
96.5 × 96.7 cm

《神话:保姆》
*Myths: Mammy*
1981

莱诺克斯博物馆纸板上丝网印刷和钻石粉末
Screen print with diamond dust on Lenox Museum Board
96.5 × 96.7 cm

"Mammy"（保姆）一词是美国对黑人家佣带有种族歧视色彩的称呼，这种刻板形象可以追溯到奴隶制时期。在那个时期，南方的黑人妇女曾被迫在富裕白人家庭中做家务和照顾孩子。南北战争结束后，黑人家佣形象便成了流行文化中的固定角色，通常被描绘成快活的、充满母性的中年妇女，并以此来粉饰奴隶制的残暴和十九世纪末至二十世纪黑人家佣备受歧视的生活状况，而那时，这往往是黑人妇女能找到的唯一工作。在《汤姆叔叔的小屋》《乱世佳人》《汤姆和杰里》等作品中可以看到这类刻板的保姆形象。

丝网印刷作品《神话：保姆》是根据沃霍尔为女演员兼歌手西尔维娅·威廉姆斯拍摄的宝丽来照片创作的，当时她正在百老汇的音乐剧《One Mo' Time》中担任主演。作为"神话"系列的一幅作品，它突出了流行文化幻想中的盲点和隐藏于此形象之后令人不安的历史。

The mammy is a racist American stereotype of a black domestic worker that dates back to the age of slavery, during which black women in the south were forced to do housework and childcare in the homes of wealthy white families. After the Civil War, the mammy became a stock character in pop culture, often portrayed as a jovial, maternal, middle-aged woman. This fiction was used to whitewash the brutality of slavery and the discriminatory conditions of black domestic workers in the late nineteenth and twentieth centuries, when this was often the only work black women could find. Famous examples of the mammy stereotype can be seen in Uncle Tom's Cabin, Gone with the Wind, and Tom and Jerry.

The silkscreen Myths: Mammy was created from a staged Polaroid Warhol took of the actress and singer Sylvia Williams, who, at the time, was starring in the off-Broadway musical One Mo' Time. As part of the Myths series, it underscores the blind spots of pop cultural fantasies and the fraught histories of such archetypes.

《神话:胡迪·都迪》
*Myths: Howdy Doody*
1981

莱诺克斯博物馆纸板上丝网印刷和钻石粉末
Screen print with diamond dust on Lenox Museum Board
96.5 × 96.7 cm

《神话:德古拉》
*Myths: Dracula*
1981

莱诺克斯博物馆纸板上丝网印刷和钻石粉末
Screen print with diamond dust on Lenox Museum Board
96.5 × 96.7 cm

《神话：米老鼠》
*Myths: Mickey Mouse*
1981

莱诺克斯博物馆纸板上丝网印刷和钻石粉末
Screen print with diamond dust on Lenox Museum Board
96.5 × 96.7 cm

《神话：圣诞老人》
*Myths: Santa Claus*
1981

莱诺克斯博物馆纸板上丝网印刷和钻石粉末
Screen print with diamond dust on Lenox Museum Board
96.5 × 96.7 cm

THE IMMATERIAL   319

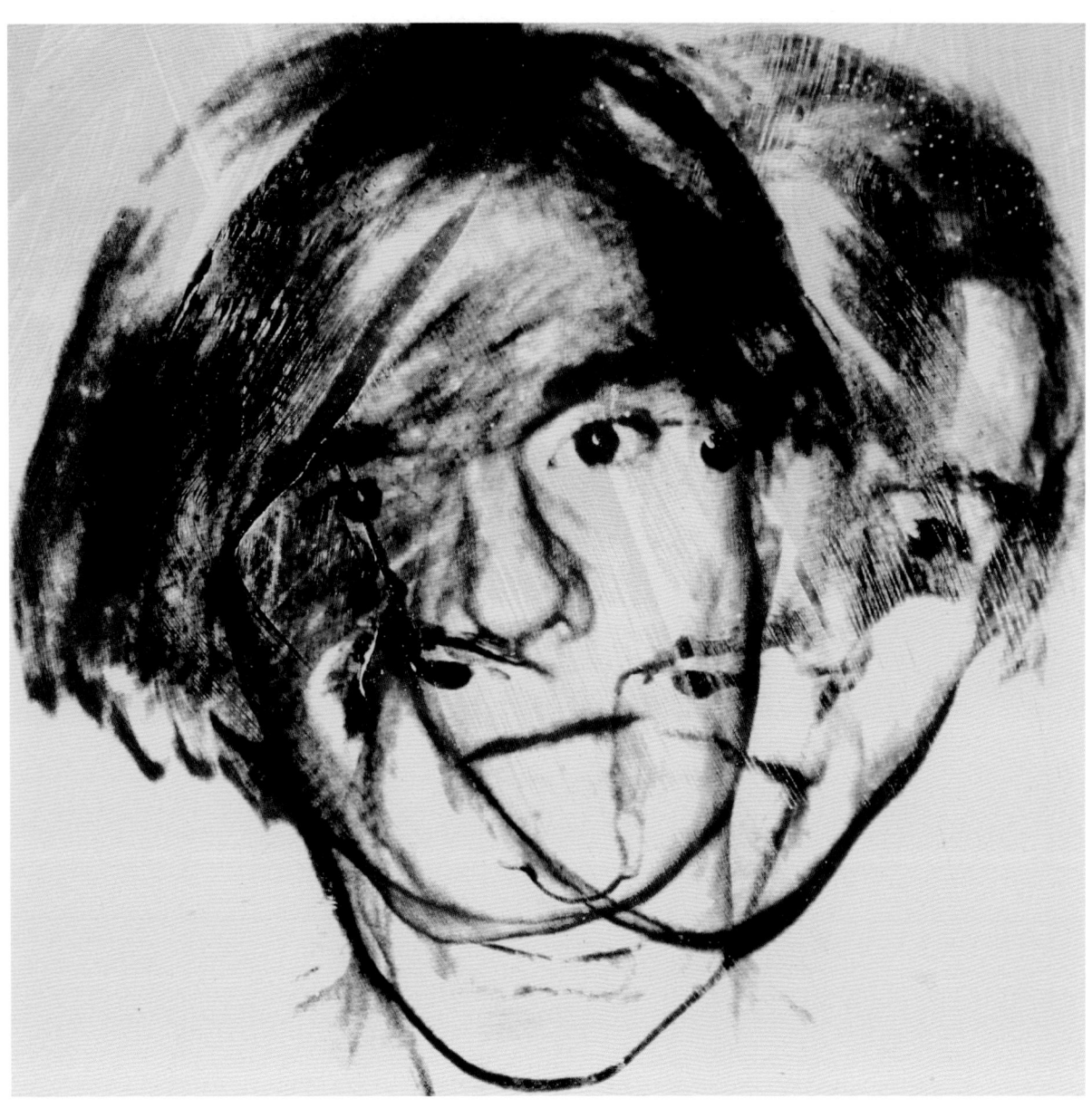

在职业生涯里,沃霍尔经常出现在自己的绘画和摄影作品中。1978 年,沃霍尔创作了 62 幅自画像,其中包括尺寸为 101.6 × 101.6 cm 的这组作品,它们与许多为彰显社会地位而委托沃霍尔创作的作品大小相似。此时期,还创作了一款以艺术家的脸为主题的壁纸。另外,他还叠加使用三张宝丽来相片创作出奇特的自画像。叠加的照片看起来像是在无声地移动,不禁让人回想起沃霍尔 1960 年代早期创作的"试镜"系列影像作品。

Warhol frequently depicted himself in paintings and photographs throughout his career. In 1978, Warhol created a total of 62 self-portraits, including this pair of 101.6 × 101.6 cm paintings, similar to the commissions many acquired for social status. Warhol superimposed three Polaroid photos to create these unusual portraits. The layered images give a sensation of silent movement, reminiscent of his early Screen Test films from the 1960s. A wallpaper featuring the artist's face was also made during this period.

《自画像》
*Self-Portrait*
1978

布上丙烯和丝印油墨
Acrylic and silkscreen ink on linen
101.6 × 101.6 cm

《自画像》
*Self-Portrait*
1978

布上丙烯和丝印油墨
Acrylic and silkscreen ink on linen
101.6 × 101.6 cm

从1961年至1963年的"死亡与灾难"系列开始，沃霍尔的作品中出现了越来越多的死亡元素。1968年，遭瓦莱丽·索拉纳斯枪击之后，死亡主题在沃霍尔的创作中开始带有个人化色彩。在1978年的一幅自画像里，沃霍尔描绘了自己被掐住脖子的样子，虽然此作品要表达的含义并不明确，但这无疑与他对死亡的恐惧有关。该系列的其他自画像则采用了独特的运笔和笔触，以及重叠的丝印技法展现运动中的混沌状态。

While Warhol's more morbid compositions began between 1961–1963 with the Death and Disaster series, the theme of death turned personal after he was shot in 1968 by Valerie Solanas. The 1978 self-portrait depicting Warhol being strangled seems ambiguous, yet the connections to the artist's fear of death are difficult to ignore. Other self-portraits in this series use gestural brushstrokes and overlapping silkscreens to show chaos through movement.

《自画像》
*Self-Portrait*
1978

布上丙烯和丝印油墨
Acrylic and silkscreen ink on linen
40.6 × 33 cm

《勒住喉咙的自画像》
*Self-Portrait Strangulation*
1978

布上丙烯和丝印油墨
Acrylic and silkscreen ink on linen
40.6 × 33 cm

1981年,沃霍尔的"美元标志"系列绘画与版画象征着这个重要符号的回归,该符号最早出现在其1960年代初创作的许多波普作品中。1962年,在他第一次尝试丝网印刷时,沃霍尔制作了几张一元美钞的作品。在后来的作品中,沃霍尔将金钱这个广泛的概念缩减为其最基本的象征元素。在此时期,他还创作了枪、刀、十字架等作品,同样也使用了要素符号代表当代社会的暴力与宗教。沃霍尔制作了多个版本的美元标志,从小型的单一图像到印有多行图像的大型画布。这些作品及其相关的艺术家书籍以一种直截了当的方式,激发观众思考金钱在我们的文化中所扮演的角色。这些作品同样也充满了戏谑的讽刺,反映了艺术世界中的经济体制。

In 1981, Warhol's Dollar Sign paintings and prints marked a return to the powerful symbol that had originally appeared in many of his Pop works in the early 1960s. In 1962, during his first use of the silkscreen process, Warhol produced several paintings of American one-dollar bills. For the later works, Warhol reduced the broad idea of money reduced to its most elemental symbol. During this period, he created the Guns, Knives, and Crosses paintings, which use key icons to represent violence and religion in contemporary society. Warhol made several versions of the Dollar Signs, from small single images to large canvases with the image printed in multiple rows. In their straightforward manner, these paintings and a related artist book invite the viewer to contemplate the role of money in our culture. They also express a playful irony that reflects the economics of the art world.

《带有美元标志的书》
*Dollar Sign Book*
年份未知 n.d.

象牙纸上石墨
Graphite on ivory paper
17.8 × 18.4 × 1.9 cm

《美元标志》
*Dollar Sign*
1981

布上丙烯和丝印油墨
Acrylic and silkscreen ink on linen
228.6 × 177.8 cm

THE IMMATERIAL

《美元标志》
*Dollar Sign*
1981

布上丙烯和丝印油墨
Acrylic and silkscreen ink on linen
228.6 × 177.8 cm

《美元标志》
*Dollar Sign*
1981

布上丙烯和丝印油墨
Acrylic and silkscreen ink on linen
228.6 × 177.8 cm

THE IMMATERIAL 327

沃霍尔的"头骨"系列画作常被视为"死亡的象征",令人回想起数百年来反复提醒我们自身死亡的艺术传统。拉丁语"Memento mori"大致可译为"记住你不是永生的"或"人终有一死"。1968年,深受精神病困扰的作家瓦莱丽·索拉纳斯因剧本丢失而精神失常,对着沃霍尔的腹部开枪。被枪击之后,沃霍尔真切感受到了人之将死的滋味。据报道,沃霍尔在被送到医院时便被宣布了死亡,但在经过五小时的手术抢救后终于脱离了生命危险。经过近两个月的治疗,沃霍尔最终出院,但在之后几年仍需要接受进一步的手术治疗。

Warhol's Skull paintings have often been seen as *memento mori*, recalling the centuries-long tradition of art that reminds us of our mortality. *Memento mori*, from Latin, translates roughly to "remember that you are mortal" or "remember you will die." Warhol's own near-death experience happened in 1968, when troubled writer Valerie Solanas shot Warhol in the abdomen from frustration around her lost script. After reportedly being declared dead upon arrival at the hospital, Warhol's life was saved during five hours of surgery. After nearly two months, he was released from the hospital but required further surgeries over the following years.

《头骨》
*Skull*
1976

布上丙烯和丝印油墨
Acrylic and silkscreen ink on linen
183.2 × 204.5 cm

《头骨》
*Skull*
1976

布上丙烯和丝印油墨
Acrylic and silkscreen ink on linen
183.2 × 204.5 cm

该系列自画像创作于沃霍尔去世前几个月,画面中的他面容枯槁,凝视着观众。许多观众和评论家倾向于将这这幅骨瘦如柴的面孔视为死亡的象征,提醒人类必有一死的命运。在创造了数十年的名人肖像后,沃霍尔以相似的打光定格自己,利用深色背景凸显其著名的标志特征——如光冕一般,看起来令人不安的假发。

Painted just a few months before his death, Warhol made a series of self-portraits depicting himself looking gaunt, intensely staring at the viewer with a blank expression. Many viewers and critics alike regard these skeletal faces as *memento mori*, reminders of human mortality. After decades of painting celebrity portraits, Warhol frames himself in a similar light, using dark background contrast to emphasize his halo-like fright wig – an iconic feature of his fame.

《自画像》
*Self-Portrait*
1986

布上丙烯和丝印油墨
Acrylic and silkscreen ink on linen
203.2 × 193 cm

《自画像》
*Self-Portrait*
1986

布上丙烯和丝印油墨
Acrylic and silkscreen ink on linen
274.3 × 274.3 × 3.8 cm

# 展览现场
**INSTALLATION VIEWS**

UCCA 尤伦斯当代艺术中心的"成为安迪·沃霍尔"展览是迄今为止安迪·沃霍尔的艺术人生在中国最为全面的展示。此次展览 2021 年 7 月 3 日至 10 月 10 日在 UCCA 北京呈现,并于 2021 年 11 月 6 日至 2022 年 3 月 6 日巡展至上海 UCCA Edge。附图是 UCCA 北京展览现场的精彩回顾。

"Becoming Andy Warhol" at UCCA Center for Contemporary Art was the most comprehensive exhibition of the artist's work organized in China to date. It was held from July 3 to October 10, 2021, at UCCA Beijing and from November 6, 2021, to March 6, 2022, at UCCA Edge in Shanghai. The following installation views document the exhibition at UCCA Beijing.

# 参考文献 Bibliography

## 书籍
## Monographs

保罗·亚历山大,《死亡与灾难:沃霍尔帝国的兴起与安迪的财富追逐》
Alexander, Paul. *Death and Disaster: The Rise of the Warhol Empire and the Race for Andy's Millions*. New York, NY: Villard, 1994.

考利·安杰尔,《安迪·沃霍尔试镜:安迪·沃霍尔电影作品》(作品全集,第一卷)
Angell, Callie. *Andy Warhol Screen Tests: The Films of Andy Warhol. Catalogue Raisonné, Volume 1*. New York: Harry N. Abrams, 2006.

斯特凡纳·阿坎编,《沃霍尔现场:安迪·沃霍尔作品中的音乐与舞蹈》
Aquin, Stéphane, ed. *Warhol Live: Music and Dance in Andy Warhol's Work*. Montreal: Montreal Museum of Fine Arts / Prestel Publishing, 2008.

浅井隆编,《安迪·沃霍尔的工厂摄影:比利·内姆的工厂照片》
Asai, Takashi, ed. *Andy Warhol's Factory Photos: Factory Foto by Billy Name*, London: Art Data; Tokyo: Uplink, 1996.

恩斯特·贝耶勒,《沃霍尔:系列作品和单件作品》
Beyeler, Ernst. *Warhol: Series and Singles*. Riehen, Basel: Fondation Beyeler; New Haven, CT: distributed by Yale University Press, 2000.

维克托·伯克里,《沃霍尔生平》
Bockris, Victor. *Warhol: The Biography*. London: Frederick Muller/Century Hutchinson, 1989.

大卫·布尔东,《沃霍尔》
Bourdon, David. *Warhol*. New York: Harry N. Abrams, 1989.

本杰明·H.D.布赫洛编,《安迪·沃霍尔:阴影与其他生命之象,安迪·沃霍尔诞辰记录》
Buchloh, Benjamin. H. D., ed. *Andy Warhol: Shadows and Other Signs of Life, Anniversary Notes for Andy Warhol*. Cologne: Walther König, 2008.

克劳迪娅·鲍尔,《安迪·沃霍尔》
Bauer, Claudia. *Andy Warhol*. Munich, Germany; New York: Prestel, 2004.

鲍勃·科拉切洛,《神圣的恐惧:安迪·沃霍尔小传》
Colacello, Bob. *Holy Terror: Andy Warhol Close Up*. New York: HarperCollins, 1990.

凯利·M.克雷萨普,《波普愚人:沃霍尔演绎天真》
Cresap, Kelly M. *Pop Trickster Fool: Warhol Performs Naiveté*. Urbana and Chicago: University of Illinois Press, 2004.

雷纳·克龙,《安迪·沃霍尔》(作品全集)
Crone, Rainer. *Andy Warhol*. (catalogue raisonné) New York: Praeger, 1970.

约翰·J.柯利,《图像的阴谋:安迪·沃霍尔,格哈德·里希特与冷战艺术》
Curley, John J. *A Conspiracy of Images: Andy Warhol, Gerhard Richter, and the Art of the Cold War*. New Haven, CT: Yale University Press, 2013.

阿瑟·C.丹托,《安迪·沃霍尔》
Danto, Arthur C. *Andy Warhol*. New Haven: Yale University Press, 2009.

简·D.迪伦贝格尔,《安迪·沃霍尔的宗教艺术》
Dillenberger, Jane D. *The Religious Art of Andy Warhol*. New York: Continuum, 1998.

珍妮弗·多伊尔,乔纳森·弗拉特利,何塞·E.穆尼奥斯编,《现:酷儿沃霍尔》
Doyle, Jennifer, Jonathan Flatley, and José E. Muñoz, eds. *Pop Out: Queer Warhol*. Durham and London: Duke University Press, 1996.

伊莎贝尔·C.迪弗雷纳,《15分钟的名望:我与安迪·沃霍尔的那些年》
Dufresne, Isabelle C. (a. k. a. Ultra Violet). *Famous For 15 Minutes: My Years With Andy Warhol*. Bloomington, IN: iUniverse, 1988.

纳特·芬克尔斯坦,《安迪·沃霍尔:工厂年间,1964–1967》
Finkelstein, Nat. *Andy Warhol: The Factory Years, 1964-1967*. New York, NY: St. Martins Press, 1989.

乔纳森·弗拉特利,《就像安迪·沃霍尔》
Flatley, Jonathan. *Like Andy Warhol*. Chicago, IL: University of Chicago Press, 2017.

马克·弗朗西斯,迪特尔·克普林,《安迪·沃霍尔绘画,1942–1987》
Francis, Mark and Dieter Koepplin. *Andy Warhol Drawings 1942-1987*. Boston, MA: Bulfinch Press, 1999.

文森特·弗里蒙特,《安迪·沃霍尔:人类最好的朋友》
Freemont, Vincent. *Andy Warhol: Man's Best Friend*. St. Louis: Lococo Fine Art, 2006.

乔治·弗赖,尼尔·普林茨,萨莉·金-内罗编,《安迪·沃霍尔作品全集,绘画与雕塑》(全五册)
Frei, George, Neil Printz, Sally King-Nero, eds. *The Andy Warhol Catalogue Raisonné, Paintings and Sculptures*. 5 vols. New York and London: Phaidon Press, 2002–2018.

莱斯利·弗罗威克等,《霍尔斯顿与沃霍尔:白银与绒皮》
Frowick, Lesley et al. *Halston & Warhol: Silver & Suede*. New York, NY: Harry N. Abrams, 2014.

加里·加雷尔斯编,《安迪·沃霍尔作品》
Garrels, Gary, ed. *The Work of Andy Warhol*. New York: Dia Art Foundation; Seattle: Bay Press, 1989.

肯尼思·戈德史密斯编,《我将是你的镜子:安迪·沃霍尔访谈选集》
Goldsmith, Kenneth, ed. *I'll Be Your Mirror: The Selected Andy Warhol Interviews*. New York: Carroll & Graf, 2004.

弗雷德·劳伦斯·吉莱斯,《舞会上的孤独者:安迪·沃霍尔的一生》
Guiles, Fred Lawrence. *Loner at the Ball: The Life of Andy Warhol*. London: Bantam Press, a division of Transworld Publishers, 1989.

布莱克·戈普尼克,《沃霍尔》
Gopnik, Blake. *Warhol*. New York: HarperCollins; London: Allen Lane, 2020.

布莱克·戈普尼克,德鲁·采巴,《爱,性,欲:安迪·沃霍尔绘画,1950–1962》
Gopnik, Blake and Drew Zeiba. *Andy Warhol. Love, Sex, and Desire. Drawings 1950–1962*. Cologne, Germany: Taschen, 2020.

安东尼·E.格鲁丁,《沃霍尔的工人阶级:波普艺术与平等主义》
Grudin, Anthony E. Warhol's *Working Class: Pop Art and Egalitarianism*. Chicago, IL: University of Chicago Press, 2017.

戴夫·希基,史蒂文·布鲁塔尔,《安迪·沃霍尔》
Hickey, Dave and Steven Bluttal. *Andy Warhol*. London, UK: Phaidon Press, 2006.

杰拉林·赫胥黎,格雷格·皮尔斯编,《安迪·沃霍尔的雀西女郎》
Huxley, Geralyn, and Greg Pierce, eds. *Andy Warhol's The Chelsea Girls*. New York: Distributed Art Publishers; Pittsburgh: The Andy Warhol Museum, 2018.

杰拉林·赫胥黎,马特·沃比肯,《安迪·沃霍尔的珍品》
Huxley, Geralyn, and Matt Wrbican. *Andy Warhol Treasures*. London: Goodman, 2009.

约瑟夫·D.凯特纳,《安迪·沃霍尔:最后十年》
Ketner II, Joseph D. *Andy Warhol: The Last Decade*. New York, NY: DelMonico Books/Prestel, 2009.

斯蒂芬·科赫,《仰望星空:安迪·沃霍尔的世界与电影》
重新修订版:《仰望星空:安迪·沃霍尔的人生,世界与电影》
Koch, Stephen. *Stargazer: Andy Warhol's World and His Films*. London: Calder and Boyars, 1974. Revised and updated as *Stargazer: The Life, World, and Films of Andy Warhol*. New York and London: Marion Boyars Publishers, 1991.

韦恩·科斯滕鲍姆,《安迪·沃霍尔》
Koestenbaum, Wayne. *Andy Warhol*. New York: Viking Penguin, A Lipper/Viking Book, 2001.

杰西·科恩布卢特,《波普前的沃霍尔》
Kornbluth, Jesse. *Pre-Pop Warhol*. New York: Panache Press, 1988.

萨拉·克拉耶夫斯基等,《安迪·沃霍尔:乔丹·D.施尼策尔家族基金会版画收藏》
Krajewski, Sara et al. *Andy Warhol: Prints: From the Collections of Jordan D. Schnitzer and his Family Foundation*. Portland, OR: Jordan Schnitzer Family Foundation, in association with Portland Art Museum; New York, NY: Distributed by Distributed Art Publishers, 2016.

马基亚·克雷默,《安迪·沃霍尔及其他:FBI的安迪·沃霍尔档案》
Kramer, Margia. *Andy Warhol et al: The FBI File on Andy Warhol*. New York: Unsub Press, 1988.

伊莎贝尔·屈尔,《安迪·沃霍尔》
Kühl, Isabel. *Andy Warhol*. Munich, Germany; New York, NY: Prestel, 2007.

科林·麦凯布,马克·弗朗西斯,彼得·沃伦编,《谁是安迪·沃霍尔?》
McCabe, Colin, Mark Francis, and Peter Wollen, eds. *Who is Andy Warhol?*. London: British Film Institute; Pittsburgh: The Andy Warhol Museum, 1997.

安妮特·米歇尔松,《安迪·沃霍尔(十月档案)》
Michelson, Annette. *Andy Warhol (October Files)*. Cambridge: MIT Press, 2001.

迈克尔·欧特曼等,《工厂直达:匹兹堡》
Oatman, Michael et al. *Factory Direct: Pittsburgh*. Pittsburgh: The Andy Warhol Museum, 2002.

佩姬·费伦等,《印相沃霍尔:无尽摄影》
Phelan, Peggy, et al. *Contact Warhol: Photography Without End*. Palo Alto, CA: Iris & Gerald Cantor Center for the Visual Arts; Boston, MA: MIT Press, 2018.

理查德·波尔斯基,《我买了安迪·沃霍尔》
Polsky, Richard. *I bought Andy Warhol*. New York, NY: H. N. Abrams, 2003.

阿兰·R.普拉特编,《对安迪·沃霍尔的批判回答》
Pratt, Alan R., ed. *The Critical Response to Andy Warhol*. Westport and London: Greenwood Press, 1997.

托尼·谢尔曼,大卫·达尔顿,《波普:安迪·沃霍尔的奇思》
Scherman, Tony and David Dalton. *POP: The Genius of Andy Warhol*. New York: HarperCollins, 2009.

尼娜·施莱夫编,《阅读沃霍尔》
Schleif, Nina, ed. *Reading Warhol*. Ostfildern: Hatje Cantz, 2013.

埃里克·沙尔斯,《沃霍尔》
Shanes, Eric. *Warhol*. New York, NY: Portland House, 1991.

罗伯特·M.肖尔,《安迪·沃霍尔》
Shore, Robert M. *Andy Warhol*. London, UK: Laurence King Publishing Ltd, 2020.

史蒂文·肖尔,琳内·蒂尔曼,《丝绒年代:沃霍尔的工厂,1965–1967》
Shore, Stephen and Lynne Tillman. *The Velvet Years: Warhol's Factory 1965-67*. London: Pavilion Books, 1995.

约翰·W.史密斯,马里奥·克雷默,马特·沃比肯,《安迪·沃霍尔的21号时间胶囊》
Smith, John W., Mario Kramer, and Matt Wrbican. *Andy Warhol's Time Capsule 21*. Cologne: Dumont, 2003.

帕特里克·S.史密斯,《沃霍尔:关于艺术家的对话》
Smith, Patrick S. *Warhol: Conversations about the Artist*. Ann Arbor: UMI Press, 1988.

安迪·沃霍尔美术馆工作人员,《安迪·沃霍尔:365场》
Staff of The Andy Warhol Museum. *Andy Warhol: 365 Takes*. New York: Harry N. Abrams, 2004.

盖尔·斯塔威兹基,《沃霍尔与车》
Stavitsky, Gail. *Warhol and Cars*. Montclair, NJ: Montclair Art Museum, 2011.

斯蒂芬妮·斯特雷,《安迪·沃霍尔》
Straine, Stephanie. *Andy Warhol*. London, UK: Tate Publishing, 2014.

菲利普·崔迪亚克,《安迪·沃霍尔》
Tretiack, Philippe. *Andy Warhol*. New York, NY: Universe Publishing, 1997.

毛里齐奥·万尼编,《安迪·沃霍尔:六十年代的炼金术士》
Vanni, Maurizio ed. *Andy Warhol: l'alchimista degli anni Sessanta = the alchemist of the Sixties*. Cinisello Balsamo, Milano: Silvana editoriale, 2019.

伊万·瓦塔尼安编,《安迪·沃霍尔五十年代的绘画与插图》
Vartanian, Ivan, ed. *Andy Warhol: Drawings and Illustrations of the 1950s*. New York: Distributed Art Publishers / Goliga Books, 2000.

安迪·沃霍尔,《a:一篇小说》
Warhol, Andy. *a: a novel*. New York: Grove Press, 1998. Originally published 1968.

安迪·沃霍尔,《美利坚》
Warhol, Andy. *America*. New York: Harper and Row, 1985.

安迪·沃霍尔,《安迪·沃霍尔的哲学(从A到B,再到A)》
Warhol, Andy. *The Philosophy of Andy Warhol (From A to B and Back Again)*. New York: Harcourt Brace Jovanovich, 1975.

安迪·沃霍尔,鲍勃·柯拉切洛,《安迪·沃霍尔的曝光》
Warhol, Andy, and Bob Colacello. *Andy Warhol's Exposures*. New York: Andy Warhol Books / Grosset & Dunlap, 1979.

安迪·沃霍尔,帕特·哈克特,《安迪·沃霍尔日记》
Warhol, Andy, and Pat Hackett. *The Andy Warhol Diaries*. New York: Warner Books, 1989.

安迪·沃霍尔,帕特·哈克特,《安迪·沃霍尔的派对指南》
Warhol, Andy, and Pat Hackett. *Andy Warhol's Party Book*. New York: Crown, 1988.

安迪·沃霍尔,帕特·哈克特,《波普主义:沃霍尔的六十年代》
Warhol, Andy, and Pat Hackett. *POPism: The Warhol Sixties*. New York: Harcourt Brace Jovanovich, 1980.

史蒂文·沃森,《工厂制造:沃霍尔与六十年代》
Watson, Steven. *Factory Made: Warhol and the Sixties*. New York: Pantheon Books, 2003.

约翰·威尔科克,《安迪·沃霍尔的自传与性生活》
Wilcock, John. *The Autobiography and Sex Life of Andy Warhol*. New York: Trela Media, 2010.

列娃·沃尔夫,《安迪·沃霍尔,六十年代的诗歌与蜚语》
Wolf, Reva. *Andy Warhol, Poetry, and Gossip in the 1960s*. Chicago: University of Chicago Press. 1997.

玛丽·沃罗诺夫,《游于地下:我在沃霍尔工厂的那些年》
Woronov, Mary. *Swimming Underground: My Years in the Warhol Factory*. London: Serpent's Tail, 1995.

马特·沃比肯,《档案:从A到Z的沃霍尔世界》
Wrbican, Matt. *A Is for Archive: Warhol's World from A to Z*. New Haven: Yale University Press; Pittsburgh: The Andy Warhol Museum, 2019.

姚强,《表里如一:安迪·沃霍尔的艺术》
Yau, John. *In the Realm of Appearances: The Art of Andy Warhol*. Hopewell, NJ: Ecco Press, 1993.

玛丽·沃罗诺夫,《游于地下:我在沃霍尔工厂的那些年》
Woronov, Mary. *Swimming Underground: My Life in the Warhol Factory*. Boston, MA: Journey Editions, 1995.

凯瑟琳·祖洛姆斯,《工厂:摄影与沃霍尔社区》
Zuromskis, Catherine. *The Factory: Photography and the Warhol Community*. Madrid: La Fábrica, 2012.

## Catalogues
画册

《安迪·沃霍尔》
*Andy Warhol*. Brisbane: Queensland Art Gallery, 2007.

《安迪·沃霍尔:十五分钟的永恒》
*Andy Warhol: 15 Minutes Eternal*. Pittsburgh: The Andy Warhol Museum, 2012.

《安迪·沃霍尔:1956—1986,时代的镜子》
*Andy Warhol: 1956–86, Mirror of His Time*. Pittsburgh: The Andy Warhol Museum; Tokyo: Asahi Shimbun, 1996.

《安迪·沃霍尔:金宝汤盒》
*Andy Warhol: Campbell's Soup Boxes*. Paris, France: Galerie Thaddaeus Ropac, 2000.

《安迪·沃霍尔:死亡与灾难》
*Andy Warhol: Death and Disasters*. Houston: Menil Collection, 1988.

《安迪·沃霍尔:1942—1987年间绘画》
*Andy Warhol: Drawings 1942-1987*. Pittsburgh: The Andy Warhol Museum, 2000.

《安迪·沃霍尔:20世纪70年代后的画作》
*Andy Warhol: Paintings from the 1970's*. New York: Skarstedt Gallery, 2012.

《安迪·沃霍尔——摄影》
*Andy Warhol – Photography*, Hamburg: Hamburger Kunsthalle; Pittsburgh: The Andy Warhol Museum; Zurich: Stemmle Publishers GmbH; New York: Edition Stemmle, Thalwil, 1999.

《安迪·沃霍尔:静物与足部研究,1956—1961》
*Andy Warhol: Still Lifes and Feet*, 1956–1961. New York: Paul Kasmin Gallery, 2010.

《安迪·沃霍尔:伟大的美国梦:图像作品 1956—1983》
*Andy Warhol: The Great American Dream: œuvres graphiques 1956–1983 = graphische Werke 1956–1983*. Milano, Italy: Mazzotta, 1996.

《安迪·沃霍尔:印第安人绘画》
*Andy Warhol: The American Indian Paintings and Drawings*. London: Skarstedt Gallery; New York, NY: Distributed Art Publishers, 2012.

《安迪·沃霍尔:霍尔收藏作品》(牛津:阿什莫林博物馆,2016.2.4–5.15)
*Andy Warhol: Works from the Hall collection: Ashmolean Museum, Oxford, 4 February to 15 May, 2016*. New York, NY: Hall Art Foundation, 2016.

沙伦·M.阿特金斯,《安迪·沃霍尔:波普政治》
Atkins, Sharon M. *Andy Warhol: Pop politics*. Harrison, NY: Neuberger Museum of Art; Manchester, N. H.: Currier Museum of Art, 2008.

雅各布·巴尔–特舒瓦,《安迪·沃霍尔展览》
Baal-Teshuva, Jacob. *Andy Warhol: An Exhibition*. New York, NY: Magidson Fine Art NYC, 1989.

戈登·鲍德温,朱迪思·凯勒,《纳达尔–沃霍尔,巴黎–纽约:摄影与名望》
Baldwin, Gordon, and Judith Keller. *Nadar-Warhol, Paris-New York: Photography and Fame*. Los Angeles: The J. Paul Getty Museum, 1999.

尼尔·鲍德温,威廉·V.加尼斯编,《安迪·沃霍尔:直穿镜头》
Baldwin, Neil, and William V. Ganis, eds. *Andy Warhol: Through a Glass Starkly*. Montclair: Montclair State University and George Segal Gallery, 2009.

玛丽·L.邦迪等,《安迪·沃霍尔:电影》
Bandy Mary L. et al. *Andy Warhol: Motion Pictures*. Berlin, Germany: KW Institute for Contemporary Art; New York, NY: D.A.P./Distributed Art Publishers, 2004.

弗朗索瓦–马里·巴尼耶,《安迪·沃霍尔:红色的书》
Banier, François-Marie. *Andy Warhol: Red Books*. New York, NY: Pace/MacGill Gallery; Göttingen, Germany: Steidl, 2004.

亚历山德拉·巴察尔等,布拉姆·奥普斯特尔腾译,《安迪·沃霍尔:〈生活〉杂志那些年,1949—1959》
Barcal, Alexandra et al. *Andy Warhol: the LIFE years 1949-1959*. Translated by Bram Opstelten. Munich, Germany: Hirmer Publishers, 2015.

海纳·巴斯蒂安等,《安迪·沃霍尔回顾展》
Bastian, Heiner, et al. *Andy Warhol: Retrospective*. London: Tate Publishing, 2001.

杰茜卡·贝克,菲利普·皮尔斯坦,《皮尔斯坦,沃霍尔,坎托:从匹兹堡到纽约》
Beck, Jessica and Philip Pearlstein. *Pearlstein, Warhol, Cantor: From Pittsburgh to New York*. Pittsburgh, PA: The Andy Warhol Museum, 2015.

杰茜卡·贝克等,《安迪·沃霍尔:我完美的身体》
Beck, Jessica et al. *Andy Warhol: My Perfect Body*. Pittsburgh: The Andy Warhol Museum, 2016.

格尔马诺·赛朗,《安迪·沃霍尔:工厂》
Celant, Germano. *Andy Warhol: A Factory*. German edition: Ostfildern: Hatje Cantz, 1998. French and Dutch editions: Brussels: Société des expositions, Palais des beaux-arts, 1999.

尼古拉斯·钱伯斯编,《阿德曼:波普之前的沃霍尔》
Chambers, Nicholas, ed. *Adman: Warhol Before Pop*. Sydney: Art Gallery of New South Wales; Pittsburgh: The Andy Warhol Museum, 2017.

鲍勃·柯拉切洛等,《安迪·沃霍尔绘画中的头部特写》
Colacello, Bob et al. *Andy Warhol: headshots: drawings and paintings*. Cologne, Germany: Jablonka Galerie; Manchester, UK: Cornerhouse 2000

雷纳·克龙,《安迪·沃霍尔,艺术家的图画秀:1942—1962年的早期作品》,原名:《安迪·沃霍尔:1942—1962年的绘画作品》
Crone, Rainer. *Andy Warhol, A Picture Show by the Artist: The Early Work 1942-1962*. Originally titled *Andy Warhol: Das Zeichnerische Werk 1942-1962*. Stuttgart: Württembergischer Kunstverein, 1976.

阿兰·屈埃夫等,《安迪·沃霍尔的大世界》
Cueff, Alain, et al. *Warhol: Le Grand Monde d'Andy Warhol*. Paris: Réunion des Musées Nationaux, 2009.

阿兰·卡明,《安迪·沃霍尔:男人》
Cumming, Alan. *Andy Warhol: Men*. San Francisco, CA: Chronicle Books, 2004.

唐纳·M.德·萨尔沃编,《安迪·沃霍尔——从A到B,再到A》
De Salvo, Donna M., ed. *Andy Warhol – From A to B and Back Again*, New York: Whitney Museum of American Art; New Haven: Yale University Press, 2018.

唐纳·M.德·萨尔沃编,《"在纽约,成功是一份工作…"安迪·沃霍尔的早期艺术与商业》
De Salvo, Donna M., ed. *"Success Is a Job in New York..." The Early Art and Business of Andy Warhol*. Pittsburgh: The Carnegie Museum of Art; New York: Grey Art Gallery, 1989.

马克斯·德拉尼,埃里克·C夏纳编,《安迪·沃霍尔/艾未未》
Delany, Max, and Eric C. Shiner, eds. *Andy Warhol / Ai Weiwei*. Melbourne: National Gallery of Victoria; New Haven: Yale University Press; Pittsburgh: The Andy Warhol Museum, 2016.

玛丽安娜·多布纳编,《安迪·沃霍尔展览:闪闪发光的另类》
Dobner, Marianne, ed. *Andy Warhol Exhibits: A Glittering Alternative*. Cologne: Walther König, 2020.

莫莉·多诺万编,《沃霍尔:头条》
Donovan, Molly, ed. *Warhol: Headlines*. New York: Prestel, 2001.

西蒙·多南,《安迪·沃霍尔:时尚》
Doonan, Simon. *Andy Warhol: Fashion*. San Francisco, CA: Chronicle Books, 2004.

伊尔马兹·杰维奥尔,格列戈尔·穆伊尔,《安迪·沃霍尔》
Dziewior, Yilmaz, and Gregor Muir. *Andy Warhol*. London: Tate Publishing, 2020.

弗瑞达·费尔德曼,约格·谢尔曼编,《安迪·沃霍尔版画:1962—1987作品全集》
Feldman, Frayda, and Jorg Schellman, eds. *Andy Warhol Prints: A Catalogue Raisonné 1962-1987*. New York: Distributed Art Publishers, 1997.

迪特马尔·埃尔格编,《安迪·沃霍尔:自画像》
Elger, Dietmar, ed. *Andy Warhol: Selbstportraits/Self-portraits*. Ostfildern: Hatje Cantz, 2004.

马克·弗朗西斯，马格丽·金编，《沃霍尔潮流：魅力，风格，时尚》
Francis, Mark, and Margery King, eds. T*he Warhol Look: Glamour, Style, Fashion*. New York: Whitney Museum of American Art; Boston: Bulfinch, 1997.

文森特·弗里蒙特，《安迪·沃霍尔：画像》
Freemont, Vincent. *Andy Warhol: Portrait Drawings*. Cologne, Germany: Jablonka Galerie, 2002.

道格拉斯·福格尔等，《安迪·沃霍尔：暗星》
Fogle, Douglas et al. *Andy Warhol: Dark Star*. London, UK: Prestel, 2017.

朱迪思·戈德曼编，《安迪·沃霍尔：绘画与相关作品，1951—1986》
Goldman, Judith, ed. *Andy Warhol: Drawings & Related Works, 1951–1986*. New York: Gagosian Gallery, 2003.

迈克尔·戈万，琳内·库克，利兹·科兹，《迪亚的安迪》
Govan, Michael, Lynne Cooke, and Liz Kotz. D*ia's Andy*. New York: Dia Art Foundation, 2005.

萨拉·尤里斯特·格林，艾利森·翁鲁编，《安迪·沃霍尔的事业》
Green, Sarah Urist, and Allison Unruh, eds. A*ndy Warhol Enterprises*. Indianapolis: Indianapolis Museum of Art, 2010.

奥托·哈恩，《安迪·沃霍尔》
Hahn, Otto. *Andy Warhol*. Paris, France: Ileana Sonnabend Gallery, 1965.

布鲁斯·海恩利，《安迪·沃霍尔绘画：小便与性》
Hainley, Bruce. A*ndy Warhol: Piss & Sex Paintings and Drawings*. New York, NY: Gagosian Gallery, 2002.

彼得·哈利，《安迪·沃霍尔：小电椅系列画作》
Halley, Peter. *Andy Warhol: Little Electric Chair Paintings*. New York, NY: Stellan Holm Gallery, 2001.

詹姆斯·霍夫迈尔，《安迪·沃霍尔：十五幅抽象画》
Hofmaier, James. *Andy Warhol: Fifteen Abstract Paintings*. New York, NY: Anton Kern Gallery, 1998.

近藤健一，佐佐木瞳，竹见洋一郎编，《安迪·沃霍尔：永远的15分》
Kondo, Kenichi, Sasaki Hitomi, and Takemi Yoichiro, eds. *Andy Warhol: 15 Minutes Eternal*. Roppongi: Mori Art Museum; Pittsburgh: The Andy Warhol Museum, 2014.

米兰达·拉希，何塞·卡洛斯·迪亚斯，《安迪·沃霍尔：启示录》
Lash, Miranda and José Carlos Diaz. *Andy Warhol: Revelation*. Pittsburgh, PA: The Andy Warhol Museum, 2019.

杰勒德·马兰加等，《安迪·沃霍尔：三十个比一个好》
Malanga, Gerard et al. *Andy Warhol: Thirty Are Better Than One*. New York, NY: Tony Shafrazi Gallery, 1997.

杰勒德·马兰加，《安迪·沃霍尔：五人死亡》
Malanga, Gerard. *Andy Warhol: 5 Deaths*. New York, NY: Stellan Holm Gallery, 2002.

保罗·马雷夏尔，作品全集《安迪·沃霍尔：全部杂志委托作品，1948–1987》
Maréchal, Paul. A*ndy Warhol: the Complete Commissioned Magazine Work 1948–1987*. Munich, Germany; London, UK; New York, NY: Prestel, 2014. Catalogue raisonné.

保罗·马雷夏尔，作品全集《安迪·沃霍尔：全部唱片封面委托作品，1949—1987》
Maréchal, Paul. *Andy Warhol: the Complete Commissioned Record Covers, 1949–1987*. Munich, Germany; London, UK; New York, NY: Prestel, 2015. Catalogue raisonné.

保罗·马雷夏尔，作品全集《安迪·沃霍尔：全部海报委托作品，1964—1987》
Maréchal, Paul. *Andy Warhol: the Complete Commissioned posters 1964–1987*. Munich, Germany; London, UK; New York, NY: Prestel, 2014. Catalogue raisonné.

让-于贝尔·马丁，《安迪·沃霍尔：晚期作品》
Martin, Jean-Hubert. *Andy Warhol: The Late Work*. New York: Prestel Publishing, 2004.

基纳斯顿·麦克夏恩编，《安迪·沃霍尔：回顾展》
McShine, Kynaston, ed. *Andy Warhol: A Retrospective*, New York: The Museum of Modern Art, New York, 1989. French edition: Paris: Centre Georges Pompidou, 1990.

伊娃·迈耶·埃尔曼编，《安迪·沃霍尔：2小时56分钟的706件作品指南》
Meyer-Hermann, Eva, ed. *Andy Warhol: A Guide to 706 Items in 2 Hours 56 Minutes*. Rotterdam: NAi Publishers, 2007.

阿斯特丽·约翰娜·奥夫纳编，《安迪·沃霍尔：电影人》
Ofner, Astrid Johanna, ed. *Andy Warhol: Filmmaker*. Vienna: Austrian Film Museum, 2005.

阿希尔·B.奥利娃，《安迪·沃霍尔：美国梦》
Oliva, Achille B. *Andy Warhol: the American Dream*. Cinisello Balsamo, Milano: Silvana Editoriale, 2014.

彼·P.帕索利尼，《安迪·沃霍尔：女士们和先生们》
Pasolini, Pier P. *Andy Warhol: Ladies and Gentlemen*. New York, N.Y.: Skarstedt Gallery, 2009.

《与安迪·沃霍尔一起突袭冰箱1》
*Raid the Icebox 1 with Andy Warhol*. Providence: Rhode Island School of Design Museum of Art, 1969.

贾恩卡洛·兰齐，多里斯·冯·德拉腾，《安迪·沃霍尔：原子弹》
Ranzi, Giancarlo and Doris von Drathen. *Andy Warhol: the Bomb*. Brescia, Italy: SHIN factory, 2006.

罗伯特·罗森布卢姆等，《安迪·沃霍尔：机械艺术》
Rosenblum, Robert et al. *Andy Warhol: The Mechanical Art*. Málaga, Spain: Museo Picasso Málaga; Madrid, Spain: La Fábrica, 2017.

朱利安·施纳贝尔，《安迪·沃霍尔：阴影绘画，1989年11月》
Schnabel, Julian. *Andy Warhol: Shadow Paintings, November 1989*. New York, NY: Gagosian Gallery, 1989.

约翰·W.史密斯编，《痴迷占有：安迪·沃霍尔与收藏》
Smith, John W. ed. *Possession Obsession: Andy Warhol and Collecting*. Pittsburgh: The Andy Warhol Museum, 2002.

阿兰·R.所罗门，《安迪·沃霍尔：展览画册，1966.10.1—11.6》
Solomon, Alan R. *Andy Warhol: Catalog of the exhibition, October 1–November 6, 1966*. Boston, MA: Institute of Contemporary Art, 1966.

贾斯廷·斯普林，《安迪·沃霍尔：声望与不幸》
Spring, Justin. *Andy Warhol: fame and misfortune*. San Antonio, TX: McNay Art Museum, 2012.

《安迪·沃霍尔美术馆开馆出版物》
*The Andy Warhol Museum: The Inaugural Publication*, Pittsburgh: The Andy Warhol Museum; New York: Distributed Art Publishers; Stuttgart: Cantz Publishers, 1994.

安迪·沃霍尔，安迪·格伦德贝里，《安迪·沃霍尔的宝丽来照片，1971–1986》
Warhol, Andy, and Andy Grundberg. *Andy Warhol Polaroids, 1971–1986*. New York, NY: Pace/MacGill Gallery, 1986.

埃尔曼·乌恩舍，《安迪·沃霍——1962—1980年图像作品》
Wunsche, Hermann. *Andy Warhol - das graphische werk 1962-1980*. Bonn, Germany: Bonner Universitats Buchdruckerei, 1980.

# 作品索引    Index of Works

作品索引中的所有作品来自安迪·沃霍尔美术馆，匹兹堡馆藏。除非另有说明，所有作品由安迪·沃霍尔（生于美国，1928—1987）创作，建馆藏品，安迪·沃霍尔美术馆，匹兹堡，安迪·沃霍尔视觉艺术基金会捐赠。

All works in the index are from the collection of The Andy Warhol Museum, Pittsburgh. Unless otherwise noted, all works are by Andy Warhol (American, 1928–1987) and credited to The Andy Warhol Museum, Pittsburgh: Founding Collection, Contribution The Andy Warhol Foundation for the Visual Arts, Inc.

《安迪·沃霍尔、茱莉娅·沃霍拉、乔治·古克和玛丽（扎瓦基）·普雷斯塔夫人》
作者未知
*Andy Warhol, Julia Warhola, George Guke, and Mrs. Mary (Zavacky) Preksta*
Unknown
1937
棕褐色原片
Sepia print
16.5 × 11.4 cm
1998.3.10540.1

《执行"烟雾控制"政策前，上午11点的匹兹堡市第五大道》
*Looking up Pittsburgh's Fifth Avenue at 11am before smoke control*
1945
明胶银盐相纸
Gelatin silver print
25.4 × 20.3 cm
阿利盖尼社区发展联盟照片，MSP 285，德特雷图书档案馆，海因茨历史中心
Allegheny Conference on Community Development Photographs, MSP 285, Detre Library and Archives, Heinz History Center
L2019.7.2

《执行"烟雾控制"政策前，上午 9 点 20 分的匹兹堡市中心》
*Downtown Pittsburgh at 9:20am before smoke control*
1945
明胶银盐相纸
Gelatin silver print
20.3 × 25.4 cm
阿利盖尼社区发展联盟照片，MSP 285，德特雷图书档案馆，海因茨历史中心
Allegheny Conference on Community Development Photographs, MSP 285, Detre Library and Archives, Heinz History Center
L2019.7.3

《鸟瞰奥克兰》
*Aerial view of Oakland*
1930–1933
明胶银盐相纸
Gelatin silver print
20.3 × 25.4 cm
阿利盖尼社区发展联盟照片，MSP 285，德特雷图书档案馆，海因茨历史中心
Allegheny Conference on Community Development Photographs, MSP 285, Detre Library and Archives, Heinz History Center
L2019.7.6

《匹兹堡湾观光游地图》
*Gulf Pittsburgh Info Map with Sight-seeing Tour*
1940年代 1940s
带框 With frame: 45.7 × 91.4 cm
德特雷图书档案馆地图收藏，海因茨历史中心
Map Collection, Detre Library and Archives, Heinz History Center
L2019.7.1

《福尔摩斯小学》
*Holmes School*
约 ca. 1950—1970
明胶银盐相纸
Gelatin silver print
20.3 × 25.4 cm
匹兹堡公立学校照片，MSP 117，德特雷图书档案馆，海因茨历史中心
Pittsburgh Public Schools Photographs, MSP 117, Detre Library and Archives, Heinz History Center
L2019.7.4

《申利高中》
*Schenley High School*
约 ca. 1950—1970
明胶银盐相纸
Gelatin silver print
20.3 × 25.4 cm
匹兹堡公立学校照片，MSP 117，德特雷图书档案馆，海因茨历史中心
Pittsburgh Public Schools Photographs, MSP 117, Detre Library and Archives, Heinz History Center
L2019.7.5

《安迪·沃霍尔申利高中班级合照》
*Homeroom picture of Andy Warhol's class at Schenley High School*
1944–1945
明胶银盐相纸
Gelatin silver print
12.7 × 18.3 cm
1998.3.5412

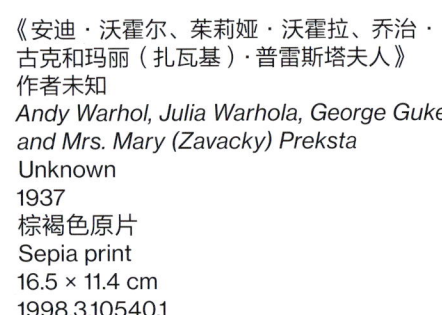

《申利高中毕业纪念册》
匹兹堡申利高中
*Schenley Journal*
*Schenley High School, Pittsburgh*
*Schenley Journal*
1945
机械装订涂布纸、黑色纸封面
Mechanical bound coated paper with black paper covers
26.7 × 20.3 × 0.6 cm
1998.3.4915

《安迪·沃霍尔》
作者未知
*Andy Warhol*
Unknown
约 ca. 1945
棕褐色原片
Sepia print
17.8 × 12.7 cm
1998.3.5219

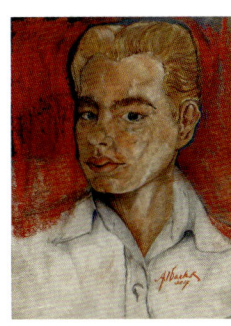
《自画像》
Self-Portrait
1944
纸板水粉
Gouache on board
40.6 × 27.9 cm
马克·沃霍拉家族收藏
Collection of Mark Warhola Family
L2014.3

《农产品卡车后面的女人和儿童》
Female and Children Behind Produce Truck
1946
马尼拉纸上墨水和石墨
Ink and graphite on manila paper
30.5 × 45.7 cm
1998.1.1614

《女人和农产品卡车》
Women and Produce Truck
1946
马尼拉纸上墨水和石墨
Ink and graphite on manila paper
33 × 47.6 cm
1998.1.1613

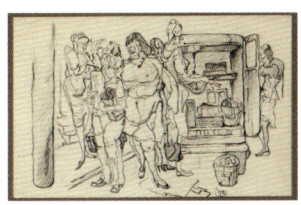
《农产品卡车后面的人》
Figures Behind Produce Truck
1946
马尼拉纸上墨水和石墨
Ink and graphite on manila paper
30.5 × 45.7 cm
1998.1.1615

《农产品卡车后面的男人》
Male Figure in Back of Produce Truck
1946
马尼拉纸上墨水和石墨
Ink and graphite on manila paper
30.5 × 45.7 cm
1998.1.1616

《人行道上的四个人》
Four Figures on Sidewalk
1946
马尼拉纸上墨水和石墨
Ink and graphite on manila paper
30.5 × 45.7 cm
1998.1.1617

《断墙前的三个人》
Three Figures Against Cracked Wall
1946
马尼拉纸上墨水和石墨
Ink and graphite on manila paper
30.5 × 45.7 cm
1998.1.1618

《卡内基理工学院学生》
Unidentified Carnegie Institute of Technology students
约 ca. 1948
明胶银盐相纸
Gelatin silver print
7 × 9.5 cm
1998.3.5413.8

《卡内基理工学院学生》
Unidentified Carnegie Institute of Technology students
约 ca. 1948
明胶银盐相纸
Gelatin silver print
7 × 9.5 cm
1998.3.5413.10

《安迪·沃霍尔(右)与多萝西·坎托在卡内基理工学院的艺术工作室》
Andy Warhol (right) and Dorothy Cantor in an art studio at Carnegie Tech
约 ca. 1948
明胶银盐相纸
Gelatin silver print
8.9 × 8.9 cm
1998.1.1613

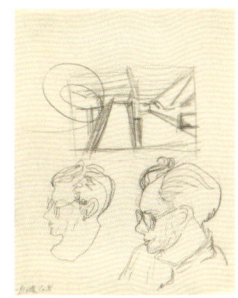
《安迪·沃霍尔素描像 I》
多萝西·坎托
Drawing of Andy Warhol I
Dorothy Cantor
约 ca. 1950—1952
纸上石墨、写生簿
Graphite on paper, sketchbook
27.6 × 21.3 cm
多萝西·坎托与菲利普·珀尔斯坦捐赠
Gift of Dorothy Cantor and Philip Pearlstein
1998.3.5220

《美术课》
菲利普·珀尔斯坦
Art Class
Philip Pearlstein
1946–1947
纸板蛋彩
Tempera on board
50.8 × 40.6 cm
多萝西·坎托与菲利普·珀尔斯坦捐赠
Gift of Dorothy Cantor and Philip Pearlstein
2017.1.3

《拉里·沃尔默与安迪·沃霍尔》
作者未知
Larry Vollmer and Andy Warhol
Unknown
1947
明胶银盐相纸
Gelatin silver print
9.5 × 11.7 cm
2017.1.1

INDEX OF WORKS 365

约瑟夫·霍恩百货公司橱窗外景照片
Exterior view of Joseph Horne Company department store window displays
1947
明胶银盐相纸
Gelatin silver print
20.3 × 25.4 cm
约瑟夫·霍恩百货公司照片，MSP 398，德特雷图书档案馆，海因茨历史中心
Joseph Horne Company Photographs, MSP 398, Detre Library and Archives, Heinz History Center
L2019.7.12

约瑟夫·霍恩百货公司"送给 情人 心之所爱"橱窗照片
Joseph Horne Company department store "Give a Valentine that Counts" window display
1947
明胶银盐相纸
Gelatin silver print
20.3 × 25.4 cm
约瑟夫·霍恩百货公司照片，MSP 398，德特雷图书档案馆，海因茨历史中心
Joseph Horne Company Photographs, MSP 398, Detre Library and Archives, Heinz History Center
L2019.7.8

约瑟夫·霍恩百货公司旅游 服饰 橱窗照片
Joseph Horne Company department store travel attire window display
1947
明胶银盐相纸
Gelatin silver print
20.3 × 25.4 cm
约瑟夫·霍恩百货公司照片，MSP 398，德特雷图书档案馆，海因茨历史中心
Joseph Horne Company Photographs, MSP 398, Detre Library and Archives, Heinz History Center
L2019.7.9

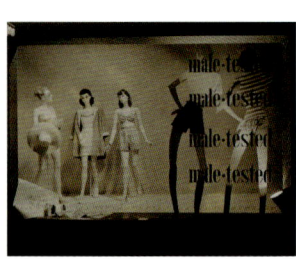

约瑟夫·霍恩百货公司"男性之选"橱窗照片
Joseph Horne Company department store "Male-tested Fashions" window display
1947
明胶银盐相纸
Gelatin silver print
20.3 × 25.4 cm
约瑟夫·霍恩百货公司照片，MSP 398，德特雷图书档案馆，海因茨历史中心
Joseph Horne Company Photographs, MSP 398, Detre Library and Archives, Heinz History Center
L2019.7.10

《安迪·沃霍尔与约瑟夫·霍恩百货商店的同事》
作者未知
Andy Warhol with unidentified co-workers from Joseph Horne's department store
Unknown
1947
明胶银盐相纸
Gelatin silver print
9.5 × 12.1 cm
1998.3.5420

《安迪·沃霍尔与同事》
作者未知
Andy Warhol and unidentified co-workers
Unknown
1947
明胶银盐相纸
Gelatin silver print
8.3 × 11.7 cm
1998.3.5418.1

《安迪·沃霍尔与同事》
作者未知
Andy Warhol and unidentified co-workers
Unknown
1947
明胶银盐相纸
Gelatin silver print
8.3 × 11.7 cm
1998.3.5418.7

《安迪·沃霍尔与同事》
作者未知
Andy Warhol and unidentified co-workers
Unknown
1947
明胶银盐相纸
Gelatin silver print
8.3 × 11.7 cm
1998.3.5418.5

《在"谷仓工作室"的安迪·沃霍尔与其两幅儿童秋千画作》
Andy Warhol in the "barn studio" with two of his paintings of children on swings
约 ca. 1948
明胶银盐相纸
Gelatin silver print
8.9 × 8.9 cm
1998.3.5221

《安迪·沃霍尔与其＜挖鼻孔的人＞画作和同学阿瑟·伊莱亚斯》
Andy Warhol with his "Nosepicker" painting and classmate Arthur Elias
约 ca. 1948
明胶银盐相纸
Gelatin silver print
8.9 × 8.9 cm
1998.3.5241.4

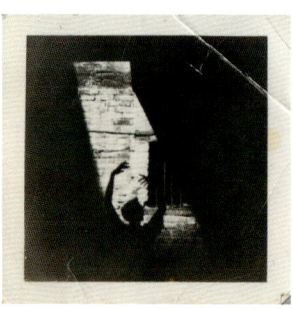

《练习现代舞的安迪·沃霍尔》
Andy Warhol practicing modern dance
约 ca. 1948
明胶银盐相纸
Gelatin silver print
8.9 × 8.9 cm
1998.3.5242

《在与同学合租的"谷仓工作室"中 摆姿势的安迪·沃霍尔》
Andy Warhol posing in the "barn studio" he rented with classmates
约 ca. 1948
明胶银盐相纸
Gelatin silver print
8.9 × 8.9 cm
1998.3.5241.1

《安迪·沃霍尔在与同学合租的"谷仓工作室"》
Andy Warhol in the "barn studio" he rented with classmates
约 ca. 1948
明胶银盐相纸
Gelatin silver print
8.9 × 8.9 cm
1998.3.5241.5

《安迪·沃霍尔(双重曝光)》
作者未知
Andy Warhol (double exposure)
Unknown
约 ca. 1950
明胶银盐相纸
Gelatin silver print
8.9 × 8.9 cm
1998.3.5222

《拿着画笔的安迪·沃霍尔》
Andy Warhol holding a paintbrush
1947
明胶银盐相纸
Gelatin silver print
7.9 × 11.1 cm
1998.3.5419

《双手撑头的安迪·沃霍尔》
梅尔顿－皮平
Andy Warhol with head cradled in hands
Melton-Pippin
约 ca. 1950
明胶银盐相纸
Gelatin silver print
24.1 × 19.1 cm
1998.3.5217

《朱莉娅·沃霍拉》
朱莉娅·沃霍拉
Julia Warhola
Julia Warhola
1955–1959
彩色印刷
Chromogenic color print
8.9 × 6 cm
T3513

《安迪·沃霍尔和母亲》
杜安·迈克尔斯
Andy Warhol and His Mother
Duane Michals
1958
明胶银盐相纸
Gelatin silver print
35.6 × 68.6 × 1.9 cm
杰伊·雷格捐赠
Gift of Jay Reeg
2011.3.2

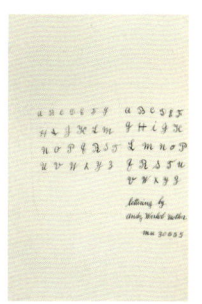

《字母表("安迪·沃霍尔母亲手写")》
朱莉娅·沃霍拉
Alphabet ("Lettering by Andy Warhol's Mother")
Julia Warhola
1953–1960
丝蒂摩纸上墨水和石墨
Ink and graphite on Strathmore Seconds paper
57.5 × 36.5 cm
1998.1.3611

《天使》
朱莉娅·沃霍拉
Angel
Julia Warhola
1952–1970
丝蒂摩纸上墨水
Ink on Strathmore paper
35.4 × 27.3 cm
1998.3.1739

《正在祈祷的两名天使》
朱莉娅·沃霍拉
Two Angels Praying
Julia Warhola
约 ca. 1957—1960
丝蒂摩纸上墨水
Ink on Strathmore paper
23.5 × 29.8 cm
1998.3.1771

《三名天使》
朱莉娅·沃霍拉
Three Angels
Julia Warhola
1952–1970
丝蒂摩纸上墨水
Ink on Strathmore paper 29.8 × 43.2 cm
1998.3.1796

《戴帽子的猫》
朱莉娅·沃霍拉
Cat with a Hat
Julia Warhola
约 ca. 1957—1960
纸上墨水
Ink on paper
37.1 × 20.6 cm
1998.3.1819

INDEX OF WORKS 367

《戴帽子的猫》
朱莉娅·沃霍拉
Cat with a Hat
Julia Warhola
约 ca. 1957—1960
丝蒂摩纸上墨水
Ink on Strathmore paper
58.4 × 37.5 cm
1998.3.1833

《五只猫》
朱莉娅·沃霍拉
Five Cats
Julia Warhola
约 ca. 1957—1961
丝蒂摩纸上墨水
Ink on Strathmore seconds paper
57.5 × 37.6 cm
1998.3.1933

《戴帽子的猫与"purr"猫叫拟声词》
朱莉娅·沃霍拉
Cat with a Hat with "Purr" Inscriptions
Julia Warhola
约 ca. 1957—1961
丝蒂摩纸上墨水
Ink on Strathmore paper
32.1 × 34.6 cm
1998.3.1851

《圣诞老人》
朱莉娅·沃霍拉
Santa
Julia Warhola
1952–1970
纸上墨水
Ink on paper
29.7 × 28.1 cm
T757.944

《猫》
朱莉娅·沃霍拉
Cat
Julia Warhola
1952–1970
丝蒂摩纸上墨水
Ink on Strathmore seconds paper
22.9 × 30.8 cm
1998.3.1870

《手持十字架的两名天使》
朱莉娅·沃霍拉
Two Angels Holding a Cross
Julia Warhola
约 ca. 1960
绿色纸上墨水
Ink on green paper
15.9 × 12.4 cm
T757.946

《戴帽子的猫》
朱莉娅·沃霍拉
Cat with a Hat
Julia Warhola
约 ca. 1957—1961
丝蒂摩纸上墨水
Ink on Strathmore paper
29.8 × 37.5 cm
T757.943

《手持十字架的天使》
朱莉娅·沃霍拉
Angel Holding Cross
Julia Warhola
约 ca. 1957—1960
金箔纸上墨水
Ink on gold paper
18.4 × 13.7 cm
T757.945

《猫和小猫咪》
朱莉娅·沃霍拉
Cat with Kittens
Julia Warhola
1952–1970
丝蒂摩纸上墨水
Ink on Strathmore paper
30.2 × 43.2 cm
T757.948

《手持十字架的天使》
朱莉娅·沃霍拉
Angel Holding Cross
Julia Warhola
约 ca. 1957—1960
金箔纸上墨水
Ink on gold paper
18.4 × 13.7 cm
1998.3.1807

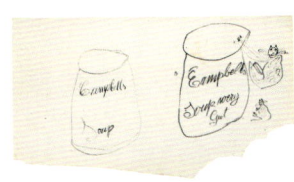
《两罐金宝汤罐头和两只猫》
朱莉娅·沃霍拉
Two Campbell's Soup Cans and Two Cats
Julia Warhola
约 ca. 1953
丝蒂摩纸上墨水
Ink on Strathmore seconds paper
33.3 × 57.5 cm
1998.3.1990

《神圣猫咪》，安迪·沃霍尔母亲绘
朱莉娅·沃霍拉
Holy Cats by Andy Warhol's Mother
Julia Warhola
1960
彩色纸上平版印刷、硬麻布封面
Offset lithograph on colored paper with buckram board cover
书 Book: 23.2 × 14.9 × 0.5 cm
1998.3.2429.1

《天使、猫和小天使》
朱莉娅·沃霍拉
Angels, Cats, and Cherubs
Julia Warhola
约 ca. 1957—1960
纸上墨水
Ink on paper
76.8 × 57.2 cm
T757.953

《手工上色的朱莉娅·沃霍拉照片》
朱莉娅·沃霍拉
Hand-colored Photograph of Julia Warhola
Julia Warhola
约 ca. 1959
重磅卡纸和手工上色照片
Heavy weight cardstock and hand-colored photograph
22.9 × 17.8 cm
T615.2

《二十五只叫山姆的猫和一只蓝色的猫》
25 Cats Name[d] Sam and One Blue Pussy
1956
纸上平版印刷和苯胺染料、硬麻布封面
Offset lithograph and Dr. Martin's aniline dye on paper with buckram board cover
23.5 × 15.6 × 1 cm
乔治·克劳伯捐赠
Gift of George Klauber
1998.2.9

《爬梯子的女士》
Females Climbing Ladders
1949
丝蒂摩纸上墨水、石墨和蛋彩
Ink, graphite, and tempera on Strathmore paper
58.4 × 50.2 cm
1998.1.1152

《五只鞋和三个女士包》
Five Shoes and Three Purses
丝蒂摩纸上墨水、石墨和水粉
20 世纪 50 年代 1950s
Ink, graphite, and gouache on Strathmore seconds paper
36.2 × 57.2 cm
1998.1.1292

《项链和两枚硬币》
Necklace and Two Coins
1957
丝蒂摩纸上墨水
Ink on Strathmore paper
38.7 × 30.5 cm
1998.1.1238

《高跟鞋》
High Heel
1955
丝蒂摩纸上墨水、石墨、蛋彩和拼贴
Ink, graphite, tempera, and printed tape collage on Strathmore paper
19.1 × 24.1 cm
1998.1.1283

《五只鞋(带印刷套准标记)》
Five Shoes (with Registration Marks)
20 世纪 50 年代 1950s
丝蒂摩纸上墨水、蛋彩和拼贴
Ink, tempera, and collage on Strathmore paper
44.1 × 29.5 cm
1998.1.1288

《女士手提包》
Purse
20 世纪 50 年代 1950s
丝蒂摩纸上墨水、石墨和蛋彩
Ink, graphite, and tempera on Strathmore paper
37.5 × 28.3 cm
1998.1.1223

《服装配饰》
Multiple Clothing Accessories
20 世纪 50 年代 1950s
木板上丝蒂摩纸上墨水
Ink on Strathmore paper on board
55.9 × 37.5 cm
1998.1.1226

《福恩斯兄弟公司手套广告》
"Fownes"
20 世纪 50 年代 1950s
丝蒂摩纸上墨水、石墨、苯胺染料和拼贴
Ink, graphite, Dr. Martin's aniline dye, and collage on Strathmore paper
39.1 × 28.9 cm
1998.1.1182

《八个戴着墨镜的女士头像》
Eight Female Heads Wearing Sunglasses
1957
丝蒂摩纸上墨水、蛋彩和醋酸盐胶片
Ink and tempera with acetate overlay on Strathmore paper
40 × 58.1 cm
1998.1.1220

INDEX OF WORKS  369

《三个翅膀的人和时尚首饰》
*Three Winged Figures and Fashion Accessories*
1950年代 1950s
丝蒂摩纸上墨水和苯胺染料
Ink and Dr. Martin's aniline dye on Strathmore paper
43.8 × 57.2 cm
1998.1.1228

《腿和可口可乐瓶》
*Pair of Legs with Coca-Cola Bottle*
约 ca. 1956
丝蒂摩纸上墨水、水粉和石墨
Ink, gouache, and graphite on Strathmore paper
30.5 × 27.3 cm
1998.1.1279

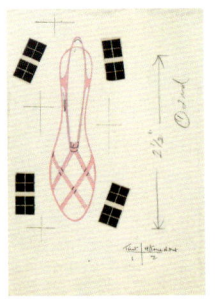

《凉鞋》
*Sandal*
1950年代 1950s
丝蒂摩纸上墨水和蛋彩
Ink and tempera on Strathmore paper
20.6 × 14 cm
1998.1.1323

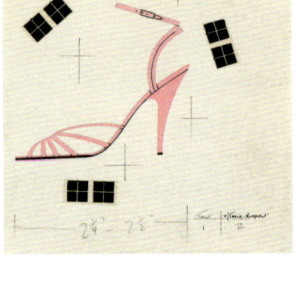

《凉鞋》
*Sandal*
1950年代 1950s
丝蒂摩纸上墨水、石墨、蛋彩和定位胶带
Ink, graphite, tempera, and registration tape on Strathmore paper
17.5 × 18.1 cm
1998.1.1322

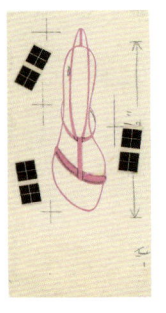

《鞋(带印刷套准标记)》
*Shoe (with Registration Marks)*
1954
丝蒂摩纸上墨水和蛋彩
Ink and tempera on Strathmore paper
20 × 10.2 cm
1998.1.1324

《八只鞋》
*Eight Shoes*
1950年代 1950s
丝蒂摩纸上墨水和苯胺染料
Ink and Dr. Martin's aniline dye on Strathmore paper
41 × 64 cm
1998.1.1045

《幻想中的鞋》
*Fantasy Shoes*
约 ca. 1956
丝蒂摩纸上墨水和苯胺染料
Ink and Dr. Martin's aniline dye on Strathmore paper
57.5 × 72.7 cm
1998.1.1055

《高跟鞋》
*High Heel Shoe*
约 ca. 1955
丝蒂摩纸上墨水和苯胺染料
Ink and Dr. Martin's aniline dye on Strathmore paper
22.9 × 27.9 cm
1998.1.1046

《高跟鞋》
*High Heeled Shoe*
1950年代 1950s
丝蒂摩纸上墨水、石墨和苯胺染料
Ink, graphite, and Dr. Martin's aniline dye on Strathmore paper
22.9 × 27.9 cm
1998.1.1057

《圣诞鞋》
*Merry Christmas Shoe*
约 ca. 1957
丝蒂摩纸和金箔纸上墨水和苯胺染料
Ink and Dr. Martin's aniline dye on Strathmore and gold paper
23.2 × 31.8 cm
1998.1.1051

《为蒂芙尼公司设计的圣诞贺卡》
*Christmas Card Design for Tiffany & Co.*
20世纪50年代 1950s
丝蒂摩纸上墨水、苯胺染料和打印材料
Ink, Dr. Martin's aniline dye, and printed material on Strathmore paper
41.6 × 31.1 cm
1998.1.1061

《为蒂芙尼公司设计的圣诞贺卡》
*Christmas Card Design for Tiffany & Co.*
20世纪50年代 1950s
丝蒂摩纸上墨水、苯胺染料和打印材料
Ink, Dr. Martin's aniline dye, and printed material on Strathmore paper
41.6 × 31.1 cm
1998.1.1060

《为蒂芙尼公司设计的圣诞贺卡》
*Christmas Card Design for Tiffany & Co.*
20世纪50年代 1950s
丝蒂摩纸上墨水和苯胺染料
Ink and Dr. Martin's aniline dye on Strathmore paper
32.1 × 43.8 cm
1998.1.1063

《鸡尾酒时间的星座运势（"虔诚的摩羯座"）》
*Horoscopes for the Cocktail Hour ("Reverent Capricorn")*
约 ca. 1961
写生纸上墨水和苯胺染料
Ink and Dr. Martin's aniline dye on sketchbook paper
61 × 45.7 cm
1998.1.1352

《鸡尾酒时间的星座运势（"香槟鸡尾酒"）》
*Horoscopes for the Cocktail Hour ("Champagne Cocktail")*
约 ca. 1961
写生纸上墨水、印墨、苯胺染料和 拼贴
Ink, stamped ink, Dr. Martin's aniline dye, and collage on sketchbook paper
61 × 45.7 cm
1998.1.1350

《鸡尾酒时间的星座运势（"明智的射手座"）》
*Horoscopes for the Cocktail Hour ("Sagacious Sagittarius")*
约 ca. 1961
写生纸上墨水、石墨和苯胺染料
Ink, graphite, and Dr. Martin's aniline dye on sketchbook paper
61 × 45.7 cm
1998.1.1351

《"彩绘蛇……为弗莱明－约菲公司"皮制品商店做的设计》
*"The Painted Serpent...Fleming Joffe"*
约 ca. 1961
纸上丝网印刷和爬行动物皮拼贴
Screen print and reptile skin collage on paper
57.2 × 43.2 cm
1998.1.1185

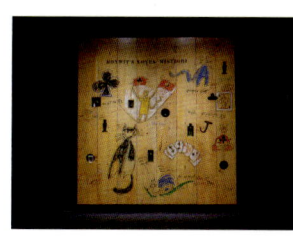

"人人都爱弗莱明－约菲牌的麂皮产品"
*"Everybody is in love with Suede at Fleming-Joffe"*
约 ca. 1958—1965
丝蒂摩纸上平版印刷、染色爬行动物皮和麂皮拼贴
Offset lithograph, dyed reptile skin, and suede collage on Strathmore paper
61.3 × 45.4 cm
特迪与阿瑟·埃德尔曼捐赠
Gift of Teddy and Arthur Edelman
2000.3.24.5

邦威特百货 Mistigri 牌香水橱窗展示
*"Bonwit's Loves Mistigri"*
1955
重制 Reproduction 2021
重制木板丙烯和蜡笔
Crayon and acrylic on wood
235 × 256.5 × 1.9 cm
IA2021.1.1a-h

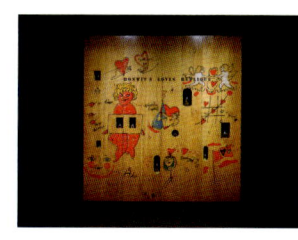

邦威特百货 Replique 牌香水橱窗展示
*"Bonwit's Loves Replique"*
1957
重制 Reproduction 2017
重制 木板丙烯和蜡笔
Crayon and acrylic on wood
235 × 256.5 × 1.9 cm
IA2017.1.1a-h

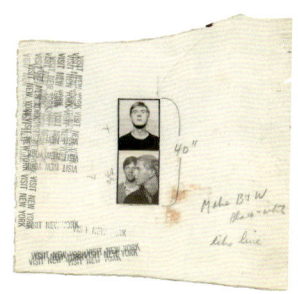

《机械感(安迪·沃霍尔快照亭自拍与迈克和鲍勃·艾布拉姆斯快照亭照片)》
*Mechanical (Andy Warhol photobooth self-portrait with Mike and Bob Abrams photobooth portraits)*
约 ca. 1964
重磅纸上快照亭照片、石墨和墨水
Photobooth photographs, graphite, and ink on heavyweight paper
25.4 × 25.7 cm
1998.3.5391

《自画像》
*Self-Portrait*
1964
布上丙烯、金属涂漆料和丝网印刷
Acrylic, metallic paint, and silkscreen ink on linen
51.1 × 41 × 1.9 cm
迪亚艺术中心捐赠
Contribution Dia Center for the Arts
2002.4.20

《机械感(安迪·沃霍尔快照亭自拍与朱迪丝·格林快照亭照片)》
*Mechanical (Andy Warhol photobooth self-portrait with Judith Green photobooth portrait)*
约 ca. 1963
重磅纸上快照亭照片和石墨
Photobooth photographs and graphite on heavyweight paper
32.4 × 27.9 cm
1998.3.5491

《自画像》
*Self-Portrait*
1963–1964
布上丙烯和丝印油墨
Acrylic and silkscreen ink on linen
50.8 × 40.6 cm
1998.1.810

《花》
*Flowers*
1964
布上丙烯、铅笔和丝网印刷
Acrylic, silkscreen ink, and pencil on linen
121.9 × 121.9 cm
1998.1.27

INDEX OF WORKS

《花》
Flowers
1964
布上丙烯、铅笔和丝网印刷
Acrylic, silkscreen ink, and pencil on linen
121.9 × 121.9 cm
1998.1.26

《简·方达》
Jane Fonda
1982
宝丽来 Polacolor 2 彩色胶片
Polaroid™ Polacolor 2
10.8 × 8.6 cm
2000.2.343

《安迪·沃霍尔给一对情侣拍照》
罗伯特·肖
Andy Warhol photographing an unidentified couple
Robert Shaw
1972
明胶银盐相纸
Gelatin silver print
27.9 × 35.6 cm
TC124.181.6

《大幅投影胶片(简·方达)》
Large acetate (Jane Fonda)
1982
聚酯膜上感光乳剂
Photo emulsion on polyester film base
137.2 × 106.7 cm
1998.3.1002.2

《安迪·沃霍尔与一位男士》
罗伯特·肖
Andy Warhol with unidentified man
Robert Shaw
1972
明胶银盐相纸
Gelatin silver print
27.9 × 35.6 cm
TC124.181.5

《简·方达》
Jane Fonda
1982
布上丙烯和丝印油墨
Acrylic and silkscreen ink on linen
121.9 × 111.8 cm
1998.1.545

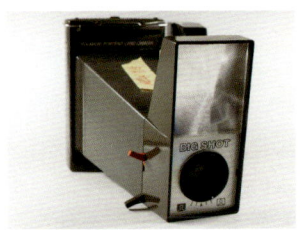

宝丽来 Big Shot 照相机
Polaroid Big Shot
约 ca. 1972
模压塑料、金属零件
Molded plastic with metal parts
26 × 15.2 × 17.1 cm
1998.3.10829.1

《简·方达》
Jane Fonda
1982
布上丙烯和丝印油墨
Acrylic and silkscreen ink on linen
121.9 × 111.8 cm
1998.1.546

宝丽来 Big Shot 照相机
Polaroid Big Shot
约 ca. 1972
模压塑料、金属零件
Molded plastic with metal parts
26 × 15.2 × 17.1 cm
1998.3.2349

《大幅描摹(简·方达)》
Large tracing (Jane Fonda)
1982
不透明聚酯板上石墨
Graphite on opaque polyester sheet
114.3 × 88.9 cm
1998.3.1002.6

《安迪·沃霍尔与一位女士》
罗伯特·肖
Andy Warhol with unidentified woman
Robert Shaw
1972
明胶银盐相纸
Gelatin silver print
35.6 × 27.9 cm
TC124.181.4

《简·方达》
Jane Fonda
1982
莱诺克斯博物馆纸板上丝网印刷
Screen print on Lenox Museum Board
101 × 80.3 cm
1998.1.2455

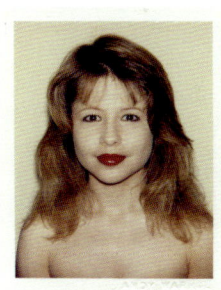

《皮娅·扎多拉》
*Pia Zadora*
1983
宝丽来 Polacolor ER 彩色胶片
Polaroid™ Polacolor ER
10.8 × 8.6 cm
2000.2.377

《马雷拉·阿涅利》
*Marella Agnelli*
1973
布上丙烯和丝印油墨
Acrylic and silkscreen ink on linen
101.6 × 101.6 cm
迪亚艺术中心捐赠
Contribution Dia Center for the Arts
1997.1.7a

《皮娅·扎多拉》
*Pia Zadora*
1983
宝丽来 Polacolor ER 彩色胶片
Polaroid™ Polacolor ER
10.8 × 8.6 cm
2000.2.378

《马雷拉·阿涅利》
*Marella Agnelli*
1973
布上丙烯和丝印油墨
Acrylic and silkscreen ink on linen
101.6 × 101.6 cm
迪亚艺术中心捐赠
Contribution Dia Center for the Arts
1997.1.7b

《安迪·沃霍尔给皮娅·扎多拉拍照》
戴维·麦高夫
*Andy Warhol photographing Pia Zadora*
David McGough
1983
明胶银盐相纸
Gelatin silver print
20.3 × 25.4 cm
TC522.119.4

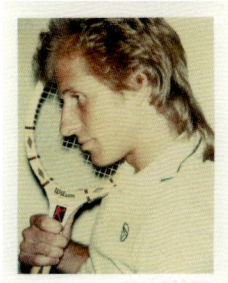

《维塔斯·格鲁莱蒂斯》
*Vitas Gerulitas*
1977
宝丽来 Polacolor (108) 彩色胶片
Polaroid™ Polacolor type 108
10.8 × 8.6 cm
2001.2.1244

《皮娅·扎多拉》
*Pia Zadora*
1983
布上丙烯和丝印油墨
Acrylic and silkscreen ink on linen
101.6 × 101.6 cm
1998.1.693

《维塔斯·格鲁莱蒂斯》
*Vitas Gerulaitis*
1977
布上丙烯和丝印油墨
Acrylic and silkscreen ink on linen
101.6 × 101.6 cm
1998.1.825

《皮娅·扎多拉》
*Pia Zadora*
1983
布上丙烯和丝印油墨
Acrylic and silkscreen ink on linen
101.6 × 101.6 cm
1998.1.694

《维塔斯·格鲁莱蒂斯》
*Vitas Gerulaitis*
1977
布上丙烯和丝印油墨
Acrylic and silkscreen ink on linen
101.6 × 101.6 cm
1998.1.824

《马雷拉·阿涅利》
*Marella Agnelli*
1972
宝丽来 Polacolor (108) 彩色胶片
Polaroid™ Polacolor type 108
10.8 × 8.6 cm
2000.2.444

《丽莎·明尼里》
*Liza Minnelli*
1977
宝丽来 Polacolor (108) 彩色胶片
Polaroid™ Polacolor type 108
10.8 × 8.6 cm
2000.2.330

《丽莎·明尼里：卡内基音乐厅演唱会》
丽莎·明尼里
Liza Minnelli: Live at Carnegie Hall
Liza Minnelli
1981
涂层唱片封套上平版印刷
Offset lithograph on coated record cover stock
31.4 × 31.1 cm
美术馆购入收藏
Museum Purchase
1994.26

《丽莎·明尼里》
Liza Minnelli
1979
布上丙烯和丝印油墨
Acrylic and silkscreen ink on linen
101.6 × 101.6 cm
迪亚艺术中心捐赠
Contribution Dia Center for the Arts
1997.1.10a

《丽莎·明尼里》
Liza Minnelli
约 ca. 1978
碎布纸上丝网印刷
Screen print on Curtis rag paper
114.3 × 88.9 cm
1998.1.2595

《丽莎·明尼里》
Liza Minnelli
1979
布上丙烯和丝印油墨
Acrylic and silkscreen ink on linen
101.6 × 101.6 cm
迪亚艺术中心捐赠
Contribution Dia Center for the Arts
1997.1.10b

《丽莎·明尼里》
Liza Minnelli
约 ca. 1978
碎布纸上丝网印刷
Screen print on Curtis rag paper
114.3 × 88.9 cm
1998.1.3912

《玛莎·葛兰姆》
Martha Graham
1980
布上丙烯和丝印油墨
Acrylic and silkscreen ink on linen
101.6 × 101.6 cm
迪亚艺术中心捐赠
Contribution Dia Center for the Arts
1997.1.13a

《小幅投影胶片(丽莎·明尼里)》
Small acetate (Liza Minnelli)
1978
聚酯膜上感光乳剂
Photo emulsion on polyester film base
31.1 × 25.4 cm
1998.3.1405.6a

《玛莎·葛兰姆》
Martha Graham
1980
布上丙烯和丝印油墨
Acrylic and silkscreen ink on linen
101.6 × 101.6 cm
迪亚艺术中心捐赠
Contribution Dia Center for the Arts
1997.1.13b

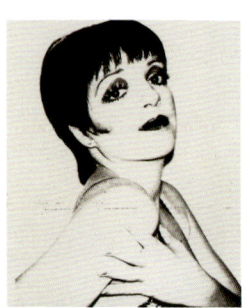

《小幅投影胶片(丽莎·明尼里)》
Small acetate (Liza Minnelli)
1978
聚酯膜上感光乳剂
Photo emulsion on polyester film base
30.5 × 25.4 cm
1998.3.1405.5a

《马里莎·贝伦森》
Marisa Berenson
1982
宝丽来 Polacolor ER 彩色胶片
Polaroid™ Polacolor ER
10.8 × 8.6 cm
2000.2.106

《小幅投影胶片(丽莎·明尼里)》
Small acetate (Liza Minnelli)
1978
聚酯膜上感光乳剂
Photo emulsion on polyester film base
30.5 × 25.4 cm
1998.3.1405.2a

《马里莎·贝伦森》
Marisa Berenson
1983–1984
布上丙烯和丝印油墨
Acrylic and silkscreen ink on linen
101.6 × 101.6 cm
1998.1.502

《马里莎·贝伦森》
*Marisa Berenson*
1983–1984
布上丙烯和丝印油墨
Acrylic and silkscreen ink on linen
101.6 × 101.6 cm
1998.1.503

《谢丽尔·提格丝》
*Cheryl Tiegs*
1984
宝丽来 Polacolor ER 彩色胶片
Polaroid™ Polacolor ER
10.8 × 8.6 cm
2000.2.373

《米盖尔·波塞》
*Miguel Bosé*
1983
莱诺克斯博物馆纸板上丝网印刷
Screen print on Lenox Museum Board
109.9 × 77.5 cm
1998.1.3925

《谢丽尔·提格丝》
*Cheryl Tiegs*
约 ca. 1984
布上丙烯和丝印油墨
Acrylic and silkscreen ink on canvas
101.6 × 101.6 cm
1998.1.667

《摩纳哥卡罗琳公主》
*Princess Caroline of Monaco*
1983
莱诺克斯博物馆纸板上丝网印刷
Screen print on Lenox Museum Board
102.6 × 102.2 cm
1998.1.3914

《谢丽尔·提格丝》
*Cheryl Tiegs*
约 ca. 1984
布上丙烯和丝印油墨
Acrylic and silkscreen ink on canvas
101.6 × 101.6 cm
1998.1.668

《米盖尔·波塞》
*Miguel Bosé*
1983
宝丽来 Polacolor ER 彩色胶片
Polaroid™ Polacolor ER
10.8 × 8.6 cm
1998.1.2943

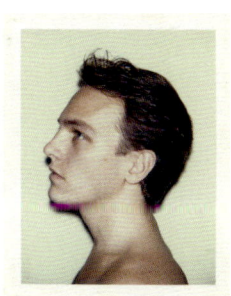

《乌尔里克·特罗亚堡》
*Ulrik Trojaborg*
1986
宝丽来 Polacolor ER 彩色胶片
Polaroid™ Polacolor ER
10.8 × 8.6 cm
1998.1.2941

《米盖尔·波塞》
*Miguel Bosé*
1983
布上丙烯和丝印油墨
Acrylic and silkscreen ink on linen
91.4 × 91.4 cm
1998.1.510

《乌尔里克·特罗亚堡》
*Ulrik Trojaborg*
1986
布上丙烯和丝印油墨
Acrylic and silkscreen ink on linen
101.6 × 101.6 cm
1998.1.669

《米盖尔·波塞》
*Miguel Bosé*
1983
布上丙烯和丝印油墨
Acrylic and silkscreen ink on linen
91.4 × 91.4 cm
1998.1.511

《乌尔里克·特罗亚堡》
*Ulrik Trojaborg*
1986
布上丙烯和丝印油墨
Acrylic and silkscreen ink on linen
101.6 × 101.6 cm
1998.1.670

INDEX OF WORKS

《瑞莉·霍尔》
*Jerry Hall*
约 ca. 1981
明胶银盐相纸
Gelatin silver print
20.3 × 25.4 cm
2001.2.128

《瑞莉·霍尔》
*Jerry Hall*
1979
明胶银盐相纸
Gelatin silver print
20.3 × 25.4 cm
1998.1.3097

《瑞莉·霍尔与生日蛋糕》
*Jerry Hall with Birthday Cake*
1980
明胶银盐相纸
Gelatin silver print
25.4 × 20.3 cm
1998.1.3103

《瑞莉·霍尔》
*Jerry Hall*
约 ca. 1981
明胶银盐相纸
Gelatin silver print
20.3 × 25.4 cm
2001.2.119

《萨尔瓦多·达利与乌尔特拉·维奥莱特，纽约》
*Salvador Dali and Ultra Violet, New York*
1970年代 1970s
明胶银盐相纸
Gelatin silver print
41 × 50.2 cm
2014.8.26

《丽莎·明尼里》
*Liza Minnelli*
1978
明胶银盐相纸
Gelatin silver print
20.3 × 25.1 cm
2001.2.814

《安迪·沃霍尔、玛莎·葛兰姆 和 生日蛋糕》
*Andy Warhol, Martha Graham, and a birthday cake*
1981
明胶银盐相纸
Gelatin silver print
20.3 × 25.4 cm
2001.2.829

《无题(周天娜与香奈儿包装盒)》
*Untitled (Tina Chow with CHANEL box)*
约 ca. 1985
明胶银盐相纸
Gelatin silver print
20.3 × 25.4 cm
1998.1.3024

《约翰·贝尼特斯、黛比·哈里 和卡尔文·克莱因》
*Jellybean Benitez, Debbie Harry, and Calvin Klein*
约 ca. 1983
明胶银盐相纸
Gelatin silver print
20.3 × 25.4 cm
2001.2.215

《葛蕾丝·琼斯》
*Grace Jones*
约 ca. 1985
明胶银盐相纸
Gelatin silver print
20.3 × 25.4 cm
1998.1.3045

《比安卡·贾格尔、丽莎·明尼里和杰奎琳·奥纳西斯在丽莎·明尼里的更衣室，纽约》
*Bianca Jagger, Liza Minnelli, and Jackie Onassis in Liza's Dressing Room, New York*
20 世纪 70 年代 1970s 明胶银盐相纸
Gelatin silver print
41 × 50.5 cm
2014.8.1

《丽莎·明尼里和约翰·列侬在沃霍尔的"工厂"，纽约》
*Liza Minnelli and John Lennon at Warhol's Factory, New York*
20 世纪 70 年代 1970s 明胶银盐相纸
Gelatin silver print
40.6 × 50.5 cm
2014.8.20

《莫妮克·范·盖德林、鲍勃·科拉切洛 和 托马斯·安曼》
*Monique van Vooren, Bob Colacello, and Thomas Ammann*
年份未知 n.d.
明胶银盐相纸
Gelatin silver print
20.3 × 25.4 cm
2001.2.234

《朱迪·福斯特与鲍勃·科拉切洛》
*Jodie Foster and Bob Colacello*
年份未知 n.d.
明胶银盐相纸
Gelatin silver print
20.3 × 25.4 cm
2001.2.688

《周天娜、弗兰·勒博维茨和一位男士》
Tina Chow, Fran Lebowitz, and
Unidentified Men
1980
明胶银盐相纸
Gelatin silver print
20.3 × 25.4 cm
2001.2.242

《杰奎琳·肯尼迪·奥纳西斯与查尔斯·亚当斯》
Jackie Kennedy Onassis and
Charles Addams
约 ca. 1980
明胶银盐相纸
Gelatin silver print
25.4 × 20.3 cm
1998.1.3057

《亨利·基辛格与伊丽莎白·泰勒·华纳,华盛顿特区》
Henry Kissinger and Elizabeth Taylor
Warner, Washington, DC
20 世纪 70 年代 1970s 明胶银盐相纸
Gelatin silver print
41 × 50.5 cm
2014.8.24

《罗伯特·梅普尔索普》
Robert Mapplethorpe
约 ca. 1978
明胶银盐相纸
Gelatin silver print
25.4 × 20.3 cm
2001.2.364

《史蒂夫·鲁贝尔》
Steve Rubell
1985
明胶银盐相纸
Gelatin silver print
25.4 × 20.3 cm
2001.2.435

《西尔维斯特·史泰龙》
Sylvester Stallone
约 ca. 1977
明胶银盐相纸
Gelatin silver print
25.4 × 20.3 cm
2001.2.444

《维克多·雨果》
Victor Hugo
年份未知 n.d.
明胶银盐相纸
Gelatin silver print
25.4 × 20.3 cm
2001.2.345

《送货员》
Unidentified Delivery Man
1980
明胶银盐相纸
Gelatin silver print 25.4 × 20.3 cm
2001.2.512

《比安卡·贾格尔与克丽丝·罗耶》
Bianca Jagger and Chris Royer
1981
明胶银盐相纸
Gelatin silver print
25.4 × 20.3 cm
TC577.79

《约翰·特拉沃尔塔与一位女士》
John Travolta and Unidentified Woman
1980
明胶银盐相纸
Gelatin silver print
20.3 × 25.4 cm
2001.2.749

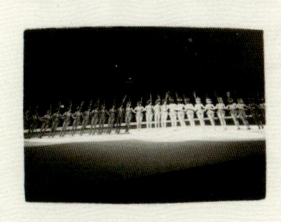
《多萝西·哈蜜尔与白雪溜冰团》
Dorothy Hamill and Ice Capades
年份未知 n.d.
明胶银盐相纸
Gelatin silver print
20.3 × 25.4 cm
2001.2.791

《卢·里德》
Lou Reed
1976–1986
明胶银盐相纸
Gelatin silver print
25.4 × 20.3 cm
2001.2.356

《克里斯·斯泰因与黛比·哈里》
*Chris Stein and Debbie Harry*
1982
明胶银盐相纸
Gelatin silver print
25.4 × 20.3 cm
2001.2.776

《米克·贾格尔》
*Mick Jagger*
1982
明胶银盐相纸
Gelatin silver print
20.3 × 25.4 cm
TC577.110.59

《马里莎·贝伦森》
*Marisa Berenson*
1981
明胶银盐相纸
Gelatin silver print
25.4 × 20.3 cm
TC577.92

《马里莎·贝伦森》
*Marisa Berenson*
约 ca. 1980
明胶银盐相纸
Gelatin silver print
25.4 × 20.3 cm
2001.2.70

《多莉·帕顿与奥莉维亚·纽顿-约翰》
*Dolly Parton and Olivia Newton-John*
年份未知 n.d.
明胶银盐相纸
Gelatin silver print
20.3 × 25.4 cm
2001.2.739

《伊恩·麦克莱恩与一位男士》
*Ian McKellen and Unidentified Man*
20 世纪 80 年代 1980s
明胶银盐相纸
Gelatin silver print
25.4 × 20.3 cm
2001.2.729

《雪儿》
*Cher*
1984–1985
明胶银盐相纸
Gelatin silver print
20.3 × 25.4 cm
2001.2.77

音乐剧《修女》派对现场
*Nunsense party*
1986
明胶银盐相纸
Gelatin silver print
25.4 × 20.3 cm
2001.2.802

《大卫·斯帕达、葛蕾丝·琼斯 和 凯斯·哈林》
*David Spada, Grace Jones, and Keith Haring*
1984
明胶银盐相纸
Gelatin silver print
25.4 × 20.3 cm
2001.2.94

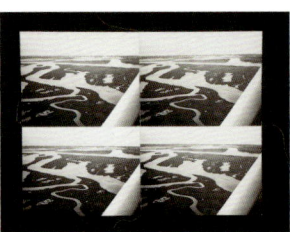

《支流(鸟瞰),1976—1986》
*Tributary (Aerial View), 1976—1986*
1986
线缝明胶银盐相纸
Gelatin silver prints sewn with thread
54.3 × 69.9 cm
1998.1.2735

《岩石海岸线,1976—1986 年》
*Rocky Shoreline, 1976—1986*
1986
线缝明胶银盐相纸
Gelatin silver prints sewn with thread
54.6 × 69.9 cm
1998.1.2709

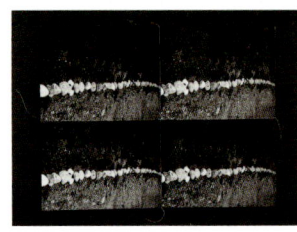

《缝制照片(蒙托克,火岛夏天)》
*Sewn Photograph (Montauk, Fire Island Summer)*
1976–1986
线缝明胶银盐相纸
Gelatin silver prints sewn with thread
69.9 × 54.3 cm
1998.1.2711

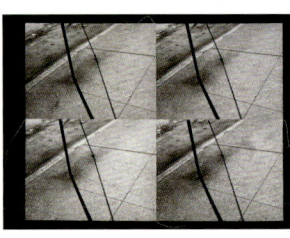

《人行道,1976—1986》
*Sidewalk, 1976—1986*
1986
线缝明胶银盐相纸
Gelatin silver prints sewn with thread
54 × 69.9 cm
1998.1.2721

《霍尔斯顿的书架,约 1978》
*Halston's Bookshelves, ca. 1978*
1986
线缝明胶银盐相纸
Gelatin silver prints sewn with thread
54.6 × 69.5 cm
1998.1.2675.10

《石滩,1976—1986》
*Beach with Stones, 1976—1986*
1986
线缝明胶银盐相纸
Gelatin silver prints sewn with thread
54.6 × 69.5 cm
1998.1.2675.4

《向后倾斜的大楼,1976—1986》
*Receding Building, 1976—1986*
1986
线缝明胶银盐相纸
Gelatin silver prints sewn with thread
69.9 × 54.3 cm
1998.1.2729

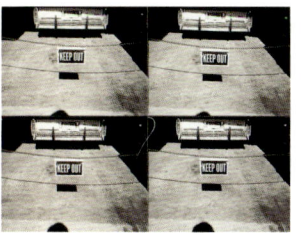

《标志("禁止入内"),1976—1986》
*Sign ("Keep Out"), 1976—1986*
1986
线缝明胶银盐相纸
Gelatin silver prints sewn with thread
54.6 × 69.1 cm
1998.1.2738

《米克·贾格尔,约 1978》
*Mick Jagger, ca. 1978*
1986
线缝明胶银盐相纸
Gelatin silver prints sewn with thread
54.3 × 70.2 cm
1998.1.2680

《多莉·帕顿和凯斯·哈林,1985》
*Dolly Parton and Keith Haring, 1985*
1986
线缝明胶银盐相纸
Gelatin silver prints sewn with thread
70.5 × 80.3 cm
1998.1.2698

《安迪·沃霍尔与克里斯·马科斯》
*Andy Warhol and Chris Makos*
1982
手工上色照片
Handcolored photograph
17.1 × 15.9 cm
1998.3.3091

《缝制照片(中国),1982》
*Sewn Photograph (China), 1982*
1986
线缝明胶银盐相纸
Gelatin silver prints sewn with thread
69.9 × 54.6 cm
1998.1.2707

《中国,1982》
*China, 1982*
1986
线缝明胶银盐相纸
Gelatin silver prints sewn with thread
54.6 × 69.9 cm
1998.1.2706

《中国(电影海报),1982》
*China (Movie Poster), 1982*
1986
线缝明胶银盐相纸
Gelatin silver prints sewn with thread
55.2 × 69.9 cm
1998.1.2705

《天窗与建筑》
*Skylight and Building*
1980
明胶银盐相纸
Gelatin silver print
20.3 × 25.4 cm
2001.2.1069

《台阶》
*Steps*
1982
明胶银盐相纸
Gelatin silver print
20.3 × 25.4 cm
2001.2.1089

《海报》
*Posters*
1980
明胶银盐相纸
Gelatin silver print
20.3 × 25.4 cm
2001.2.1092

《苏维埃战争纪念碑》
*Soviet War Memorial*
约 ca. 1982
明胶银盐相纸
Gelatin silver print
25.4 × 20.3 cm
TC577.111.26

INDEX OF WORKS

《结构》
Structure
年份未知 n.d.
明胶银盐相纸
Gelatin silver print
20 × 25.4 cm
2001.2.1020

《佛罗里达州棕榈滩上方的飞机》
Airplane over Palm Beach, Florida
约 ca. 1982
明胶银盐相纸
Gelatin silver print
20.3 × 25.4 cm
TC577.109.2

《结构》
Structure
年份未知 n.d.
明胶银盐相纸
Gelatin silver print
20 × 25.4 cm
2001.2.1021

《成排的明胶银盐相纸相片》
Rows of Gelatin Silver Prints
约 ca. 1980–1984
明胶银盐相纸
Gelatin silver print
20.3 × 25.4 cm
TC577.110.40

《建筑》
Buildings
年份未知 n.d.
明胶银盐相纸
Gelatin silver print
20 × 25.4 cm
2001.2.1008

《纪念碑上的树》
Trees at an undetermined monument
约 ca. 1980–1984
明胶银盐相纸
Gelatin silver print
25.4 × 20.3 cm
TC577.109.20

《建筑(阳台)》
Building (Balconies)
年份未知 n.d.
明胶银盐相纸
Gelatin silver print
20 × 25.4 cm
2001.2.1019

《树》
Tree
约 ca. 1980—1984
明胶银盐相纸
Gelatin silver print
20.3 × 25.4 cm
TC577.109.50

《盥洗室》
Bathroom
年份未知 n.d.
明胶银盐相纸
Gelatin silver print
20.3 × 25.4 cm
2001.2.262

《跳蚤市场(鸡蛋盒中的高尔夫球)》
Flea market (golf balls in egg cartons)
年份未知 n.d.
明胶银盐相纸
Gelatin silver print
20.3 × 25.2 cm
2001.2.930

《佛罗里达州棕榈沙滩上的脚》
Feet in the sand in Palm Beach, Florida
约 ca. 1982
明胶银盐相纸
Gelatin silver print
20.3 × 25.4 cm
TC577.108.5

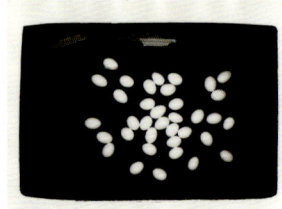

《蛋》
Eggs
1982
明胶银盐相纸
Gelatin silver print
20.3 × 25.4 cm
2001.2.637

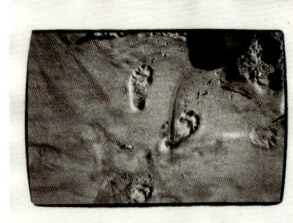

《沙滩上的脚印》
Footprints on a beach
约 ca. 1982
明胶银盐相纸
Gelatin silver print
20.3 × 25.4 cm
TC577.109.22

《成排的相片》
Rows of Prints
约 ca. 1980—1984
明胶银盐相纸
Gelatin silver print
25.4 × 20.3 cm
TC577.110.30

《框》
Frames
1982
明胶银盐相纸
Gelatin silver print
25.4 × 20.3 cm
2001.2.951

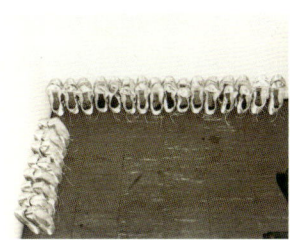

《芭蕾舞鞋》
Ballet Slippers
年份未知 n.d.
明胶银盐相纸
Gelatin silver print
20.3 × 25.4 cm
2001.2.888

《静物(可口可乐产品)》
Still-life (Coca-Cola merchandise)
1980年代 1980s
明胶银盐相纸
Gelatin silver print
20.3 × 25.4 cm
2001.2.926

《鞋》
Shoes
约 ca. 1980
明胶银盐相纸
Gelatin silver print
25.4 × 20.3 cm
2001.2.869

《成排的物体》
Serial Objects
20 世纪 80 年代 1980s
明胶银盐相纸
Gelatin silver print
25.4 × 20.3 cm
2001.2.927

《头骨》
Skulls
1986
明胶银盐相纸
Gelatin silver print
20 × 25.2 cm
2001.2.806

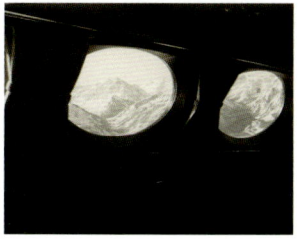

《鸟瞰》
Aerial view
1984
明胶银盐相纸
Gelatin silver print
20.3 × 25.4 cm
2001.2.990

《中国(可口可乐瓶)》
China (Coca-Cola Bottles)
1982
明胶银盐相纸
Gelatin silver print
20.2 × 25.4 cm
2001.2.961

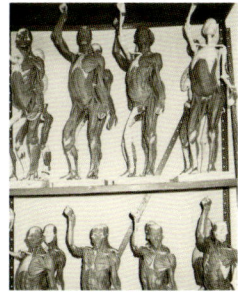

《雕塑模型》
Sculpture Models
1984
明胶银盐相纸
Gelatin silver print
25.4 × 20.3 cm
2001.2.987

《毛线》
Italian yarn
1982–1983
宝丽来 Polacolor ER 彩色胶片
Polaroid™ Polacolor ER
10.8 × 8.6 cm
2001.2.1495

《灯泡》
Light bulbs
1980
宝丽来 Polacolor ER 彩色胶片
Polaroid™ Polacolor ER
10.8 × 8.6 cm
2001.2.1514

《葡萄》
Grapes
1981
宝丽来 Polacolor 2 彩色胶片
Polaroid™ Polacolor 2
10.8 × 8.6 cm
2001.2.1515

《葡萄》
Grapes
1981
宝丽来 Polacolor 2 彩色胶片
Polaroid™ Polacolor 2
10.8 × 8.6 cm
2001.2.1516

《鞋》
*Shoes*
1980
宝丽来 Polacolor 2 彩色胶片
Polaroid™ Polacolor 2
38.1 × 35.6 cm
2001.2.1607

《钥匙》
*Keys*
1980
宝丽来 Polacolor 2 彩色胶片
Polaroid™ Polacolor 2
10.8 × 8.6 cm
2001.2.1511

《鞋(女式)》
*Shoes (Women's group)*
1980
宝丽来 Polacolor 2 彩色胶片
Polaroid™ Polacolor 2
38.1 × 35.6 cm
2001.2.1482

《布里洛盒子》
*Brillo boxes*
1979
宝丽来 Polacolor 2 彩色胶片
Polaroid™ Polacolor 2
38.1 × 35.6 cm
2001.2.1483

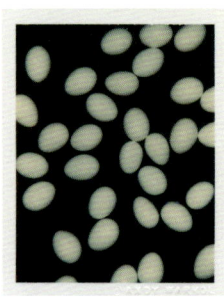

《复活节彩蛋》
*Easter Eggs*
1982
宝丽来 Polacolor 2 彩色胶片
Polaroid™ Polacolor 2
10.8 × 8.6 cm
2001.2.1694

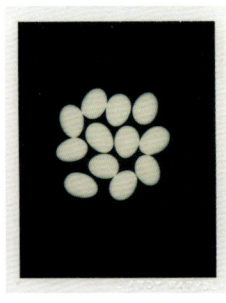

《复活节彩蛋》
*Easter Eggs*
1982
宝丽来 Polacolor 2 彩色胶片
Polaroid™ Polacolor 2
10.8 × 8.6 cm
2001.2.1693

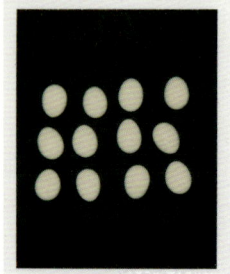

《复活节彩蛋》
*Easter Eggs*
1982
宝丽来 Polacolor 2 彩色胶片
Polaroid™ Polacolor 2
10.8 × 8.6 cm
2001.2.1692

《安迪·沃霍尔用宝莱克斯电影摄像机拍摄》
弗雷德·麦克达拉
*Andy Warhol filming with Bolex movie camera*
Fred McDarrah
1964
明胶银盐相纸
Gelatin silver print
30 × 40 cm
弗雷德·麦克达拉捐赠
Gift of The Estate of Fred W. McDarrah
2016.1.27

奥瑞康 CM-72A 摄像机
*Auricon CM-72A*
约 ca. 1964
混合档案材料
胶片盒:33 × 63.5 cm
Mixed archival material
Film cannister: 33 × 63.5 cm
1998.3.7861.1a-c

三脚架
*Tripod*
约 ca. 1964
木材、金属、塑料
高度:116.8 cm
Wood, metal, and plastic
Folded: 116.8 cm
2000.2.3019

《安迪·沃霍尔正在拍摄电影〈泰勒·米德之臀〉》
弗雷德·麦克达拉
*Andy Warhol Filming Taylor Mead's Ass*
Fred McDarrah
1964
明胶银盐相纸
Gelatin silver print
40 × 30 cm
弗雷德·麦克达拉捐赠
Gift of The Estate of Fred W. McDarrah
2016.1.24

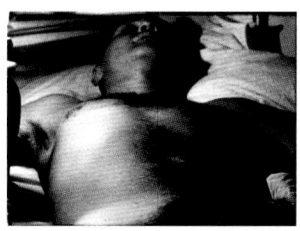

《沉睡》
*Sleep*
1964
16 毫米黑白无声电影，16fps
5 小时 21 分
16 mm film, black and white, silent, 16fps
321'

《伊迪·塞奇威克》
*Edie Sedgwick*
约 ca. 1965
快照亭照片
Photobooth photograph
20 × 4.1 cm
1998.1.2767
1998.1.2765
1998.1.2798

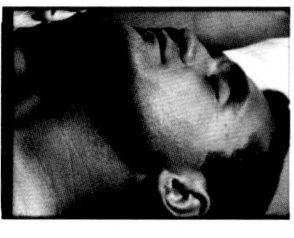

《帝国大厦》
*Empire*
1964
16 毫米黑白无声电影，16fps
8 小时 5 分
16 mm film, black and white, silent, 16fps
485'

《泰勒·米德》
*Taylor Mead*
1963 – 1964
快照亭照片
Photobooth photograph
20 × 4.1 cm
1998.1.2804

《比利·内姆给安迪·沃霍尔拍照》
斯蒂芬·肖尔
*Billy Name Photographing Andy Warhol*
Stephen Shore
1965
明胶银盐相纸
Gelatin silver print
12.7 × 20 cm
1998.3.14748

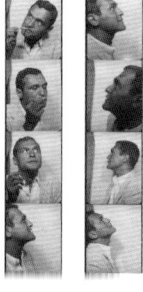

《约翰·焦尔诺》
*John Giorno*
约 ca. 1963
快照亭照片
Photobooth photograph
20 × 4.1 cm
1998.1.2822
1998.1.2818

《安迪·沃霍尔与杰拉德·马兰加》
斯蒂芬·肖尔
*Andy Warhol and Gerard Malanga*
Stephen Shore
1965
明胶银盐相纸
Gelatin silver print
12.7 × 20.3 cm
1998.3.14700

《自画像》
*Self-Portrait*
约 ca. 1963
明胶银盐相纸
Gelatin silver print
19.8 × 4.1 cm
TC25.2

《莎莉·柯克兰德》
斯蒂芬·肖尔
*Sally Kirkland*
Stephen Shore
1965
明胶银盐相纸
Gelatin silver print
12.7 × 20.3 cm
1998.3.14691

《莎莉·柯克兰德》
斯蒂芬·肖尔
*Sally Kirkland*
Stephen Shore
1965
明胶银盐相纸
Gelatin silver print
12.7 × 20.3 cm
1998.3.14577

《杰拉德·马兰加》
*Gerard Malanga*
约 ca. 1965
快照亭照片
Photobooth photograph
19.4 × 3.8 cm
1998.1.2833

《伊迪·塞奇威克与莎莉·柯克兰德》
斯蒂芬·肖尔
*Edie Sedgwick and Sally Kirkland*
Stephen Shore
1965
明胶银盐相纸
Gelatin silver print
12.7 × 20.3 cm
1998.3.14548

《伊迪·塞奇威克》
斯蒂芬·肖尔
*Edie Sedgwick*
Stephen Shore
1965
明胶银盐相纸
Gelatin silver print
12.7 × 20.3 cm
1998.3.14600

《莎莉·柯克兰德》
斯蒂芬·肖尔
*Sally Kirkland*
Stephen Shore
1965
明胶银盐相纸
Gelatin silver print
12.7 × 20.3 cm
1998.3.14729

《杰拉德·马兰加与艾薇·尼科尔森》
斯蒂芬·肖尔
*Gerard Malanga and Ivy Nicholson*
Stephen Shore
1965
明胶银盐相纸
Gelatin silver print
12.7 × 20.3 cm
1998.3.14590

《贝弗利·格兰特和杰克·史密斯在安迪·沃霍尔的电影＜蝙蝠侠 德古拉＞中 (1964)》
丹尼斯·霍珀
*Beverly Grant and Jack Smith on the set of Andy Warhol's film Batman Dracula (1964)*
Dennis Hopper
1964
明胶银盐相纸
Gelatin silver print
17.5 × 25.2 cm
1998.3.4569

《1965年，安迪·沃霍尔和保罗·莫里西等人正在拍摄 电影＜我的小白脸＞》
斯蒂芬·肖尔
*Andy Warhol, Paul Morrissey, and others during the filming of My Hustler, 1965*
Stephen Shore
重印 Reprint 1997
明胶银盐相纸
Gelatin silver print
25.4 × 20.3 cm
斯蒂芬·肖尔捐赠
Gift of Stephen Shore
1997.11.TC10.539.1

《安迪·沃霍尔、查克·魏因、杰拉德·马兰加和伊迪·塞奇威克在戴维·麦凯布工作室内摆出波普造型，纽约市，1965年春》
戴维·麦凯布
*Andy Warhol, Chuck Wein, Gerard Malanga and Edie Sedgwick as composite Pop creature at David McCabe's studio, New York City, spring 1965*
David McCabe
明胶银盐相纸
Gelatin silver print
50.5 × 40.6 cm
T592

《安迪·沃霍尔和奥瑞康摄像机在"工厂"的＜乙烯＞片场，纽约市，1965年4月初》
戴维·麦凯布
*Andy Warhol and the Auricon newsreel camera on the set of VINYL at the Factory, New York City, early April 1965*
David McCabe
重印 Reprint 1996
明胶银盐相纸
Gelatin silver print 27.9 × 35.2 cm
美术馆购入收藏
Museum Purchase
1996.9.101

《伊迪·塞奇威克、罗杰·特鲁多和勒内·里卡德（远端）在《厨房》片场（巴德·维特沙夫特公寓内），纽约市，1965年5月》
戴维·麦凯布
*Edie Sedgwick, Roger Trudeau and Rene Ricard (in background) on the set of KITCHEN (in the apartment of Bud Wirtschafter, New York City, May 1965*
David McCabe
重印 Reprint 1996
明胶银盐相纸
Gelatin silver print 35.6 × 27.9 cm
美术馆购入收藏
Museum Purchase
1996.9.105

《艾薇·尼科尔森试镜，1966》
比利·内姆
*Ivy Nicholson's Screen Test, 1966*
Billy Name
重印 Reprint 1996
明胶银盐相纸
Gelatin silver print
27.9 × 35.6 cm
美术馆购入收藏
Museum Purchase
1996.9.71

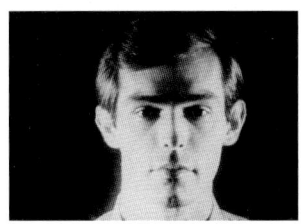
《彼得·于亚尔》[ST157]
*Peter Hujar* [ST157]
1964
16 毫米黑白无声电影，16fps
16 mm film, black and white, silent, 16fps
4'24"

《埃米·托宾》[ST335]
*Amy Taubin* [ST335]
1964
16 毫米黑白无声电影，16fps
16 mm film, black and white, silent, 16fps
4'24"

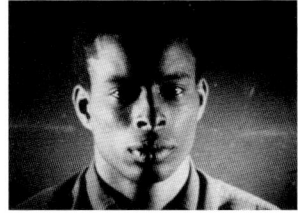
《鲁弗斯·科林斯》[ST61]
*Rufus Collins* [ST61]
1964
16 毫米黑白无声电影，16fps
16 mm film, black and white, silent, 16fps
4'30"

《弗朗索瓦·德梅尼尔》[ST212]
*Francois de Menil* [ST212]
1965
16 毫米黑白无声电影，16fps
16 mm film, black and white, silent, 16fps
4'30"

《比利·林奇》[ST194]
*Billy Linich* [ST194]
1964
16 毫米黑白无声电影，16fps
16 mm film, black and white, silent, 16fps
4'24"

《艾薇·尼科尔森》[ST230]
*Ivy Nicholson* [ST230]
1964
16 毫米黑白无声电影，16fps
16 mm film, black and white, silent, 16fps
4'30"

《泰勒·米德》[ST209]
*Taylor Mead* [ST209]
1964
16 毫米黑白无声电影，16fps
16 mm film, black and white, silent, 16fps
4'24"

《简·霍尔泽》[ST142]
*Jane Holzer* [ST142]
1964
16 毫米黑白无声电影，16fps
16 mm film, black and white, silent, 16fps
4'30"

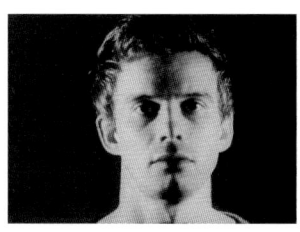
《沃尔特·戴恩伍德》[ST65]
*Walter Dainwood* [ST65]
1964
16 毫米黑白无声电影，16fps
16 mm film, black and white, silent, 16fps
4'24"

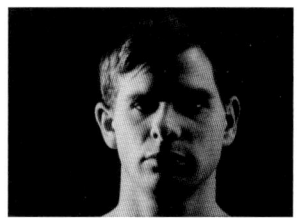
《凯莉·埃迪》[ST89]
*Kelly Edey* [ST89]
1964
16 毫米黑白无声电影，16fps
16 mm film, black and white, silent, 16fps
4'30"

《伊迪·塞奇威克》[ST308]
*Edie Sedgwick* [ST308]
1965
16 毫米黑白无声电影，16fps
16 mm film, black and white, silent, 16fps
4'36"

《布鲁克·海沃德》[ST132]
*Brooke Hayward* [ST132]
1964
16 毫米黑白无声电影，16fps
16 mm film, black and white, silent, 16fps
4'30"

《男孩》[ST31]
*Boy* [ST31]
1964
16 毫米黑白无声电影，16fps
16 mm film, black and white, silent, 16fps
4'30"

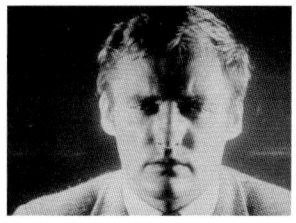
《丹尼斯·霍珀》[ST154]
*Dennis Hopper* [ST154]
1964
16 毫米黑白无声电影，16fps
16 mm film, black and white, silent, 16fps
4'24"

《多尼尔·卢纳》[ST195]
*Donyale Luna* [ST195]
1965
16 毫米黑白无声电影，16fps
16 mm film, black and white, silent, 16fps
4'30"

贝泽勒 Vu-Lyte 反射式放映机
*Beseler Vu-Lyte*
约 ca. 1960
混合档案材料
Mixed archival material
66.7 × 38.7 × 51.4 cm
T3831

《弗雷迪·赫科》[ST137]
*Freddy Herko* [ST137]
1964
16 毫米黑白无声电影，16fps
16 mm film, black and white, silent, 16fps
4'36"

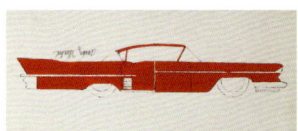

《车》
*Car*
1950 年代1950s
丝蒂摩纸上墨水和苯胺染料
Ink and Dr. Martin's aniline dye on Strathmore paper
33.7 × 65.1 cm
1998.1.1096

《杰拉德·马兰加》[ST198]
*Gerard Malanga* [ST198]
1964
16 毫米黑白无声电影，16fps
16 mm film, black and white, silent, 16fps
4'36"

《四名着戏装的男士全身像》
*Four Male Costumed Full Figures*
1950 年代 1950s
丝蒂摩纸上墨水和苯胺染料
Ink and Dr. Martin's aniline dye on Strathmore Seconds paper
57.2 × 72.4 cm
1998.1.973

《格雷戈里·巴特库克》[ST18]
*Gregory Battcock* [ST18]
1964
16 毫米黑白无声电影，16fps
16 mm film, black and white, silent, 16fps
4'30"

《凯迪拉克》
*Cadillac*
1962
写生纸上石墨
Graphite on sketchbook paper
61 × 45.7 cm
1998.1.2292

《莎莉·柯克兰德》[ST181]
*Sally Kirkland* [ST181]
1964
16 毫米黑白无声电影，16fps
16 mm film, black and white, silent, 16fps
4'30"

《七辆凯迪拉克》
*Seven Cadillacs*
1962
布上丝网印刷
Silkscreen ink on linen
142.2 × 48.3 cm
1998.1.23

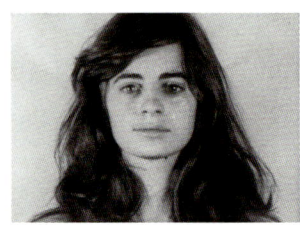

《安妮·布坎南》[ST33]
*Ann Buchanan* [ST33]
1964
16 毫米黑白无声电影，16fps
16 mm film, black and white, silent, 16fps
4'30"

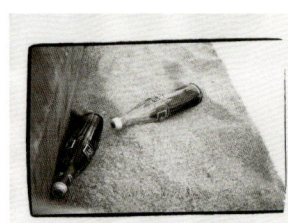

《可口可乐瓶》
*Coca-Cola Bottles*
约 ca. 1982
明胶银盐相纸
Gelatin silver print
20.3 × 25.4 cm
TC577.107.46

《可口可乐 2》
Coca-Cola 2
1961
布上酪蛋白颜料和蜡笔
Casein and crayon on linen
176.5 × 132.7 cm
迪亚艺术中心捐赠
Contribution Dia Center for the Arts
1997.1.20

《金宝汤罐头》
Campbell's Soup Can
1962
布上酪蛋白颜料、纸胶带和石墨
Casein, masking tape, and graphite on linen
181 × 135.9 cm
1998.3.1990

《标签撕开的大金宝汤罐头 (胡椒浓汤味)》
Big Torn Campbell's Soup Can (Pepper Pot)
1962
布上酪蛋白颜料和石墨
Casein and graphite on canvas
181.9 × 132.1 cm
1998.1.31

《挤压过的金宝汤罐头(牛肉面味)》
Crushed Campbell's Soup Can (Beef Noodle)
1962
棉布上酪蛋白颜料和石墨
Casein and graphite on cotton canvas
182.6 × 132.1 cm
1998.1.30

《金宝汤罐头 II：传统蔬菜味》
Campbell's Soup II: Old Fashioned Vegetable
1969
纸上丝网印刷
Screen print on paper
88.9 × 58.4 cm
1998.1.2394.1

《金宝汤罐头 II：切达奶酪味》
Campbell's Soup II: Cheddar Cheese
1969
纸上丝网印刷
Screen print on paper
88.9 × 58.4 cm
1998.1.2394.10

《金宝汤罐头 II：苏格兰浓汤味》
Campbell's Soup II: Scotch Broth
1969
纸上丝网印刷
Screen print on paper
88.9 × 58.4 cm
1998.1.2394.2

《金宝汤罐头 II：素食蔬菜味》
Campbell's Soup II: Vegetarian Vegetable
1969
纸上丝网印刷
Screen print on paper
88.9 × 58.4 cm
1998.1.2394.3

《金宝汤罐头 II：番茄牛肉圈形面味》
Campbell's Soup II: Tomato - Beef Noodle O's
1969
纸上丝网印刷
Screen print on paper
88.9 × 58.4 cm
1998.1.2394.8

《金宝汤罐头 II：新英格兰蛤蜊浓汤味》
Campbell's Soup II: New England Clam Chowder
1969
纸上丝网印刷
Screen print on paper
88.9 × 58.4 cm
1998.1.2394.4

《金宝汤罐头 II：鸡肉面糊味》
Campbell's Soup II: Chicken 'n Dumplings
1969
纸上丝网印刷
Screen print on paper
88.9 × 58.4 cm
1998.1.2394.5

《金宝汤罐头 II：黄金蘑菇味》
Campbell's Soup II: Golden Mushroom
1969
纸上丝网印刷
Screen print on paper
88.9 × 58.4 cm
1998.1.2394.9

INDEX OF WORKS

《金宝汤罐头 II：热狗豆味》
Campbell's Soup II: Hot Dog Bean
1969
纸上丝网印刷
Screen print on paper
88.9 × 58.4 cm
1998.1.2394.6

《金宝汤盒(洋葱蘑菇味)》
Campbell's Onion Mushroom Soup Box
1986
布上丙烯和丝印油墨
Acrylic and silkscreen ink on linen
50.8 × 50.8 cm
1998.1.360

《金宝汤罐头 II：生蚝浓汤味》
Campbell's Soup II: Oyster Stew
1969
纸上丝网印刷
Screen print on paper
88.9 × 58.4 cm
1998.1.2394.7

《金宝汤盒》
Campbell's Noodle Soup Box
1986
布上丙烯和丝印油墨
Acrylic and silkscreen ink on linen
50.8 × 50.8 cm
1998.1.361

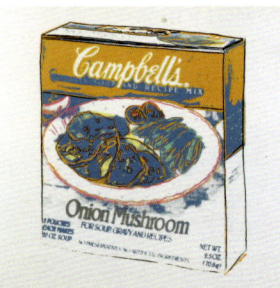

《金宝汤盒(洋葱蘑菇味)》
Campbell's Onion Mushroom Soup Box
1986
布上丙烯和丝印油墨
Acrylic and silkscreen ink on linen
50.8 × 50.8 cm
1998.1.365

《金宝汤盒》
Campbell's Noodle Soup Box
1986
布上丙烯和丝印油墨
Acrylic and silkscreen ink on linen
50.8 × 50.8 cm
1998.1.362

《金宝汤盒》
Campbell's Noodle Soup Box
1986
布上丙烯和丝印油墨
Acrylic and silkscreen ink on linen
50.8 × 50.8 cm
1998.1.366

《金宝汤盒》
Campbell's Noodle Soup Box
1986
布上丙烯和丝印油墨
Acrylic and silkscreen ink on linen
50.8 × 50.8 cm
1998.1.359

《金宝汤盒》
Campbell's Noodle Soup Box
1986
布上丙烯和丝印油墨
Acrylic and silkscreen ink on linen
50.8 × 50.8 cm
1998.1.363

《金宝汤盒(鸡肉面味)》
Campbell's Soup Box (Chicken Noodle)
1986
手工纸上石墨
Graphite on HMP paper
80 × 60.3 cm
1998.1.2083

《金宝汤盒(鸡肉米汤味)》
Campbell's Chicken Rice Soup Box
1986
布上丙烯和丝印油墨
Acrylic and silkscreen ink on linen
50.8 × 50.8 cm
1998.1.364

《金宝汤罐头(云吞)》
Campbell's Soup Can (Wonton)
约 ca. 1981
手工纸上石墨
Graphite on HMP paper
80 × 62.2 cm
1998.1.2086

《布里洛含皂钢丝棉包装盒》
*Brillo Soap Pads Box*
1964
胶合板上丝网油墨和建筑漆
Silkscreen ink and house paint on plywood
43.2 × 43.2 × 35.6 cm
1998.1.709

《玛丽莲·梦露（玛丽莲）》
*Marilyn Monroe (Marilyn)*
1967
纸上丝网印刷
Screen print on paper
91.4 × 91.4 cm
1998.1.2386

《金宝汤番茄汁包装箱》
*Campbell's Tomato Juice Box*
1964
胶合板上丝网油墨和建筑漆
Silkscreen ink and house paint on plywood
25.4 × 48.3 × 24.1 cm
1998.1.762

《玛丽莲·梦露（玛丽莲）》
*Marilyn Monroe (Marilyn)*
1967
纸上丝网印刷
Screen print on paper
91.4 × 91.8 cm
1998.1.2383

《亨氏番茄酱包装箱》
*Heinz Tomato Ketchup Box*
1964
胶合板上丝网油墨和建筑漆
Silkscreen ink and house paint on plywood
21.6 × 39.4 × 26.7 cm
1998.1.756

《玛丽莲·梦露（玛丽莲）》
*Marilyn Monroe (Marilyn)*
1967
纸上丝网印刷
Screen print on paper
91.4 × 91.4 cm
1998.1.2387

《德尔蒙桃罐头包装箱》
*Del Monte Peach Halves Box*
1964
胶合板上丝网油墨和建筑漆
Silkscreen ink and house paint on plywood
30.5 × 38.1 × 24.1 cm
1998.1.771

《玛丽莲·梦露（玛丽莲）》
*Marilyn Monroe (Marilyn)*
1967
纸上丝网印刷
Screen print on paper
91.4 × 91.4 cm
1998.1.2388

《玛丽莲·梦露：玛丽莲（"反转"系列）》
*Marilyn Monroe: Marilyn (Reversal series)*
约 ca. 1978
碎布纸上丝网印刷
Screen print on Curtis rag paper
57.2 × 44.5 cm
1998.1.2622

《玛丽莲·梦露（玛丽莲）》
*Marilyn Monroe (Marilyn)*
1967
纸上丝网印刷
Screen print on paper
91.4 × 91.4 cm
1998.1.2390

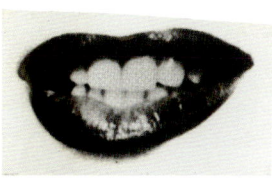

《投影胶片（玛丽莲·梦露的嘴唇）》
玛丽莲·梦露
*Acetate (Marilyn Monroe's lips)*
*Marilyn Monroe*
1962–1964
聚酯膜上感光乳剂
Photo emulsion on polyester film base
17.8 × 28.9 cm
TC30.46

《玛丽莲·梦露书本设计小样》
*Marilyn Monroe Book Maquette*
约 ca. 1968
综合媒介
Mixed media
15.2 × 24.1 × 1.9 cm
TC55.101a-c

《玛丽莲·梦露（玛丽莲）》
*Marilyn Monroe (Marilyn)*
1967
纸上丝网印刷
Screen print on paper
91.4 × 91.4 cm
1998.1.2384

INDEX OF WORKS

《牛》壁纸
*Cow Wallpaper*
1966
纸上丝网印刷
Screenprint on paper
安迪·沃霍尔美术馆重制，© 安迪·沃霍尔视觉艺术基金会
Refabricated by The Andy Warhol Museum, ©The Andy Warhol Foundation for the Visual Arts, Inc.

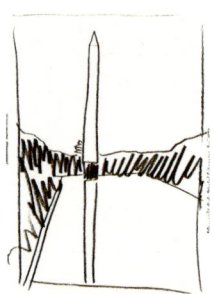

《华盛顿纪念碑》壁纸
*Washington Monument Wallpaper*
1974
纸上丝网印刷
Screenprint on paper
安迪·沃霍尔美术馆重制，© 安迪·沃霍尔视觉艺术基金会
Refabricated by The Andy Warhol Museum, ©The Andy Warhol Foundation for the Visual Arts, Inc.

《自画像》壁纸
*Self-Portrait Wallpaper*
1978
纸上丝印油墨
Screenprint on paper
安迪·沃霍尔美术馆重制，© 安迪·沃霍尔视觉艺术基金会
Refabricated by The Andy Warhol Museum, ©The Andy Warhol Foundation for the Visual Arts, Inc.

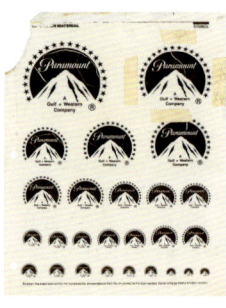

《派拉蒙影业公司商标标志》
作者未知
*Paramount Pictures trademark symbols*
Unknown
1980s
涂布纸上油墨印刷、纸胶带、石墨标记
Printed ink on coated paper with masking tape and graphite markings
27.8 × 21.4 cm
美术馆购入收藏，杰伊·雷格捐赠
Museum Purchase, Gift of Jay Reeg
2003.5.3

《广告：派拉蒙影业》
*Ads: Paramount*
1985
布上丙烯和丝印油墨
Acrylic and silkscreen ink on linen
55.9 × 55.9 cm
1998.1.475

《广告：派拉蒙影业》
*Ads: Paramount*
1985
莱诺克斯博物馆纸板上丝网印刷
Screen print on Lenox Museum Board
96.5 × 96.5 cm
1998.1.2484.3

《免税》
*Duty Free*
约ca. 1982 年
布上丙烯和丝印油墨
Acrylic and silkscreen ink on canvas
101.6 × 101.6 cm
1998.1.389

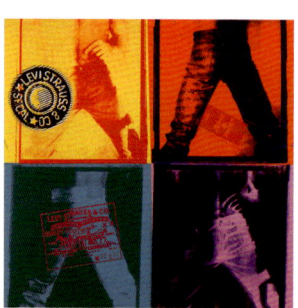

《李维斯牛仔裤（四幅）》
*Levi's (Four Images)*
1984
布上丙烯和丝印油墨
Acrylic and silkscreen ink on linen
101.6 × 101.6 cm
1998.1.400

《绝对伏特加》
*Absolut Vodka*
1985
手工纸上丙烯
Acrylic on HMP paper
80.6 × 61 cm
1998.1.393

《绝对伏特加》
*Absolut*
年份未知 n.d.
明胶银盐相纸
Gelatin silver print
20.3 × 25.4 cm
2001.2.577

《绝对伏特加》
*Absolut Vodka*
1985
布上丙烯和丝印油墨
Acrylic and silkscreen ink on linen
101.6 × 101.6 cm
1998.1.393

《巴黎水包装瓶》
Perrier Bottles
1983
布上丙烯和丝印油墨
Acrylic and silkscreen ink on linen
50.8 × 76.2 cm
1998.1.417

《巴黎水包装瓶》
Perrier Bottles
1983
布上丙烯和丝印油墨
Acrylic and silkscreen ink on linen
76.2 × 50.8 cm
1998.1.420

《巴黎水包装瓶》
Perrier Bottles
1983
布上丙烯和丝印油墨
Acrylic and silkscreen ink on linen
76.2 × 50.8 cm
1998.1.419

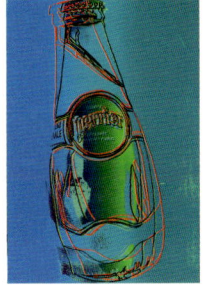
《巴黎水包装瓶》
Perrier Bottles
1983
布上丙烯和丝印油墨
Acrylic and silkscreen ink on linen
76.2 × 50.8 cm
1998.1.418

《新可口可乐》
New Coke
约 ca. 1985
手工纸上丝网印刷
Screen print on HMP paper
80.6 × 62.2 cm
1998.1.2505

《新可口可乐》
New Coke
约 ca. 1985
粘贴彩色美术纸上丝网印刷
Screen print on taped sheets
of colored graphic art paper
90.5 × 60.6 cm
1998.1.2506

《广告：苹果》
Ads: Apple
1985
布上丙烯和丝印油墨
Acrylic and silkscreen ink on linen
55.9 × 55.9 cm
1998.1.483

纽约 Esquire 公司
Esquire, *Inc.*, New York
《杂志广告（香奈儿 5 号香水，
<Esquire> 杂志，1955 年 1 月刊）》
Magazine Advertisement (CHANEL N°5,
Esquire magazine, January 1955)
1955
涂布纸上油墨印刷
Printed ink on coated paper
33.5 × 25.7 cm
美术馆购入收藏，杰伊·雷格捐赠
Museum Purchase, Gift of Jay Reeg
2003.5.5.2

《广告：香奈儿》
Ads: CHANEL
1985
布上丙烯和丝印油墨
Acrylic and silkscreen ink on linen
55.9 × 55.9 cm
1998.1.478

《安迪·沃霍尔十五分钟访谈（第 4 集）》
Andy Warhol's Fifteen Minutes (episode 4)
1987
1 英寸彩色有声录像带
1-inch videotape, color, sound
30'

《安迪·沃霍尔十五分钟访谈（第 4 集）》
Andy Warhol's Fifteen Minutes (episode 4)
1987
1 英寸彩色有声录像带
1-inch videotape, color, sound
30'

《安迪·沃霍尔电视秀
（第 1 季，第 10 集）》
Andy Warhol's T.V. (season 1, episode 10)
1981
¾ 英寸彩色有声录像带
¾-inch videotape, color, sound
30'

INDEX OF WORKS 391

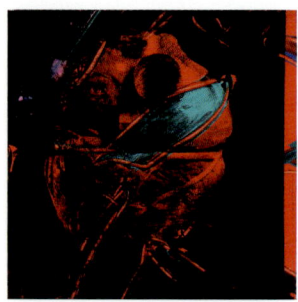

《人类心脏》
*Human Heart*
约 ca. 1979
布上丙烯和丝印油墨
Acrylic and silkscreen ink on canvas
55.9 × 55.9 cm
1998.1.447

《人类心脏》
*Human Heart*
约 ca. 1979
布上丙烯和丝印油墨
Acrylic and silkscreen ink on canvas
55.9 × 55.9 cm
1998.1.448

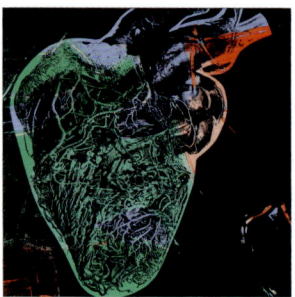

《人类心脏》
*Human Heart*
约 ca. 1979
布上丙烯和丝印油墨
Acrylic and silkscreen ink on canvas
55.9 × 55.9 cm
1998.1.449

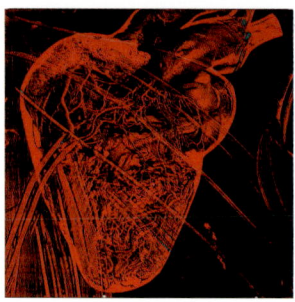

《人类心脏》
*Human Heart*
约 ca. 1979
布上丙烯和丝印油墨
Acrylic and silkscreen ink on canvas
55.9 × 55.9 cm
1998.1.450

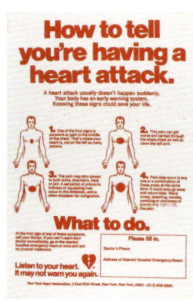

《情人节心脏健康宣传广告（……"心动"的感觉）》
*Valentine's Hearts Ads (...Having a Heart Attack)*
1982–1983
布上丙烯和丝印油墨
Acrylic and silkscreen ink on linen
38.1 × 25.4 cm
1998.1.461

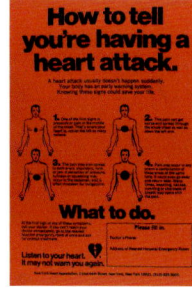

《情人节心脏健康宣传广告（……"心动"的感觉）》
*Valentine's Hearts Ads (...Having a Heart Attack)*
1982–1983
布上丙烯和丝印油墨
Acrylic and silkscreen ink on linen
38.1 × 25.4 cm

《迷彩》
*Camouflage*
1986
布上丙烯和丝印油墨
Acrylic and silkscreen ink on linen
203.2 × 203.2 cm
1998.1.350

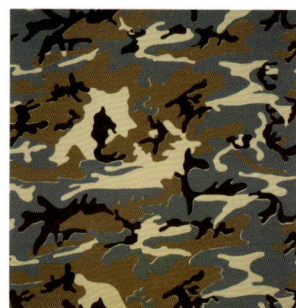

《迷彩》
*Camouflage*
1986
布上丙烯和丝印油墨
Acrylic and silkscreen ink on linen
203.8 × 193.7 cm
1998.1.351

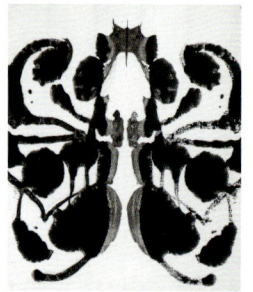

《罗夏墨迹测验》
*Rorschach*
1984
布上丙烯和丝印油墨
Acrylic and silkscreen ink on linen
50.8 × 40.6 cm
1998.1.302

《罗夏墨迹测验》
*Rorschach*
1984
布上丙烯和丝印油墨
Acrylic and silkscreen ink on linen
50.8 × 40.6 cm
1998.1.304

《罗夏墨迹测验》
*Rorschach*
1984
布上丙烯和丝印油墨
Acrylic and silkscreen ink on linen
50.8 × 40.6 cm
1998.1.299

《罗夏墨迹测验》
*Rorschach*
1984
布上丙烯和丝印油墨
Acrylic and silkscreen ink on linen
50.8 × 40.6 cm
1998.1.300

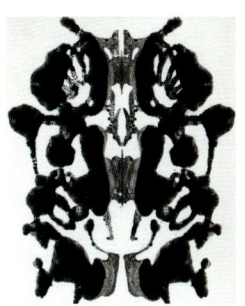

《罗夏墨迹测验》
*Rorschach*
1984
布上丙烯和丝印油墨
Acrylic and silkscreen ink on linen
50.8 × 40.6 cm
1998.1.303

《神话：女巫》
*Myths: The Witch*
1981
莱诺克斯博物馆纸板上丝网印刷和钻石粉末
Screen print with diamond dust on Lenox Museum Board
96.5 × 96.7 cm
1998.1.2452.4

《罗夏墨迹测验》
*Rorschach*
1984
布上丙烯和丝印油墨
Acrylic and silkscreen ink on linen
50.8 × 40.6 cm
1998.1.301

《神话：保姆》
*Myths: Mammy*
1981
莱诺克斯博物馆纸板上丝网印刷和钻石粉末
Screen print with diamond dust on Lenox Museum Board
96.5 × 96.7 cm
1998.1.2452.5

《神话：阴影》
*Myths: The Shadow*
1981
莱诺克斯博物馆纸板上丝网印刷和钻石粉末
Screen print with diamond dust on Lenox Museum Board
96.5 × 96.7 cm
1998.1.2452.10

《神话：胡迪·都迪》
*Myths: Howdy Doody*
1981
莱诺克斯博物馆纸板上丝网印刷和钻石粉末
Screen print with diamond dust on Lenox Museum Board
96.5 × 96.7 cm
1998.1.2452.6

《神话：明星》
*Myths: The Star*
1981
莱诺克斯博物馆纸板上丝网印刷和钻石粉末
Screen print with diamond dust on Lenox Museum Board
96.5 × 96.7 cm
1998.1.2452.1

《神话：德古拉》
*Myths: Dracula*
1981
莱诺克斯博物馆纸板上丝网印刷和钻石粉末
Screen print with diamond dust on Lenox Museum Board
96.5 × 96.7 cm
1998.1.2452.7

《神话：山姆大叔》
*Myths: Uncle Sam*
1981
莱诺克斯博物馆纸板上丝网印刷和钻石粉末
Screen print with diamond dust on Lenox Museum Board
96.5 × 96.7 cm
1998.1.2452.2

《神话：米老鼠》
*Myths: Mickey Mouse*
1981
莱诺克斯博物馆纸板上丝网印刷和钻石粉末
Screen print with diamond dust on Lenox Museum Board
96.5 × 96.7 cm
1998.1.2452.8

《神话：超人》
*Myths: Superman*
1981
莱诺克斯博物馆纸板上丝网印刷和钻石粉末
Screen print with diamond dust on Lenox Museum Board
96.5 × 96.7 cm
1998.1.2452.3

《神话：圣诞老人》
*Myths: Santa Claus*
1981
莱诺克斯博物馆纸板上丝网印刷和钻石粉末
Screen print with diamond dust on Lenox Museum Board
96.5 × 96.7 cm
1998.1.2452.9

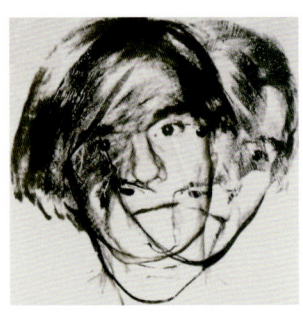

《自画像》
*Self-Portrait*
1978
布上丙烯和丝印油墨
Acrylic and silkscreen ink on linen
101.6 × 101.6 cm
1998.1.807

《美元标志》
*Dollar Sign*
1981
布上丙烯和丝印油墨
Acrylic and silkscreen ink on linen
228.6 × 177.8 cm
1998.1.248

《自画像》
*Self-Portrait*
1978
布上丙烯和丝印油墨
Acrylic and silkscreen ink on linen
101.6 × 101.6 cm
1998.1.806

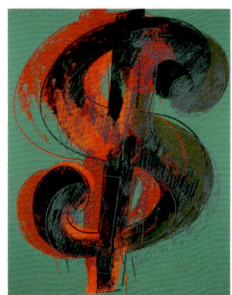

《美元标志》
*Dollar Sign*
1981
布上丙烯和丝印油墨
Acrylic and silkscreen ink on linen
228.6 × 177.8 cm
1998.1.247

《自画像》
*Self-Portrait*
1978
布上丙烯和丝印油墨
Acrylic and silkscreen ink on linen
40.6 × 33 cm
1998.1.811

《头骨》
*Skull*
1976
布上丙烯和丝印油墨
Acrylic and silkscreen ink on linen
183.2 × 204.5 cm
迪亚艺术中心捐赠
Contribution Dia Center for the Arts
2002.4.28

《勒住喉咙的自画像》
*Self-Portrait Strangulation*
1978
布上丙烯和丝印油墨
Acrylic and silkscreen ink on linen
40.6 × 33 cm
1998.1.812

《头骨》
*Skull*
1976
布上丙烯和丝印油墨
Acrylic and silkscreen ink on linen
183.2 × 204.5 cm
迪亚艺术中心捐赠
Contribution Dia Center for the Arts
2002.4.30

《带有美元标志的书》
*Dollar Sign Book*
年份未知 n.d.
象牙纸上石墨
Graphite on ivory paper
17.8 × 18.4 × 1.9 cm
1998.1.2275

《自画像》
*Self-Portrait*
1986
布上丙烯和丝印油墨
Acrylic and silkscreen ink on linen
203.2 × 193 cm
1998.1.817

《美元标志》
*Dollar Sign*
1981
布上丙烯和丝印油墨
Acrylic and silkscreen ink on linen
228.6 × 177.8 cm
1998.1.249

《自画像》
*Self-Portrait*
1986
布上丙烯和丝印油墨
Acrylic and silkscreen ink on linen
274.3 × 274.3 × 3.8 cm
1998.1.814

# UCCA 尤伦斯当代艺术中心成员
# UCCA Center for Contemporary Art Staff

馆长兼CEO
田霏宇

**Director and Chief Executive Officer**
Philip Tinari

首席运营官
朱玮琦

**Chief Operating Officer**
Windy Zhu

副馆长
尤洋

**Deputy Director**
You Yang

馆长办公室
黄文璇
张雅歌
张杨
黄天蓉
张丽婷
唐棠

**Director's Office**
Huang Wenxuan
Melody Zhang
Zhang Yang
Isak Huang
Amber Zhang
Taffe Tang

展览部
郭希
栾诗璇
关健
施瑶
杜帆
张南昭
杨翛然
刘楷韵
王紫薇
林妍

**Exhibitions Department**
Guo Xi
Luan Shixuan
Edward Guan
Shi Yao
Duffy Du
Neil Zhang
Anna Yang
Liu Kaiyun
Wang Ziwei
Yvonne Lin

研究部
赖柏圣
黄洁华
西门·法兰克
滕依霏
丁昕霓
李潇逸

**Research Department**
Patrick Rhine
Huang Jiehua
Simon Frank
Teng Yifei
Cindy Ding
Li Xiaoyi

公共实践部
韩馨逸
林立
蔺青霞
张罗威

**Public Practice Department**
Liya Han
Wild Lin
Anna Lin
Larry Zhang

UCCA Edge
卞卡
韩楠
秋韵
查旻恩
方言
林鹭琪
张尧
钱梦妮
徐子涵
李晓璇
蒋静忆
薛冰砚
王以真
庄诗琪
种婉耘
黄旖琳
王嫣然
刘越峰
庞雨晨
黄丽洁
孙雯婷
王倩影

品牌市场部
孔令祎
徐丹羽
袁嘉敏
潘玲丽
王继源
王可
李思慧
许诺
房小冉
王玲玲
胡健楠
朱乔昕
王天雨

发展部
游骁
魏红箫

**UCCA Edge**
Bian Ka
Han Nan
Ara Qiu
Mason Zha
Fang Yan
Lin Luqi
Zhang Yao
Qian Mengni
Nicole Xu
Li Xiaoxuan
Jiang Jingyi
Laura Xue
Wang Yizhen
Zhuang Shiqi
Chong Wanyun
Elaine Huang
Wang Yanran
Liu Yuefeng
Pang Yuchen
Esther Huang
Sun Wenting
Wang Qianying

**Communications and Marketing Department**
Kong Lingyi
Xu Danyu
Yuan Jiamin
Fatina Pan
Wang Jiyuan
Wang Ke
Li Sihui
Xu Nuo
Frank Fang
Willa Wang
Hu Jiannan
Jaime Chu
Brittany Wang

**Development Department**
Christina You
Ann Wei

李琳
李淙淙
施怡然
巫雨伦

Alin Li
Cindy Li
Hilary Shi
Alan Wu

张赫群
崔佳琦
傅蕾
雷潇潇

Silvia Zhang
Jessie Cui
Faye Fu
Michelle Lei

**基金会**
陈睿
郭晓虹
李舰
高浪浪

**UCCA Foundation**
Alex Chen
Guo Xiaohong
Li Jian
Gao Langlang

**UCCA商店**
沈蕾
关莹莹
吕峥
梁媛媛
张占春
王丁丁
彭乙轩
刘寅
王素萍
于佳宁
李俊仁
杨雯怡
邓丽维
吴诗羽

**UCCA Store**
Nikki Shen
Guan Yingying
Lyu Zheng
Liang Yuanyuan
Zhang Zhanchun
Wang Dingding
Peter Peng
Liu Yin
Wang Suping
Yu Jianing
Vader Li
Yang Wenyi
Deng Liwei
Wu Shiyu

**观众部**
杜英临
江弋舟
刘新月
闫笑
王鬈心
李仪
李慧娟
刘莹
许琳
关皓月
张明明

**Visitor Services Department**
Joanna Du
Jiang Yizhou
Luna Liu
Lulu Yan
Chelsea Wang
Li Yi
Li Huijuan
Liu Ying
Xu Lin
Grace Guan
Zhang Mingming

**教育部**
赵梦颖
张书轲
王思思
王晓玲
郑燕
张雪飞
张宝英
宋晓茜
吕汇洋
孟庆艳
刘欣悦
李江
米娜
商艳淼
刘潇
李立圆
毛新钰
王萌
李莎润梓
冯子凡
于欣月
刘朝

**UCCA Kids**
Zhao Mengying
Lisa Zhang
Sisi Wang
Wang Xiaoling
Zheng Yan
Zhang Xuefei
Zhang Baoying
Song Xiaoqian
Leticia Lyu
Meng Qingyan
Joy Liu
Matteo Li
Mina Mi
Lucy Shang
Daisy Liu
Li Liyuan
Lody Mao
Mona Wang
Runzi Li
Feng Zifan
Yu Xinyue
Liu Chao

**数字化战略部**
包雯璐

**Digital Strategy Department**
Wenlu Bao

**运营部**
李洋
安闯

**Operations Department**
Li Yang
An Chuang

**技术部**
李朗
李晔

**IT Department**
Li Lang
Li Ye

**人力资源部**
孙侃
韩晓萌
钱亚非
王玉凤

**Human Resources Department**
Terry Sun
Han Xiaomeng
Echo Qian
Wang Yufeng

**财务部**
邓舟源
宋奎奎
魏振玲
王晓红
谢忱
李宁
刘瑞芬
谢思琦

**Finance Department**
James Deng
Cathy Song
Wei Zhenling
Wang Xiaohong
Ivy Xie
Li Ning
Liu Ruifen
Xie Siqi

2021年7月3日

July 3, 2021

**UCCA Lab**
吴奕萱
刘雪丽
吴颜如
金禾昀
张佩伦
王上源
张家睿
曲博阳
谭皓泽
马子涵
黄昕昀
刘轩
张鑫
唐誉祯
王子侨

**UCCA Lab**
Wu Yixuan
Shirley Liu
Wu Yanru
Gillian Jin
Helena Zhang
Wang Shangyuan
Zhang Jiarui
Qu Boyang
Tan Haoze
Alain Ma
Huang Xinyun
Xuan Liu
Johnson Zhang
Yoojin Tang
Wang Ziqiao

**IP授权发展部**
冯颖
吕天瑀

**Intellectual Property Development Department**
Carmen Feng
Raven Lyu

# 鸣谢 Acknowledgments

| 尤伦斯艺术基金会理事会 | UCCA Foundation Council |
|---|---|
| 曹雅薇 | Sarah Cao |
| 陈丹霞 | Dio Chen |
| Jack Chen | Jack Chen |
| 陈晓雨 | Vivian Chen |
| 仇浩然 | Hallam Chow |
| 邓宇聪 | Eugene Tang |
| 方涛 | Paul Fang |
| 江南春 | Jason Jiang |
| Ivy Le | Ivy Le |
| 李晖 与 辛浩鹰 | Frank Lee & Chris Xin |
| 李琳 | Li Lin |
| 李锐 与 梁涛 | Michael Li & Liang Tao |
| 黎万强 | Alee |
| 刘兰 | Liu Lan |
| 刘千里 与 秦致 | Lily Liu & James Qin |
| 马寅 | Ma Yin |
| 茅矛 与 史佩婧 | Jerry Mao & Laura Shi |
| 沙烨 | Sha Ye |
| 尚云华 | Shang Yunhua |
| 苏丹瑞 与 梁琨如 | Derek & Michelle Leung Sulger |
| 涂雅芳 | Carmen Tu |
| 尤伦斯夫妇 | Guy & Myriam Ullens |
| 杰克·沃兹沃思 与 苏茜·沃兹沃思 | Jack & Susy Wadsworth |
| 王思勉 | Simian Collection |
| 王信文 | Kenny Wang |
| 谢伟 | Alina Xie |
| 杨滨 | Yang Bin |
| 余晚晚 | Wendy Yu |
| 曾宝宝 | Zeng Baobao |
| 曾子墨 | Zeng Zimo |
| 吴萌 与 张荷 | Wu Meng & Zhang He |
| 郑烜乐 | Leo Zheng |
| 周航 | Herman Zhou |

| UCCA国际委员会 | UCCA International Circle |
|---|---|
| 欧瑞思公主 | Princess Alia Al-Senussi |
| 董堂荣 | DTR (Dong Tangrong) |
| 杜妍 | Du Yan |
| 葛丹妮 | Nini Ge |
| 郭佳鑫 | Vince Guo |
| 金辰思 | Catriona Jin |
| 李铮 | James Li |
| 练峰 | Lian Feng |
| 梁舒乔 | Monique Leong |
| 刘宏剑 | Liu Hongjian |
| 刘晓丹 与 George Wang | Diane Liu & George Wang |
| 马东 | Ma Dong |
| | Dino Sadhwani |
| | Mei & Allan Warburg |
| 汪斌 | Robin Wang |
| 王睿 | Wang Rui |
| 文心 | Kevin Wen |
| 吴丰恒 | Henry Wu |
| 吴心竹 | Wu Xinzhu |
| 项倢婧 | Cici Xiang |
| 谢蓉 | Sophia Xie |
| 张卫平 | Tony Zhang |
| 张雪凝 | Sherry Zhang |

| UCCA青年赞助人 | UCCA Young Associates |
|---|---|
| 毕裕 | Bi Yu |
| 蔡秉桥 | Paula Tsai |
| 蔡逸胅 | Cai Yizhen |
| Click #15 | Click #15 |
| 曾瀛 | David Zeng |
| 陈安宇 | Chen Anyu |
| 陈碧何 | Bonnie Chen |
| 陈辰 | Claire Chen |
| 陈思园 | Eva Chen |
| 陈婉婷 | Chen Wanting |
| 陈一冰 | Ava Chen |
| 陈瀛洲 | Chen Yingzhou |
| 陈咏潞 | Nyx Chen |
| 陈宇曦 | Emilie Chen |
| 陈正 | Samuel Chen |
| 邓婷 | Lorina Deng |
| 杜凯睿 | Kerry Du |
| 杜欣然 | Doris Du |
| 段庄苒 | Danning Nichole |
| 方笛 | Iris Fang |
| 方证钧 | James Fang |
| 傅寒春 | Rebekah Fu |
| 付晓东 | Fu Xiaodong |
| 顾伟 | Damon Gu |
| 顾小骞 | Candice Gu |
| 顾耀 | Yod Gu |
| 国颖 | Guo Ying |
| 高子晴 | Ziqing Gao |
| Jonathan Ha | Jonathan Ha |
| 韩昕洺 | Han Xinming |
| Olivier Hervet | Olivier Hervet |
| 何祖琳 | He Zulin |
| 洪帆 | Stephanie Hong |
| Michelle Ho | Michelle Ho |
| 胡祎 | Hu Yi |

| | | | |
|---|---|---|---|
| 黄蕾 | Julie Huang | 王聪琳 | Marble Wang |
| 黄雅琼 | Huang Yaqiong | 王大骐 | CHI |
| 黄一峰 | William Huang | 汪海凝 | Wang Haining |
| 贾海宁 | Jia Haining | 王皓琳 | Wang Haolin |
| 蒋汉锡 | Justin Jiang | 王慧籽 | Sally Wang |
| 蒋梦婕 | Jiang Mengjie | 王珏 | Lydia Wang |
| 金翎语 | Jin Lingyu | 王莲仪 | Lotus Wang |
| 孔唯佳 | Weijia Chloe Kong | 王谅晨 | Jessica Wang |
| 来梦馨 | Sherry Lai | 王果果 | Celina Wang |
| 李楚珩 | Jenna Li | 王天也 | Wang Tianye |
| Jay Li | Jay Li | 王晓暄 | Annie Wang |
| 李婕 | Rachel Li | 王艺丹 | Wang Yidan |
| 黎晴之 | Candice Li | 王祎宁 | Elaine Wang |
| 李雯 | Li Wen | 王玥伦 | Wang Yuelun |
| 李文驹 | Brandon Li | 魏令斐 | Wei Lingfei |
| 李夏特 | Li Xiate | 韦熠 | Derek Wei |
| 李晓春 | Spring Li | 吴佳蓺 | Flora Wu |
| 李烨 | Roman Li | 吴谦 | Wu Qian |
| 李雨涵 | Li Yuhan | 吴雨珊 | Wu Yushan |
| 李志强 | Andy Li | 武釜 | Ayur Wu |
| 李宗琳 | Zonglin Li | 肖盾 | Xiao Dun |
| 林默 | Moon Lin | 小麦 | Rene Meile |
| 刘传 | Max Liu | 谢旖心 | Alda Xie |
| 刘玫君 | Mellie Liu | 许昊天 | Frank Xu |
| 刘沁敏 | Liu Qinmin | 徐珏 | Rita Xu |
| 刘水音 | Sylvia Liu | 许舒靖 | Andrea Xu |
| 刘苇航 | Dear Liu | 徐怡琛 | Rebecca Xu |
| 刘玮妍 | Liu Weiyan | 薛博中 | BoBo Xue |
| 刘雅芸 | Jenny Liu | 晏旺 | Yan Wang |
| 刘以恒 | Amber Liu | Grace Yang | Grace Yang |
| 卢婷婷 | Lu Tingting | 杨蓉 | Yang Rong |
| 陆洋 | Naomi Ru | 杨天渡 | Tian D. Yang |
| Claire Ma | Claire Ma | 杨雅麟 | Yang Yalin |
| 马豪 | Nick Ma | 杨轶 | Poppy Yang |
| 马赫 | Rory Ma | 叶晓薇 | Shaway Yeh |
| 马晶晶 | Ma Jingjing | 于庆新 | Yu Qingxin |
| 马青山 | Ma Qingshan | 于芷若 | Fiona Yu |
| 马小雨 | Rainie Ma | 原来是西门大嫂 | 原来是西门大嫂 |
| Lu Meng | Lu Meng | 袁宁杰 | Yuan NingJei |
| 孟露 | Lulu Meng | 云磊 | Yun Lei |
| 苗欣荣 | Stella Miao | Annabel Zhang | Annabel Zhang |
| 倪南 | Lana Ni | 张靖平 | Jackie Zhang |
| 彭雪 | Peng Xue | 张敬唯 | Sophie Zhang |
| 平良雨晴 | Melody Taira | 张均昱 | Jason Zhang |
| 浦奕柳 | Pu Yiliu | 张梦涵 | Henry Zhang |
| 邱伯谦 | Qiu Boqian | 张文昭 | Wenzhao Zhang |
| 曲晓东 | Jenny Qu | 张杨洋 | Amber Zhang |
| 曲直 | Kerry Qu | 郑涵 | Han Zheng |
| 宋墨馨 | Song Moxin | 郑俊豪 | LiL How |
| 宋特 | Song Te | 郑瑞昀 | Rui Zheng |
| 苏德中 | Timothy So | 郑思维 | Zheng Siwei |
| 苏晴 | Sunny Su | 郑宇希 | Celia Zheng |
| 孙博涵 | Sun Bohan | 郑云峰 | Vincent Zheng |
| 孙家欣 | Sun Jiaxin | 周密子 | Zhou Mizi |
| 滕悦 | Chloe Teng | 朱彬露 | Zhu Binlu |
| 田甜 | Tina Tian | 朱婧汐 | JING |
| 涂芷萱 | Elphe Tu | 祝开凝 | Zhu Kaining |
| Christian Johannes Voss | Christian Johannes Voss | 朱珠 | Zhu Zhu |
| 万婷 | Nicole Wan | 邹骋 | Rex Zou |
| 傲然时光 | Aoran Wang | 邹倚天 | Zou Yitian |
| 汪慧 | Yi Baratier | 1003 POLO | 1003 POLO |

| | | | |
|---|---|---|---|
| 荣誉呈现<br>Proudly<br>Presented By |  | 首席赞助<br>Executive<br>Sponsor | CHANEL |
| 联合赞助<br>Presenting<br>Sponsors | Morgan Stanley 摩根士丹利  Sotheby's 蘇富比 | 独家环保墙面方案支持<br>Exclusive Wall<br>Solutions Support |  |

# 版权信息 / Colophon

| 版权信息 | Colophon |
|---|---|
| 作者<br>何塞·卡洛斯·迪亚兹<br>布莱克·戈普尼克<br>周婉京 | Authors<br>José Carlos Diaz<br>Blake Gopnik<br>Stefanie Chow |
| 画册设计<br>休伯特&费希尔公司 | Catalogue Design<br>Hubert & Fischer |
| 中文排版<br>李家明 | Chinese Typesetting<br>Kaming Lee |
| 执行主编<br>赖柏圣 | Managing Editor<br>Patrick Rhine |
| 中文编辑<br>黄洁华<br>李潇逸<br>张钟尹 | Chinese Editing<br>Huang Jiehua<br>Li Xiaoyi<br>Shelly Zhang |
| 版权协调<br>丁昕霓 | Rights Clearance<br>Cindy Ding |
| 翻译<br>陈玺安<br>刁卓<br>高芷青<br>寇淮禹 | Translation<br>Zian Chen<br>Zoey Diao<br>Gao Zhiqing<br>Kou Huaiyu |
| 印刷<br>雅昌文化（集团）有限公司 | Printing<br>Artron Art (Group) Co., Ltd. |

本书为展览"成为安迪·沃霍尔"相关出版物，展览于2021年7月3日至10月10日在UCCA北京呈现，并于2021年11月6日至2022年3月6日巡展至上海UCCA Edge。

艺术家、作者和出版方向允许他们在本书中使用版权所有材料的版权方表示感激。我们已竭尽所能地试图与版权持有人取得联系，以获得他们对材料使用的许可。出版方为书中可能有的错误或遗漏致歉，并向所有为此书提供勘误信息的读者表示衷心的感谢，我们将在本出版物未来的再印或再版版本中对其进行更正。

©2021版权归尤UCCA伦斯当代艺术中心。未经授权，任何单位和个人不得擅自对本出版物进行复制、销售、翻译、出版和使用，违者必究。

所有安迪·沃霍尔作品版权归©安迪·沃霍尔视觉艺术基金会所有/艺术家权益协会（ARS）授权，纽约

安迪·沃霍尔影像及视频版权归©匹兹堡安迪·沃霍尔美术馆（隶属卡内基博物馆）。版权所有，翻版必究。

第26、214（上）、215页：弗雷德·麦克达拉/华盖创意高级档案
第53（右）页：©多萝西·坎托
第55页：©菲利普·珀尔斯坦/艺术家权益协会（ARS）授权，纽约
第67页：©杜安·迈克尔斯
第125页：©戴维·麦高夫
第225、227—233、235页：©斯蒂芬·肖尔，由303画廊提供，纽约
第234页：©丹尼斯·霍珀，由霍珀艺术信托提供
第237—239页：©图片由西波拉画廊提供
第240页：©比利·内姆遗产/艺术家权益协会（ARS）授权，纽约
第272—276页：玛丽莲·梦露™；形象权及人格权归玛丽莲·梦露遗产有限责任公司所有 marilynmonroe.com
第295页：商标使用权由苹果公司提供

封面与封底：《自画像》（局部）
衬页：《机械感（安迪·沃霍尔快照亭自拍与朱迪丝·格林快照亭照片）》（局部）
第34页：《双手撑头的安迪·沃霍尔》
第106页：《安迪·沃霍尔与一位女士》
第210页：《安迪·沃霍尔，1965》
第246页：《1982年9月21日，安迪·沃霍尔在纽约市百老汇大道860号"工厂"的办公室打电话》（局部）
第300页：《自画像》（局部）

封面及封底图经UCCA尤伦斯当代艺术中心调整，2021年。

This catalogue is published on the occasion of the exhibition "Becoming Andy Warhol," held at UCCA Beijing from July 3 to October 10, 2021, and at UCCA Edge in Shanghai from November 6, 2021, to March 6, 2022.

The artists, authors, and publisher gratefully acknowledge permission granted them to reproduce the copyrighted material in this book. Every effort has been made to contact copyright holders and to obtain their permission for the use of this material. The publisher apologizes for any errors or omissions and would be grateful if notified of any corrections that should be incorporated in future reprints or editions of this publication.

©2021 UCCA Center for Contemporary Art. All rights reserved. No part of this publication may be reproduced, stored in a retrieval system, or transmitted in any form or by any means electronic, mechanical, photocopying, recording, or otherwise, without the prior permission of the publisher.

All artworks by Andy Warhol © 2021 The Andy Warhol Foundation for the Visual Arts, Inc. / Licensed by Artists Rights Society (ARS), New York

Andy Warhol films and videos © The Andy Warhol Museum, Pittsburgh, PA, a museum of Carnegie Institute. All rights reserved

Pp. 26, 214 (top), 215: Fred W. McDarrah/Premium Archive via Getty Images
P. 53, right: © Dorothy Cantor
P. 55: © 2021 Philip Pearlstein / Artists Rights Society (ARS), New York
P. 67: © Duane Michals
P. 125: © David McGough
Pp. 225, 227–233, 235: © Stephen Shore. Courtesy 303 Gallery, New York
P. 234: © Dennis Hopper, Courtesy of The Hopper Art Trust
Pp. 237–239: © All images provided by CIPOLLA GALLERY
P. 240: © 2021 Billy Name Estate / Artists Rights Society (ARS), New York
Pp. 272–276, Marilyn Monroe™; Rights of Publicity and Persona Rights: The Estate of Marilyn Monroe LLC. marilynmonroe.com
P. 295: Courtesy of Apple Inc.

Front and back covers: Self-Portrait (details)
Endpapers: Mechanical (Andy Warhol photobooth self-portrait with Judith Green photobooth portrait) (details)
P. 34: Andy Warhol with head cradled in hands
P. 106: Andy Warhol with unidentified woman
P. 210: Andy Warhol, 1965
P. 246: Andy Warhol on the phone in his personal office at the Factory, 860 Broadway, on September 21, 1982 in New York City, New York. (detail)
P. 300: Self-Portrait (detail)

Front and back cover modified from the original by UCCA Center for Contemporary Art in 2021.

责任编辑：程　禾
文字编辑：王家豪
责任校对：朱晓波
责任印制：汪立峰

**图书在版编目（CIP）数据**

成为安迪·沃霍尔 / UCCA尤伦斯当代艺术中心编
. -- 杭州：浙江摄影出版社，2021.9
 ISBN 978-7-5514-3438-6

Ⅰ. ①成… Ⅱ. ①U… Ⅲ. ①沃霍尔(Warhol, Andy 1928-1987) — 人物研究 Ⅳ. ①K837.125.72

中国版本图书馆CIP数据核字(2021)第181536号

CHENGWEI ANDI WOHUOER

## 成为安迪·沃霍尔

UCCA 尤伦斯当代艺术中心　编

全国百佳图书出版单位
浙江摄影出版社出版发行
地址：杭州市体育场路 347 号
邮编：310006
电话：0571-85151082
网址：www.photo.zjcb.com
制版：北京雅昌艺术印刷有限公司
印刷：北京雅昌艺术印刷有限公司
开本：710 mm × 1000 mm　1/8
印张：50
2021 年 9 月第 1 版　2021 年 9 月第 1 次印刷
ISBN 978-7-5514-3438-6
定价：288.00 元

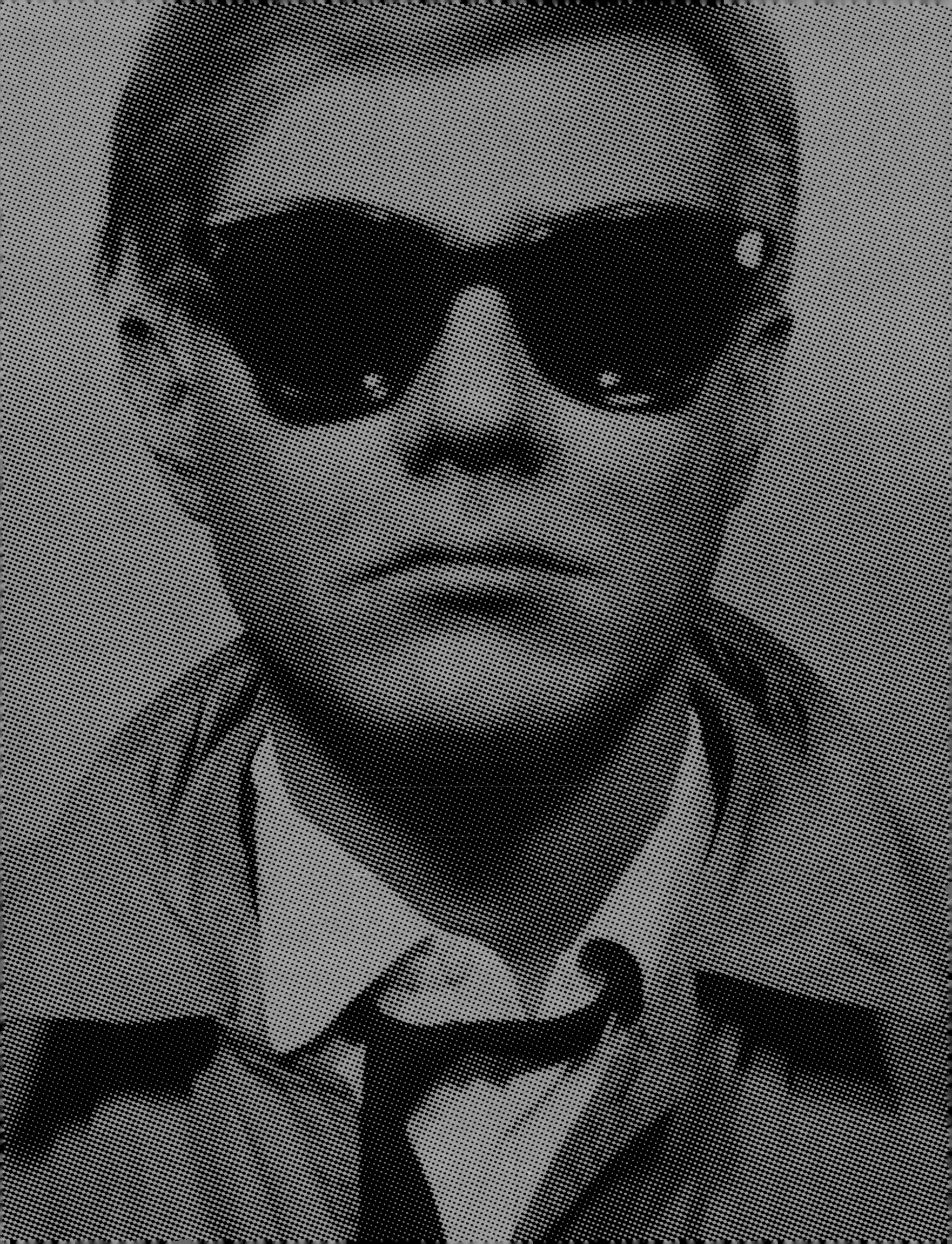